The Knauss Music Curriculum

BOOK 1A
RHYTHM & TONAL SKILL EXERCISES

Classroom (General) Music for Elementary and Middle Level: Supplement to Book 1

Dr. David E. Knauss

Published by:
Music Excellence Publishing
knaussde@gmail.com

THE KNAUSS MUSIC CURRICULUM
BOOK 1A RHYTHM & TONAL SKILL EXERCISES
CLASSROOM (GENERAL) MUSIC FOR ELEMENTARY AND MIDDLE LEVEL: SUPPLEMENT TO BOOK 1

First Printing, 2001, by Music Excellence Publishers, David E. Knauss
Every print edition is a single printing revised with the latest research and advances in music education.

ISBN-13: 978-1-955820-02-8

PRINTED IN THE UNITED STATES OF AMERICA

Cover Design by:

Author | Designer | Photographer
Hannah Linder Creations LLC

www.hannahlinderbooks.com
www.hannahlinderdesigns.com
www.hannahlinderphotography.com
hannah@hannahlinderdesigns.com

PERMISSION FOR BOOK 1A: You (the purchaser of this Book 1A) have my permission (the author of this book's rhythm and tonal exercises) to make one 8.5x11 copy of each of these pages for teaching in general music classes. I suggest laminating the copies to create individual flash cards.
—David E. Knauss

"Making music, in fact, is the very best way of learning about music."
—Richard Baker

"Music does not exist until it is performed."
—Benjamin Britten

"I hear (Tell me), I forget,
I see (Show me), I remember,
I do (Involve me), I understand!"
—Chinese Proverb

"If your vision is for a year, plant wheat.
If your vision is for ten years, plant trees.
If your vision is for a lifetime, plant people."
—Chinese Proverb

"Excellence is not an act, but a habit."
—Aristotle

This music skills book is dedicated to Dr. Kenneth R. Raessler, my first music supervisor and sensei who saw hidden ability in a beginning teacher and patiently perfected it; to Dr. Joyce C. Wunderlich, my master's degree professor who opened the doors to Orff-Schulwerk; and foremost to my wife Joanne for her never-ending patience and support.

Contact info: knaussde@gmail.com
Music education inservices and master classes are available.

About the author:
Dr. David Knauss taught inner-city K-12 general music for 3 decades, helped to develop an award-winning music department and general music curriculum, led his students to relate to each other as family members and become outstanding musicians, and saw the community's artist values change as the music program became the city's icon. Dr. Knauss then taught undergraduate and graduate music education methods and master classes to classroom (general) music teachers and elementary teachers. In retirement, Dr. and Mrs. Knauss now travel across states teaching praise and worship (general) music.

David E. Knauss
Ph. D. in Music Education, Penn State University
Doc. of Humane Letters, The Wesley Synod International

"In a lifelong search for my students' learning limits, I only ever found my teaching limits!"
—D. Knauss

Book 1A: Rhythm & Tonal Music Skill Exercises
(Supplement to Book 1)

Duple #1

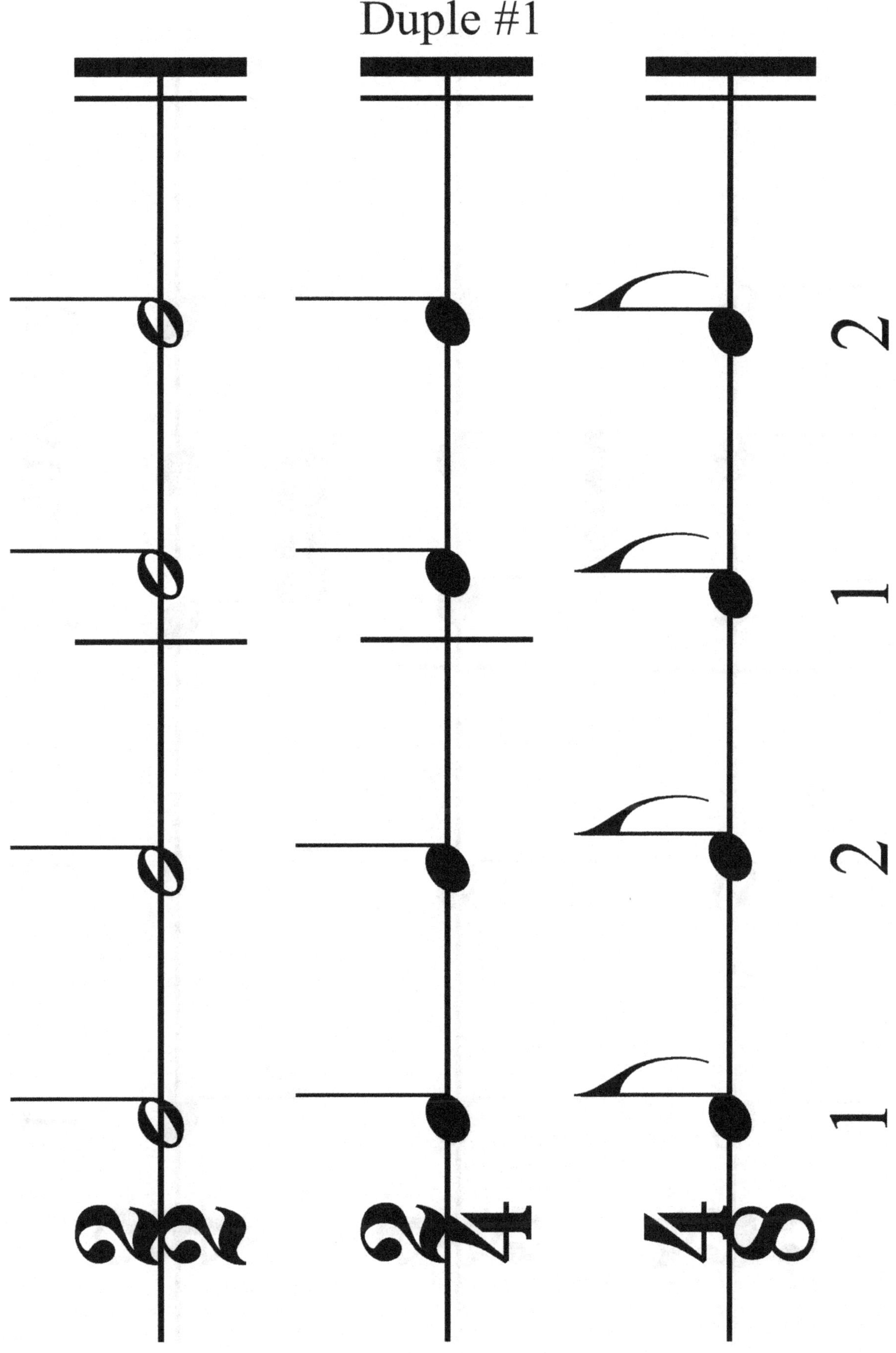

Duple #2

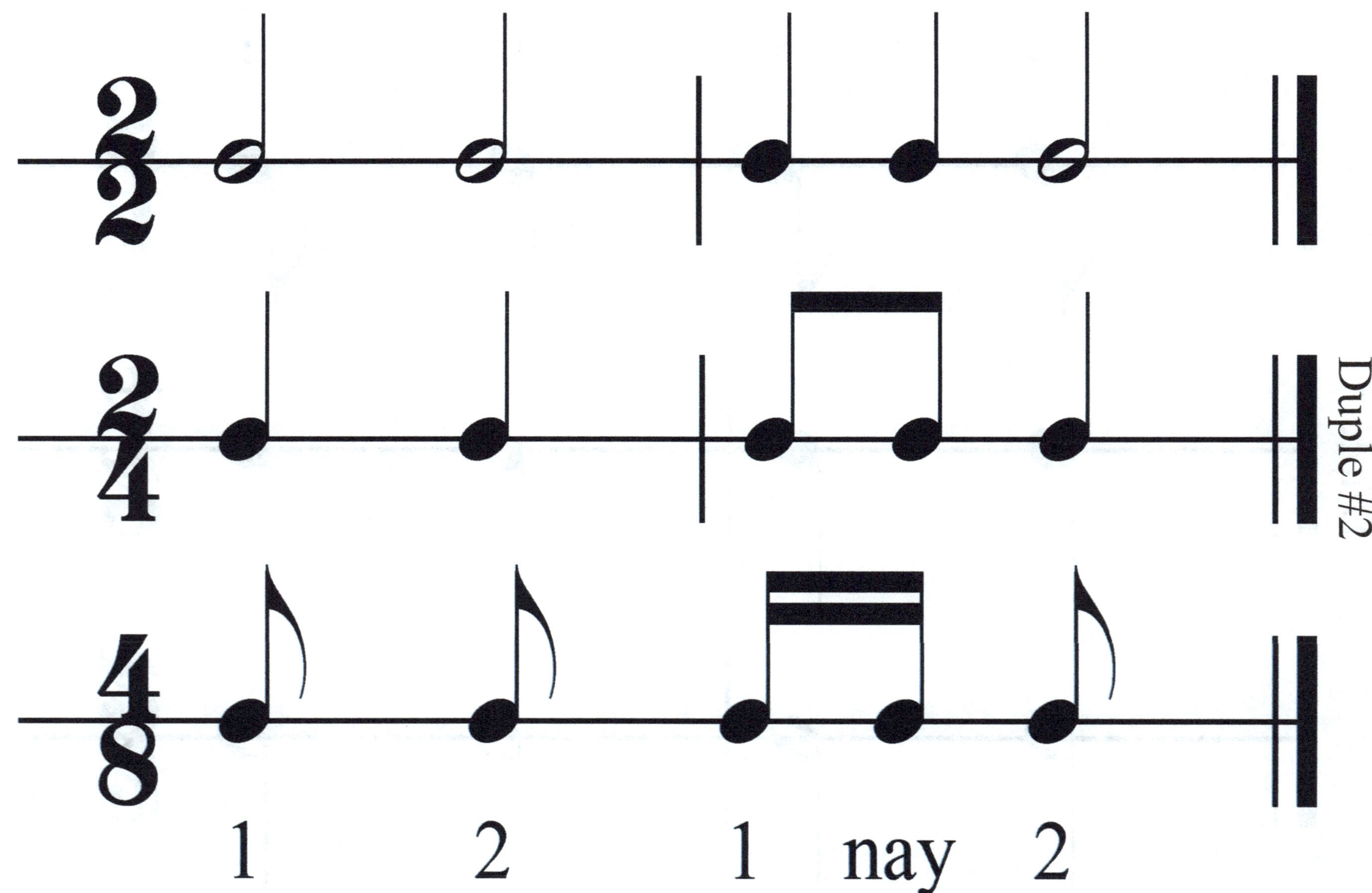

Duple #3

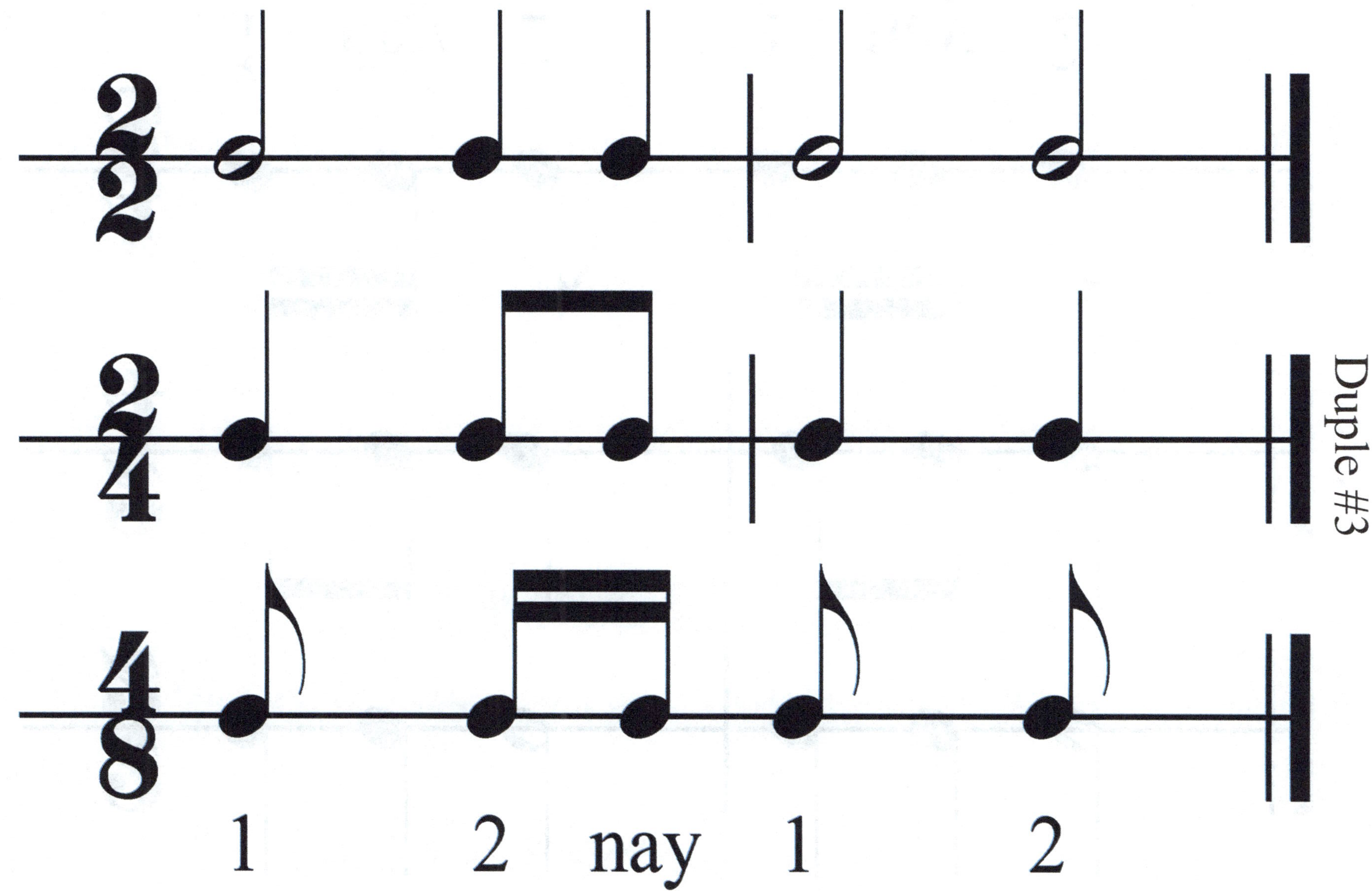

Duple #4

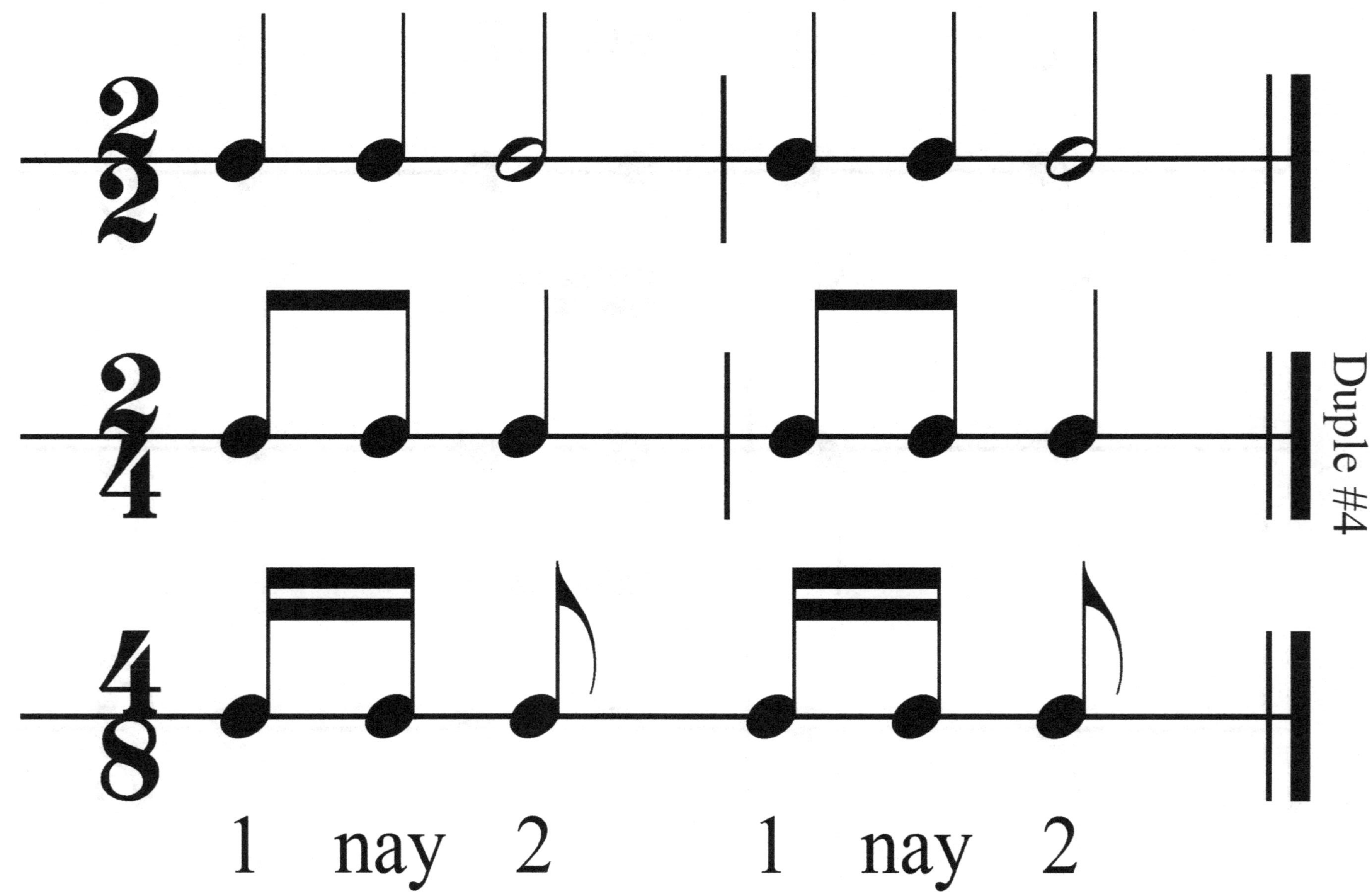

Duple #5

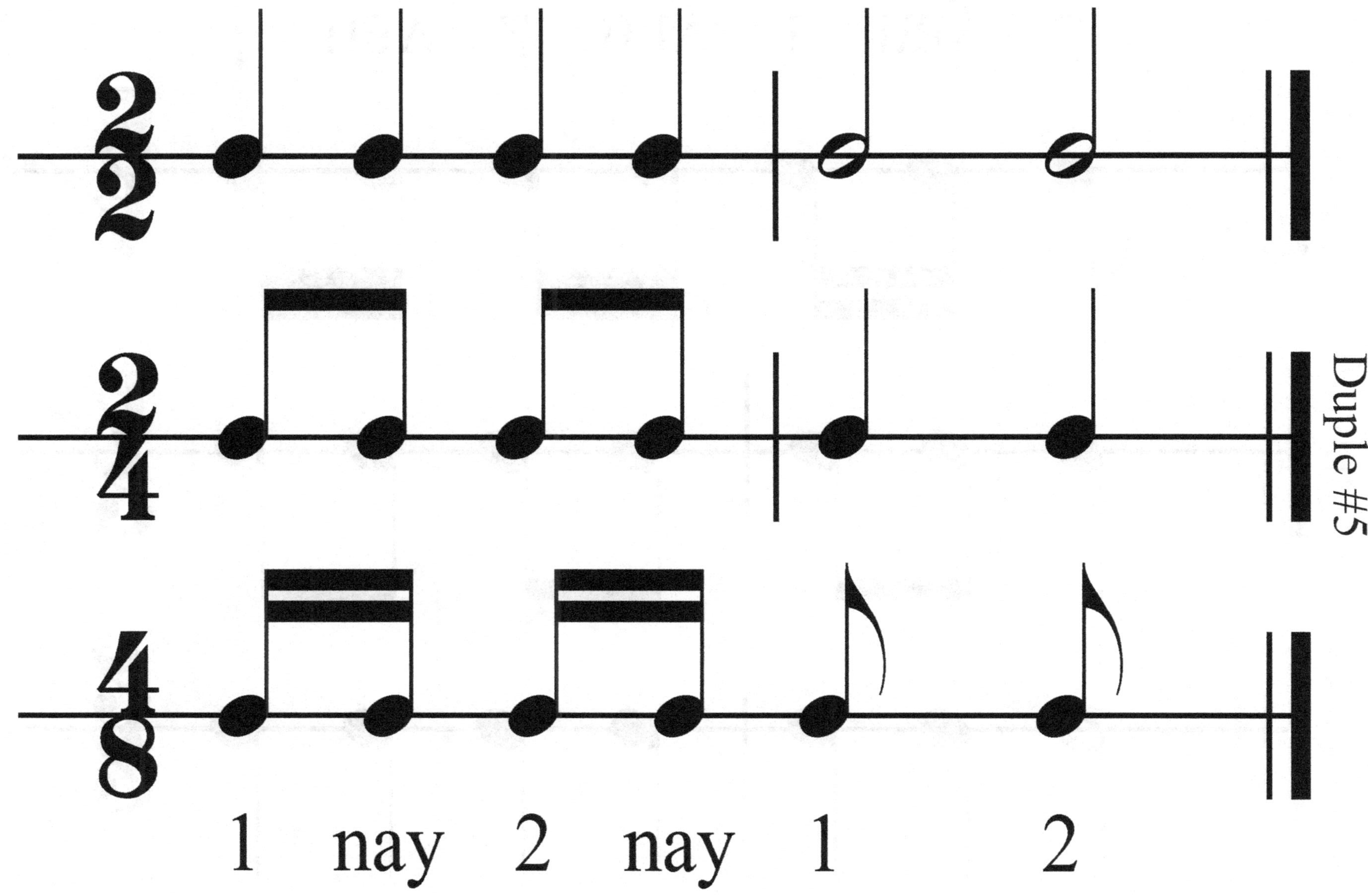

Duple #6

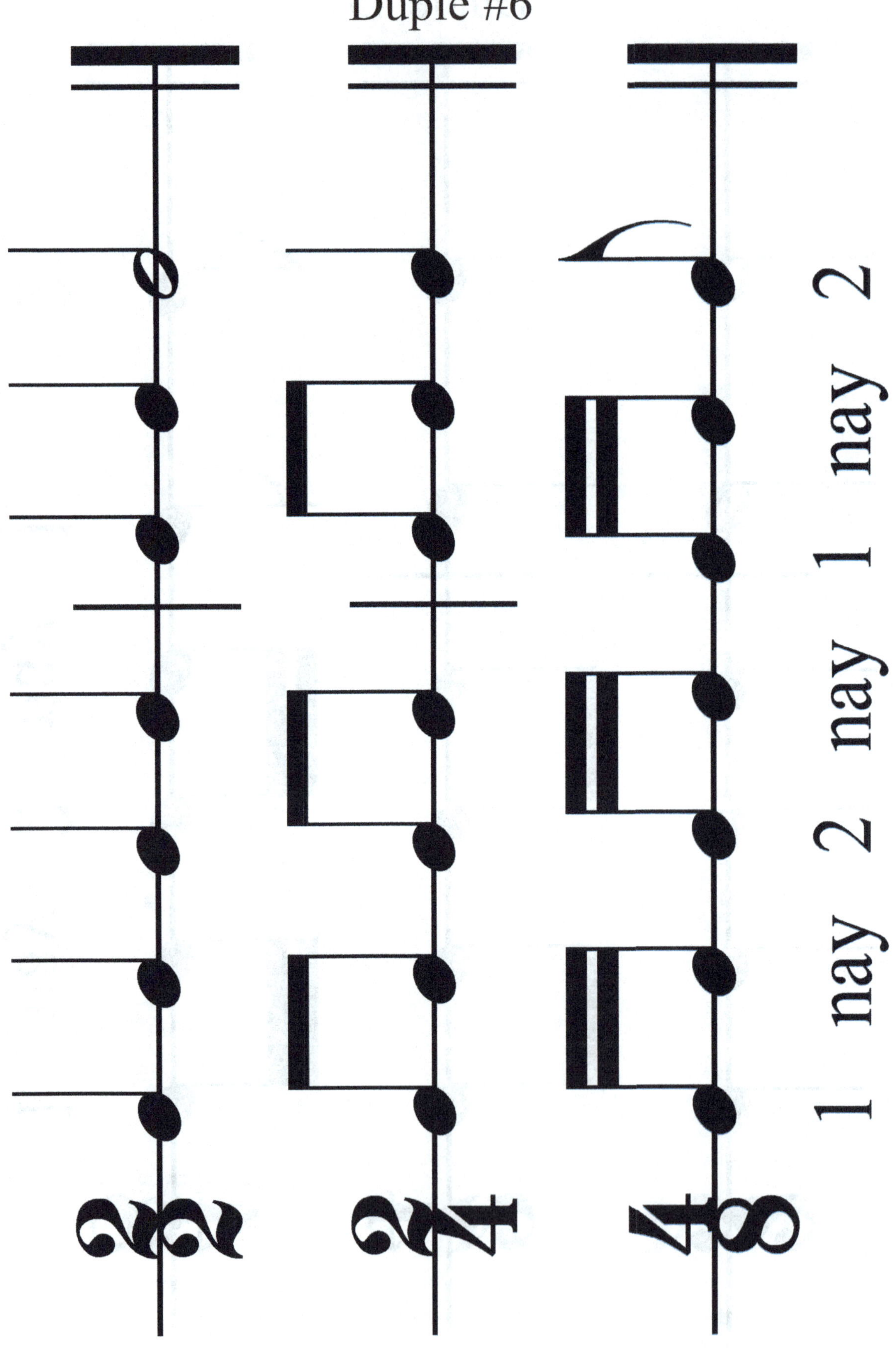
1 nay 2 nay 1 nay 2

Duple #7

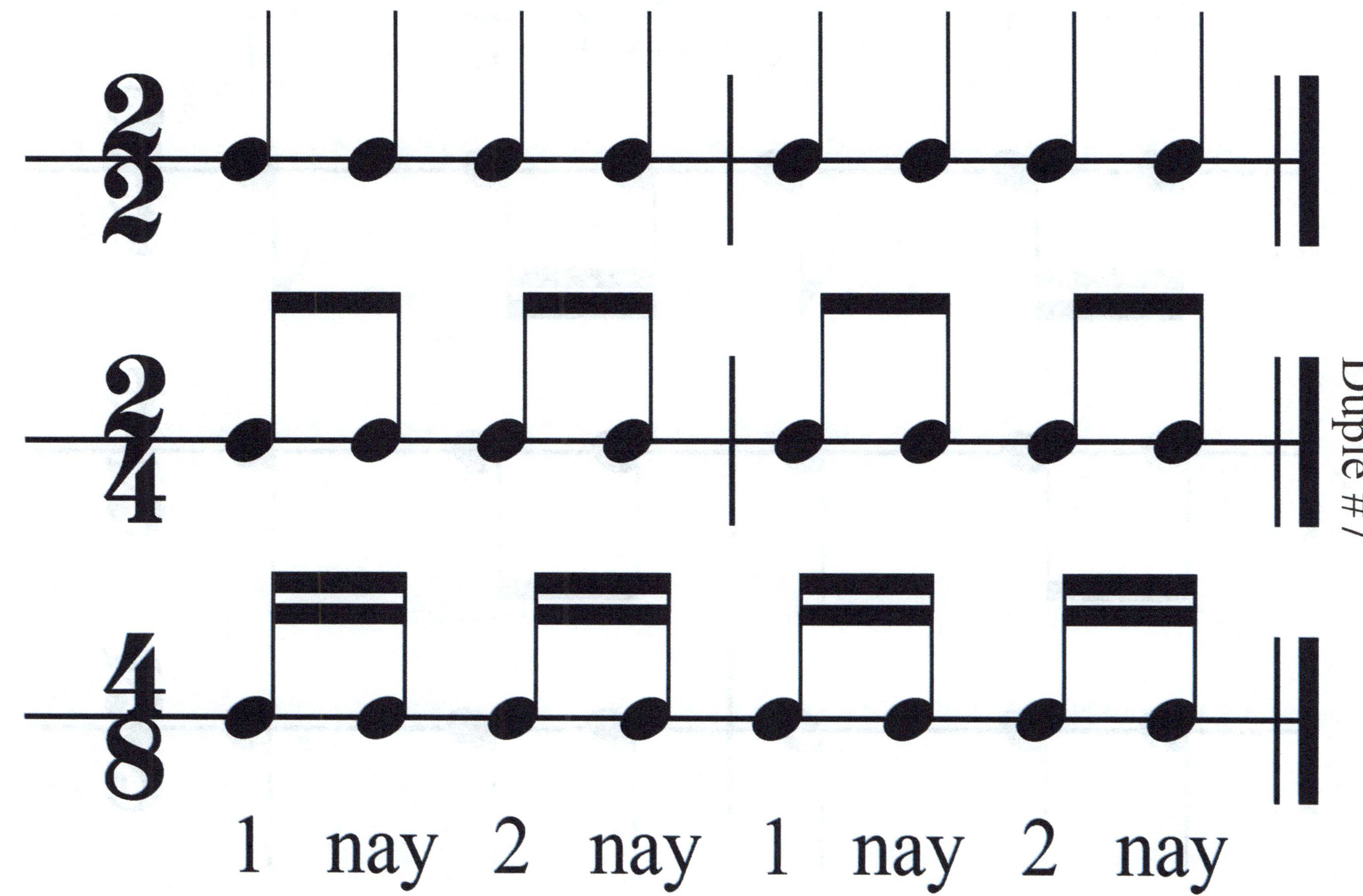
1 nay 2 nay 1 nay 2 nay

Duple #8

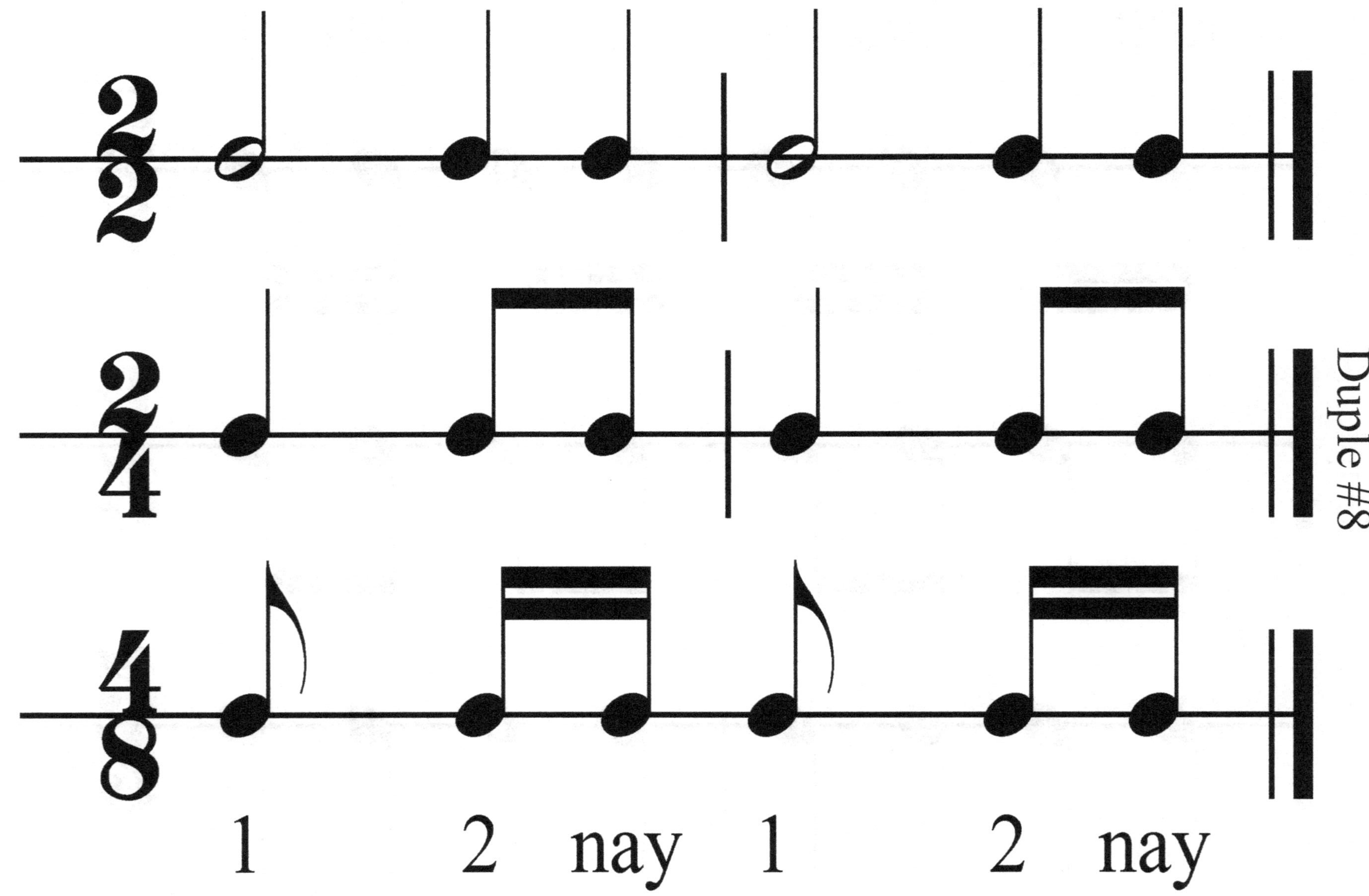

Duple #9

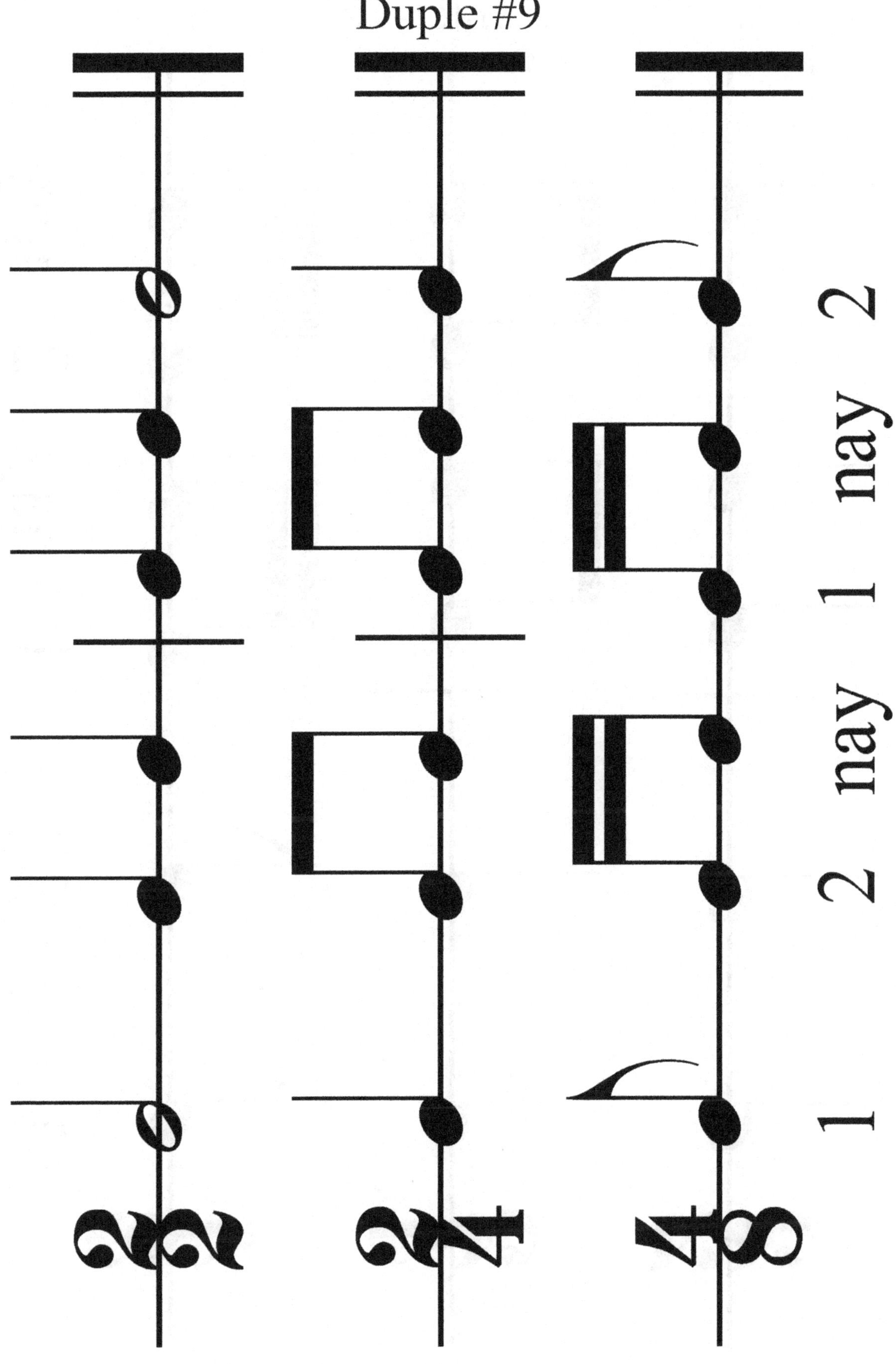

Duple #10

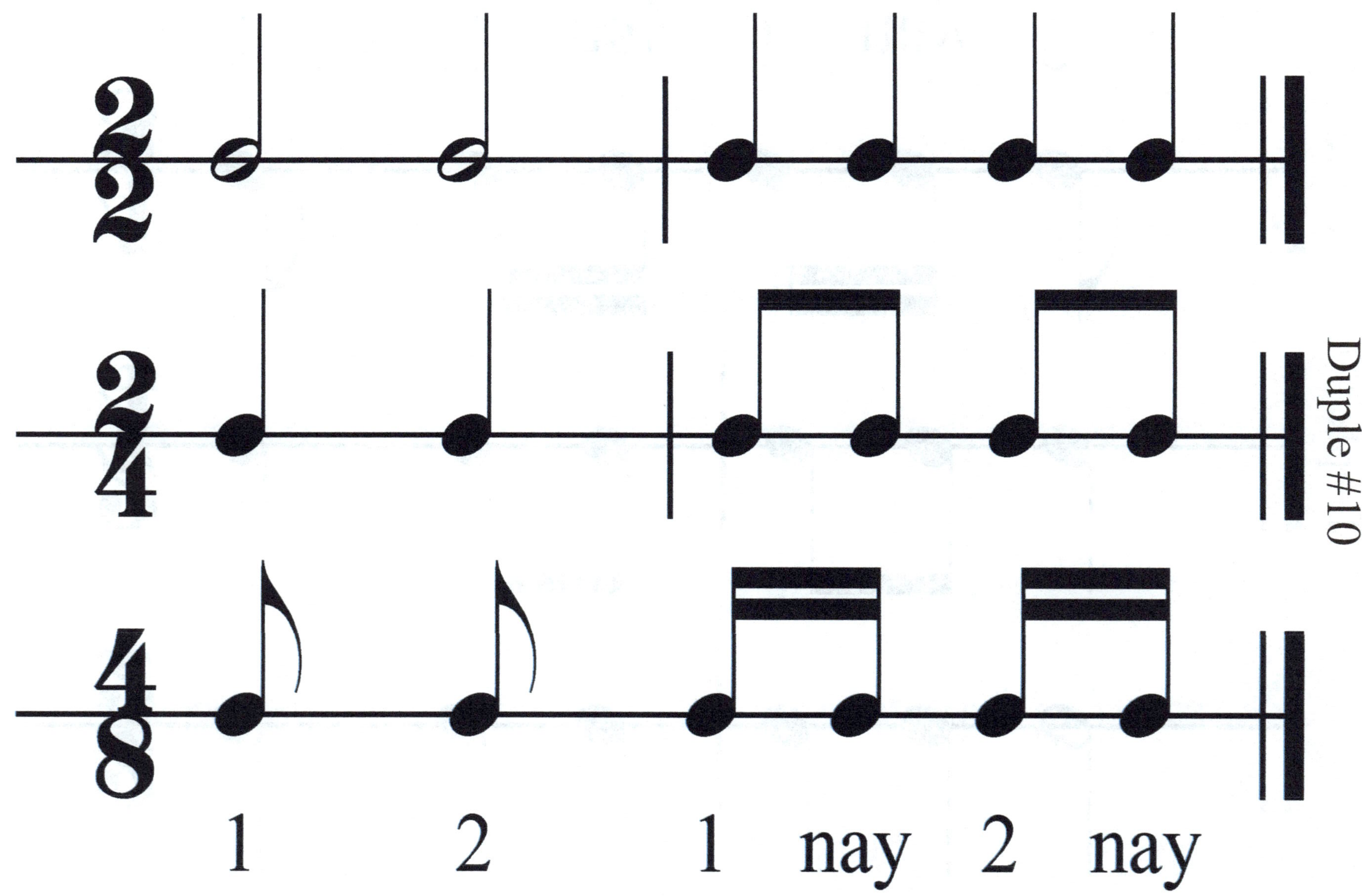

Duple #11

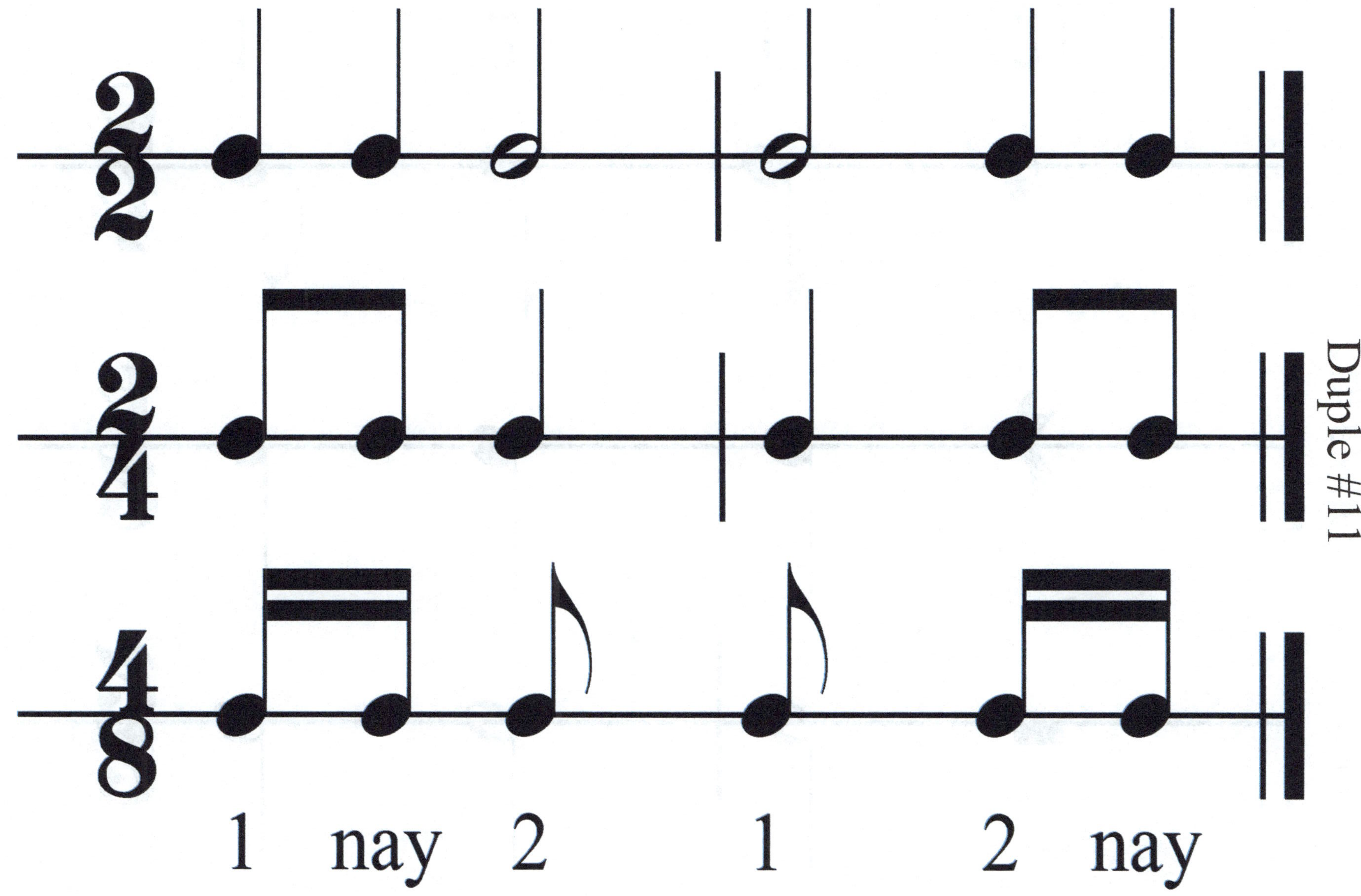

Duple #12

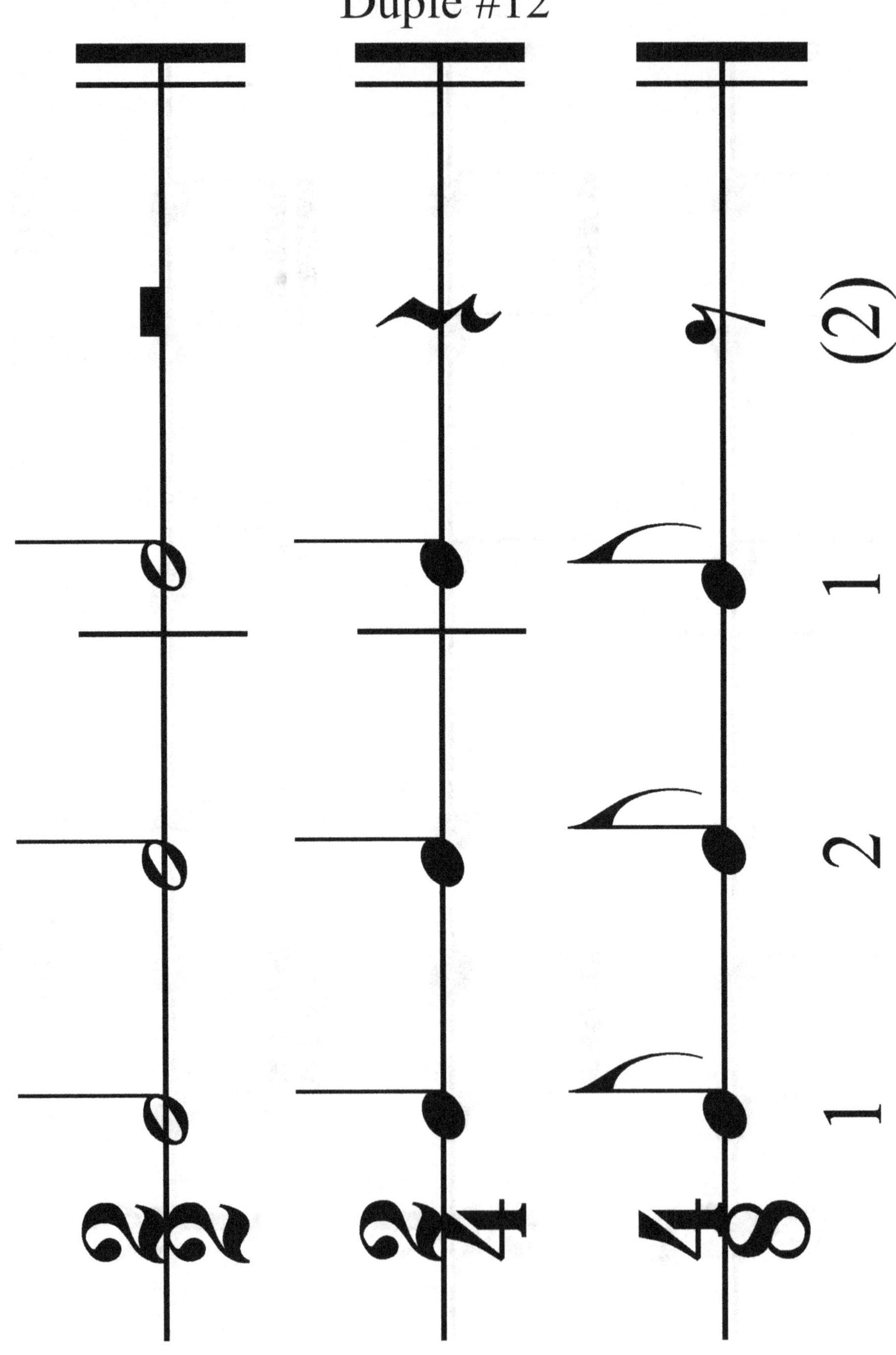

Duple #13

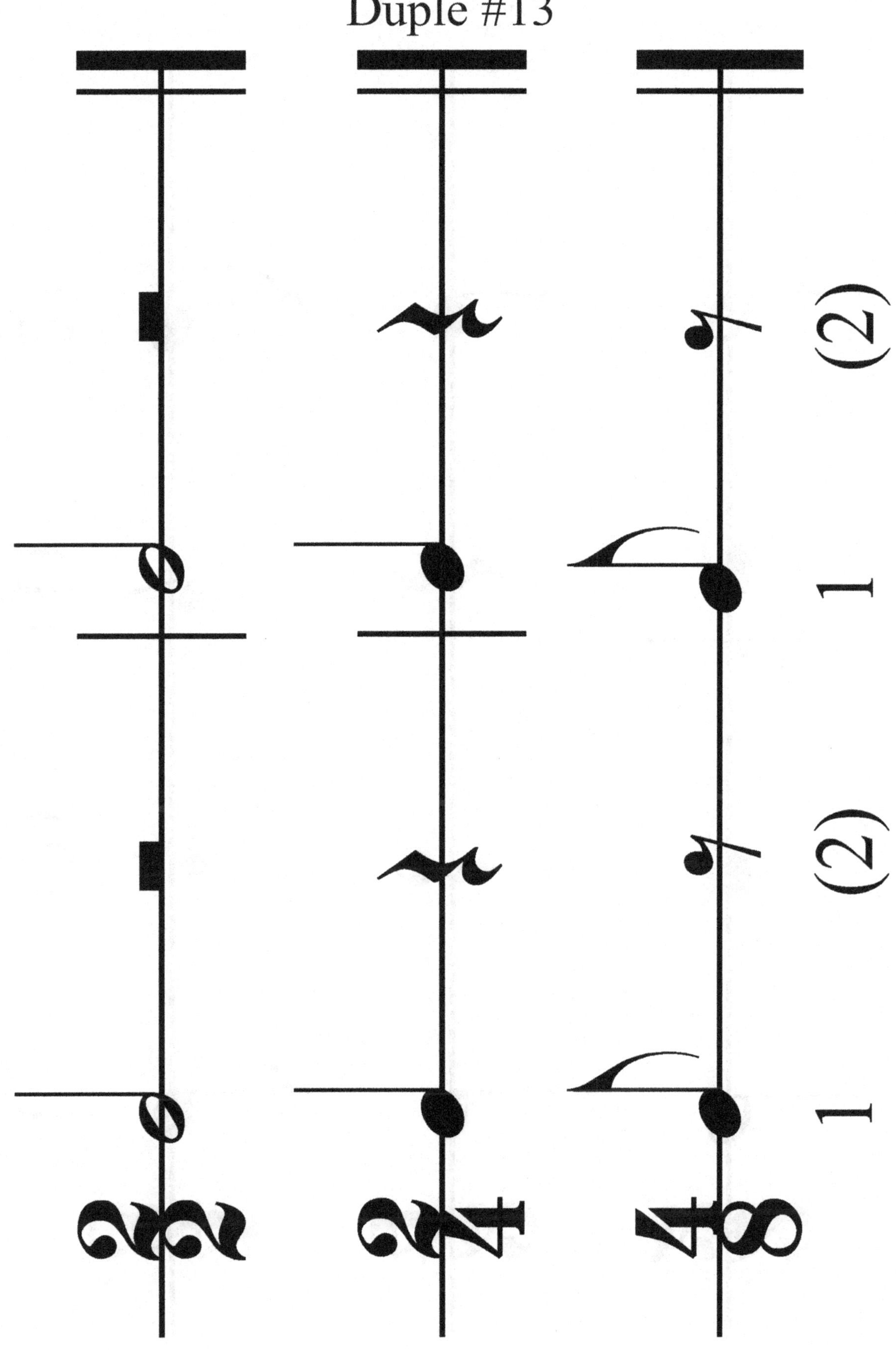

Duple #14

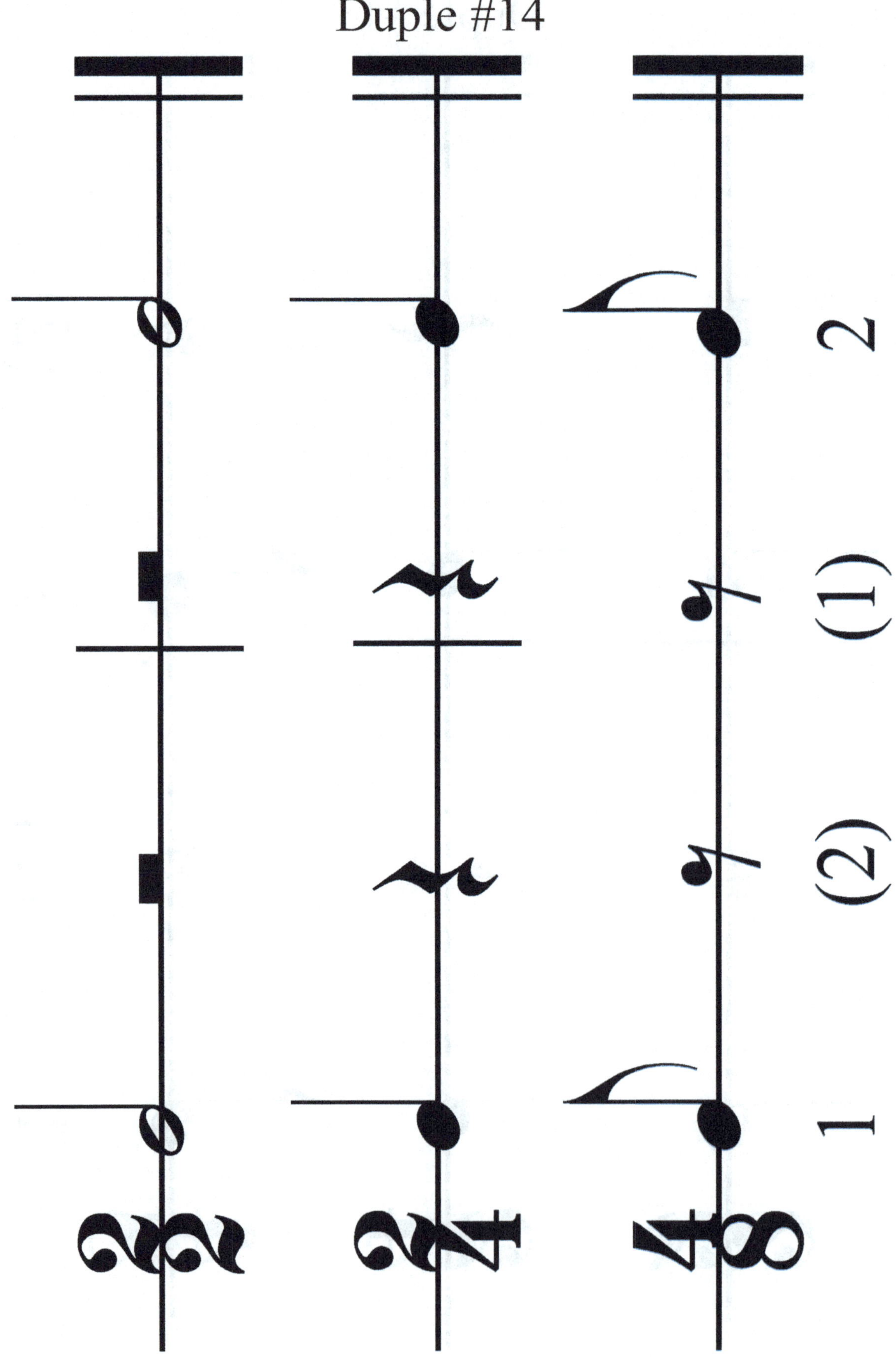

Duple #15

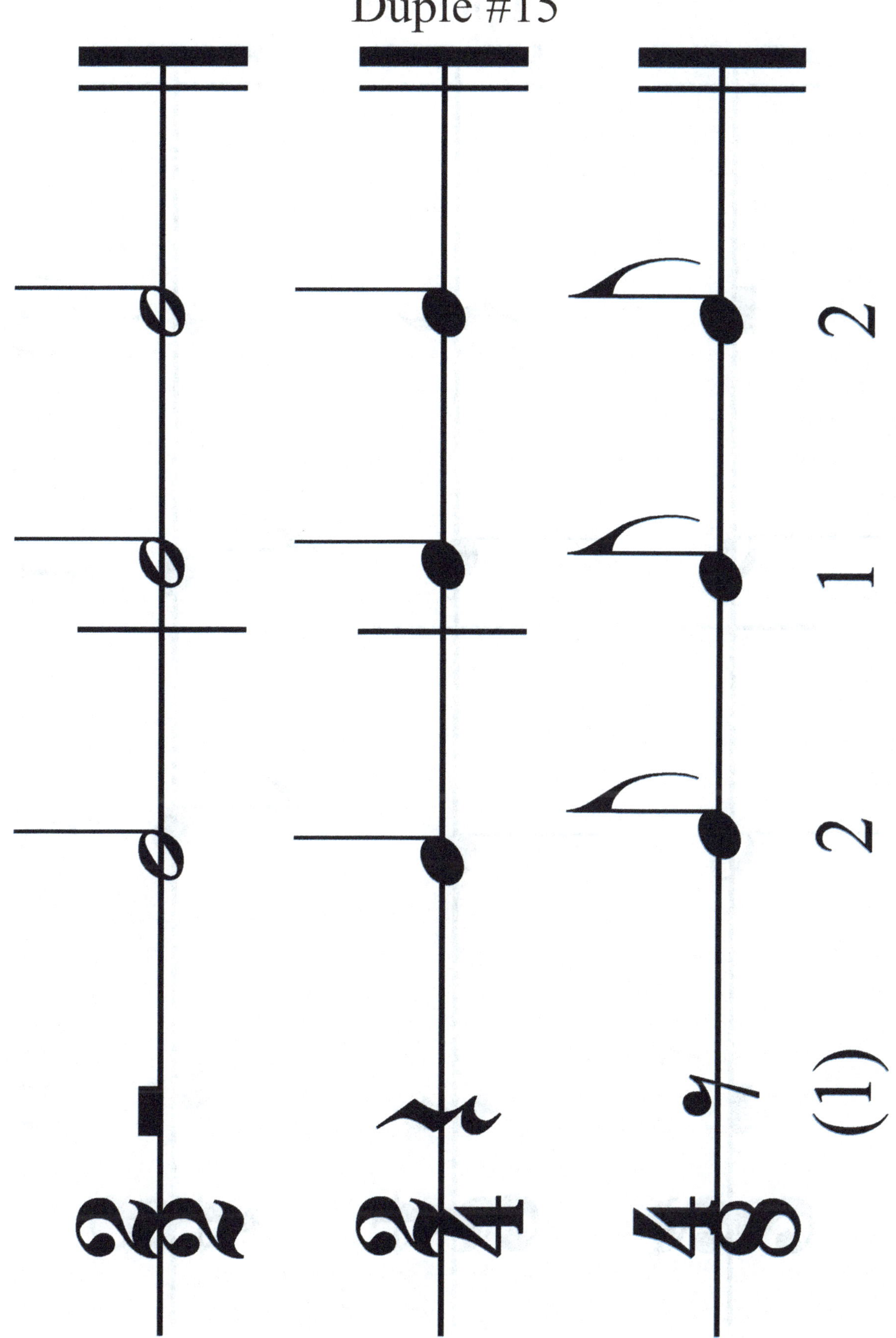

Duple #16

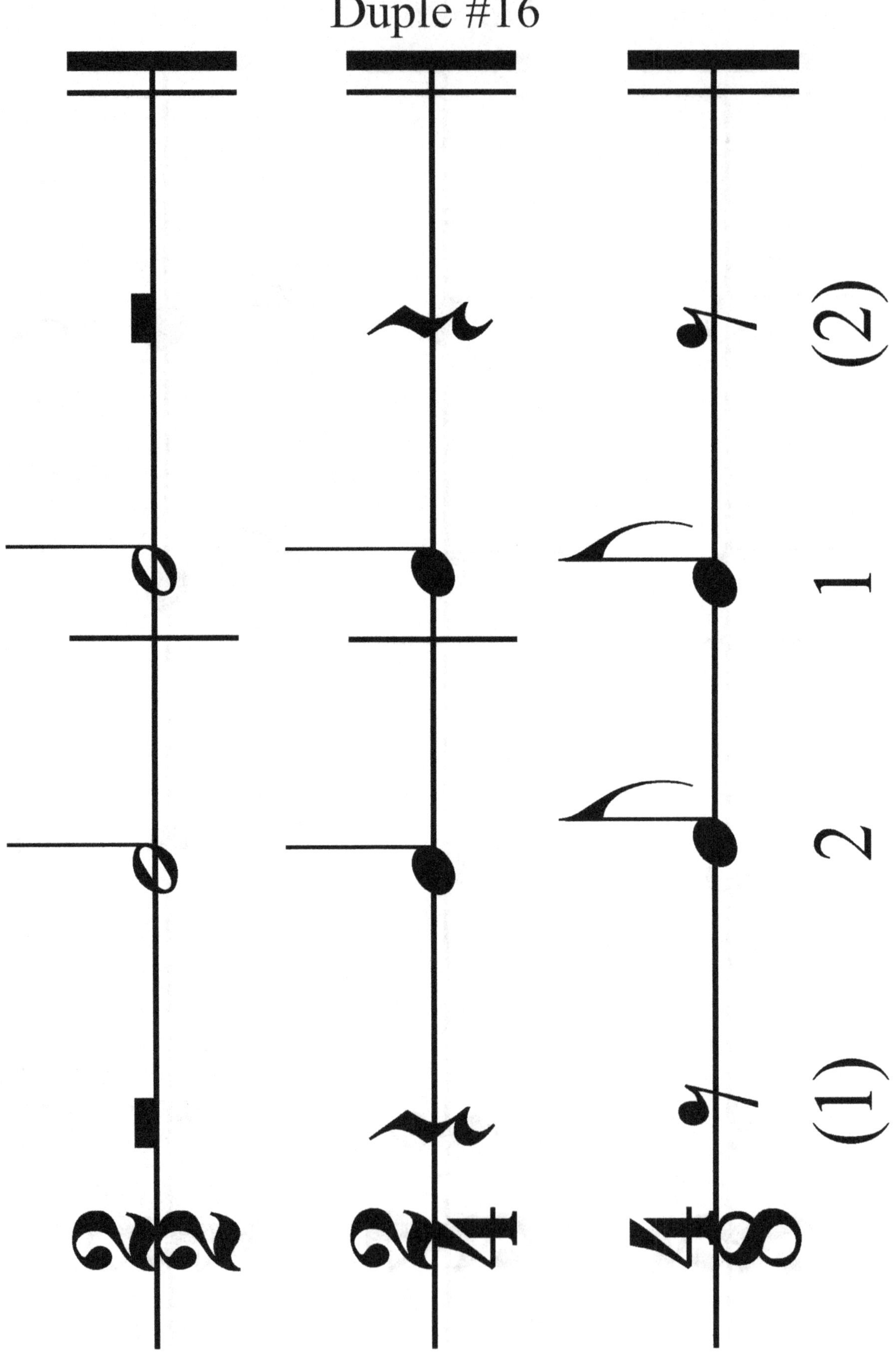

Duple #17

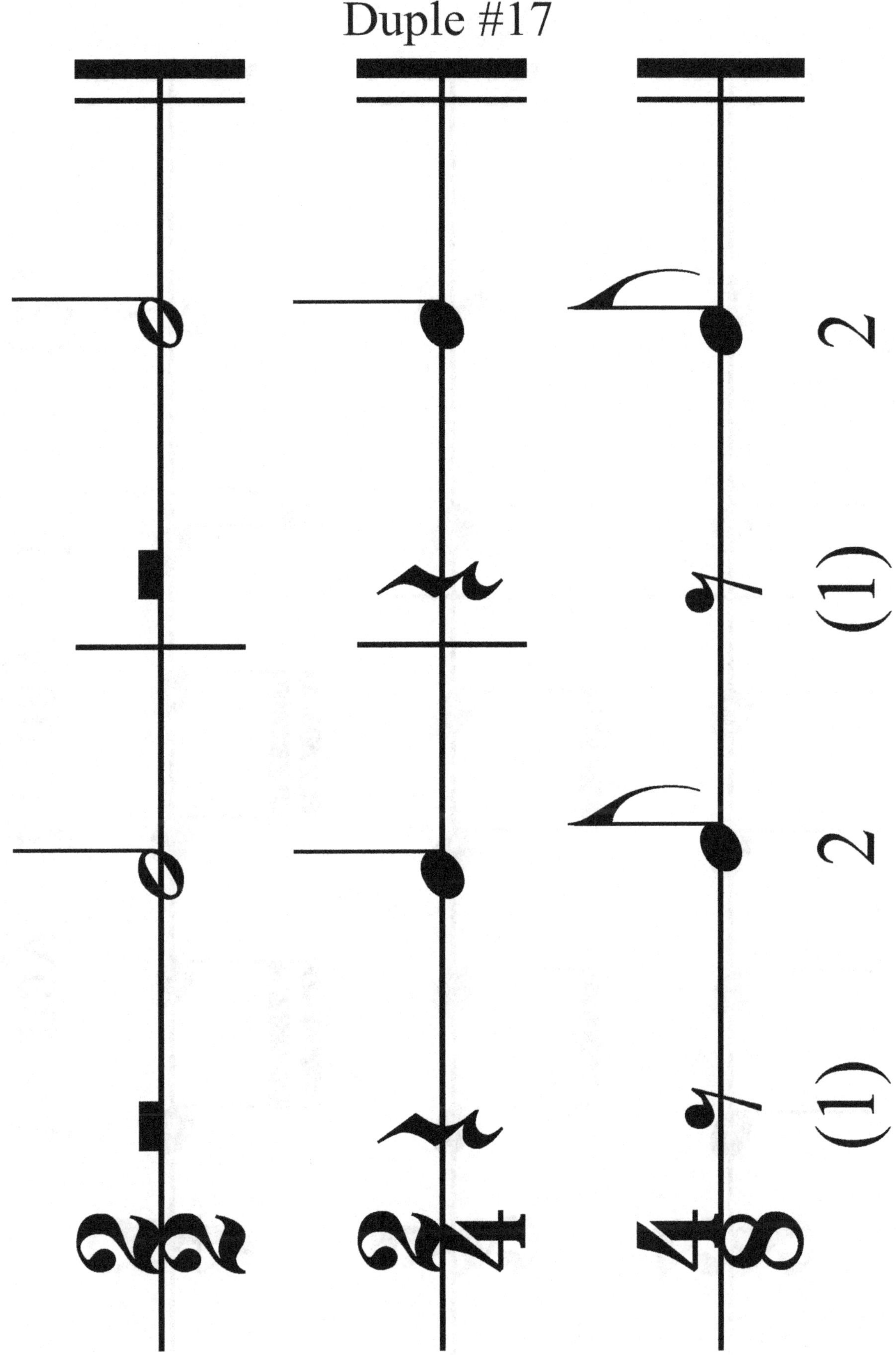

Duple #18

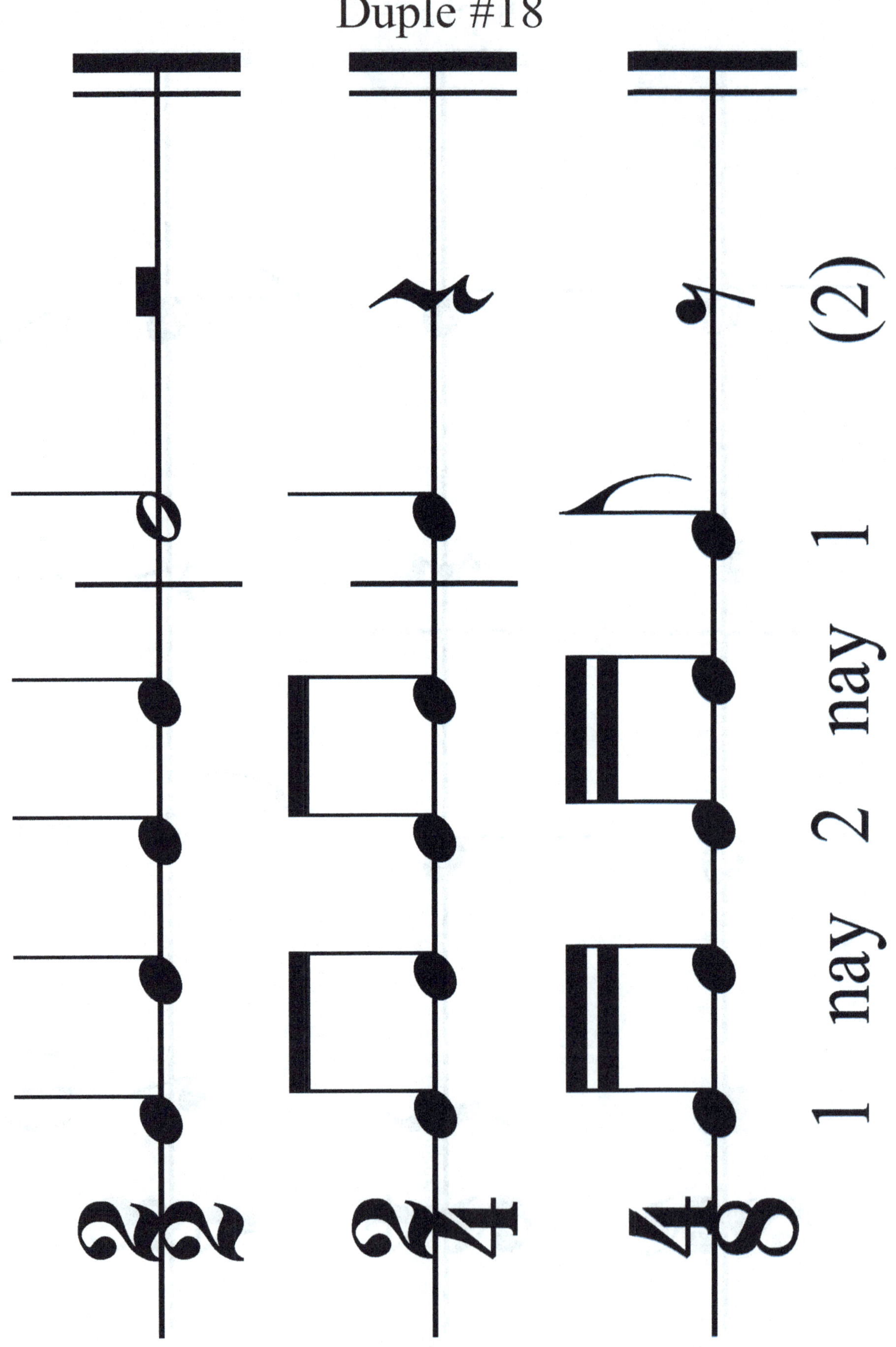

Duple #19

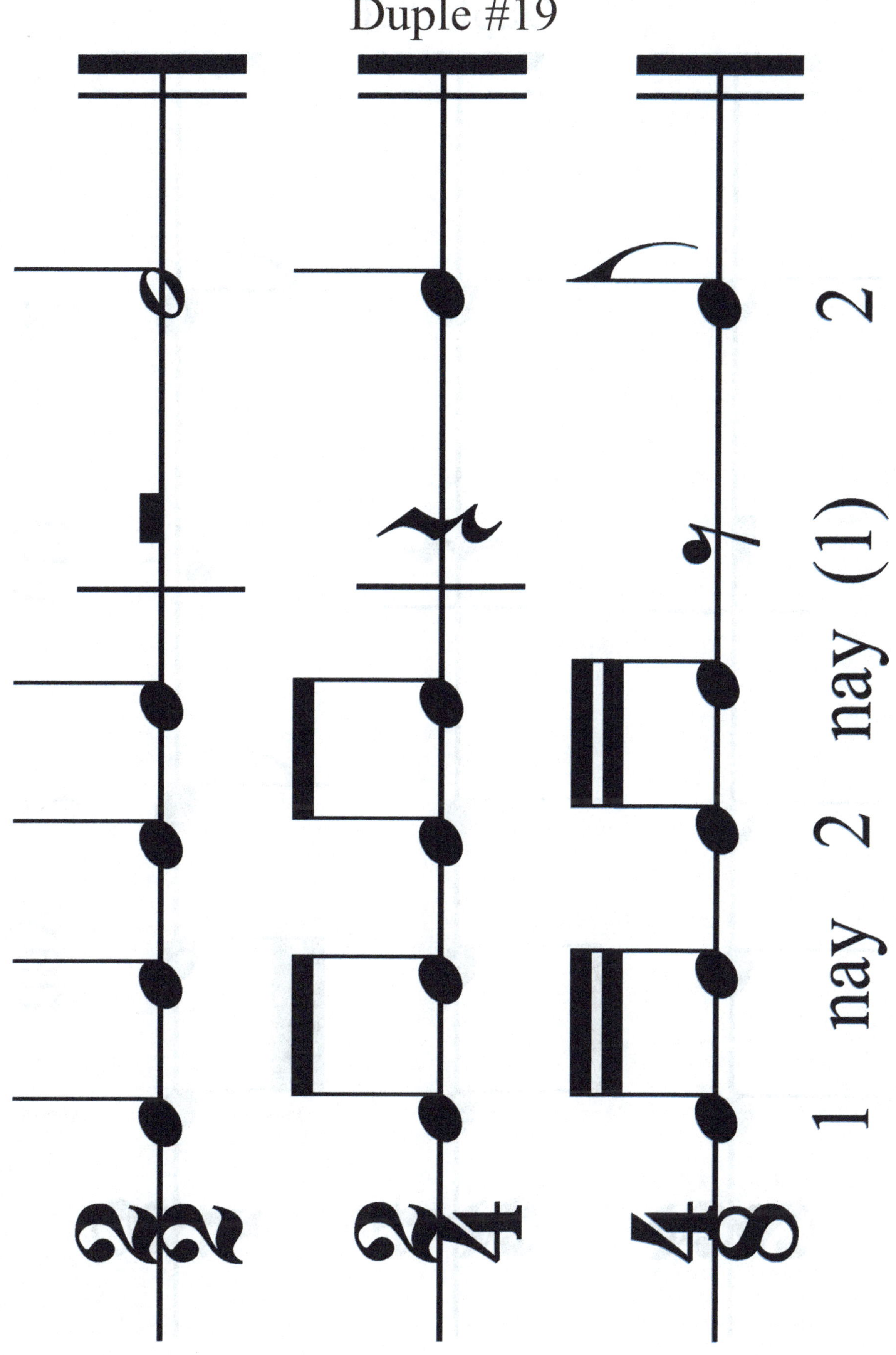

Duple #20

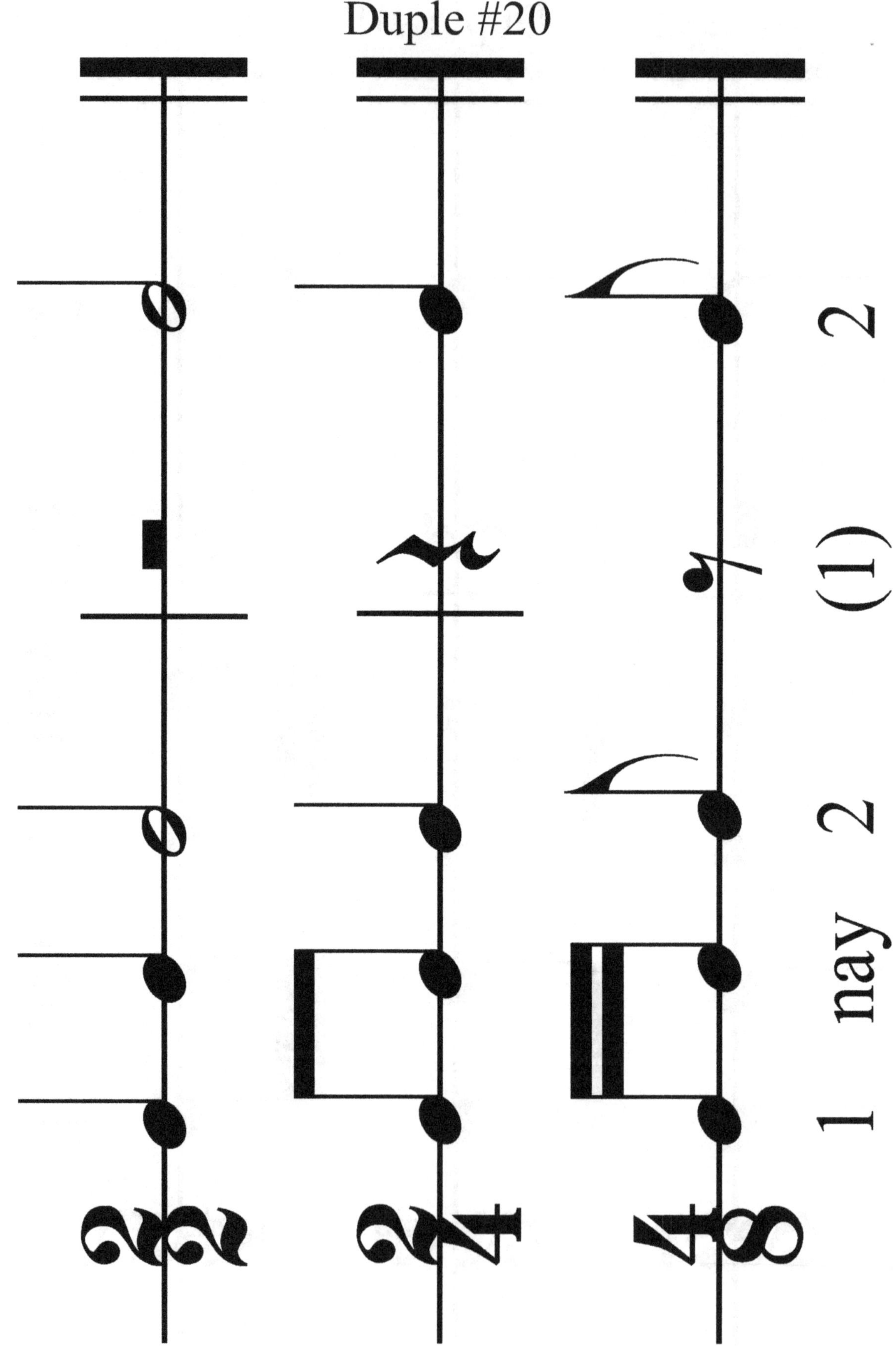

Duple #21

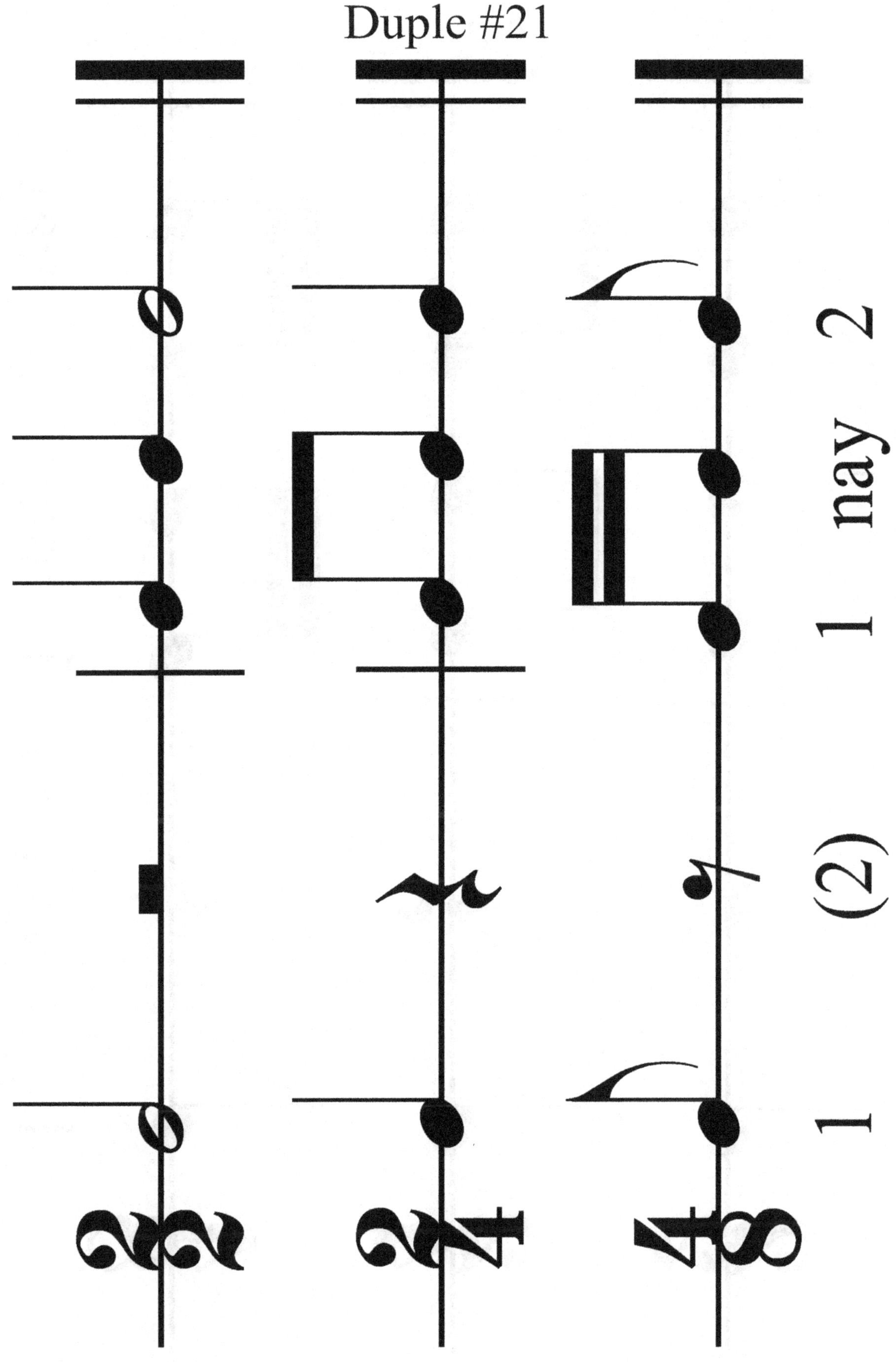

Duple #22

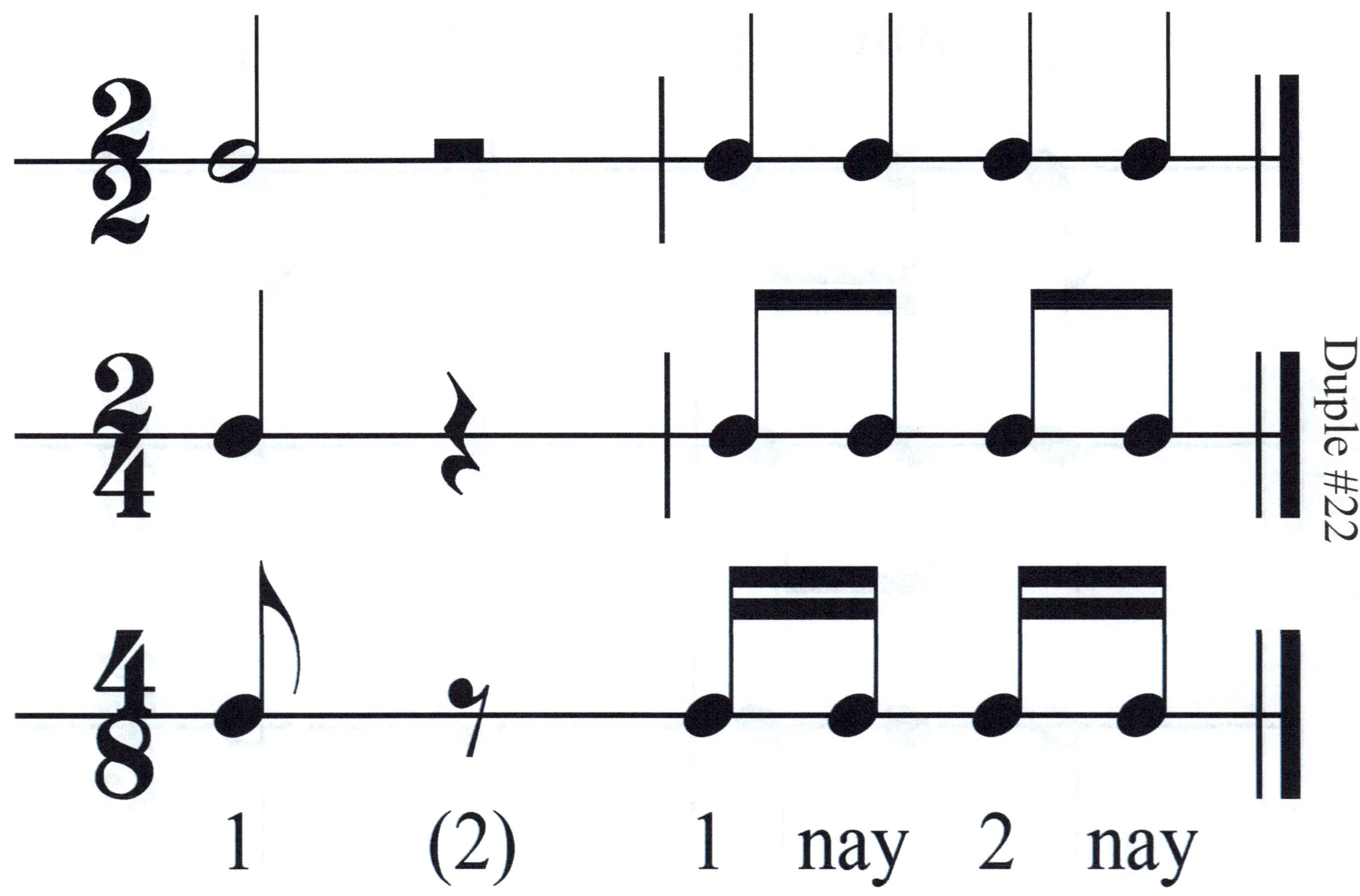

Duple #23

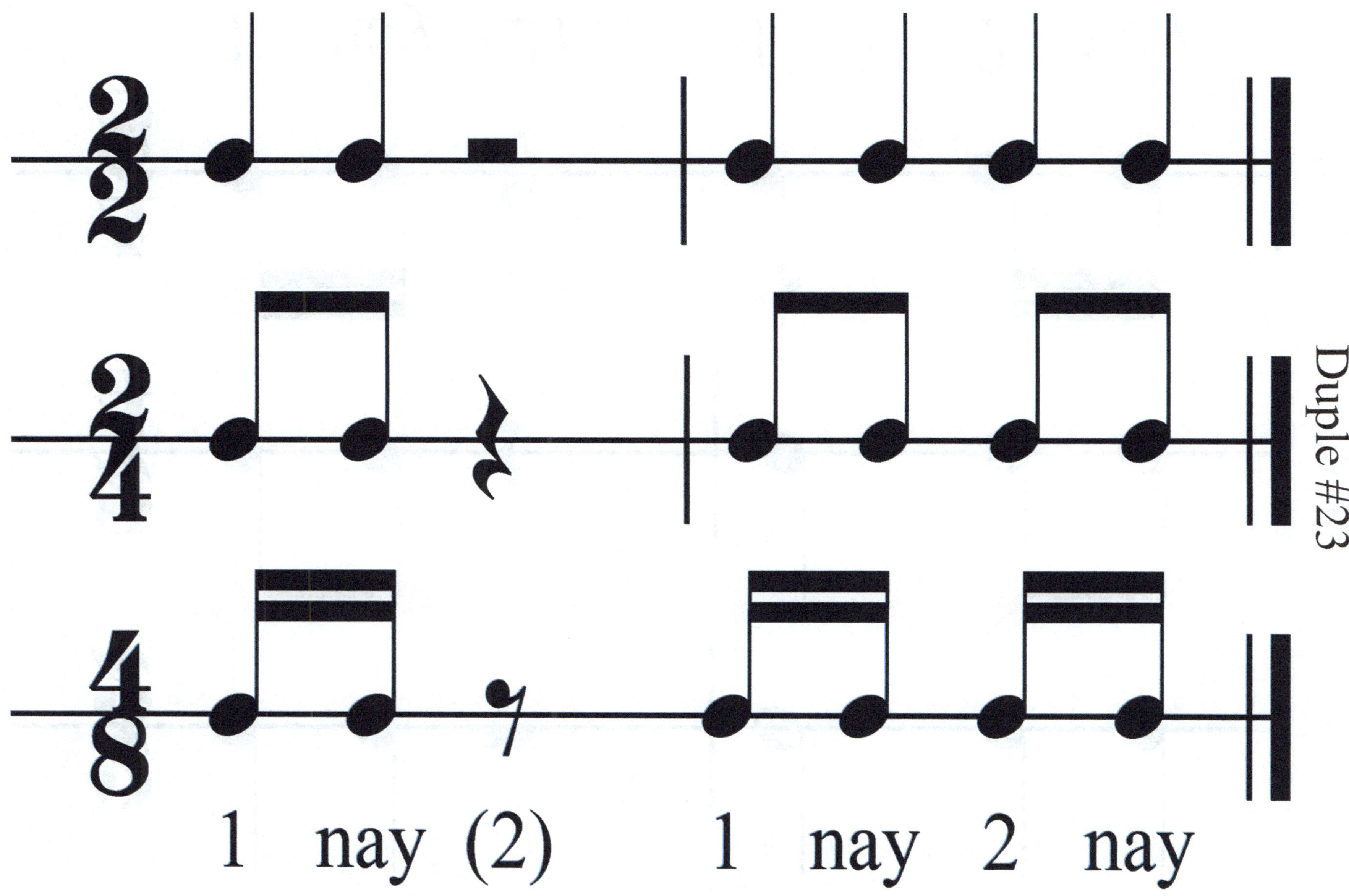
1 nay (2) 1 nay 2 nay

Duple #24

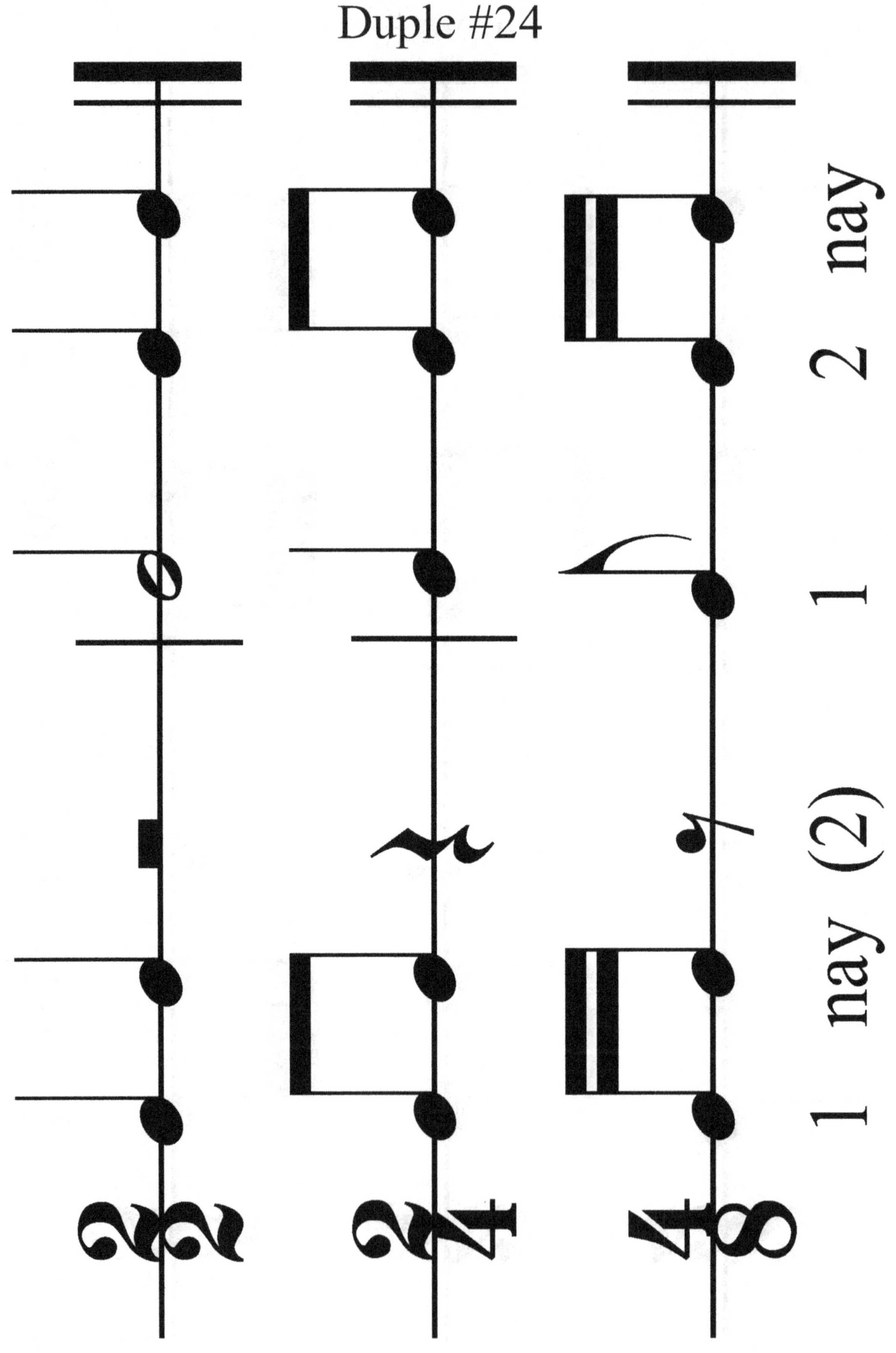

Duple #25

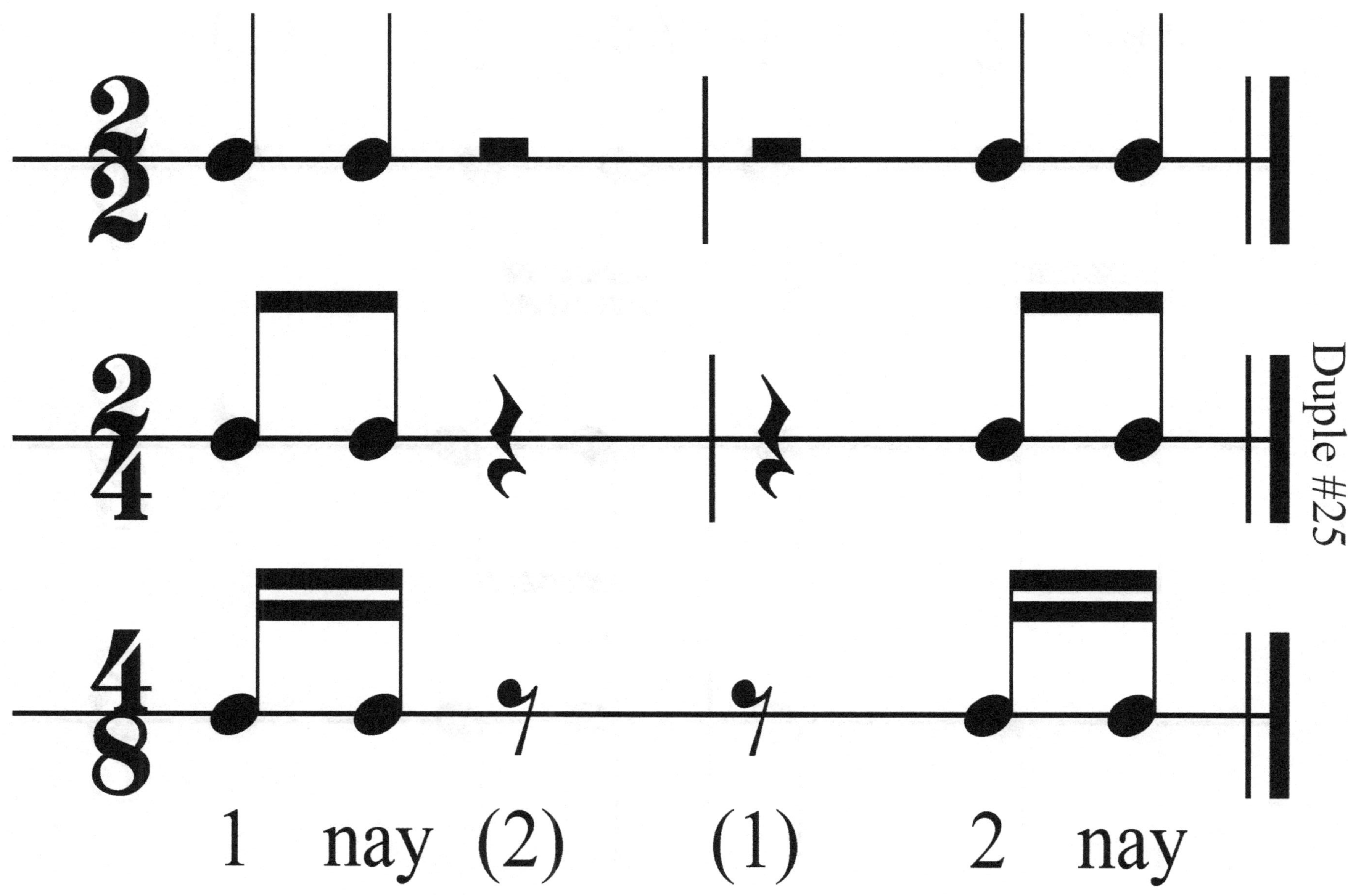
2/2
2/4
4/8
1 nay (2) (1) 2 nay

Duple #26

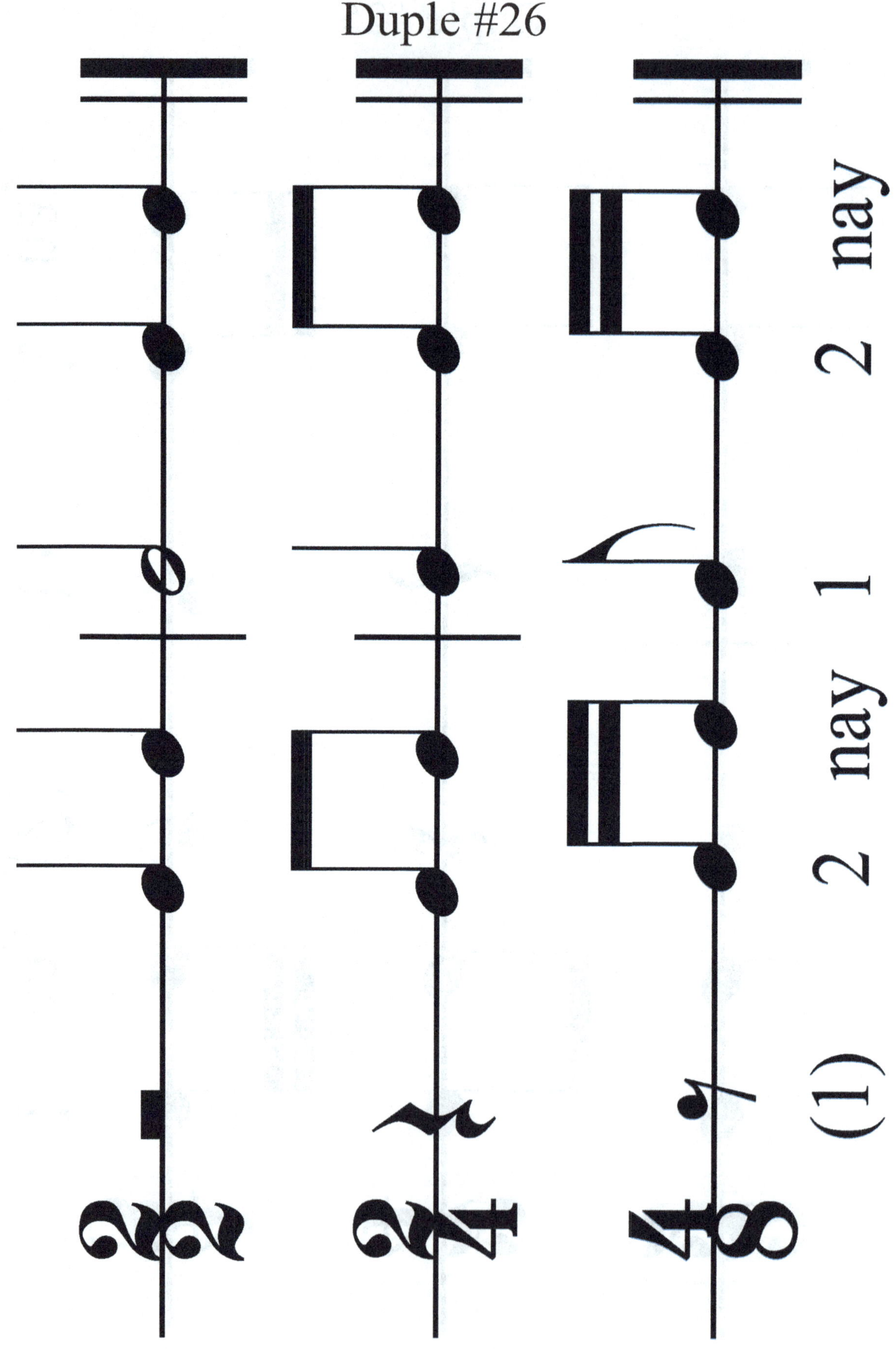

Duple #27

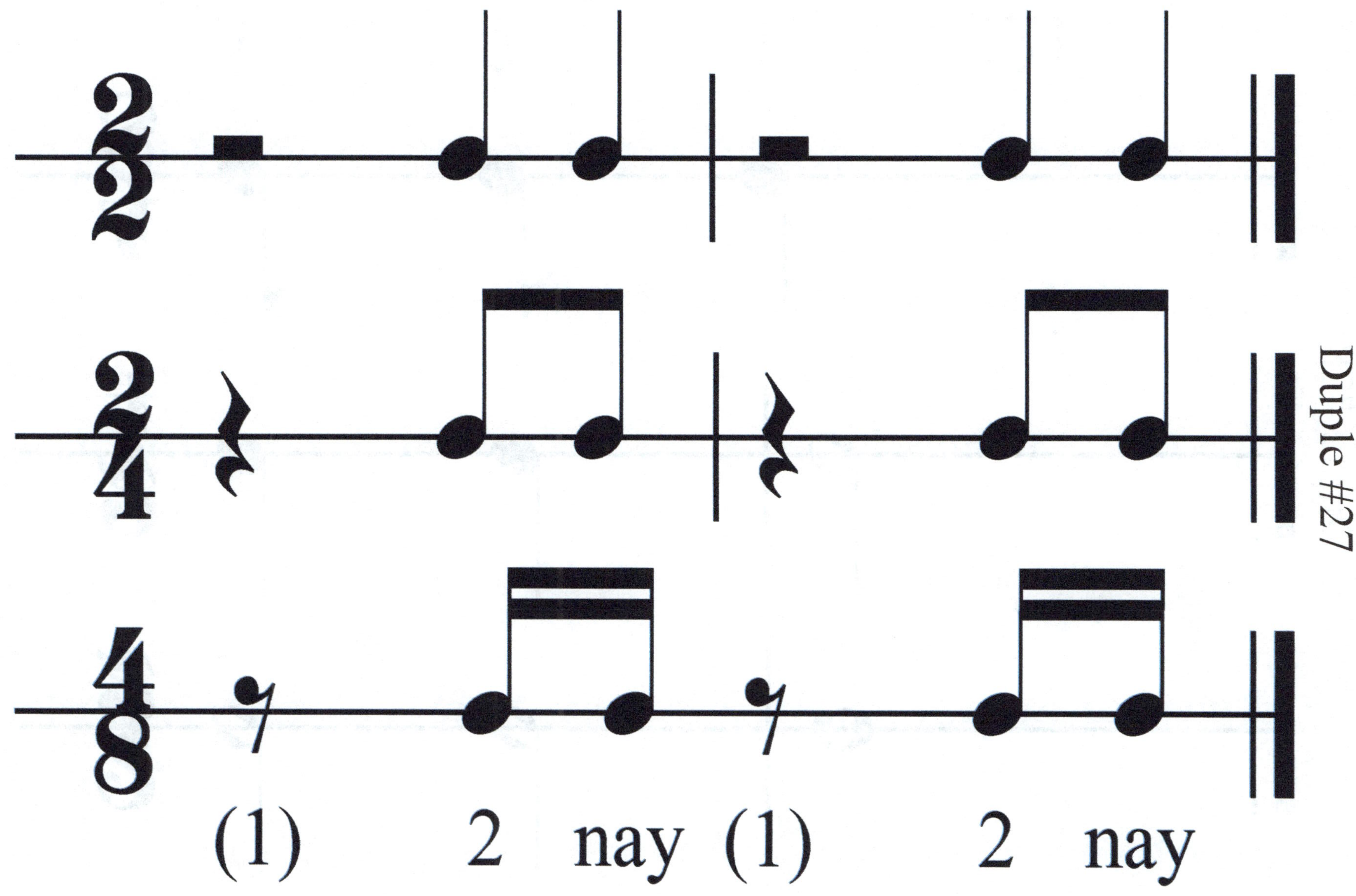

Duple #28

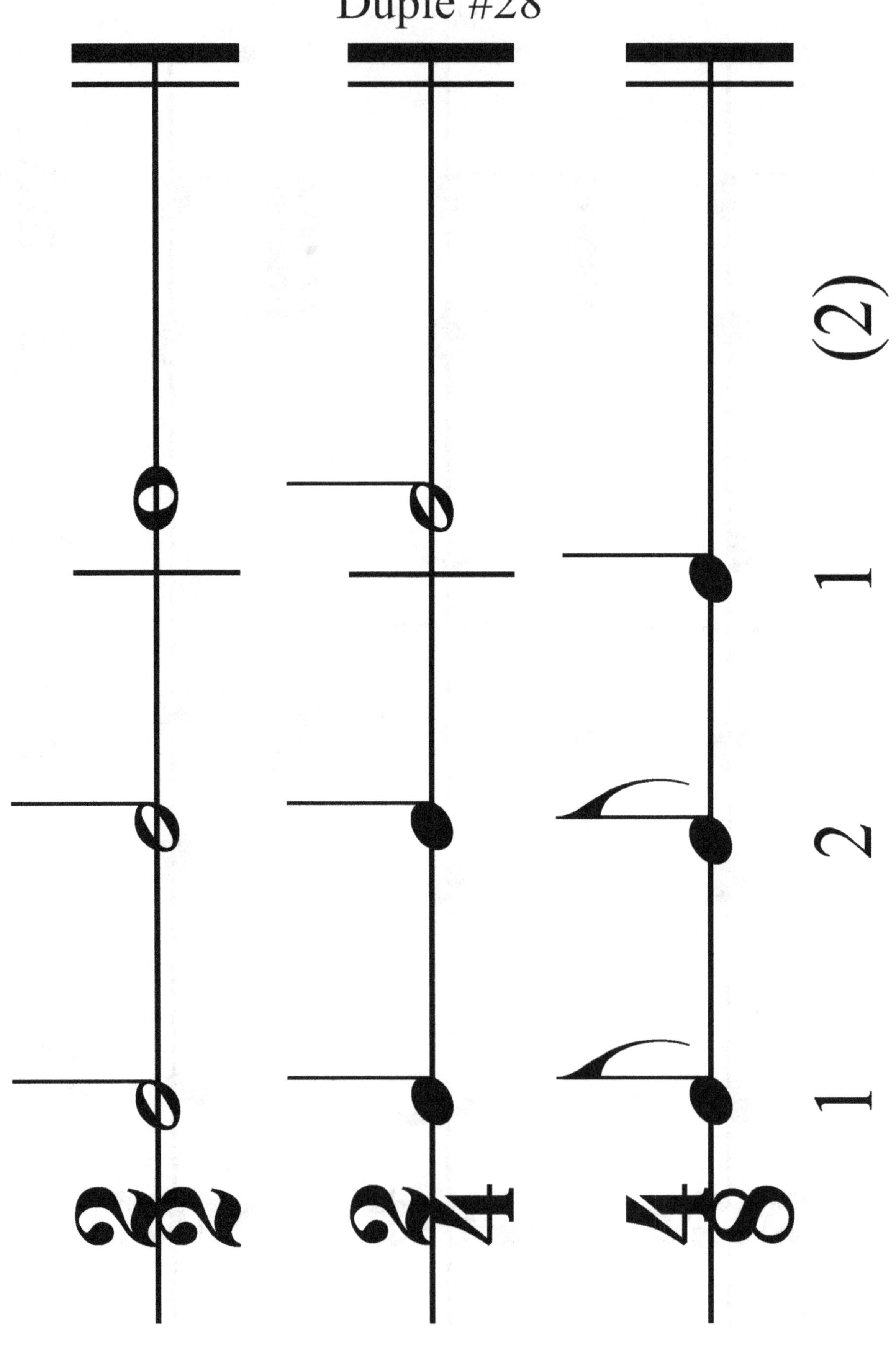

Duple #29

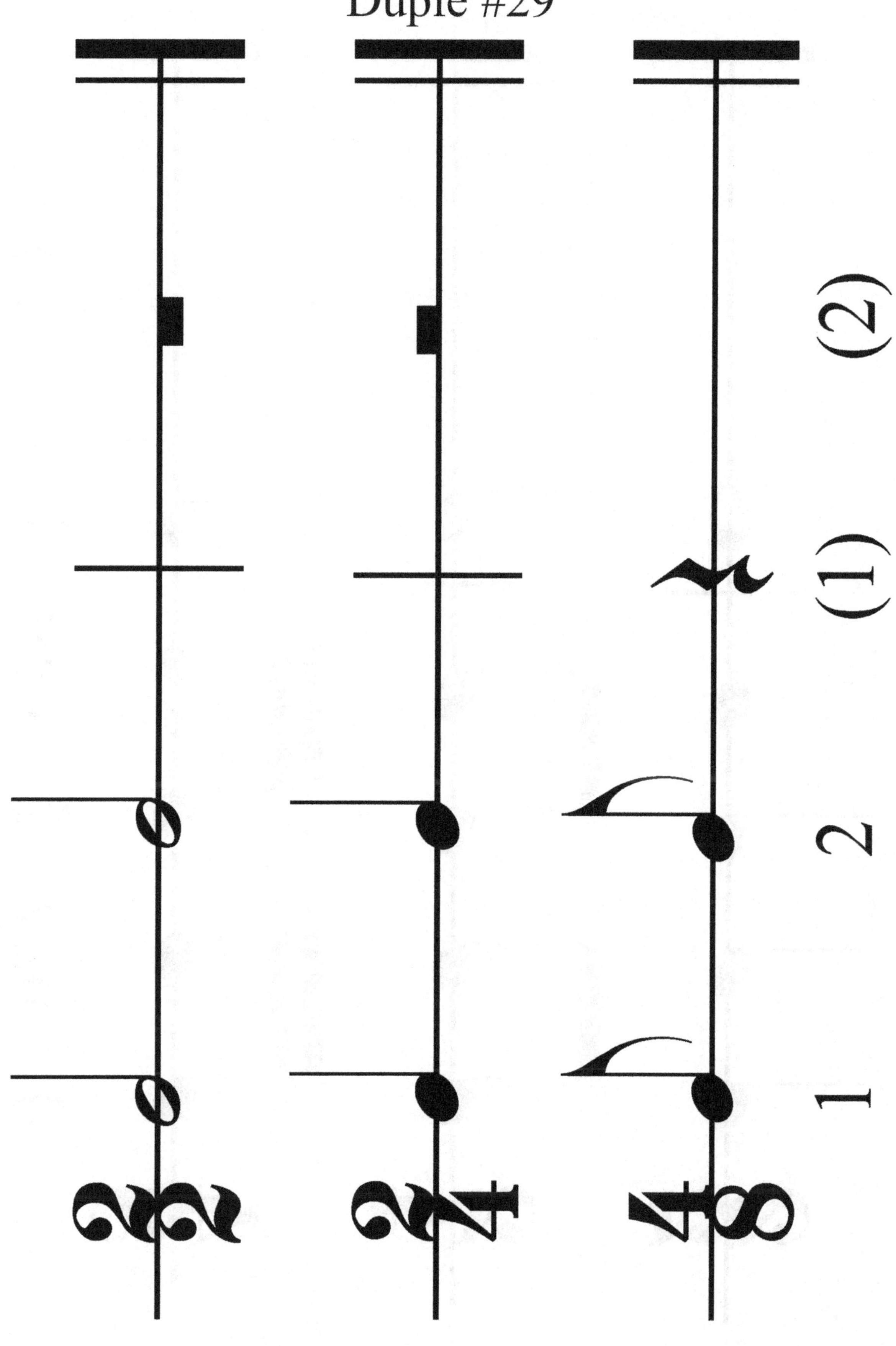

Duple #30

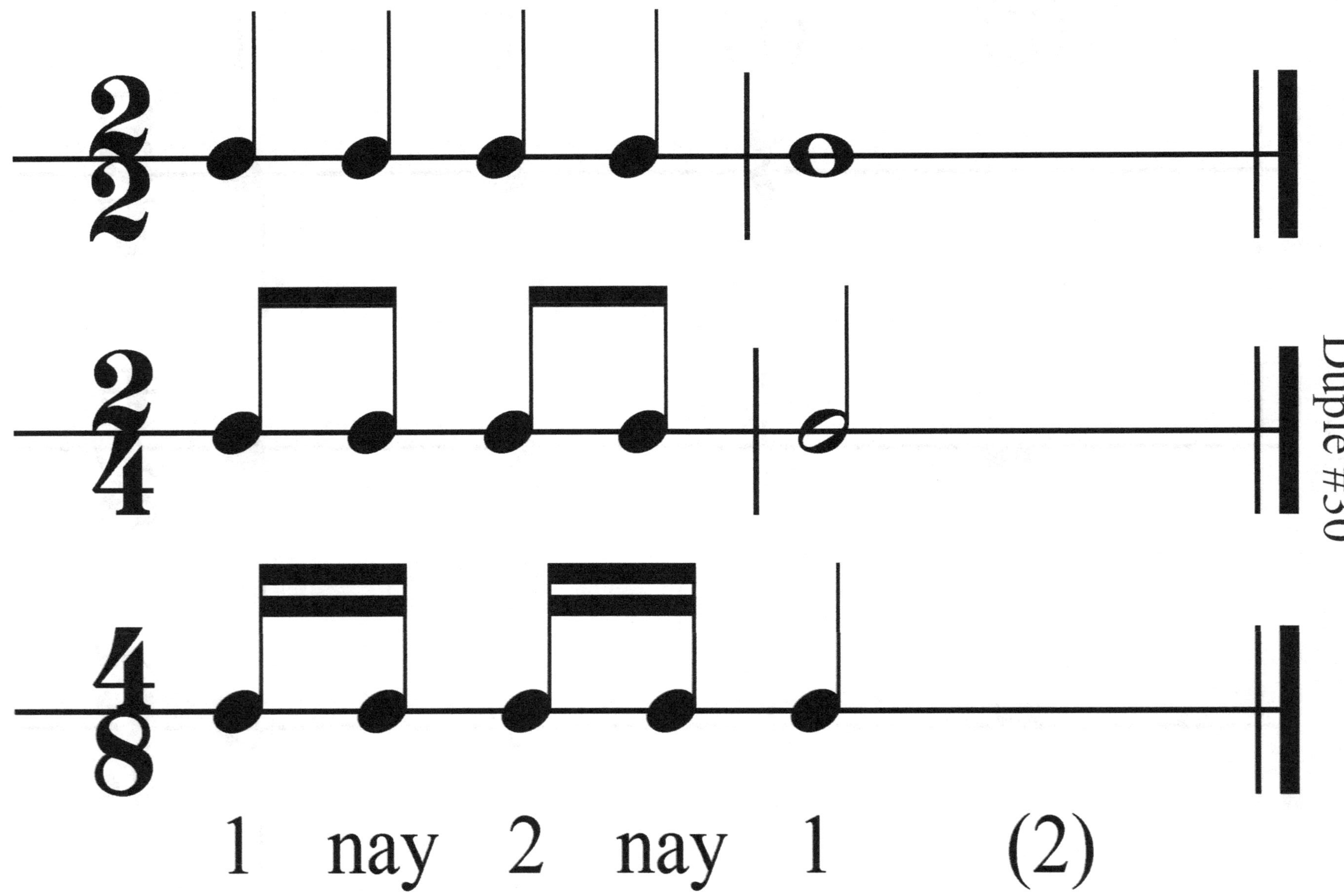

Duple #31

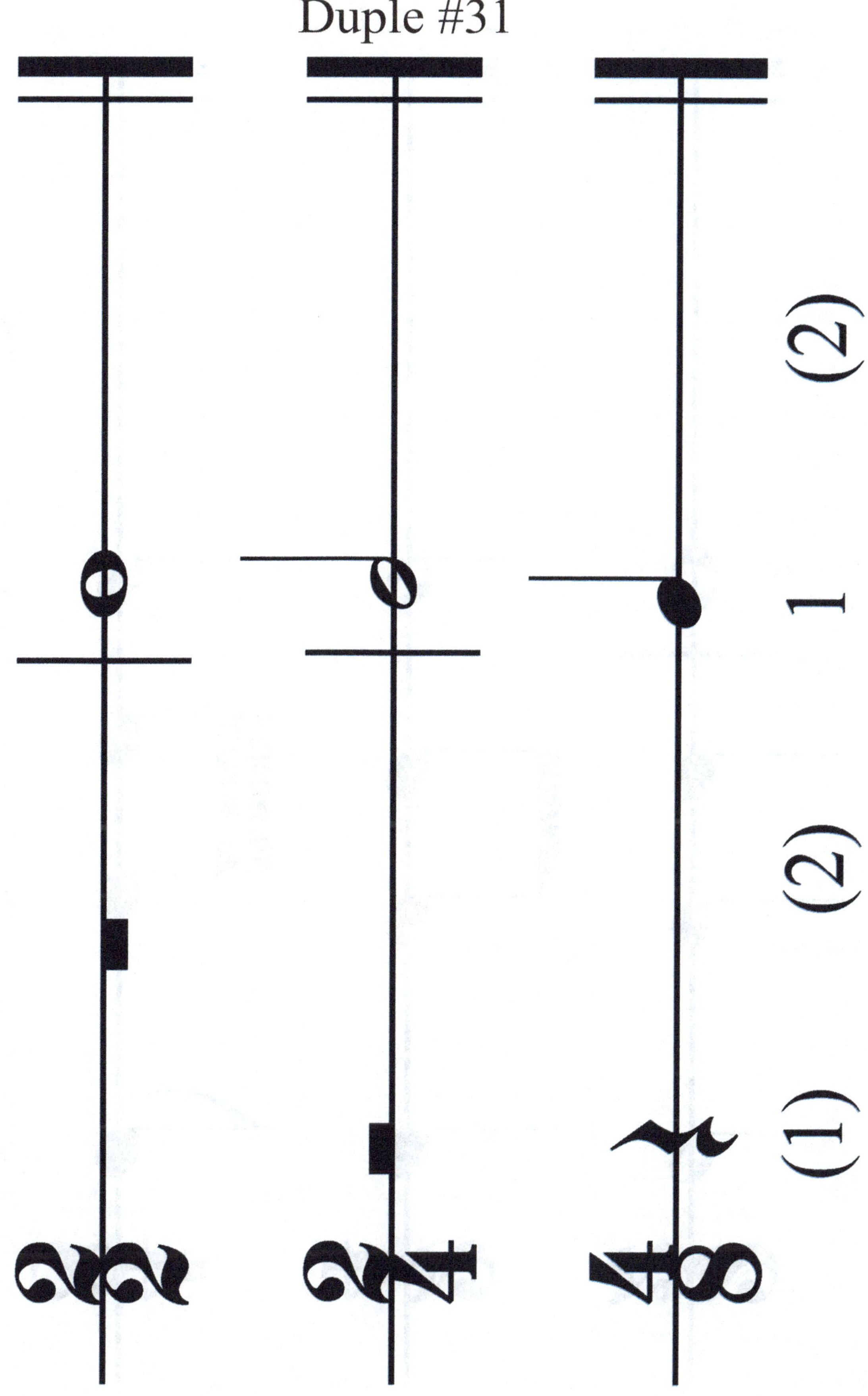

Duple #32

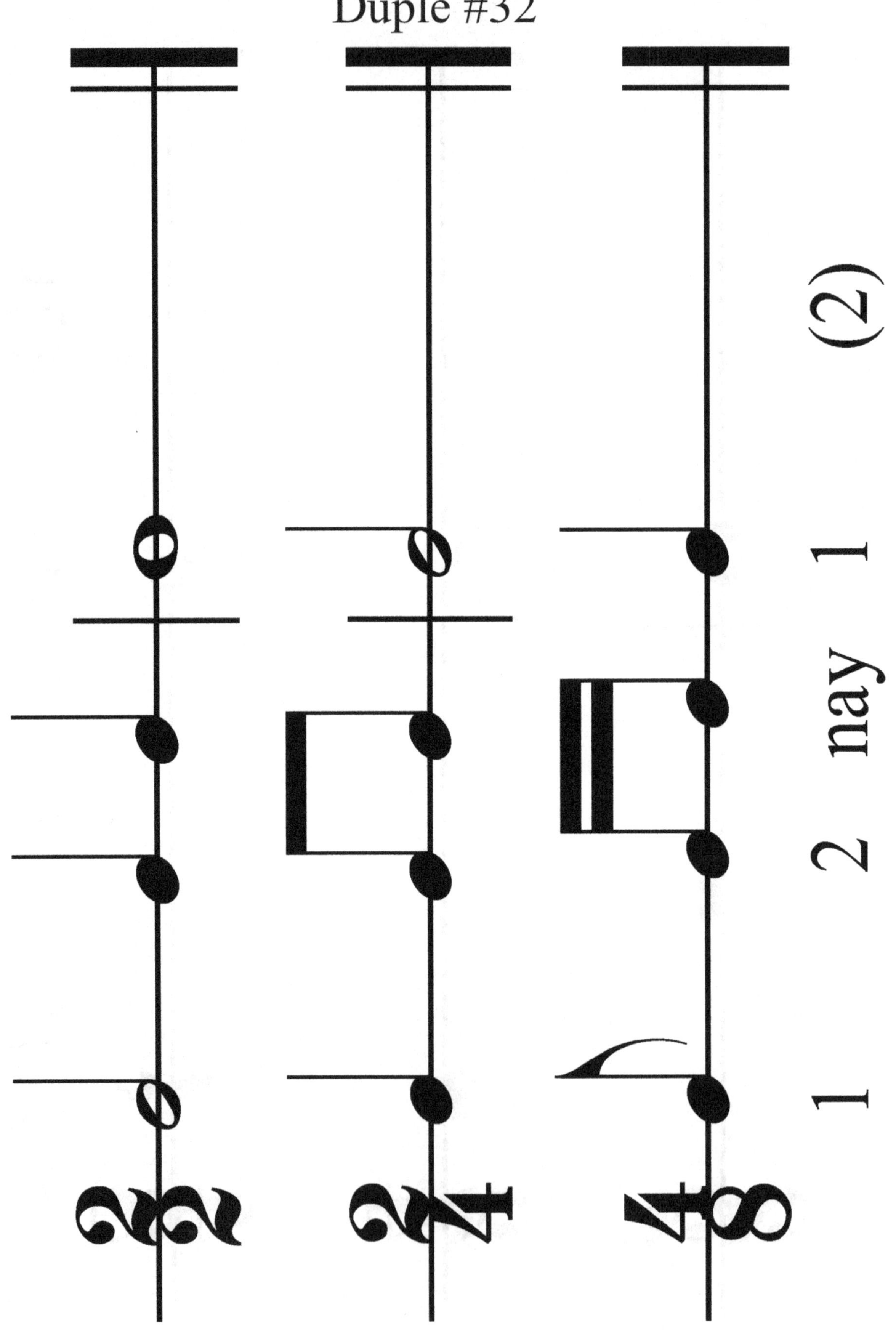

Duple #33

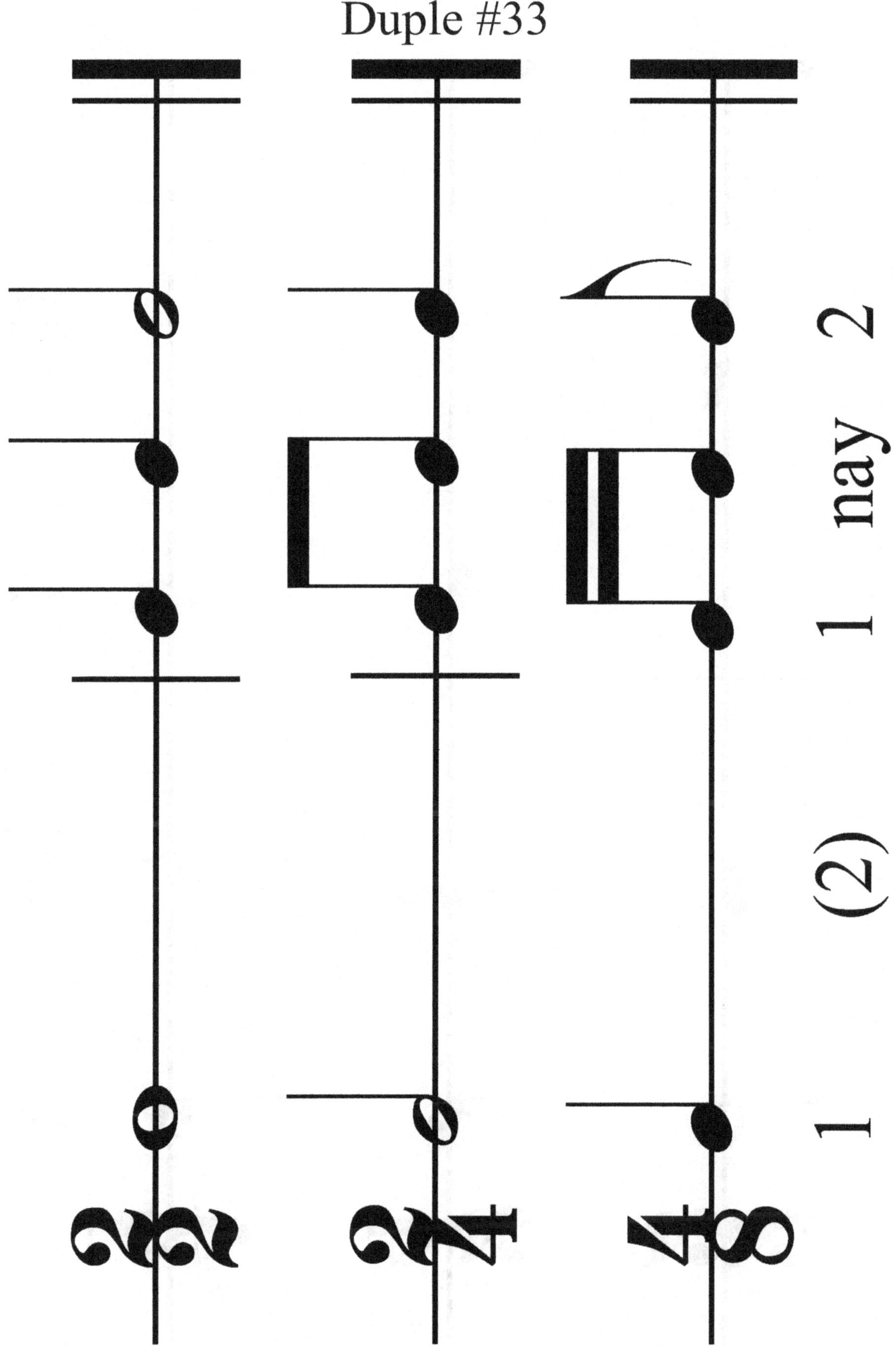

Duple #34

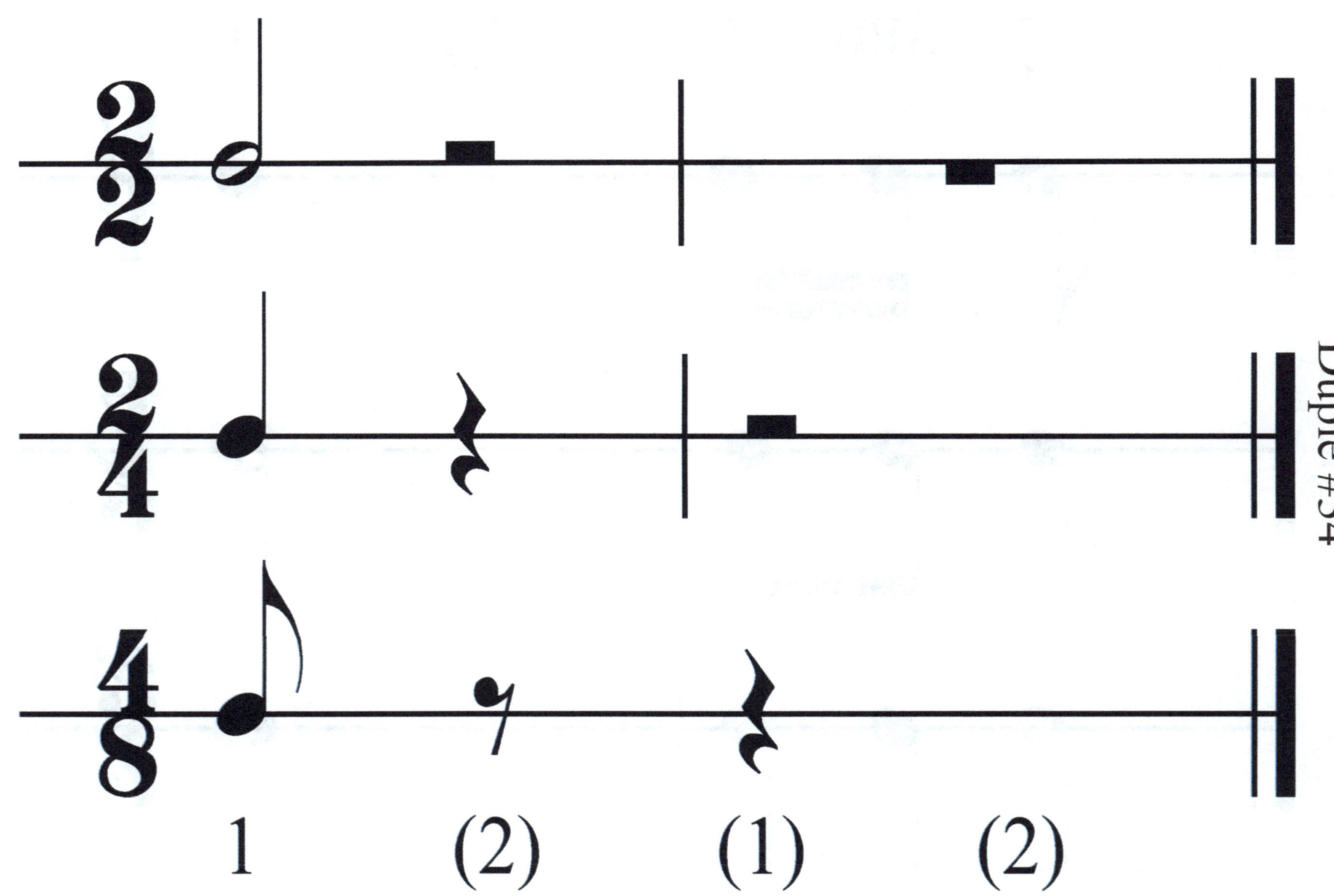

Duple #35

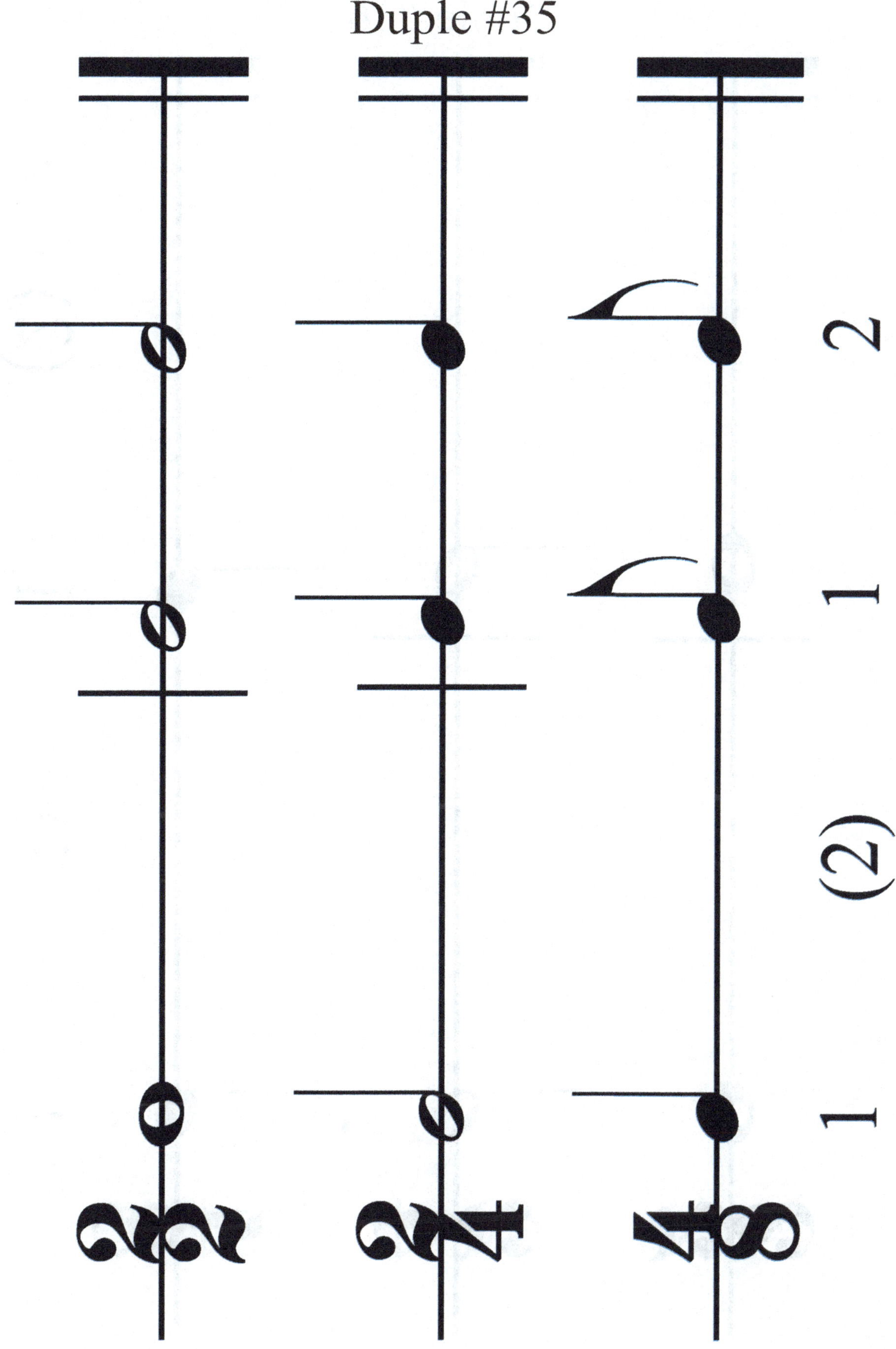

Duple #36

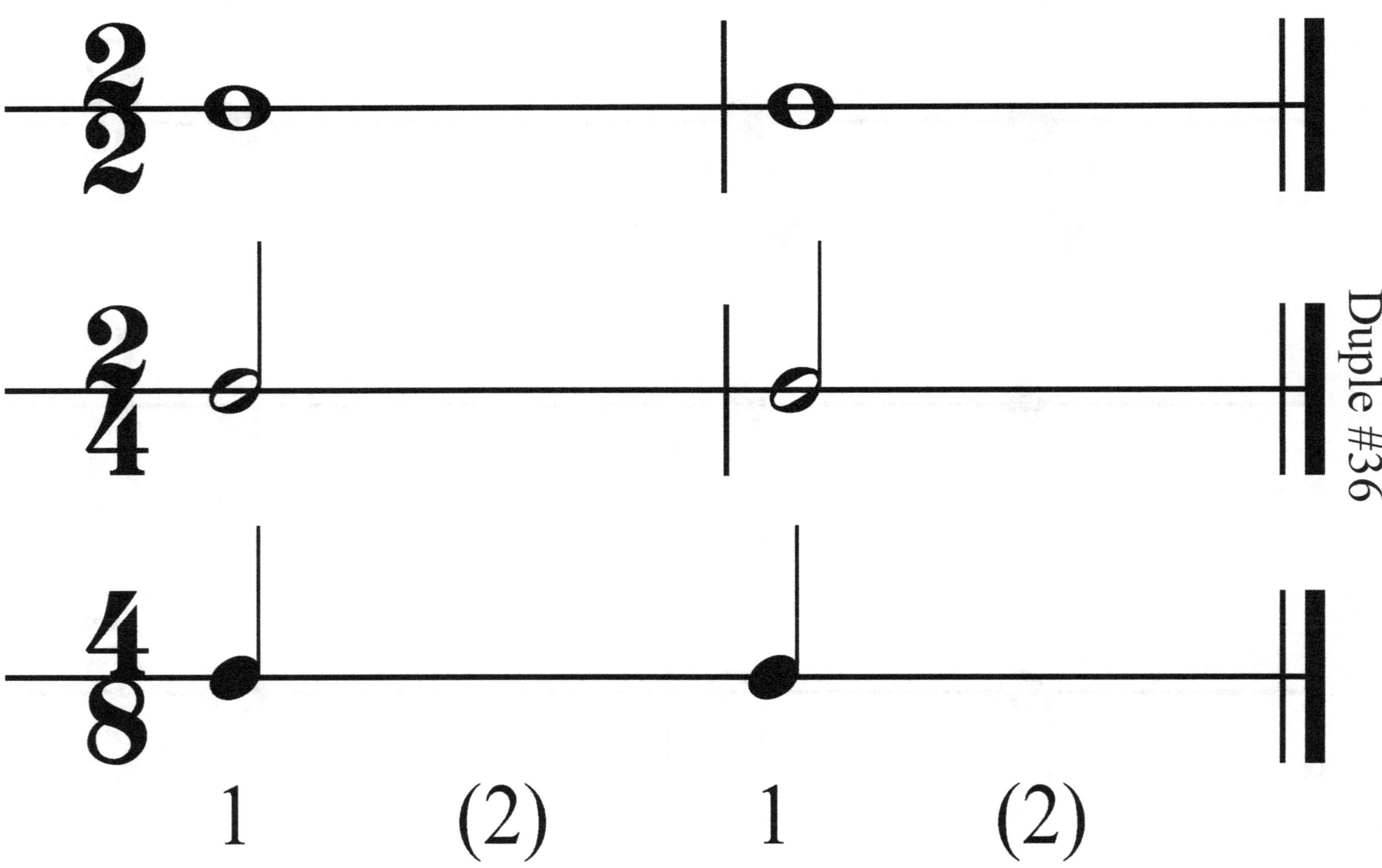

Duple #37

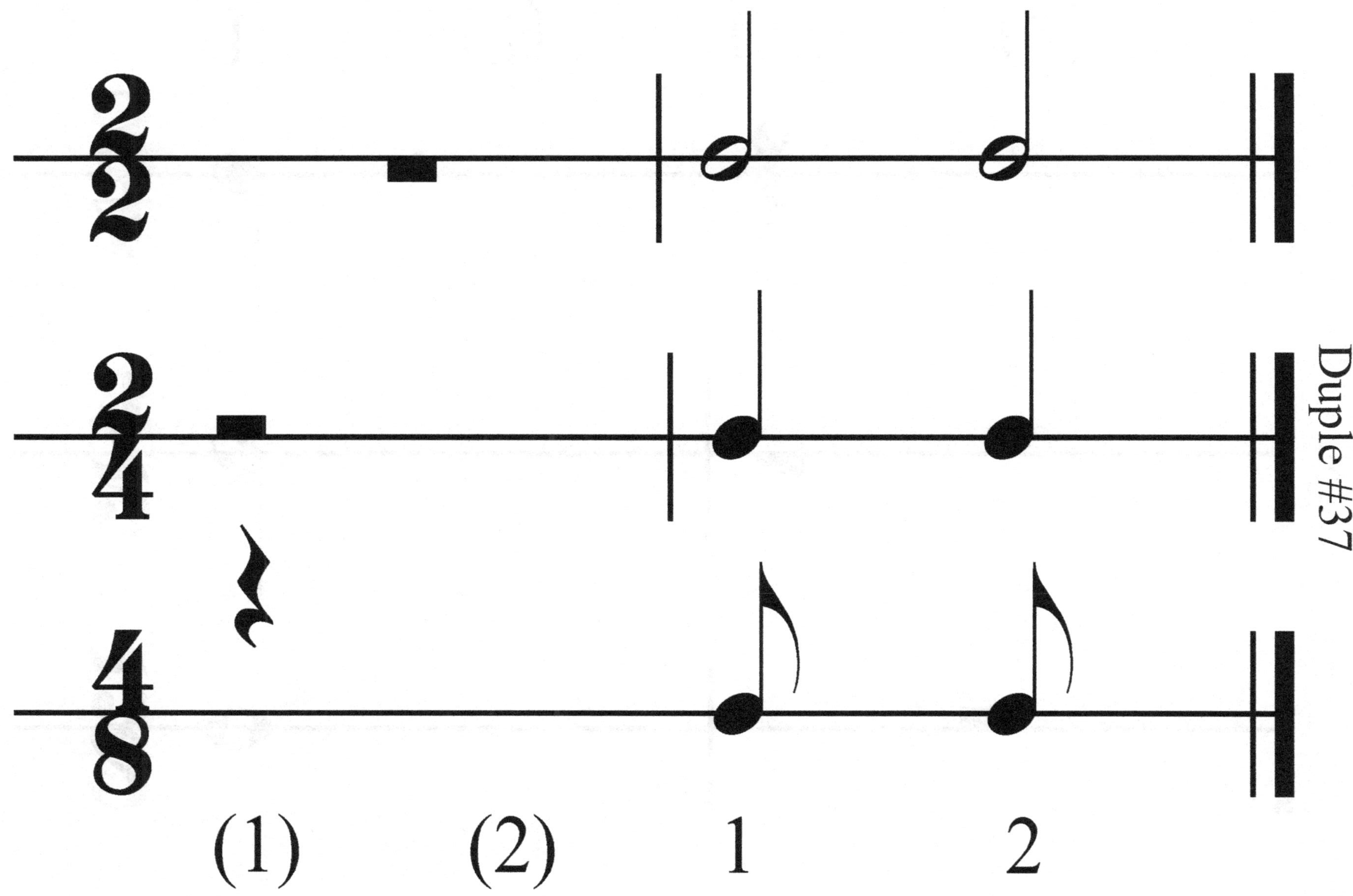

Duple #38

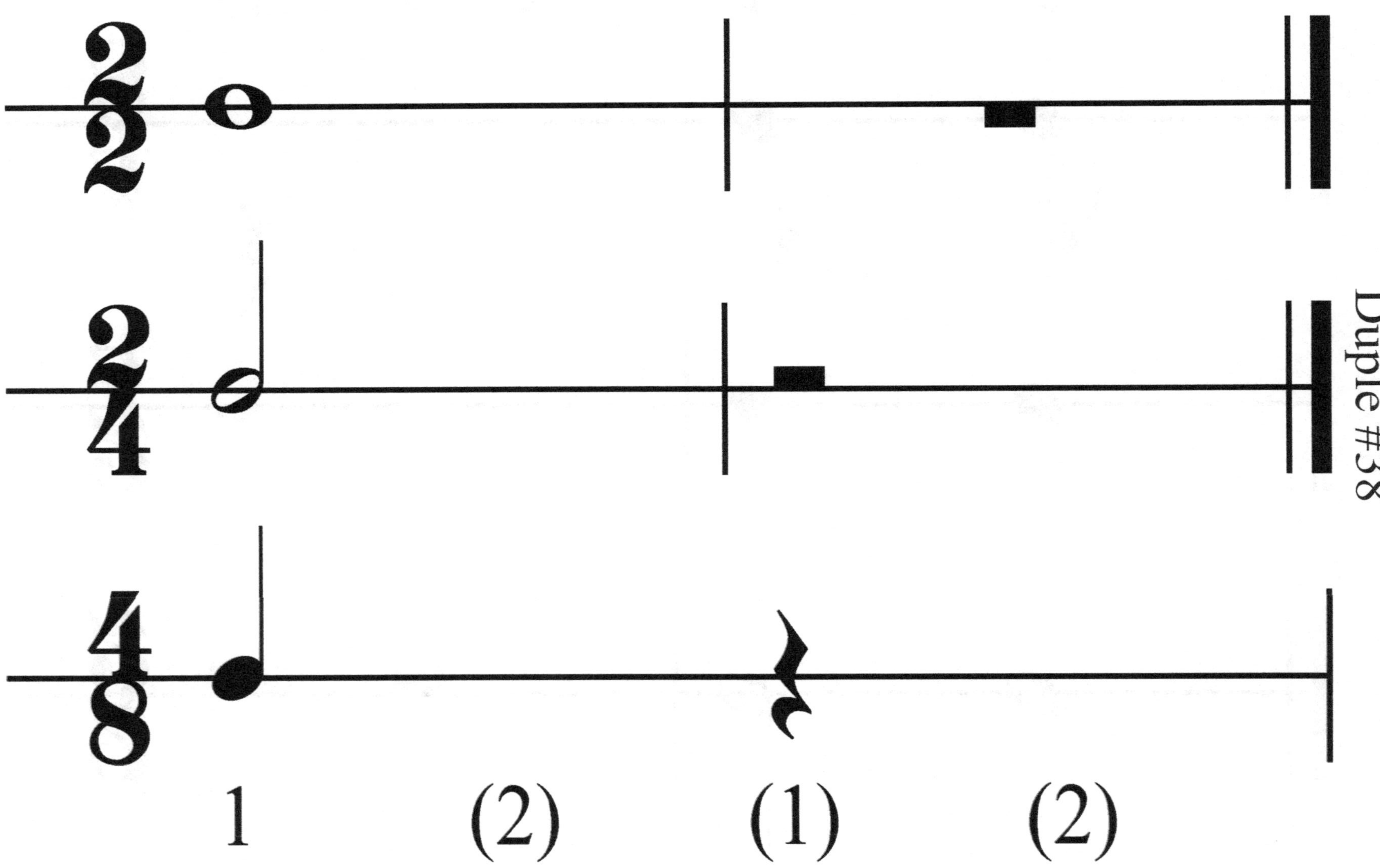

Duple #39

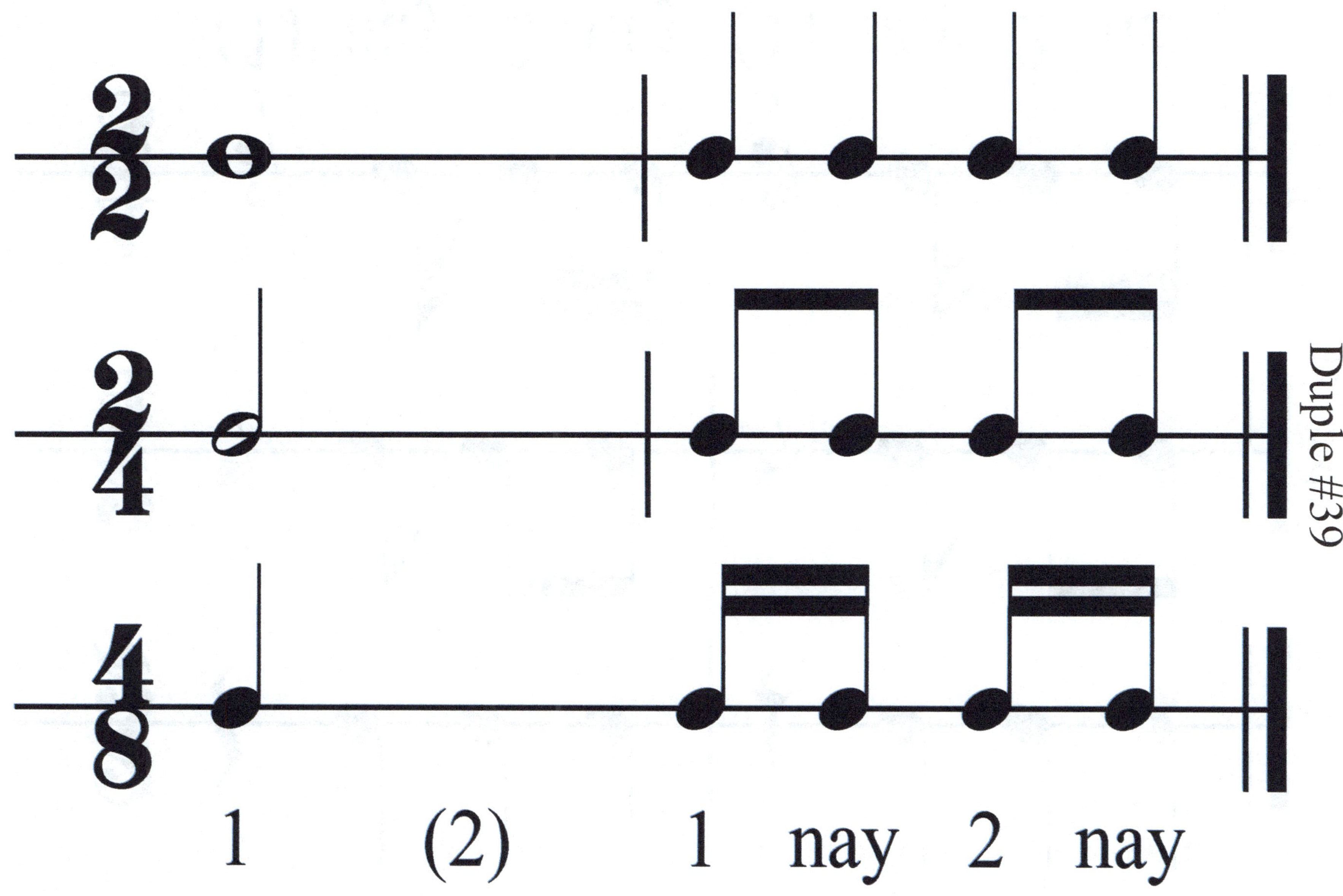

Duple #40

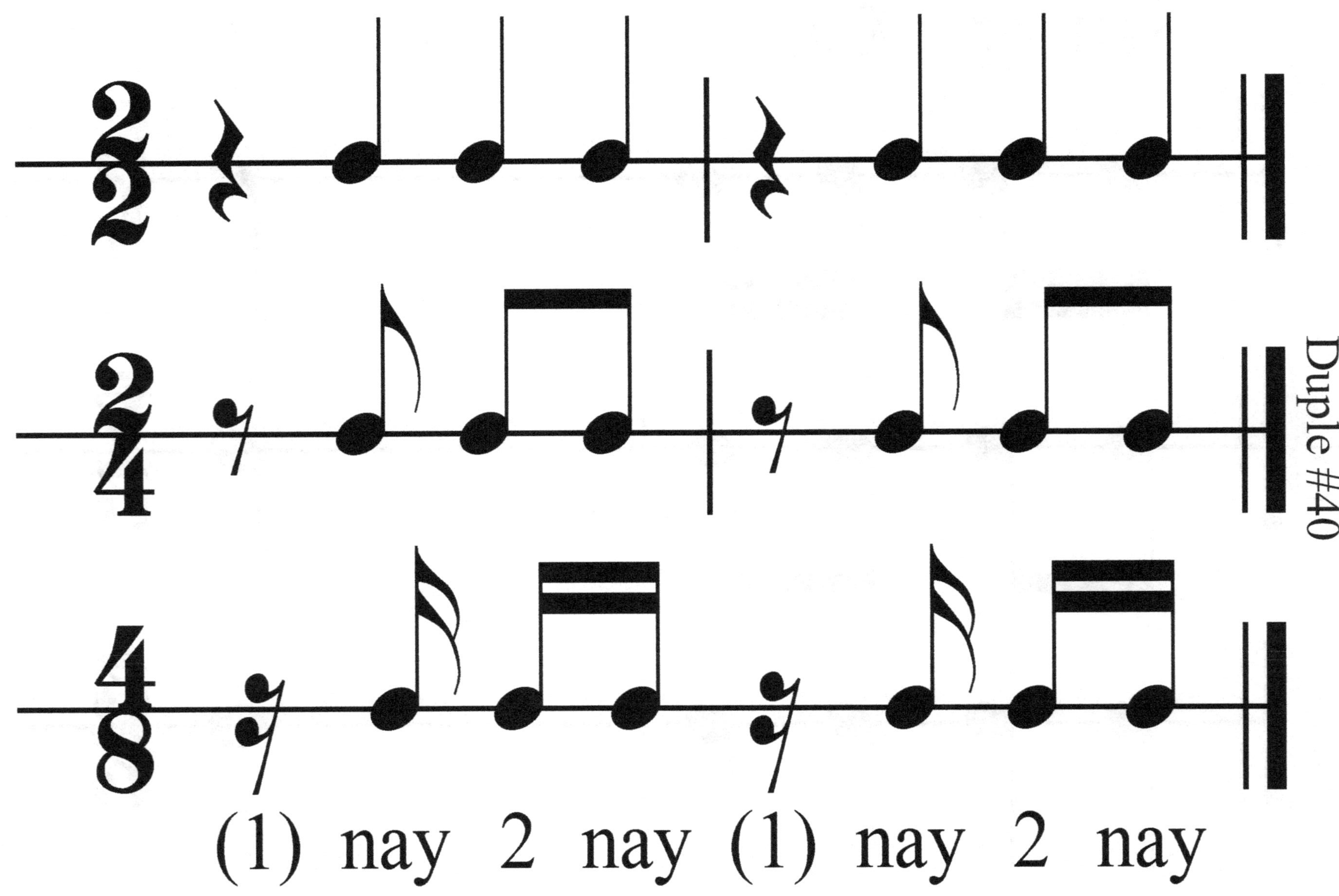
(1) nay 2 nay (1) nay 2 nay

Duple #41

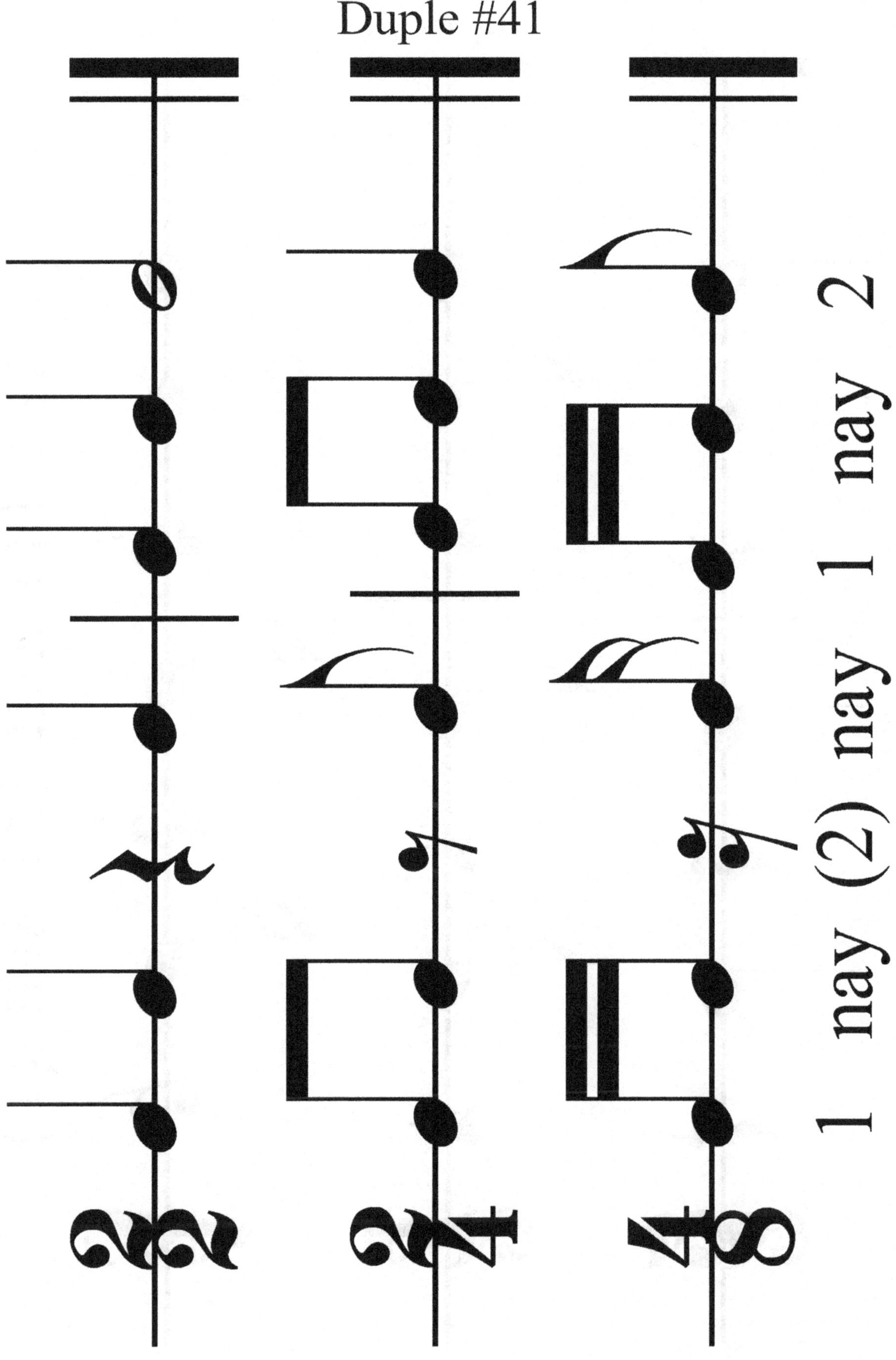
1 nay (2) nay 1 nay 2

Duple #42

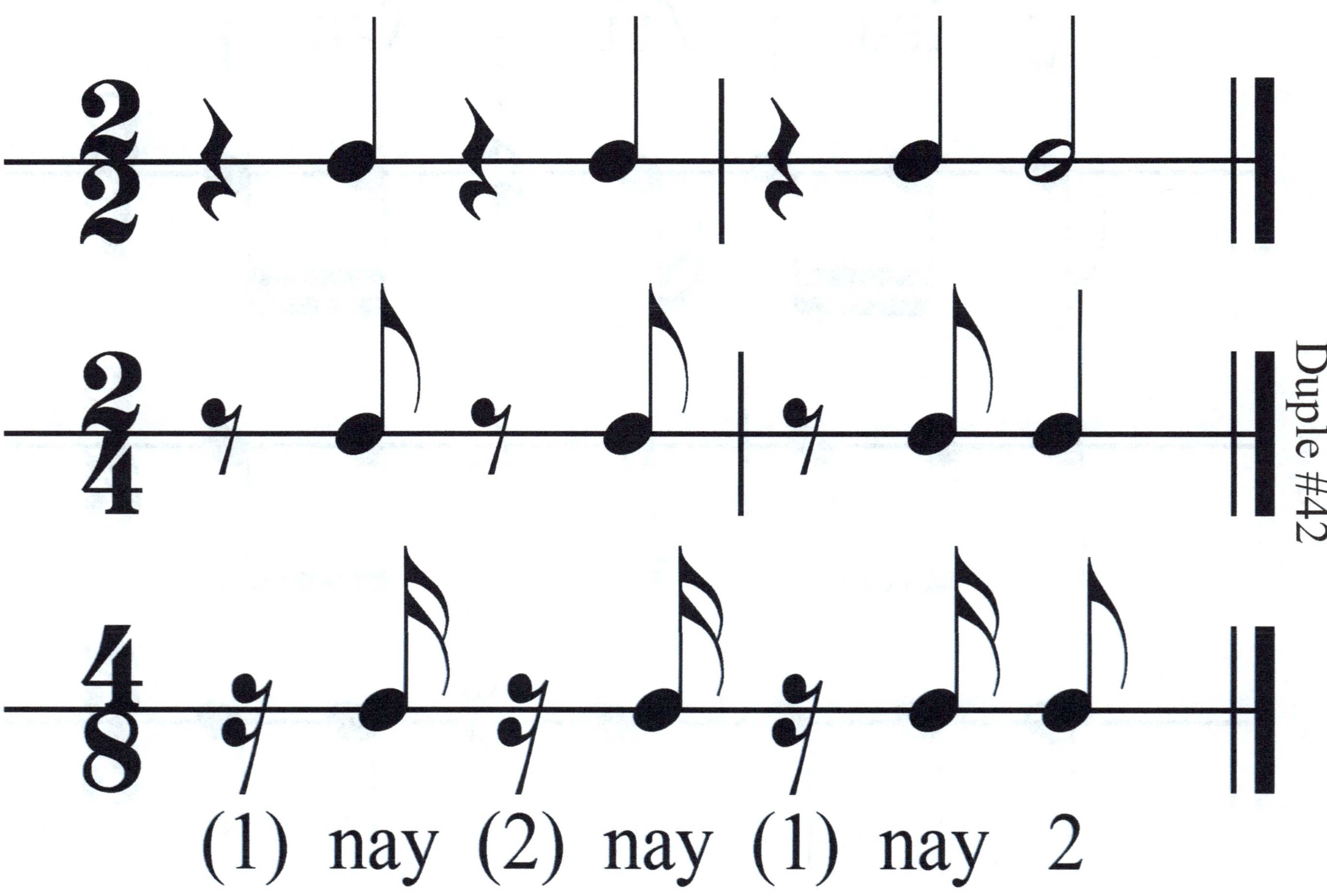

Duple #43

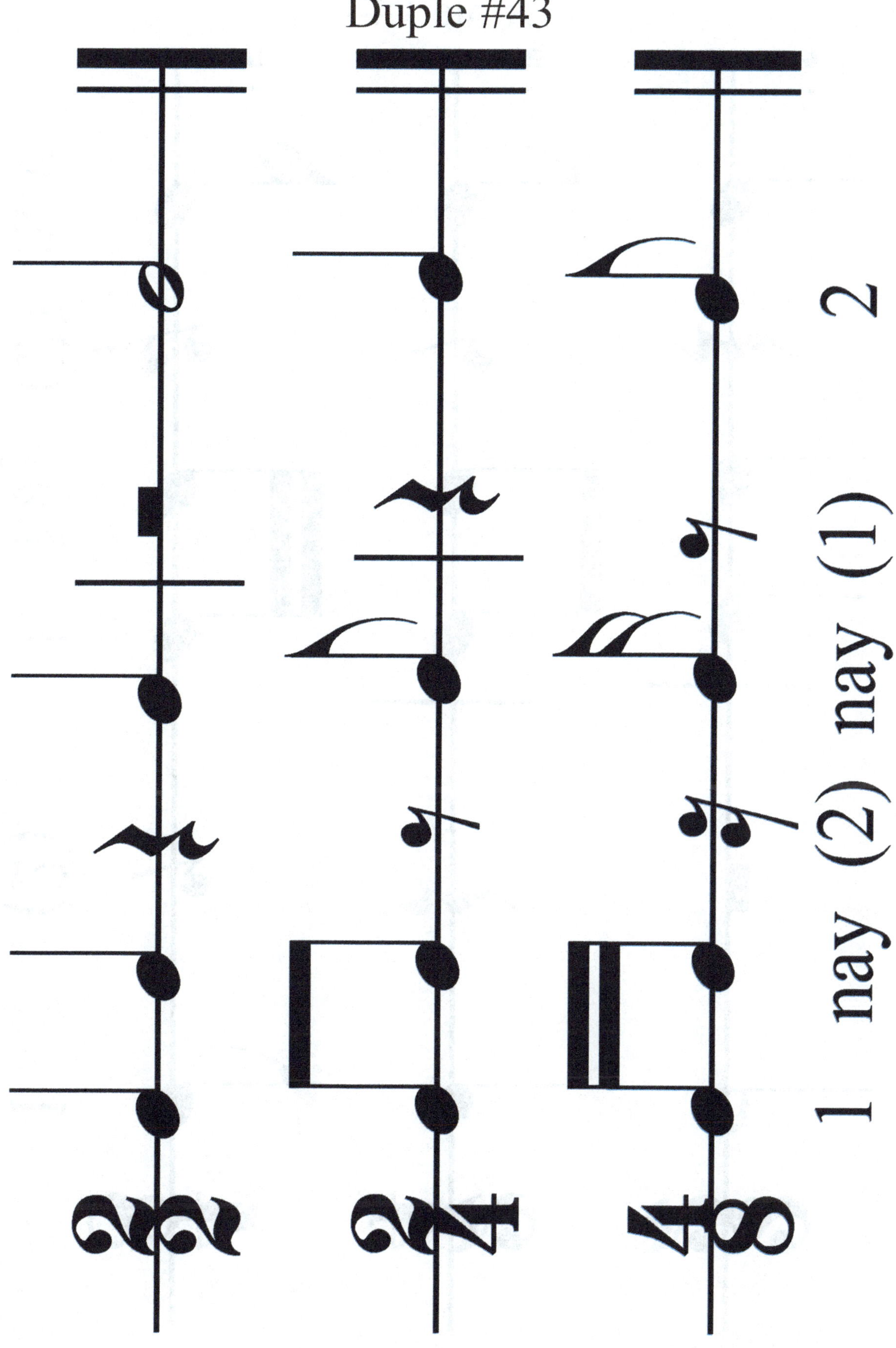

Duple #44

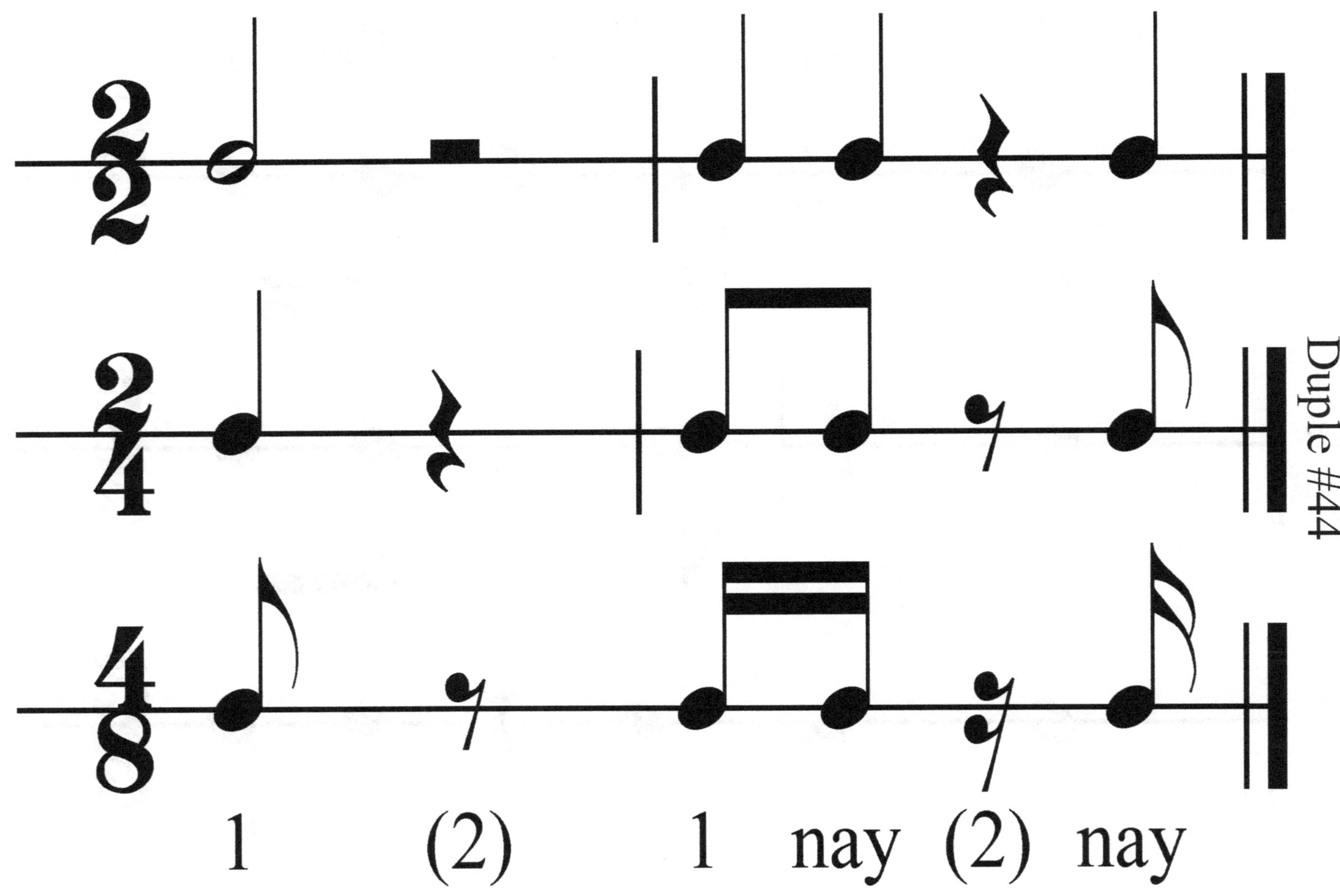

Duple #45

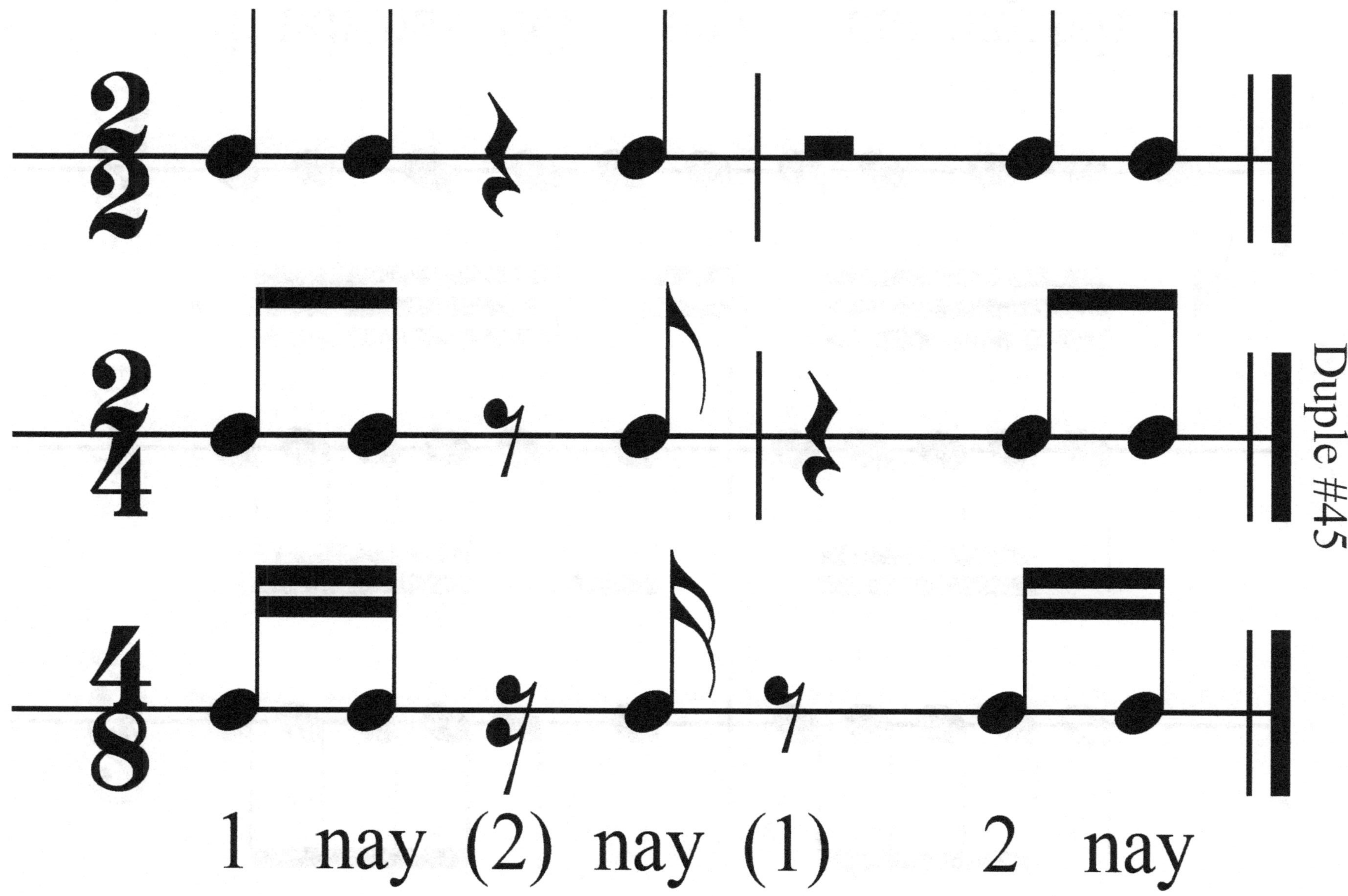
1 nay (2) nay (1) 2 nay

Duple #46

Duple #47

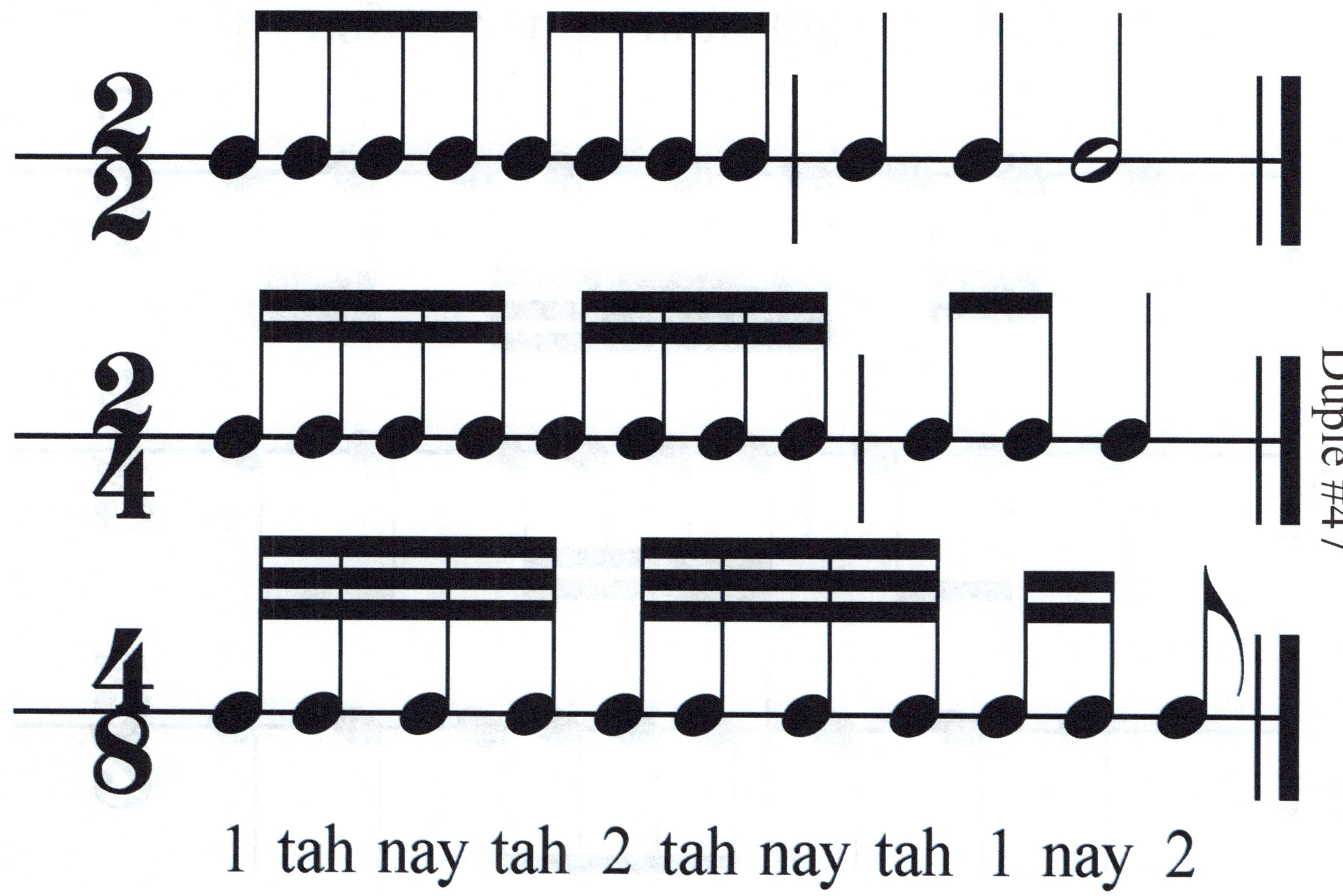
1 tah nay tah 2 tah nay tah 1 nay 2

Duple #48

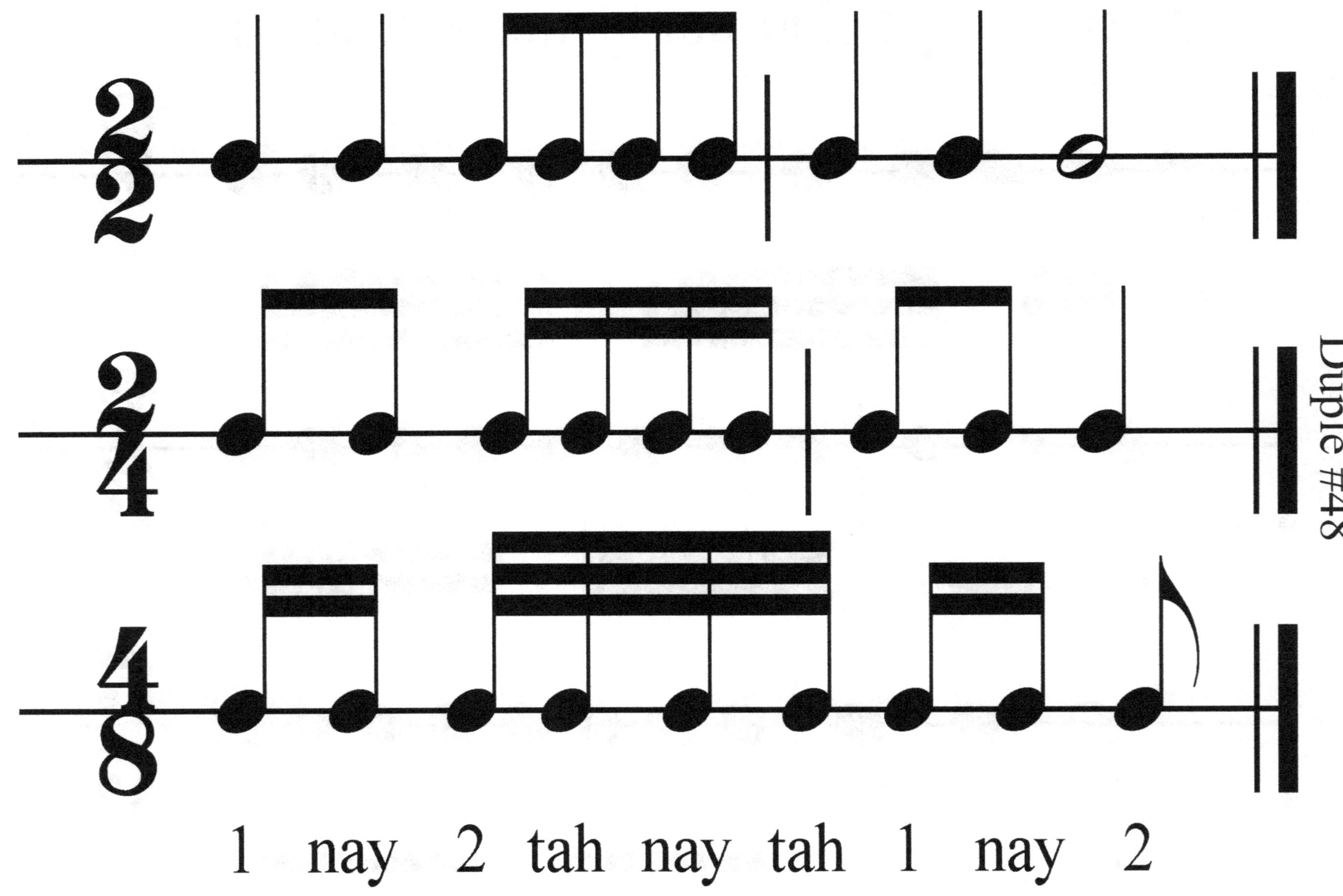
1 nay 2 tah nay tah 1 nay 2

Duple #49

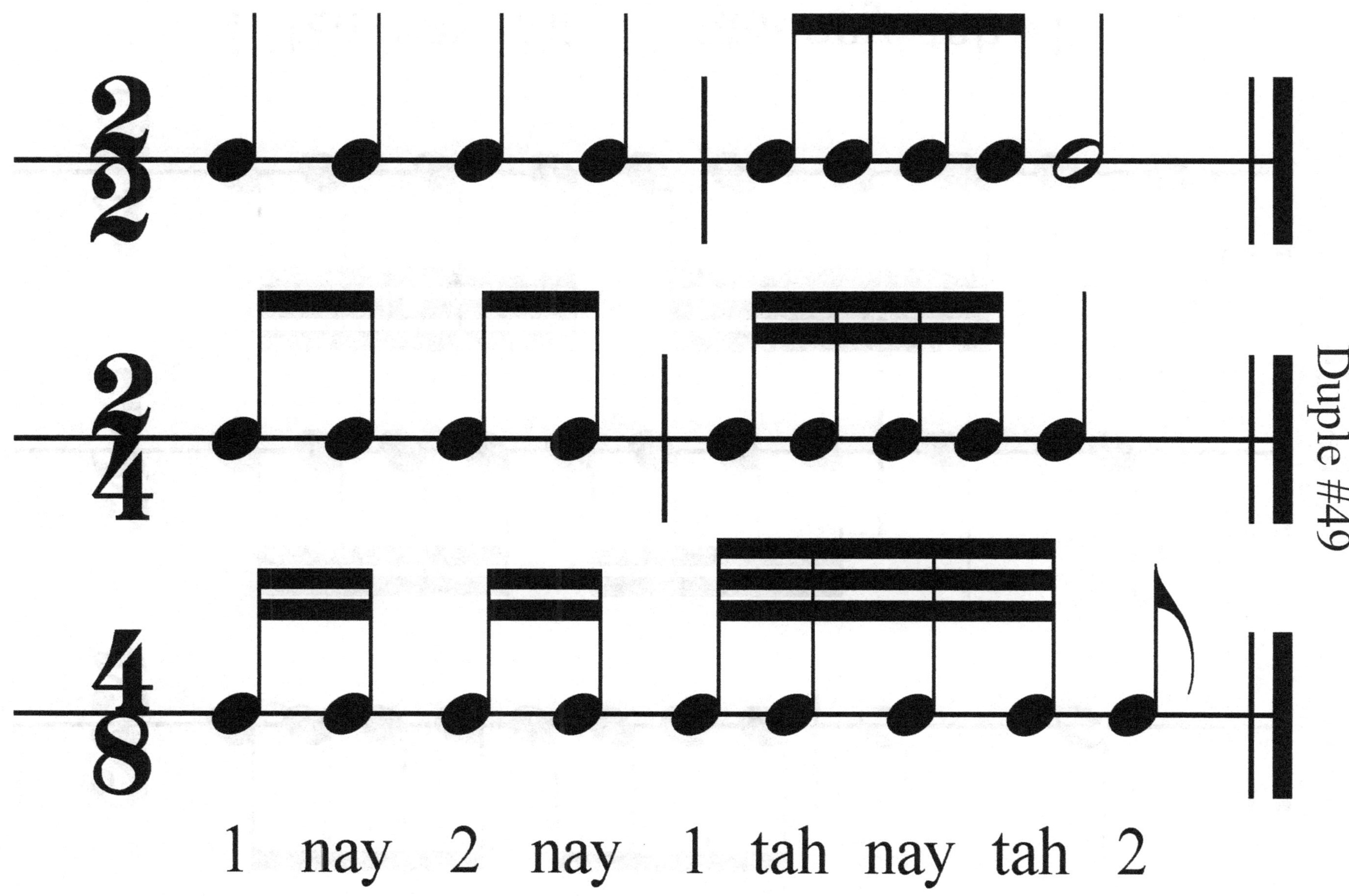
1 nay 2 nay 1 tah nay tah 2

Duple #50

Duple #51

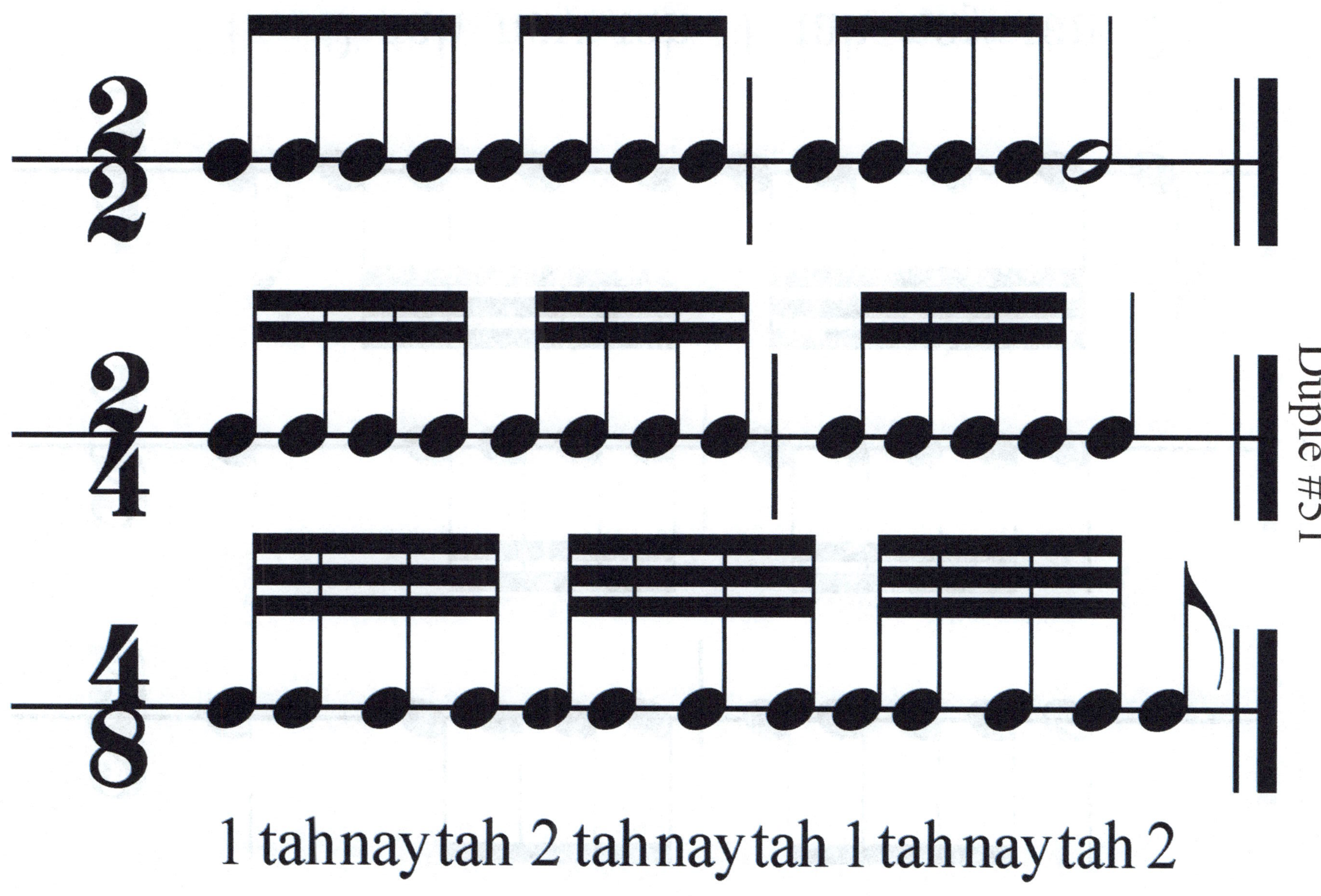
1 tahnaytah 2 tahnaytah 1 tahnaytah 2

Duple #52

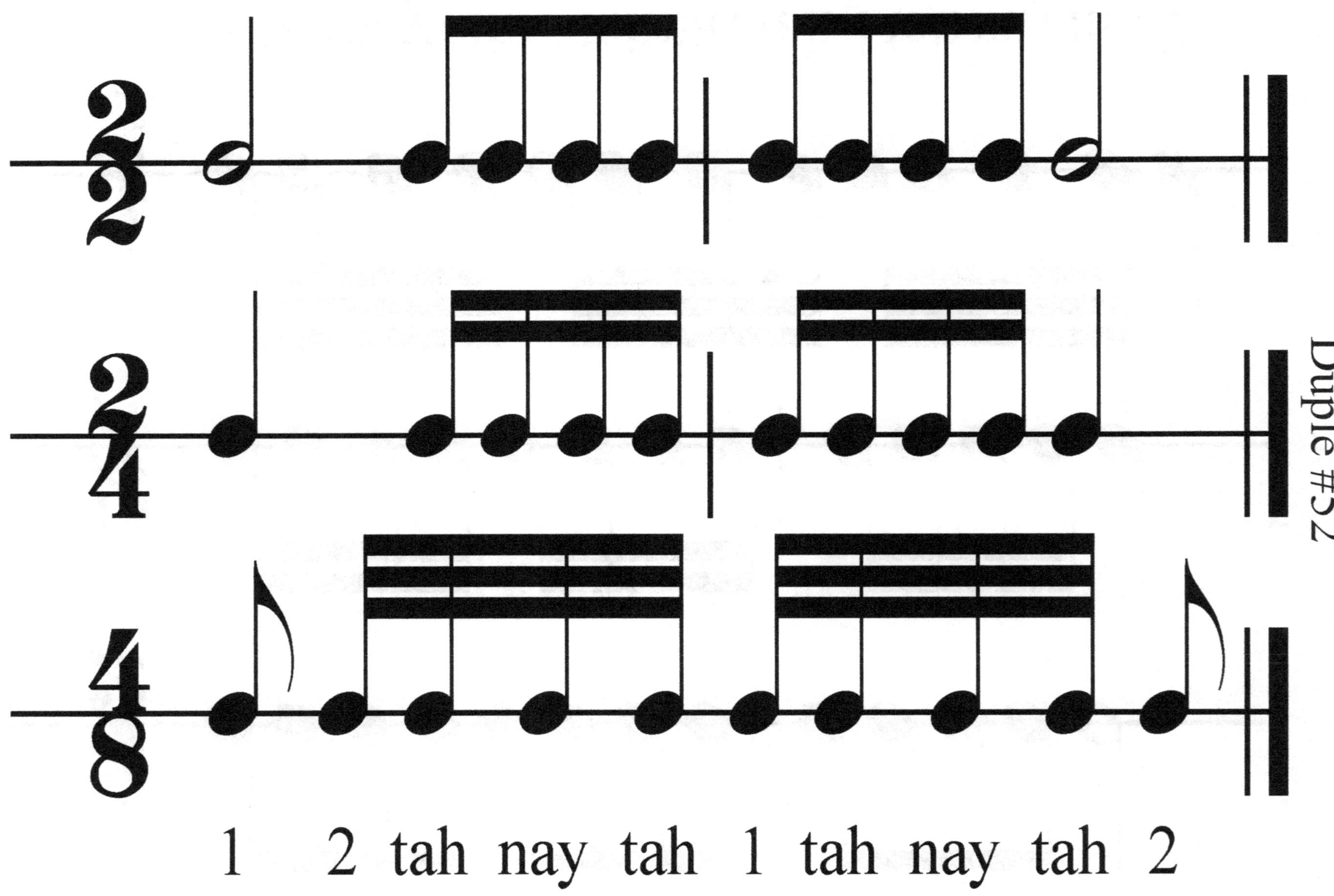
2
2
2
4
4
8
1 2 tah nay tah 1 tah nay tah 2

Duple #53

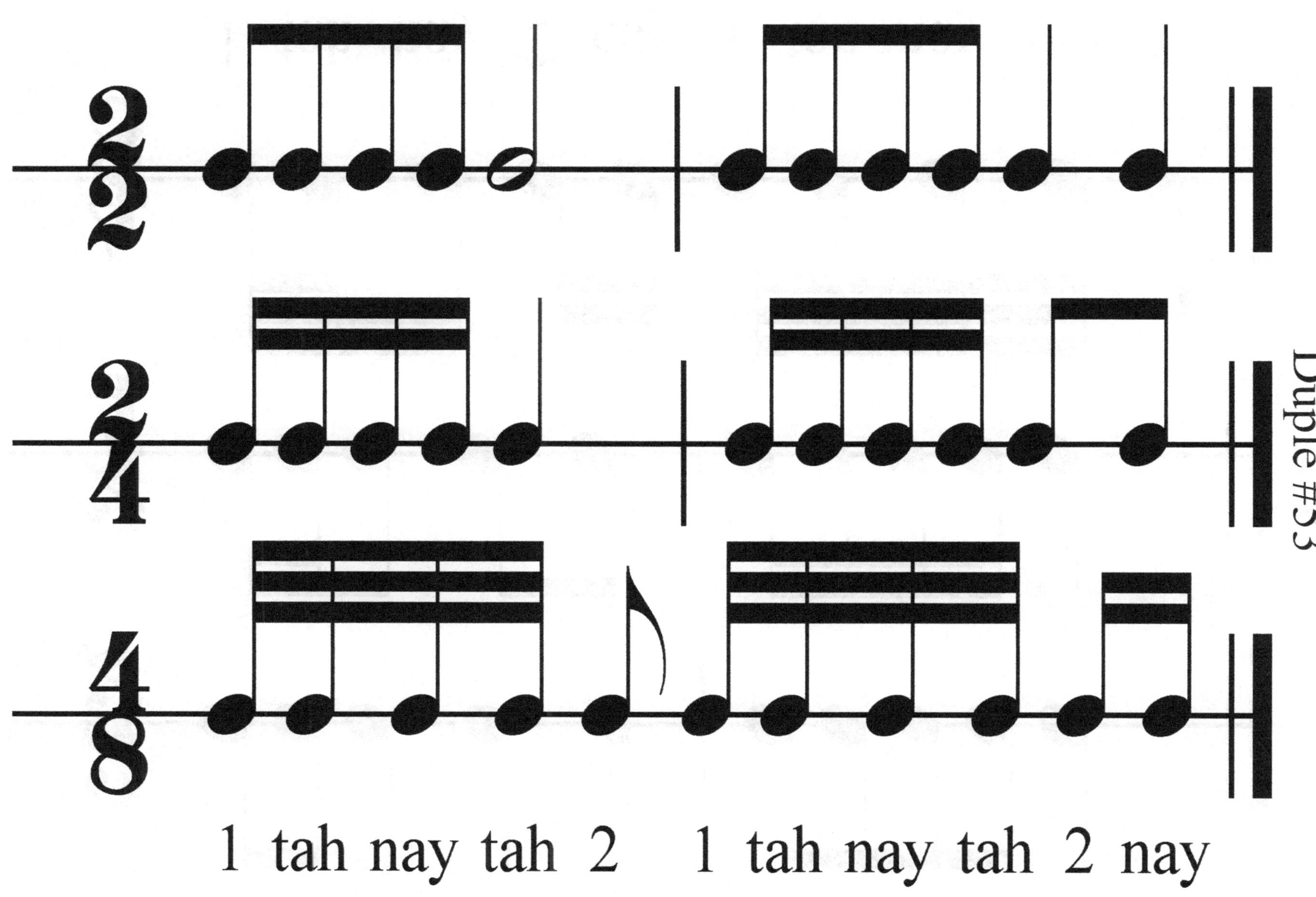
1 tah nay tah 2 1 tah nay tah 2 nay

Duple #54

Duple #55

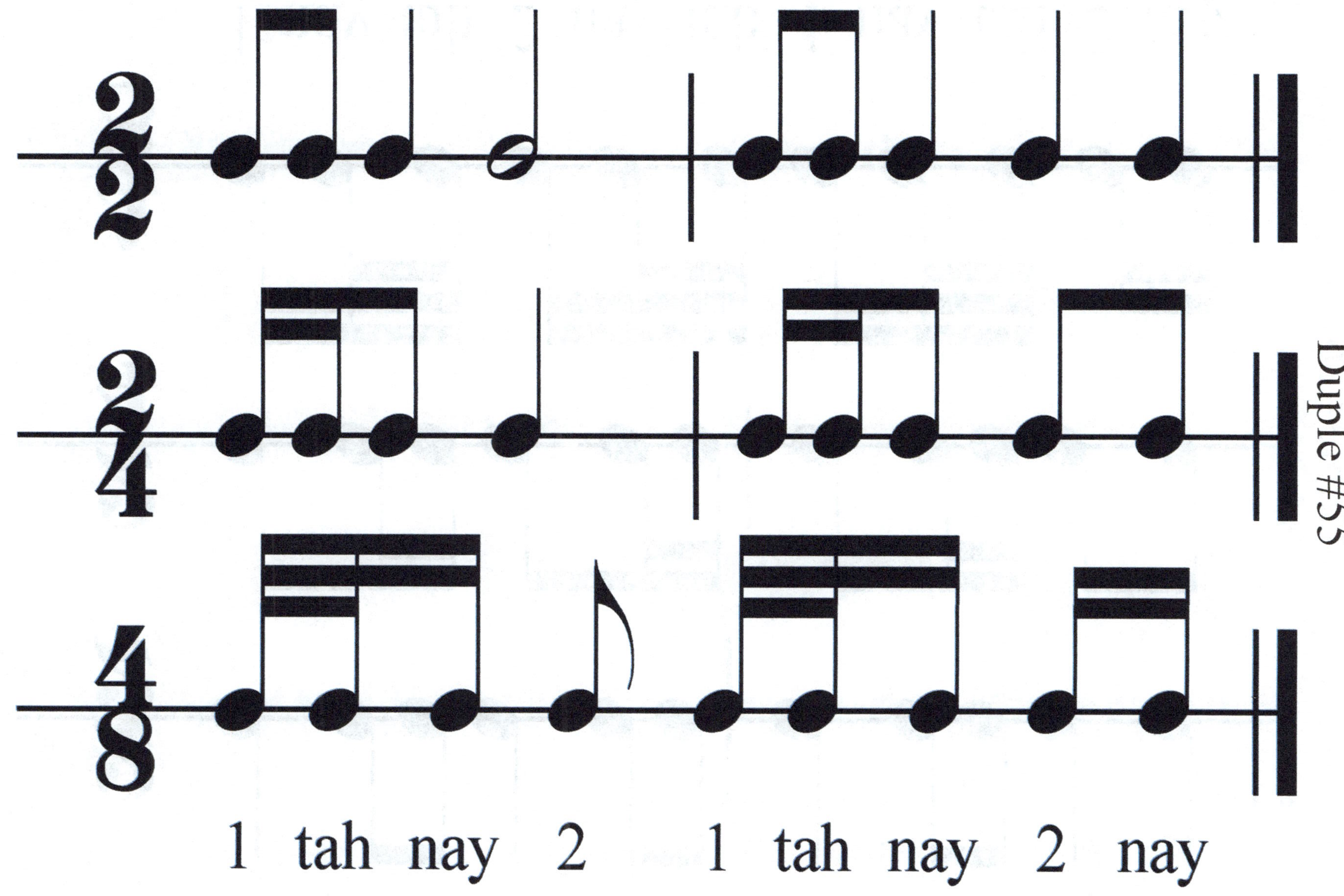

Duple #56

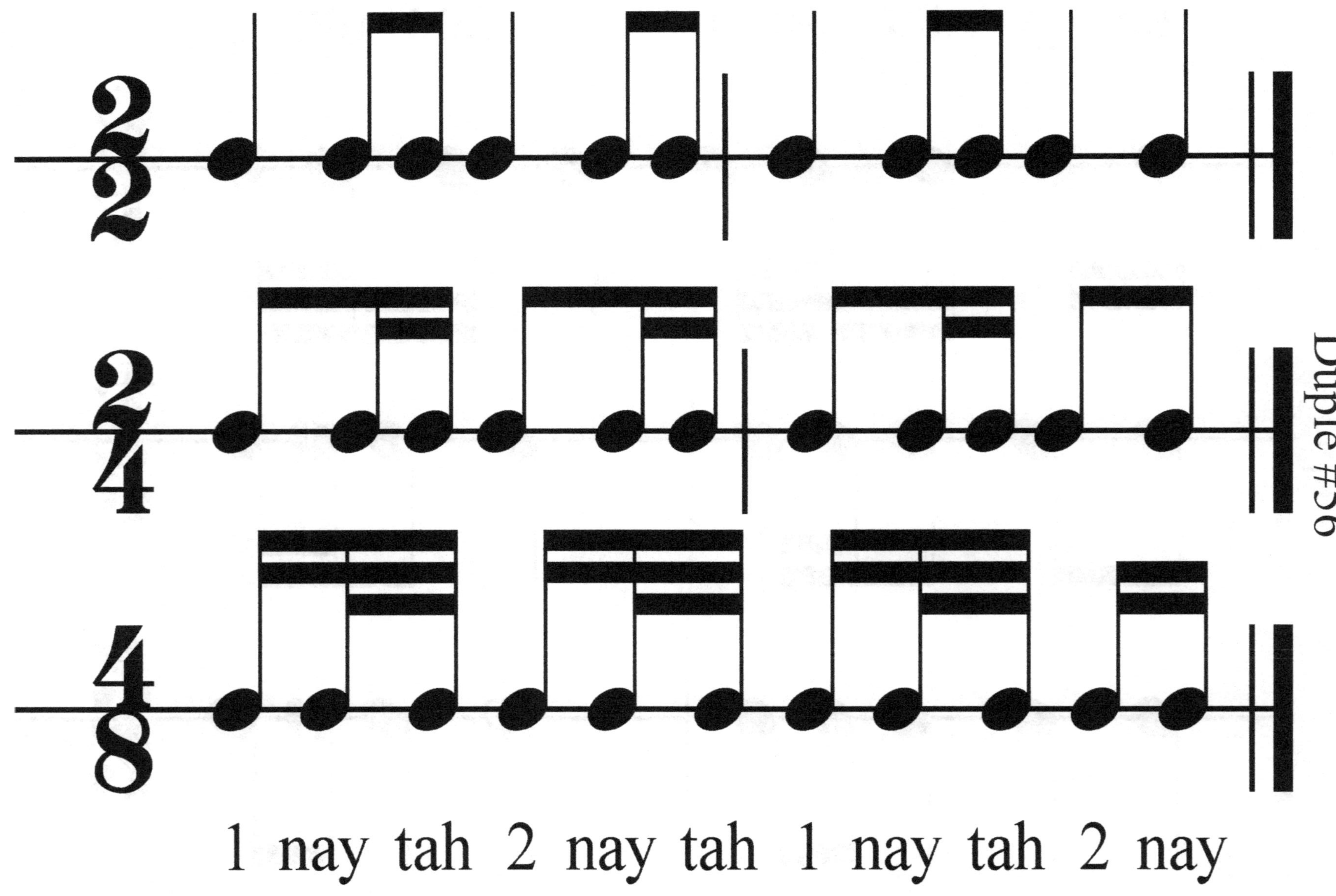
2/2
2/4
4/8
1 nay tah 2 nay tah 1 nay tah 2 nay

Duple #57

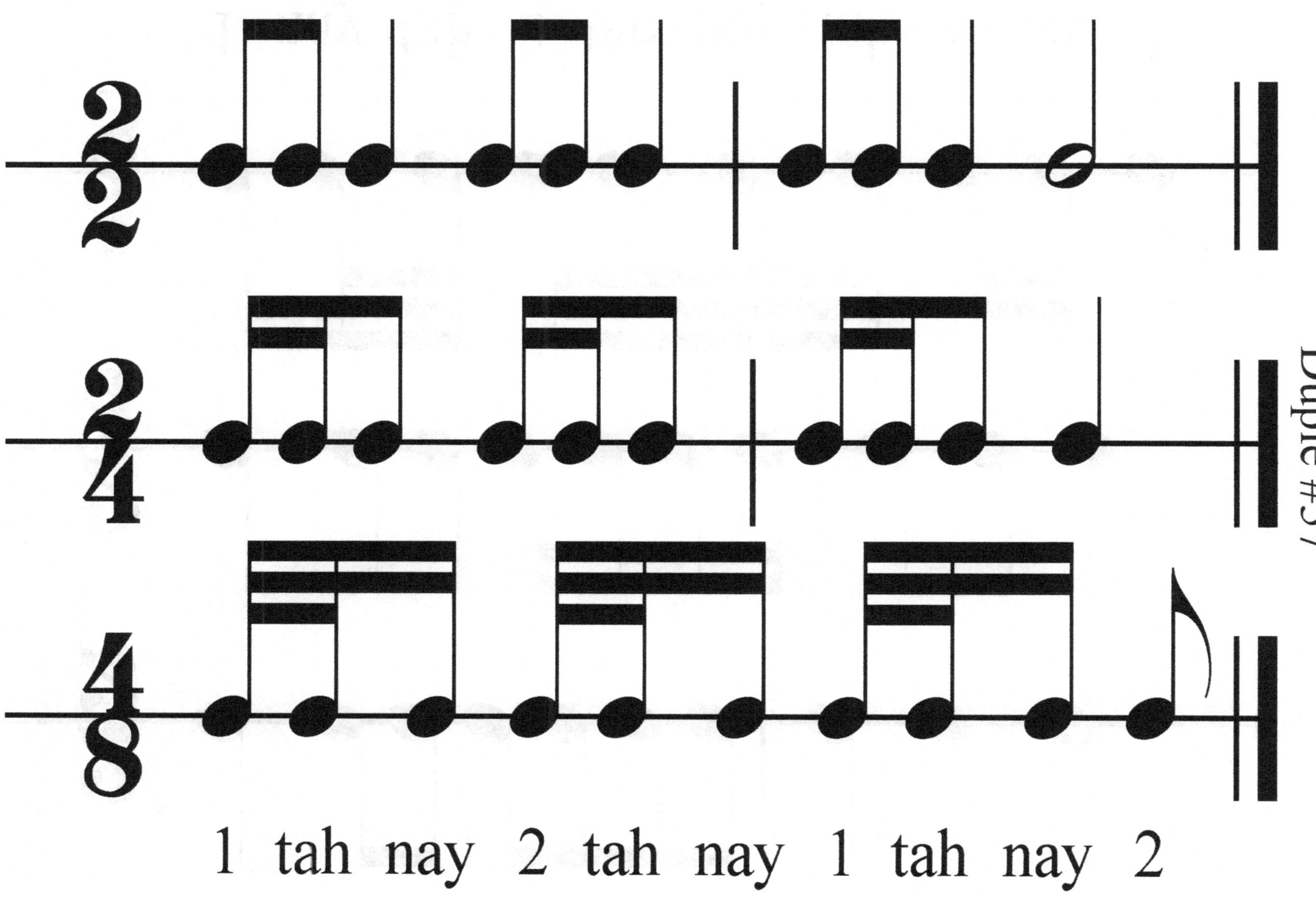
2/2
2/4
4/8
1 tah nay 2 tah nay 1 tah nay 2

Duple #58

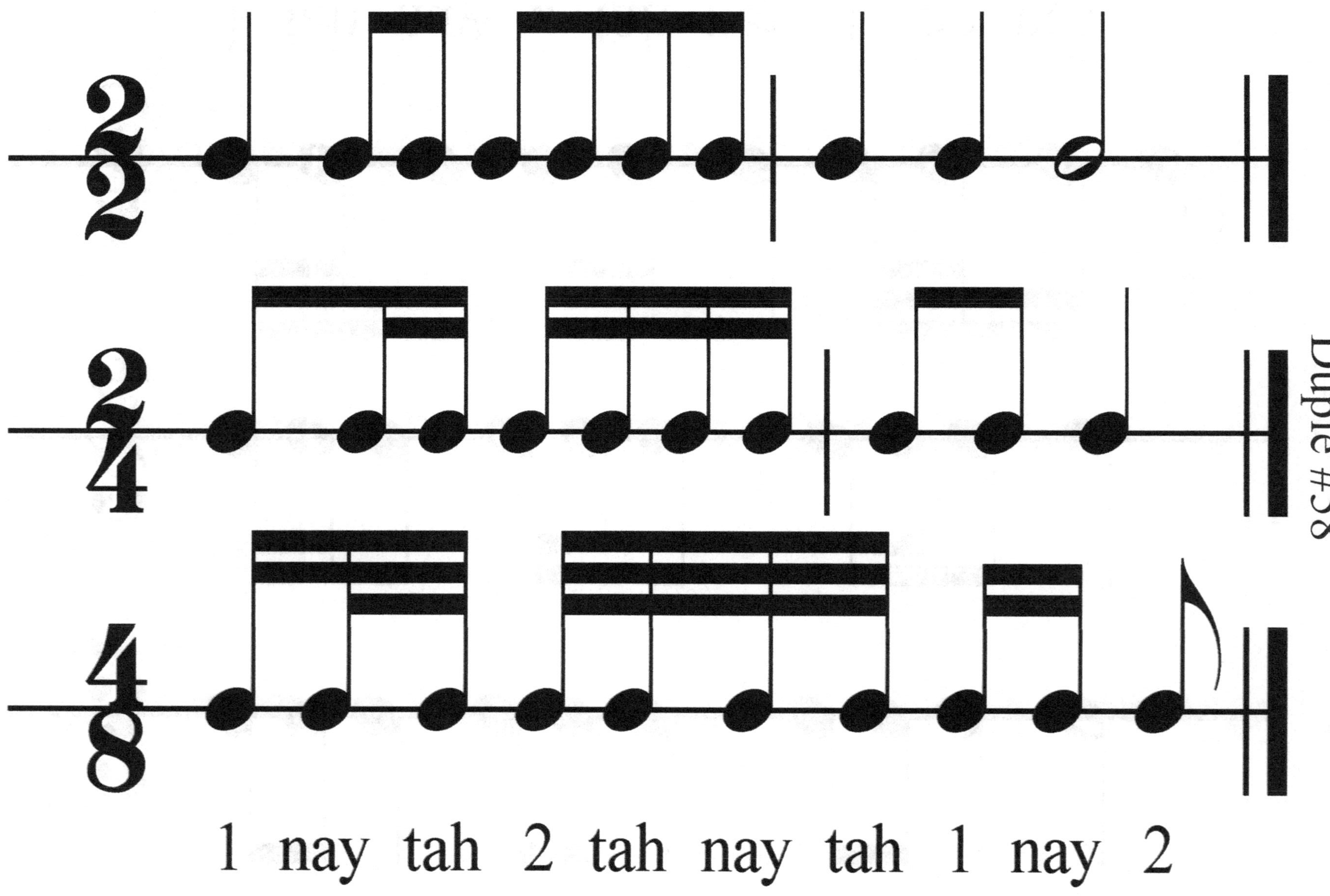
1 nay tah 2 tah nay tah 1 nay 2

Duple #59

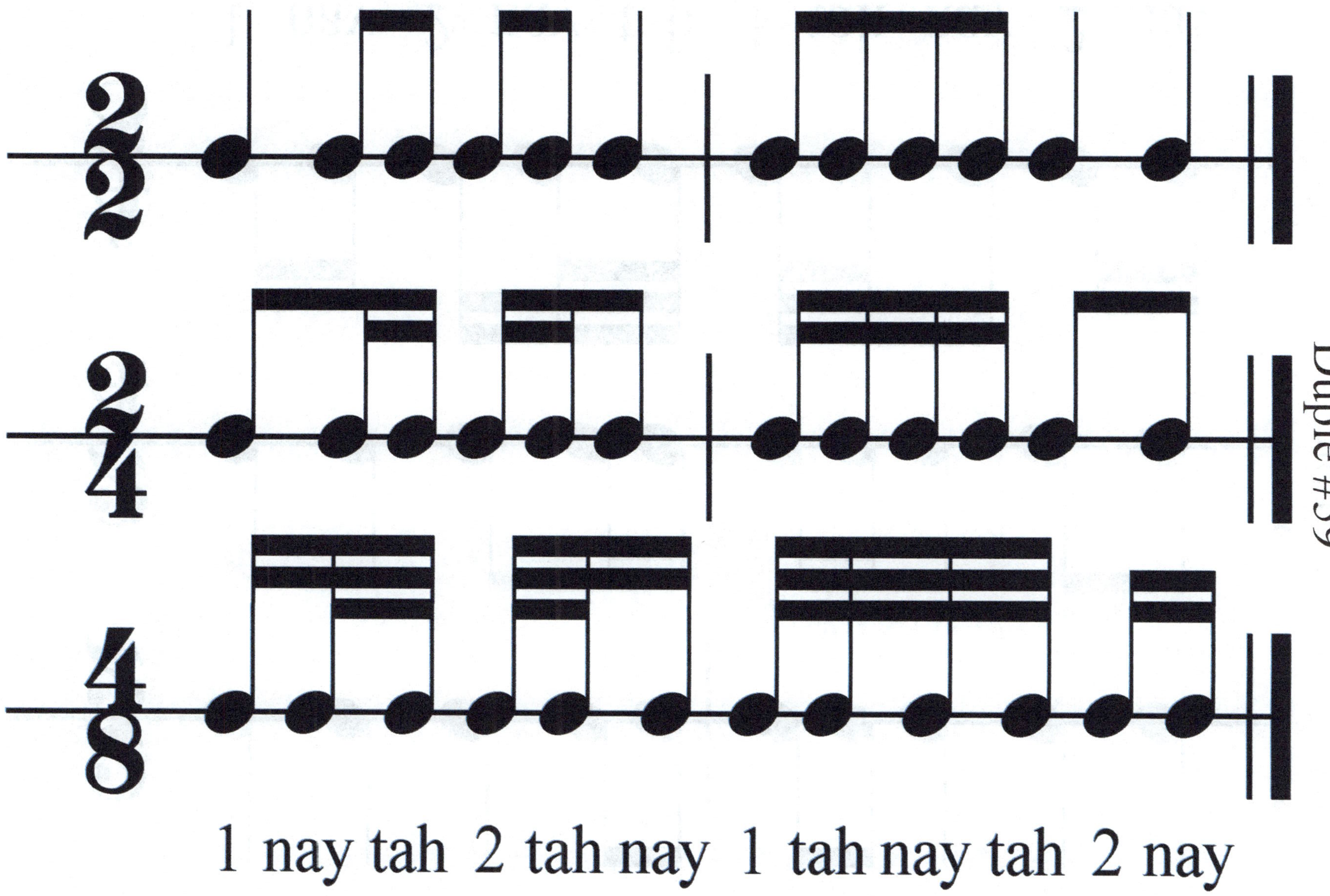
2/2
2/4
4/8
1 nay tah 2 tah nay 1 tah nay tah 2 nay

Duple #60

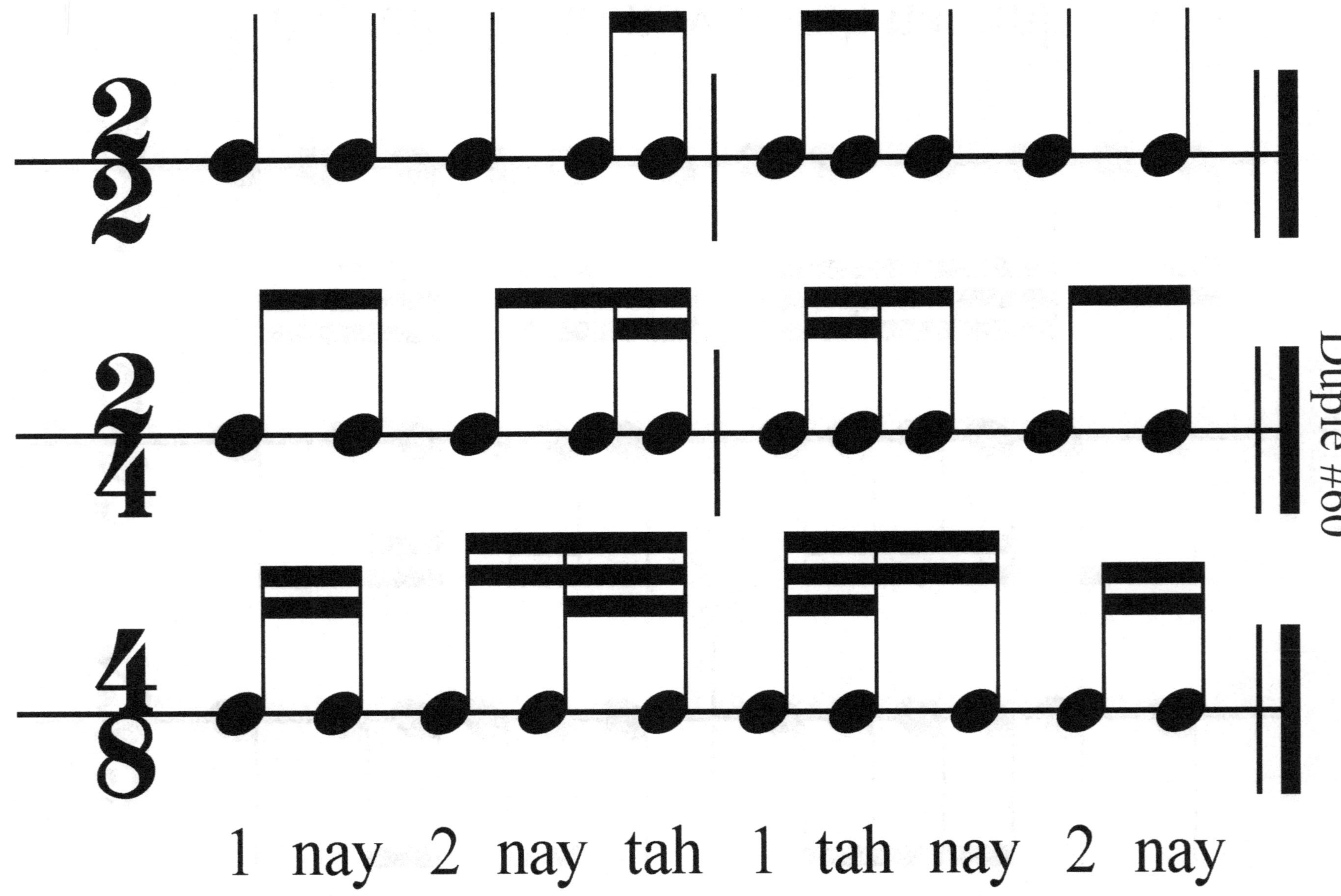
1 nay 2 nay tah 1 tah nay 2 nay

Duple #61

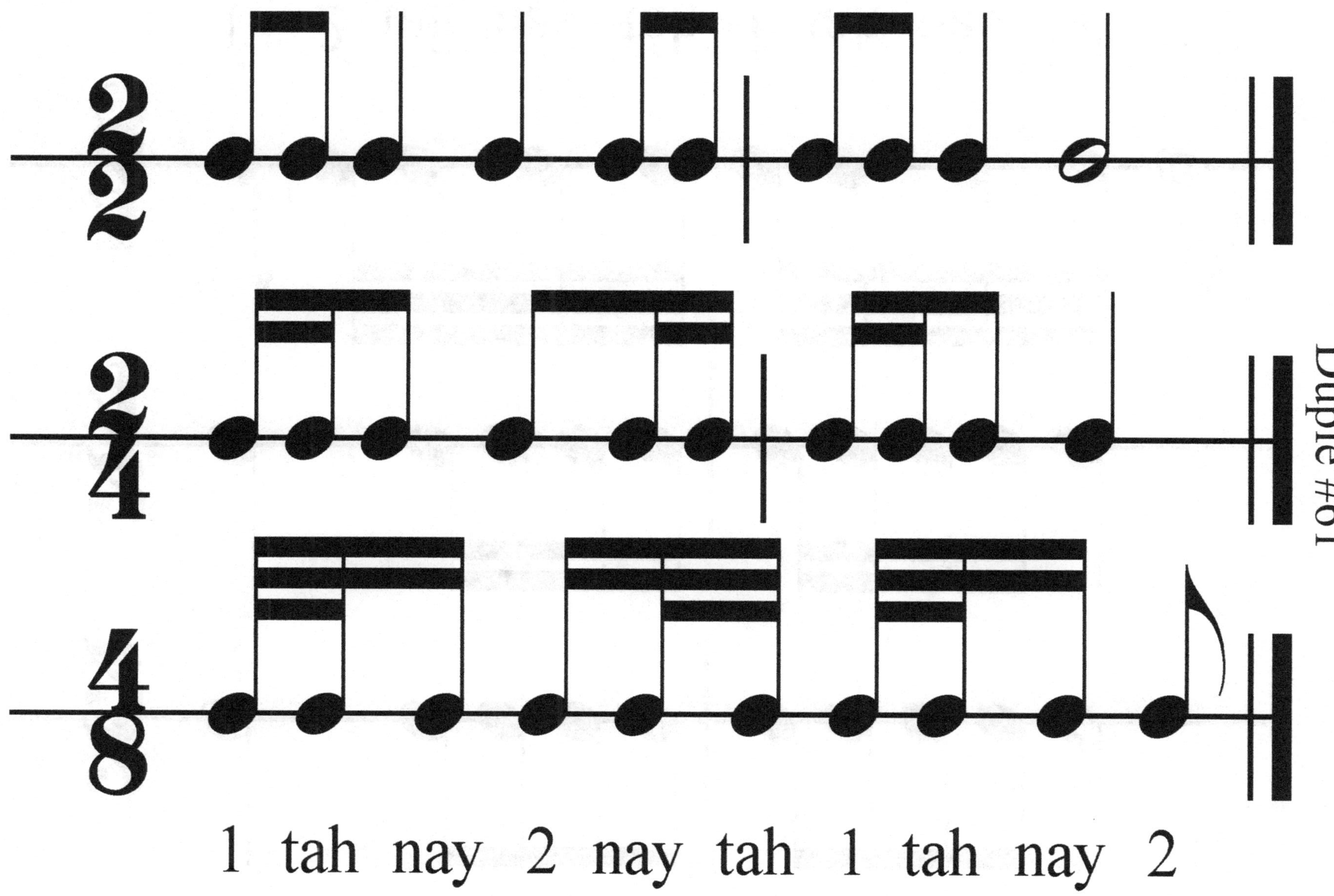
1 tah nay 2 nay tah 1 tah nay 2

Duple #62

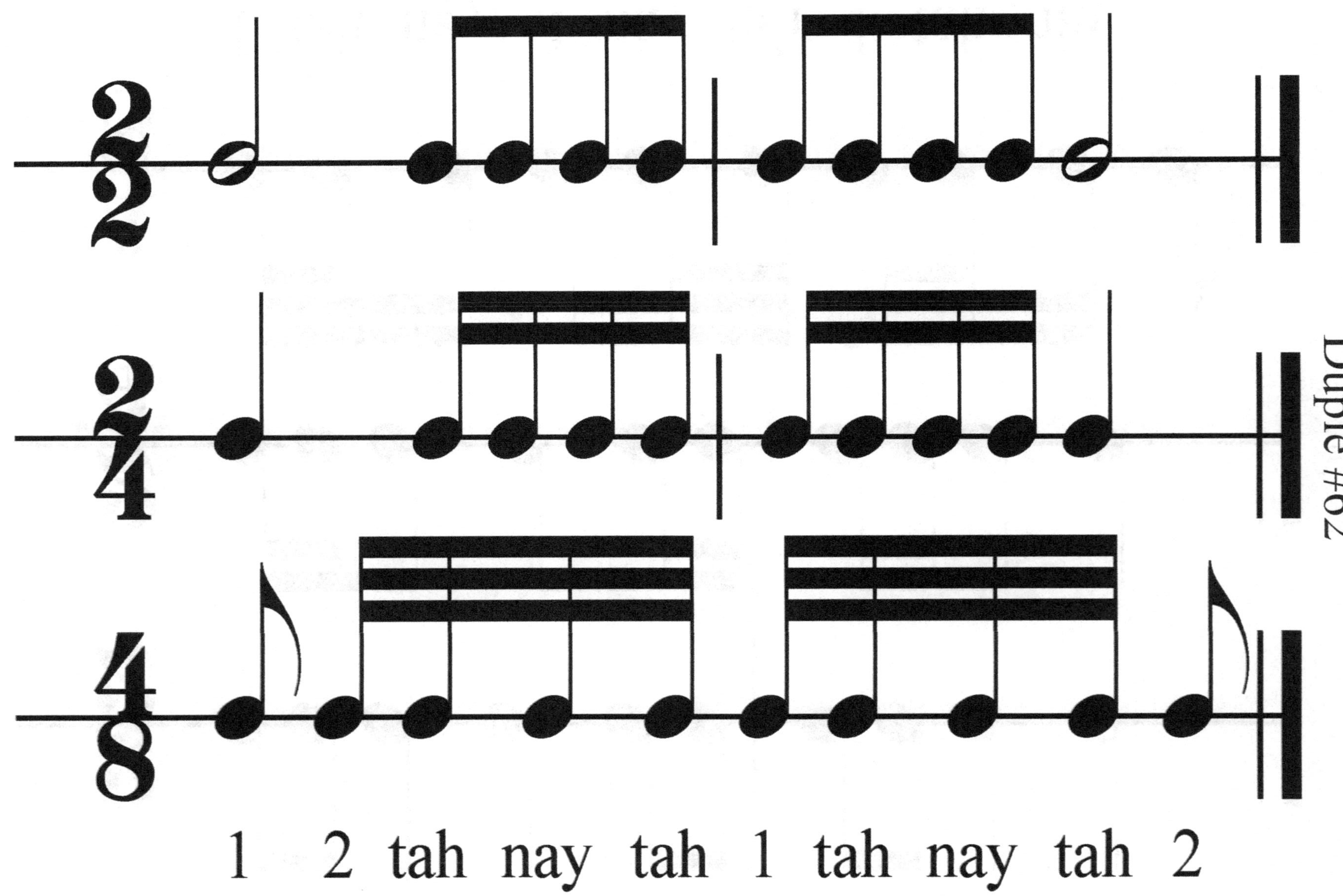
1 2 tah nay tah 1 tah nay tah 2

Duple #63

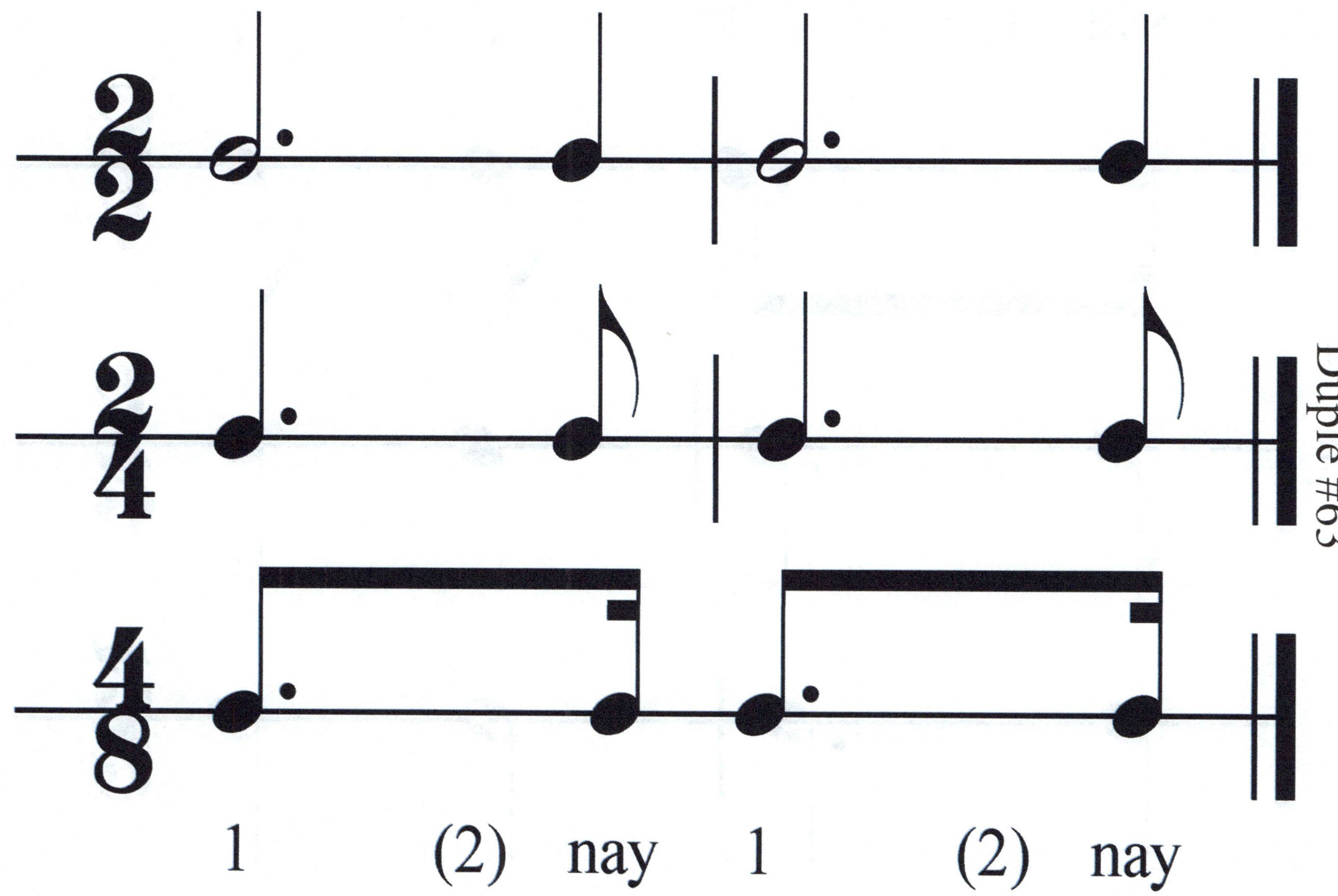

Duple #64

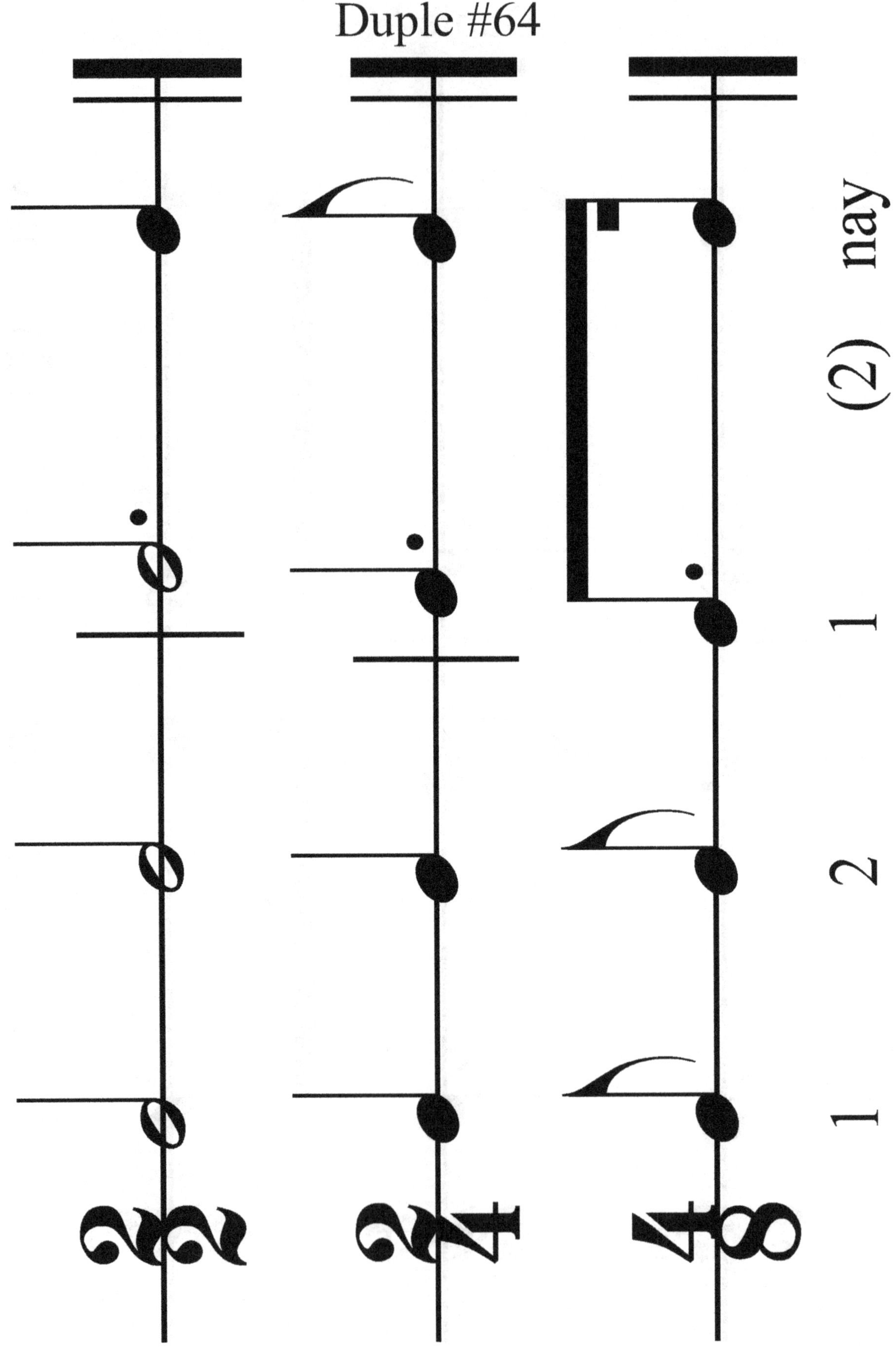

Duple #65

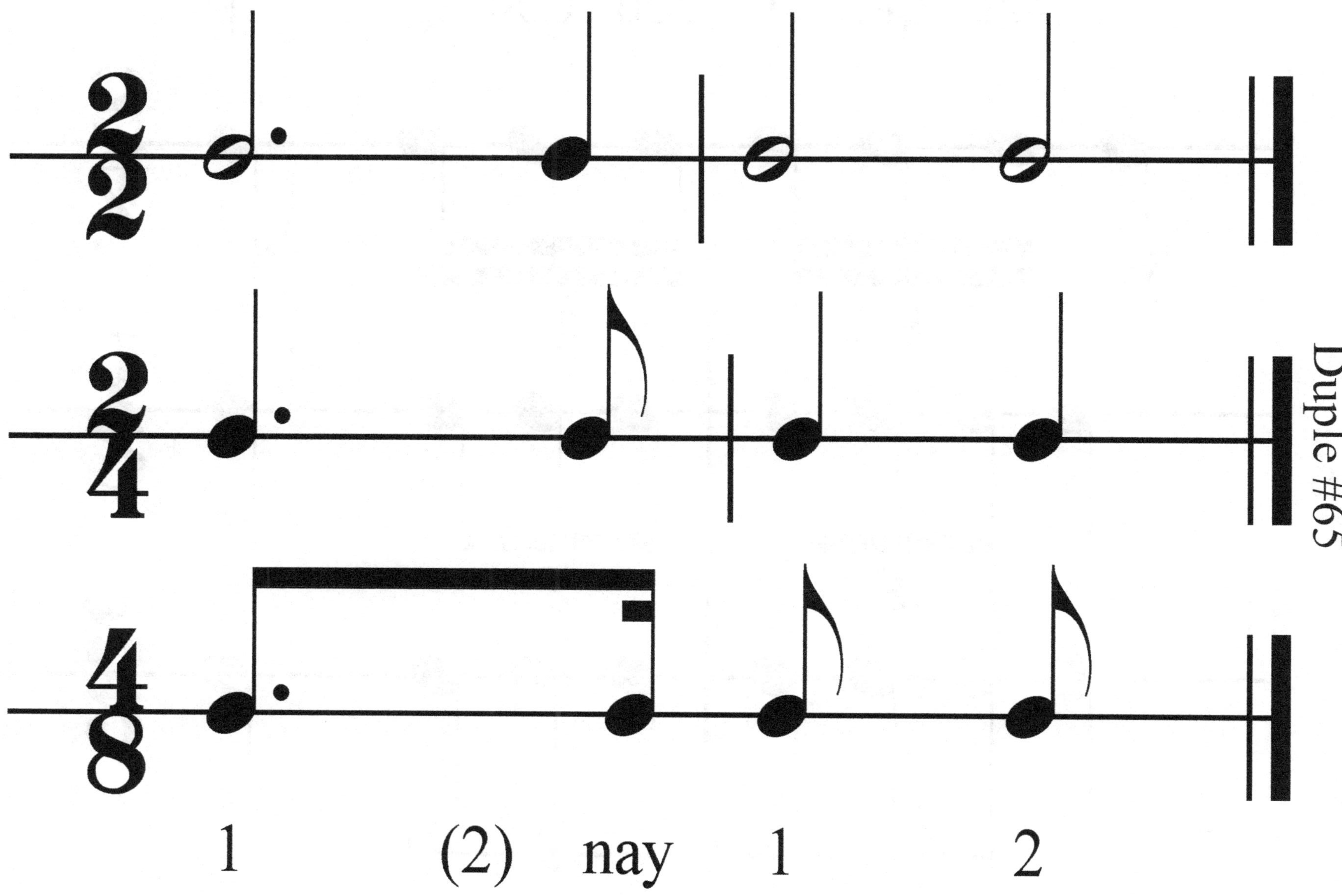

Duple #66

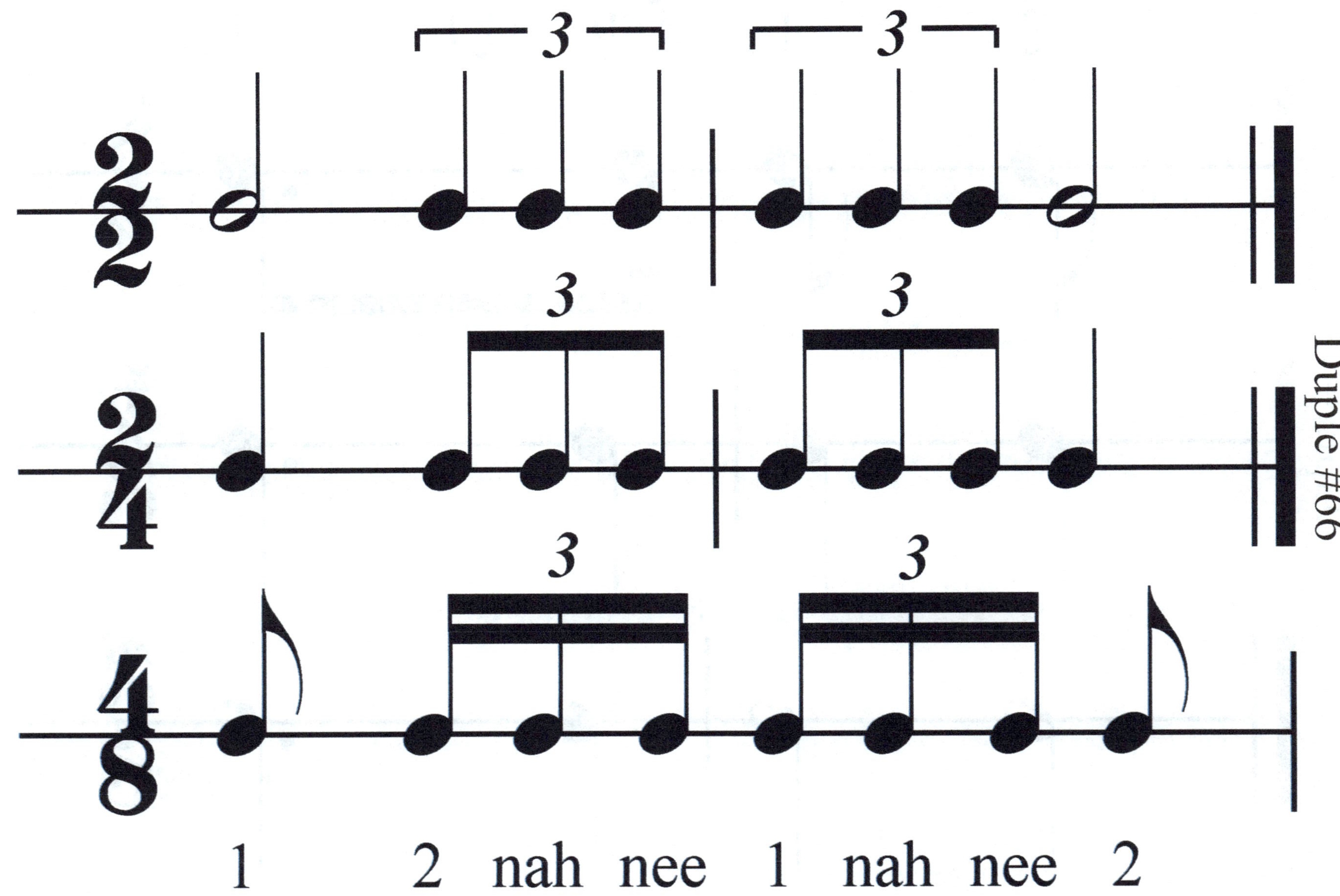
3
3
3
3
3
3
1 2 nah nee 1 nah nee 2

Duple #67

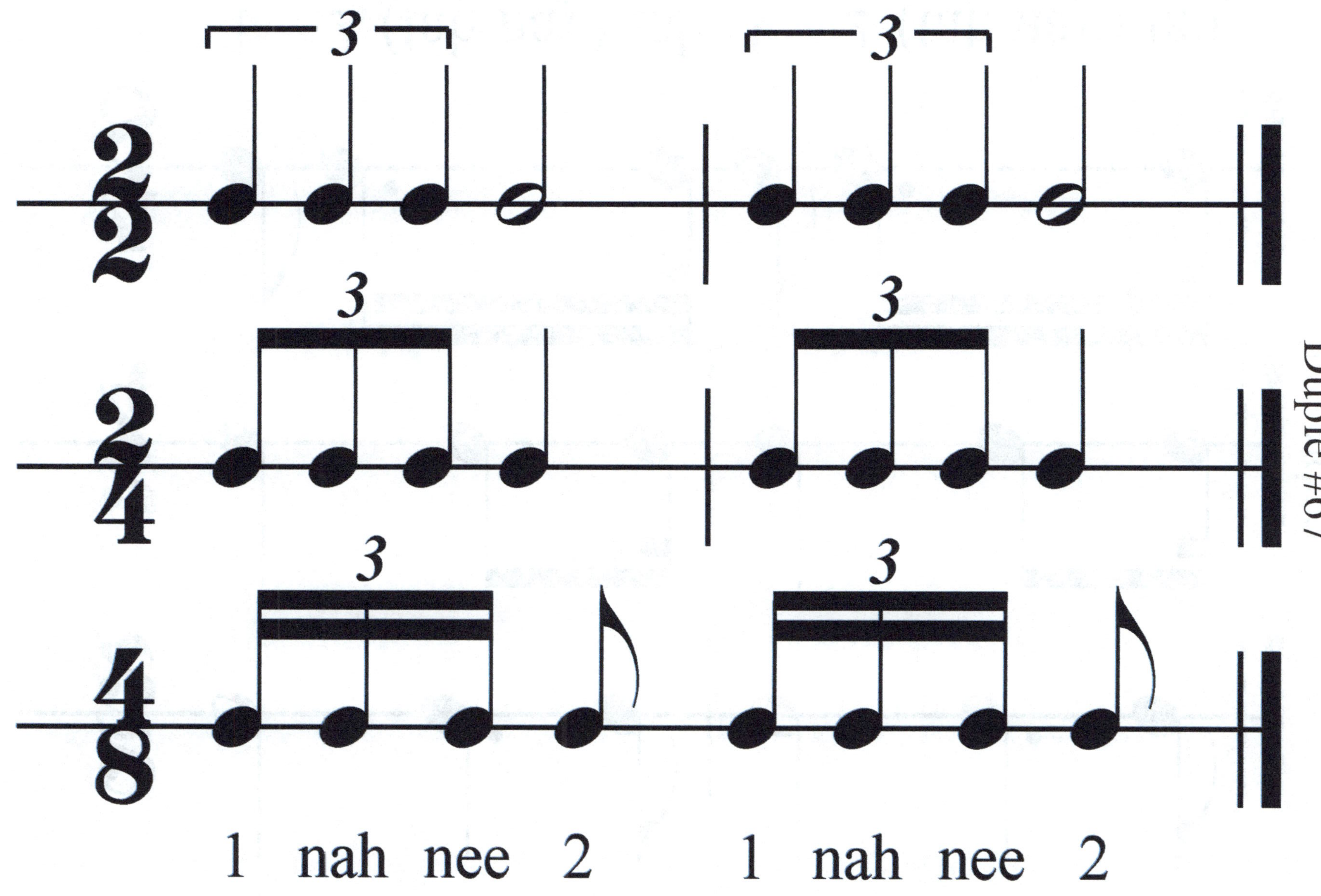

Duple #68

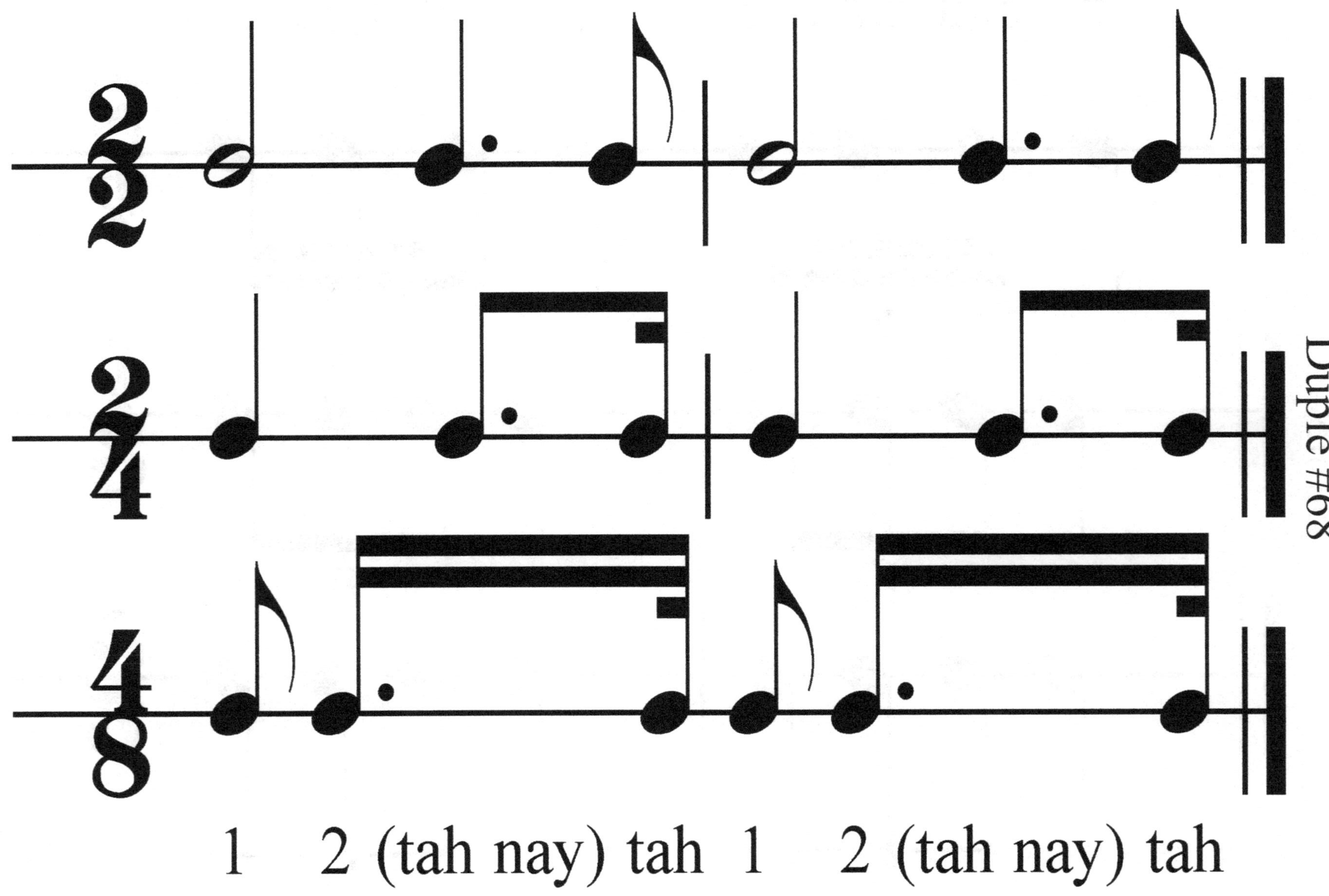

1 2 (tah nay) tah 1 2 (tah nay) tah

Duple #69

Duple #70

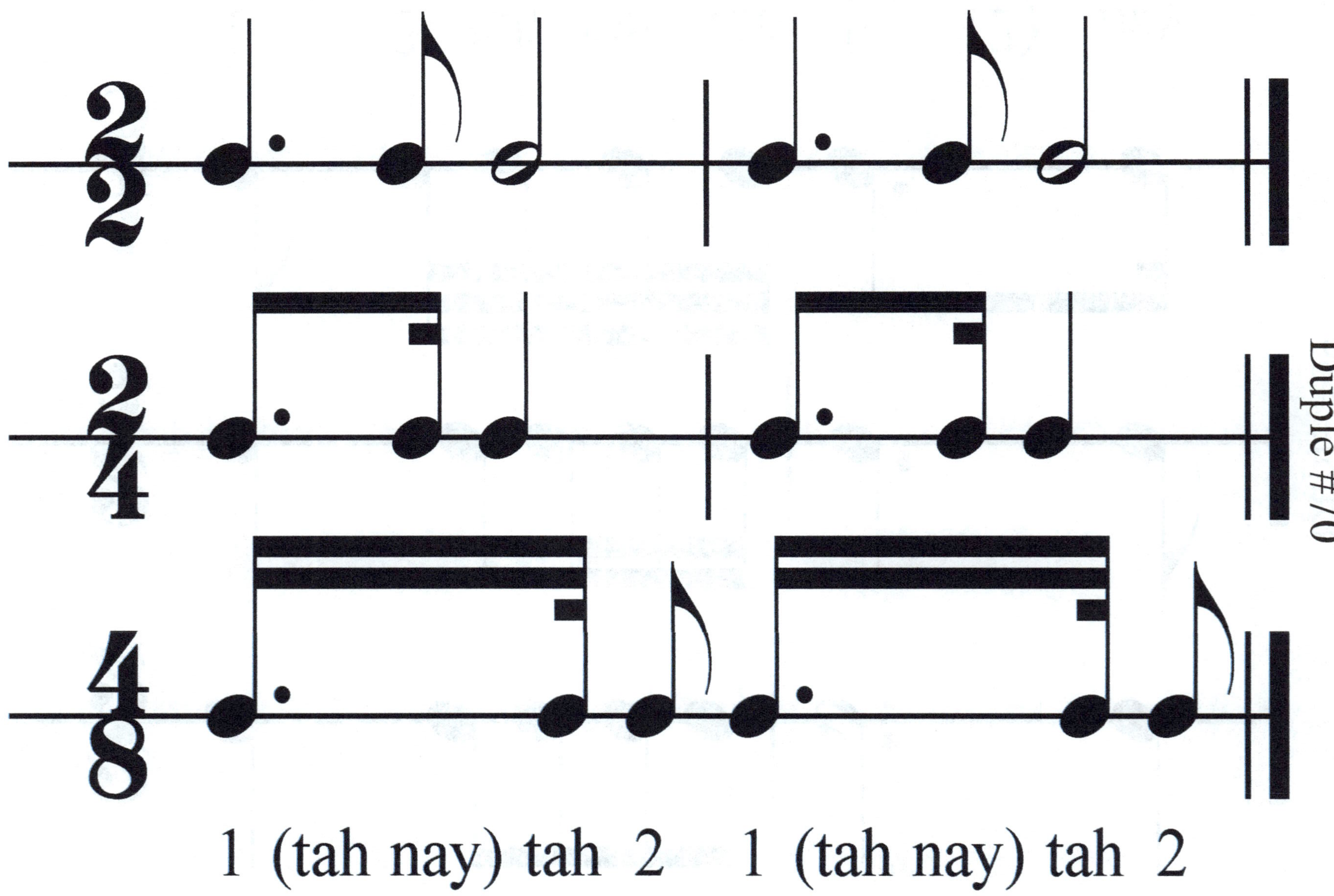

Duple #71

Duple #72

Duple #73

Duple #74

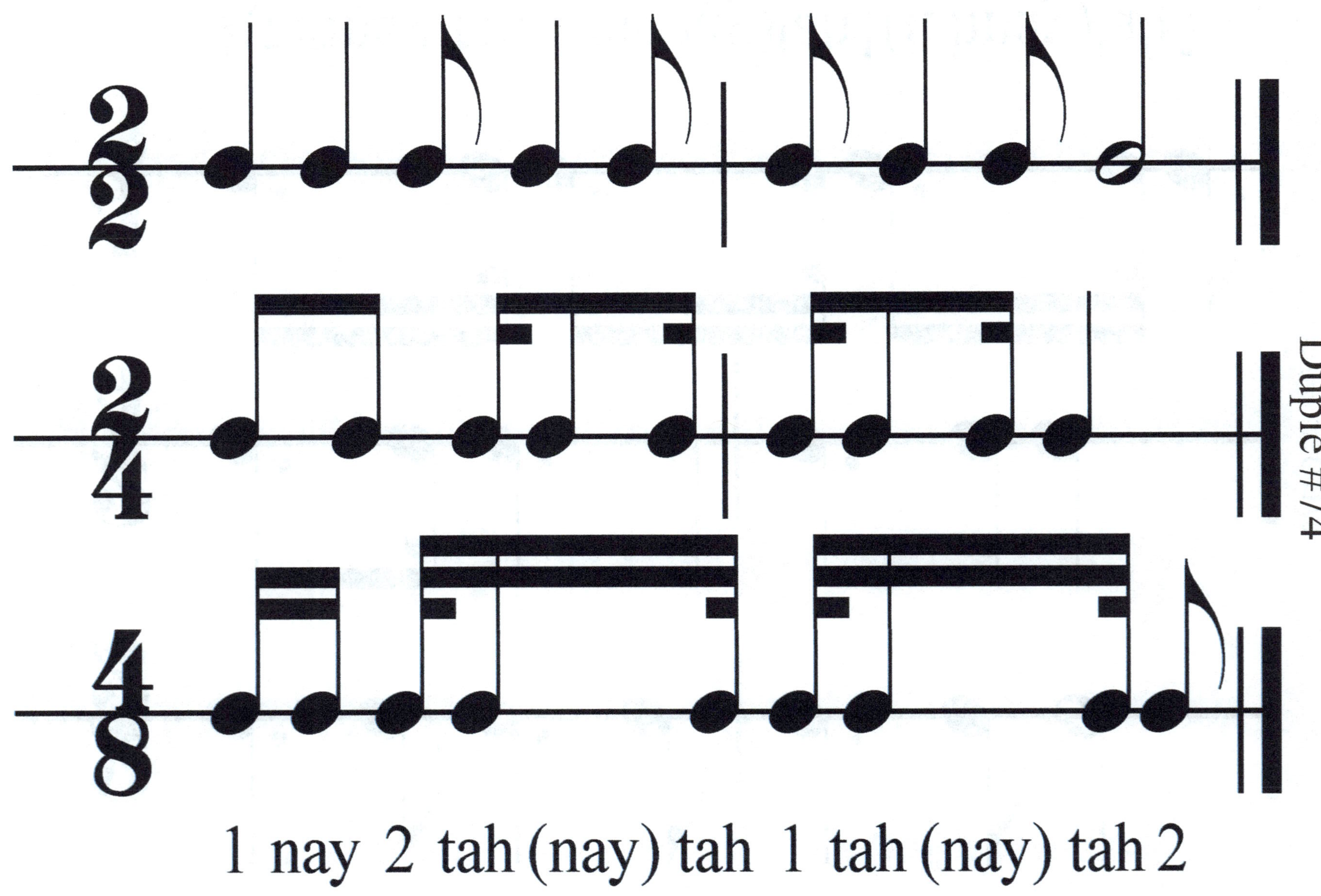
1 nay 2 tah (nay) tah 1 tah (nay) tah 2

Duple #75

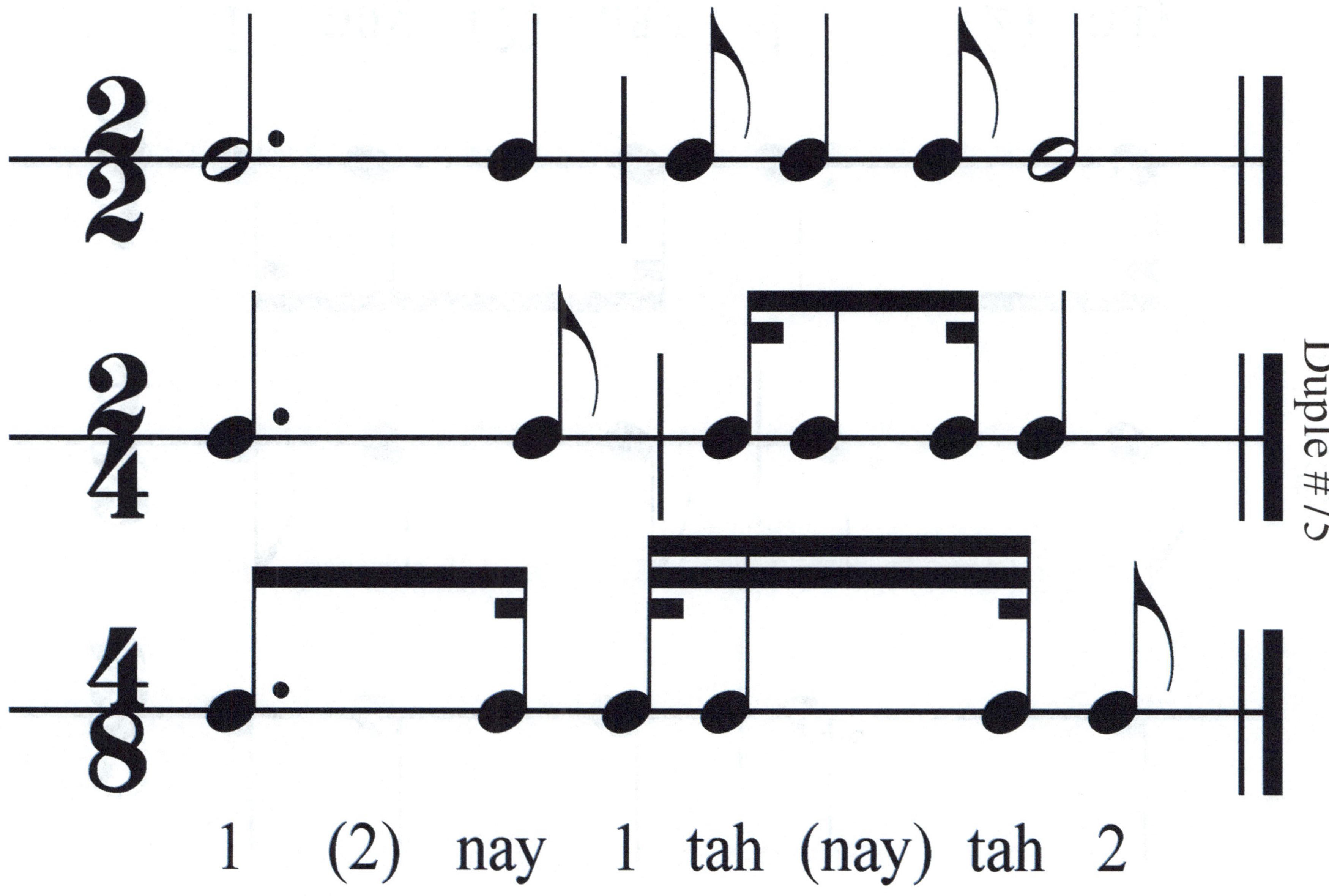
1 (2) nay 1 tah (nay) tah 2

Duple #76

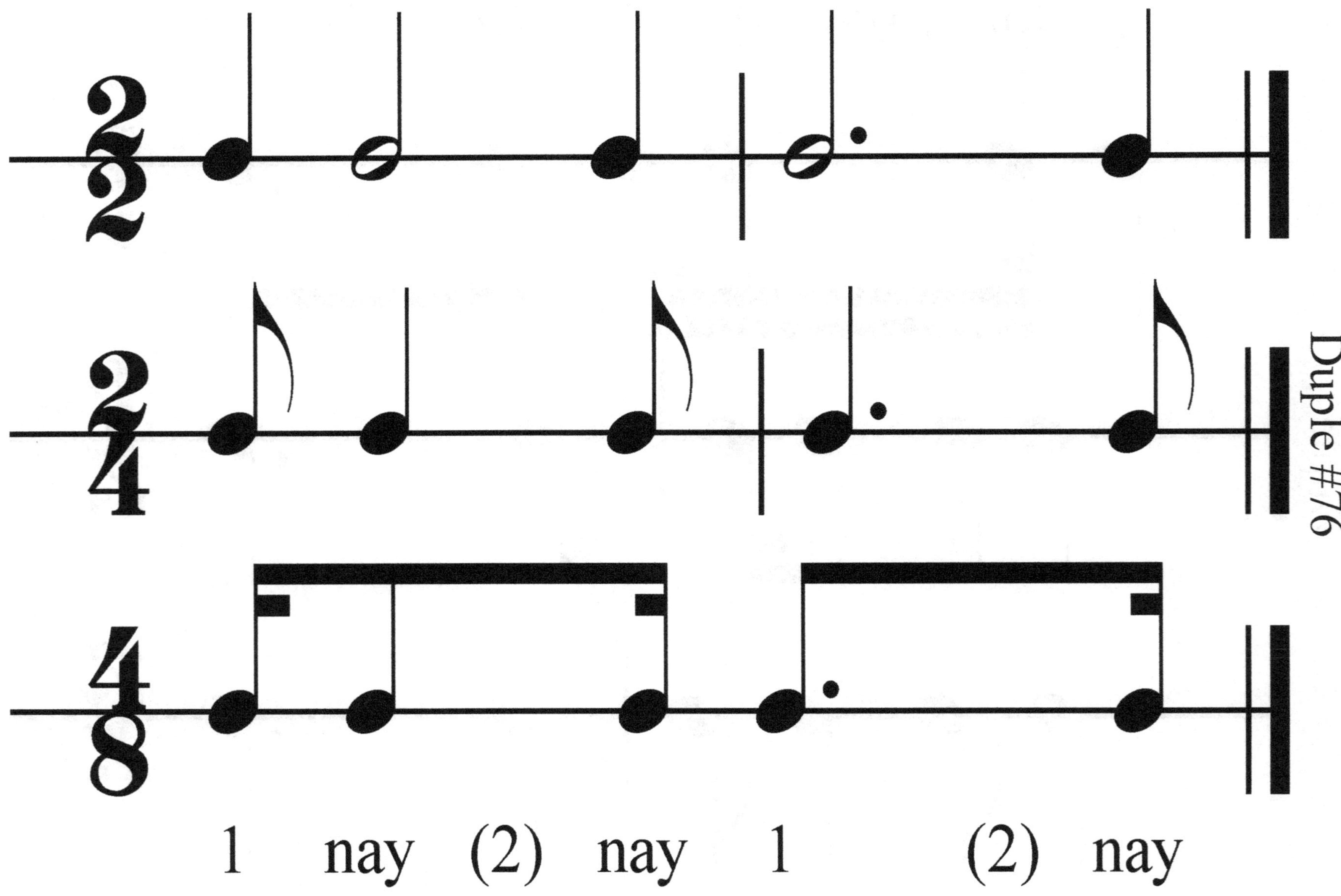

1 nay (2) nay 1 (2) nay

Duple #77

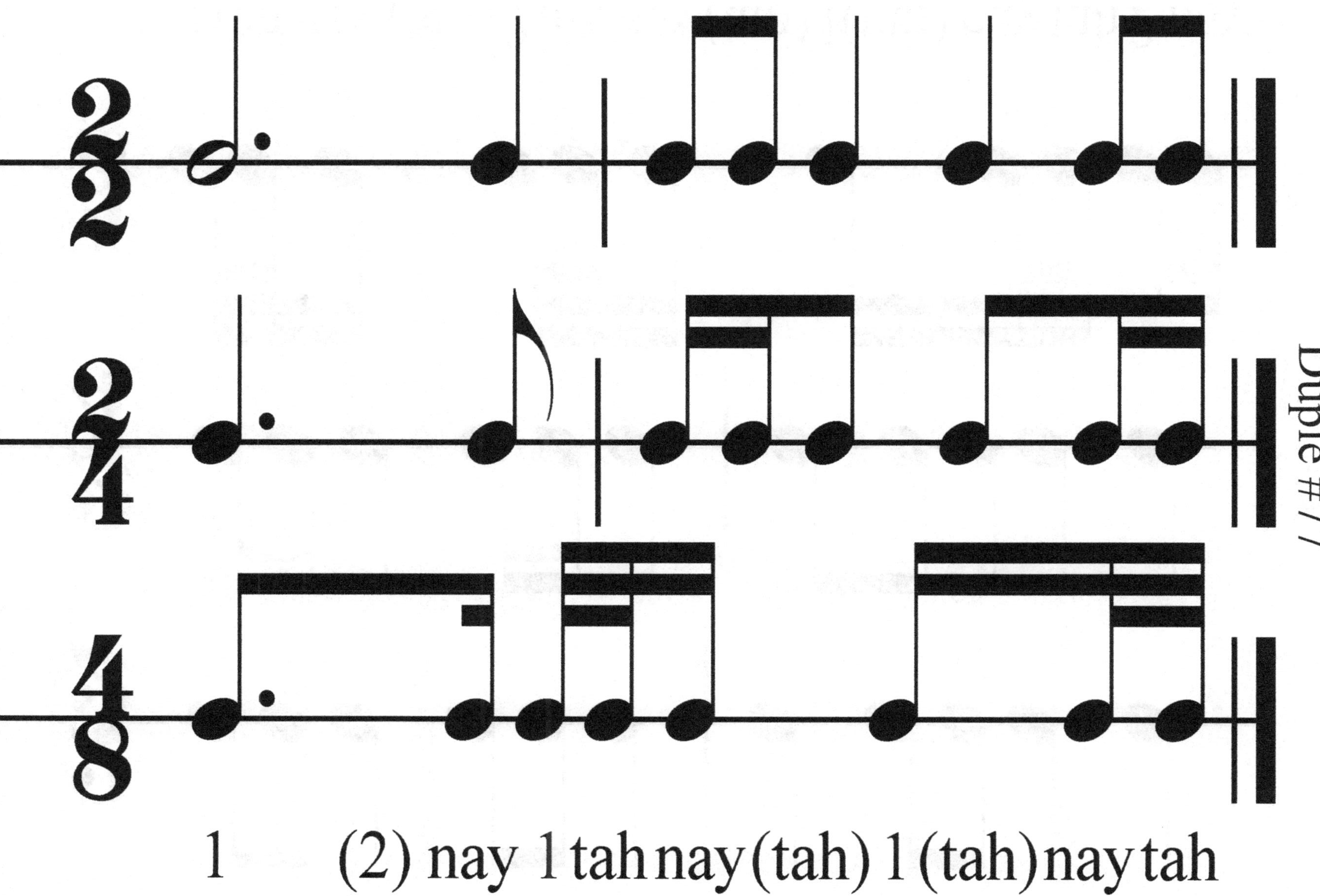
1 (2) nay 1 tahnay(tah) 1 (tah)naytah

Duple #78

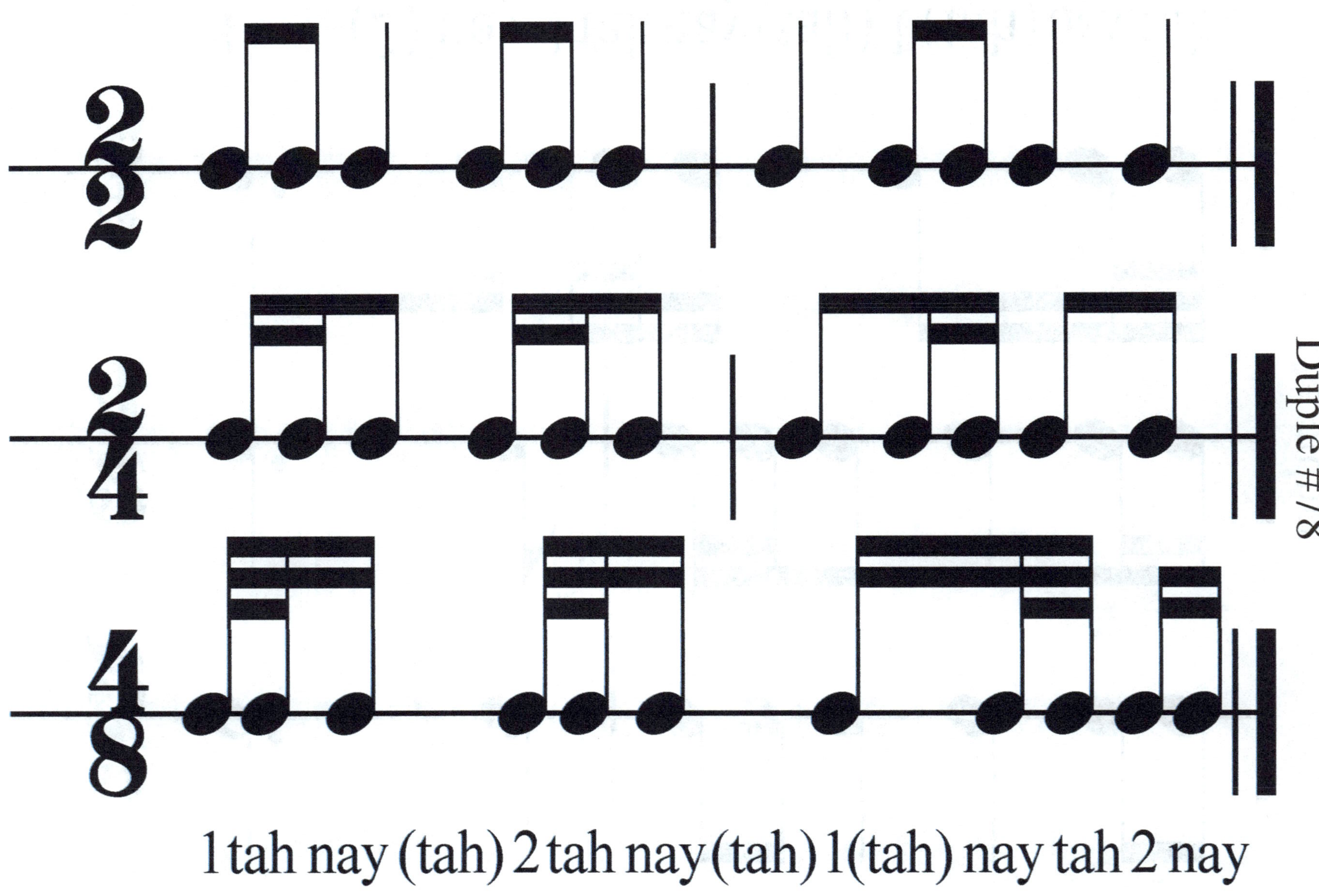
2/2
2/4
4/8
1 tah nay (tah) 2 tah nay (tah) 1 (tah) nay tah 2 nay

Duple #79

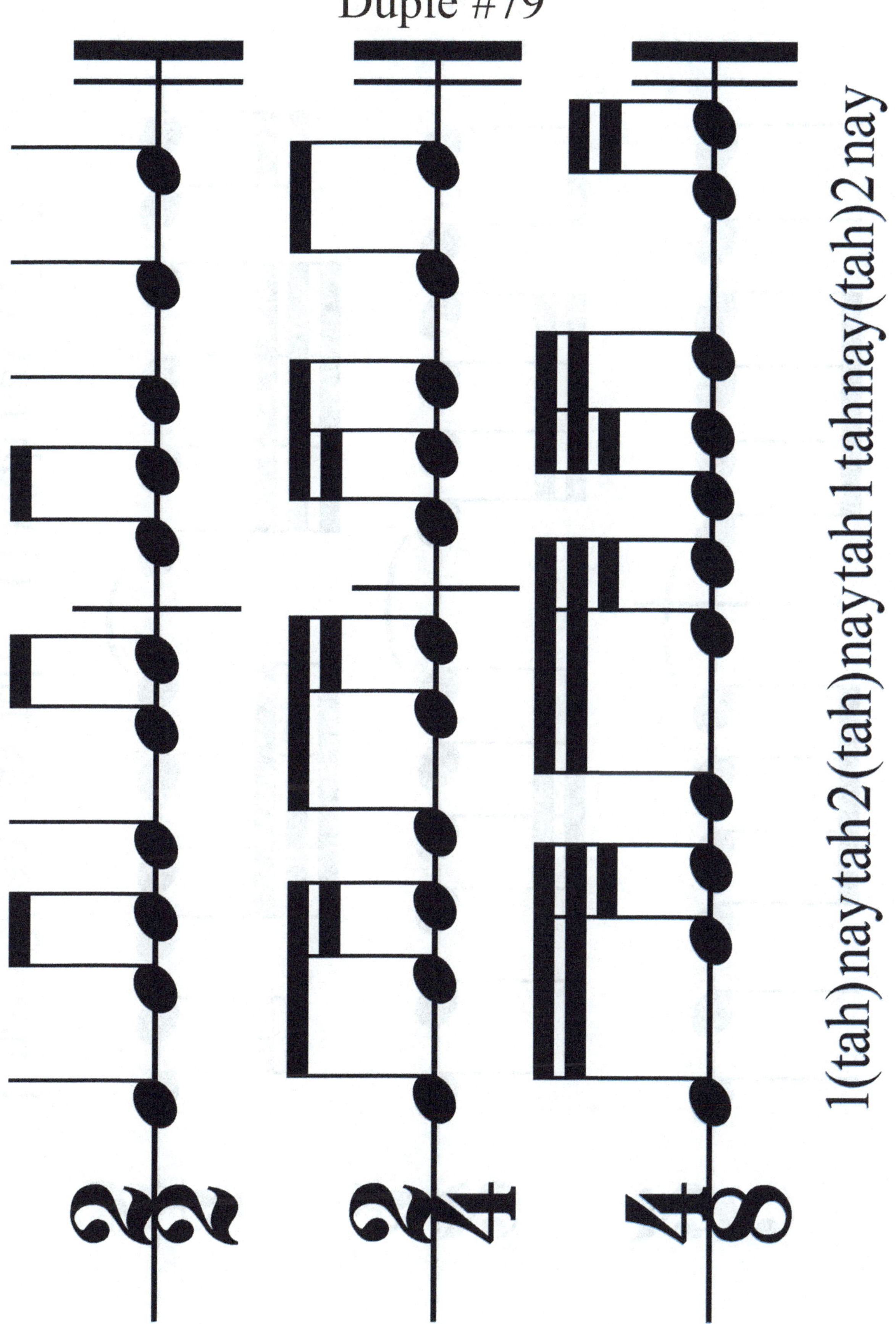
1(tah)naytah2(tah)naytah 1 tahnay(tah)2nay

Duple #80

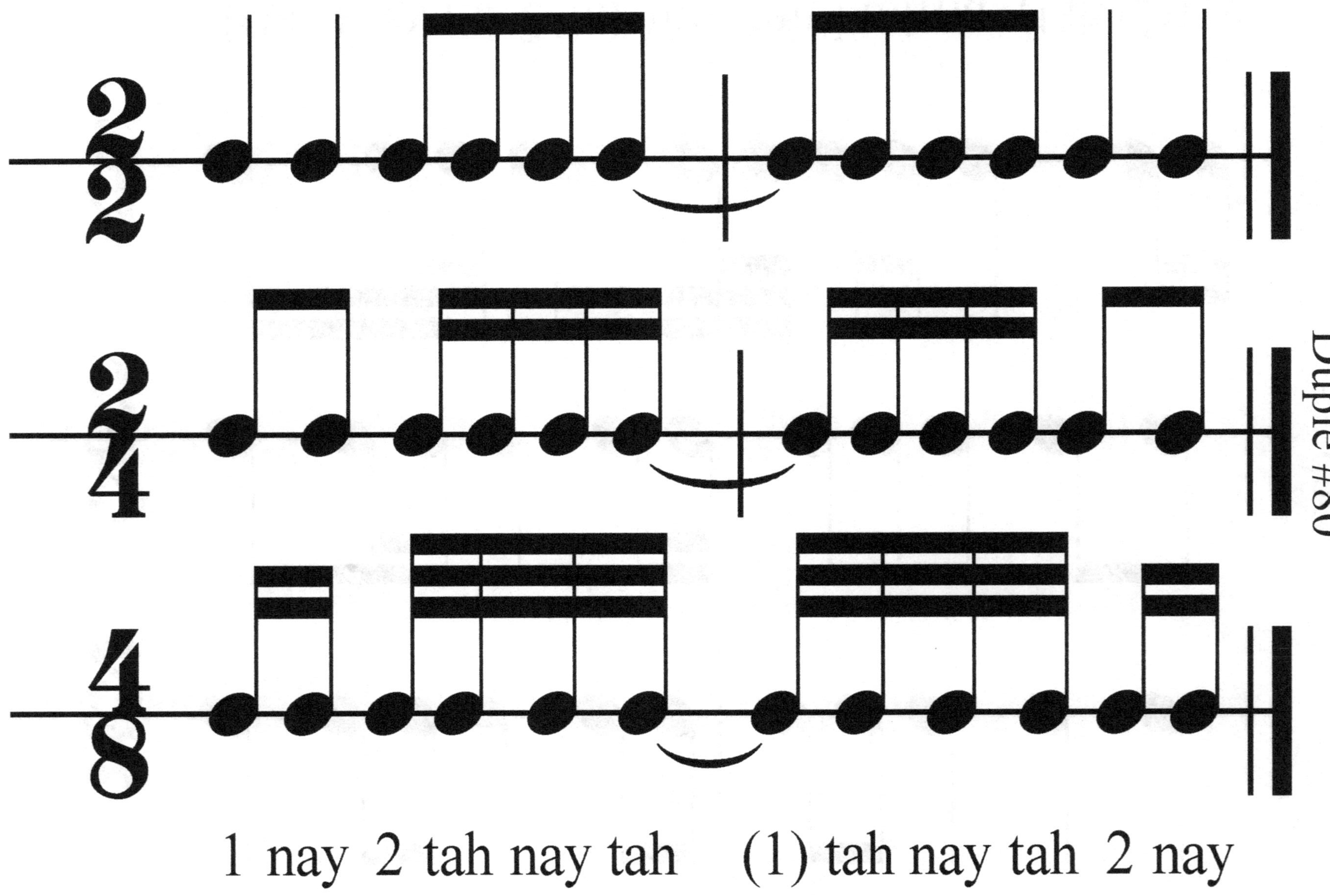

Duple #81

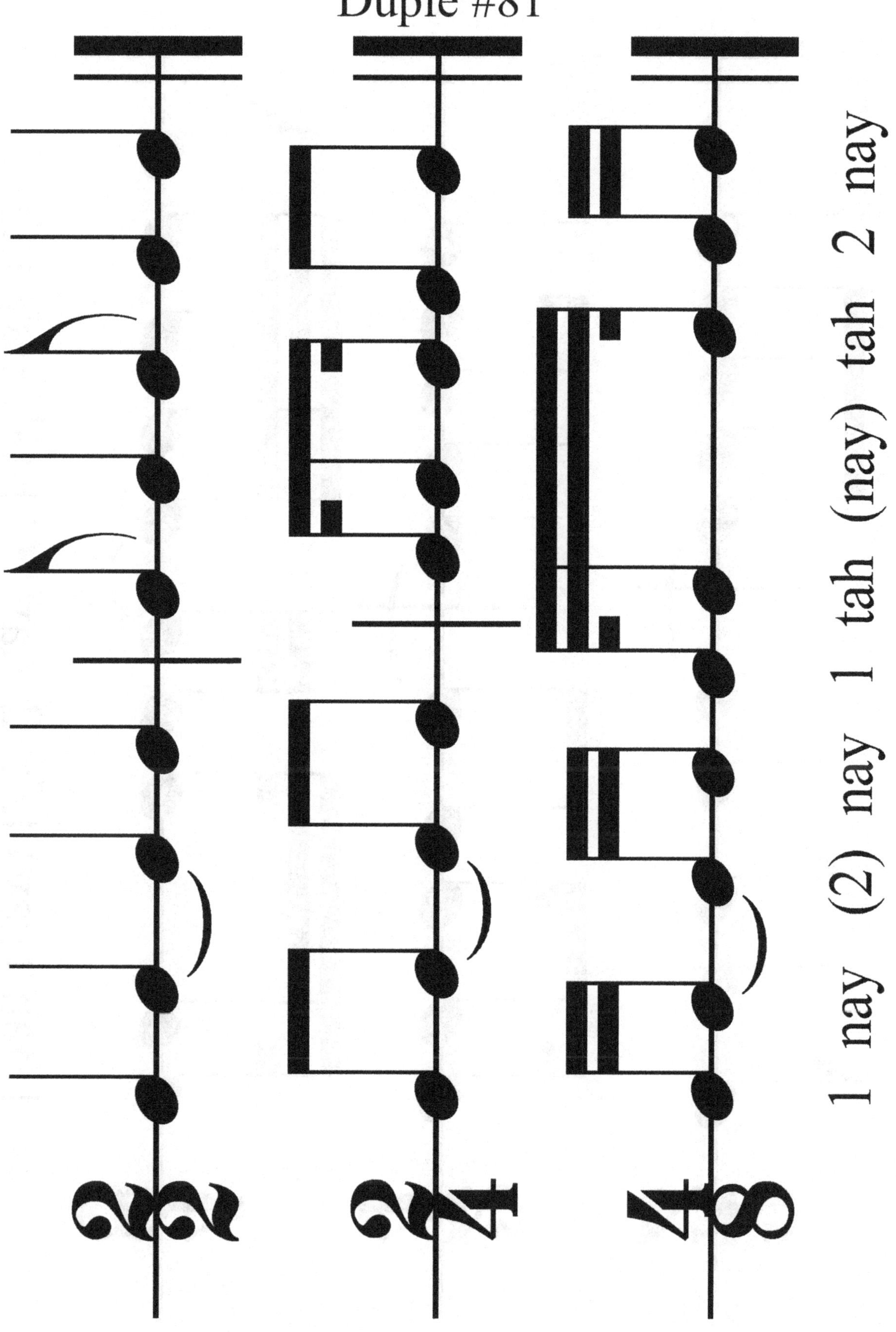
2/2
2/4
4/8
1 nay (2) nay 1 tah (nay) tah 2 nay

Duple #82

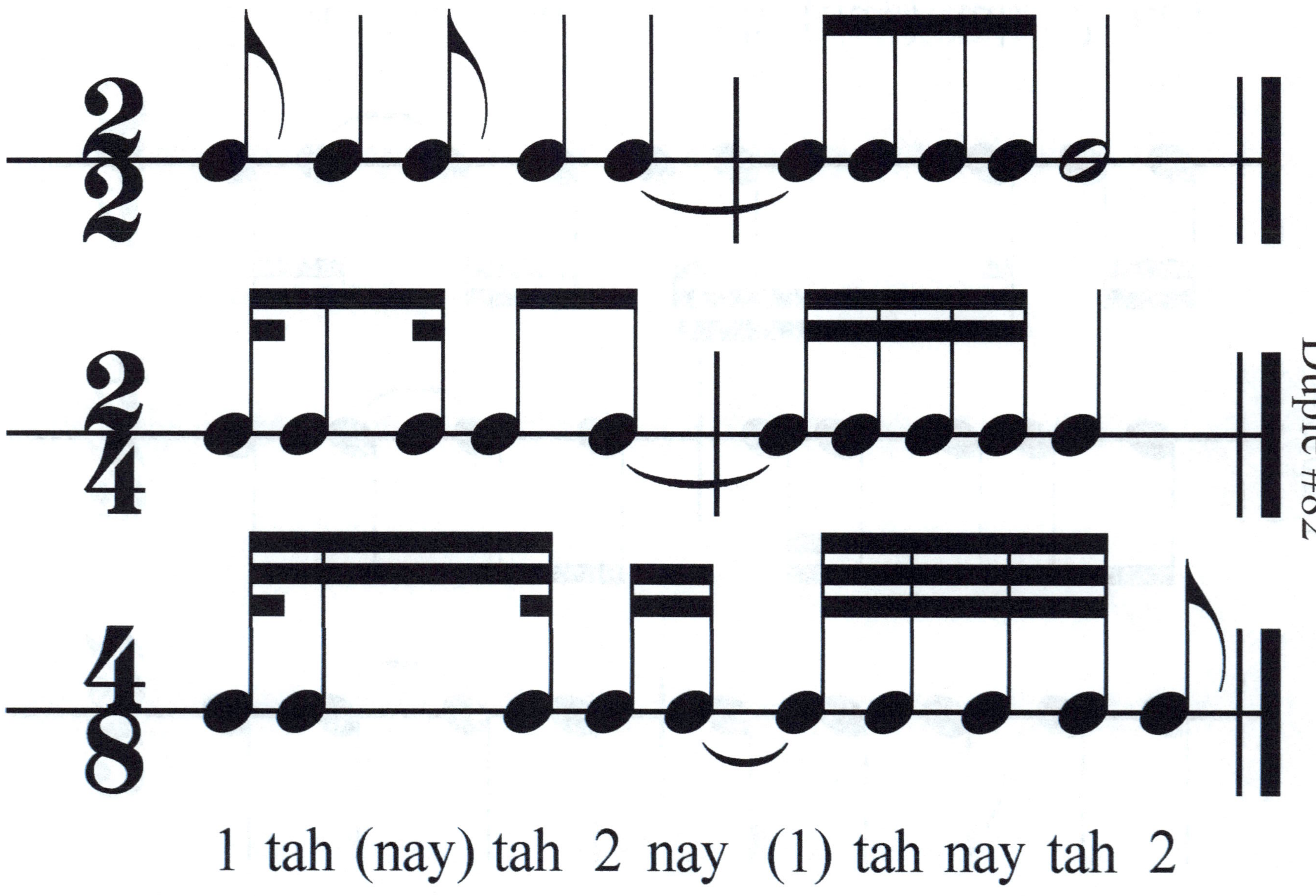
1 tah (nay) tah 2 nay (1) tah nay tah 2

Duple #83

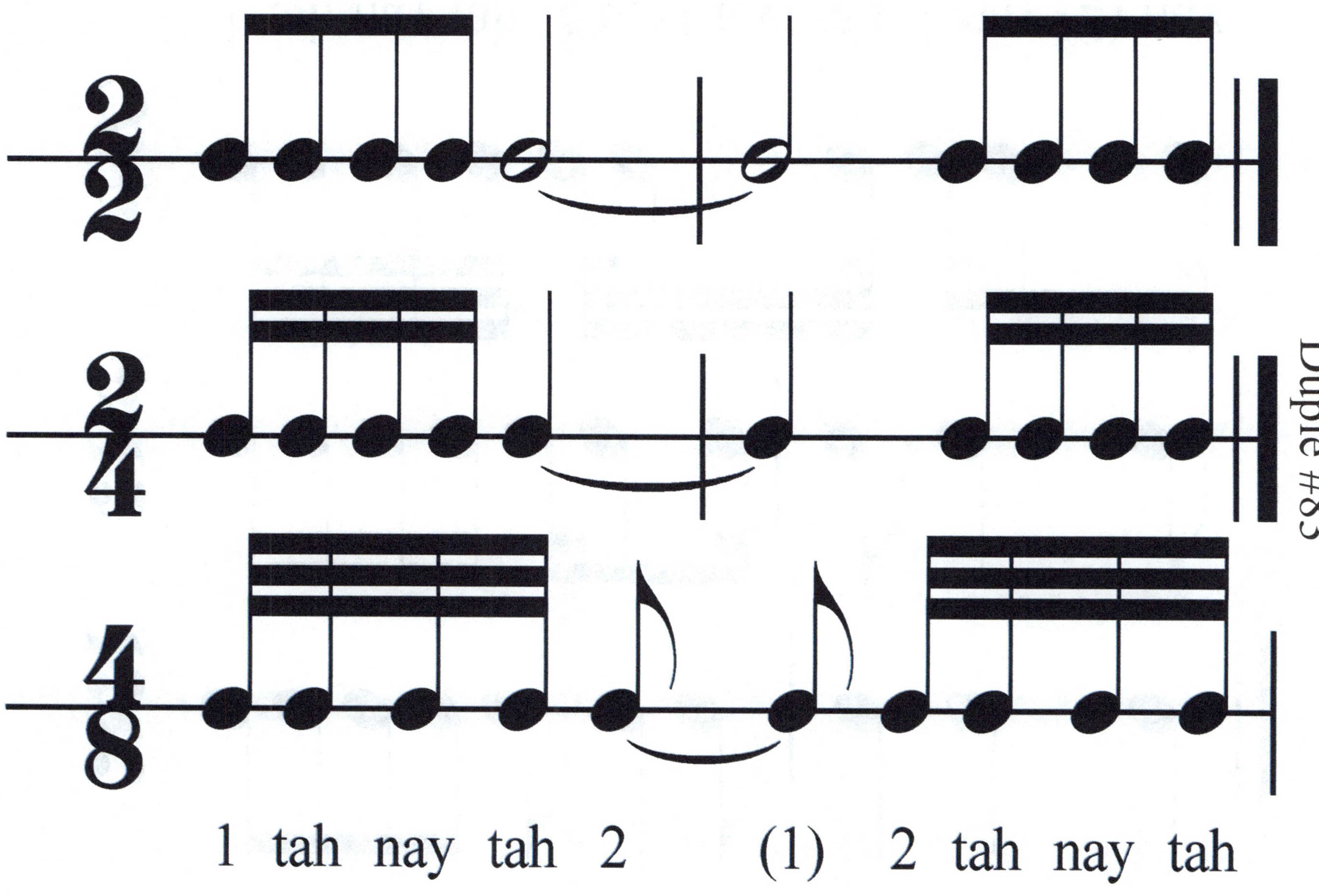

Duple #84

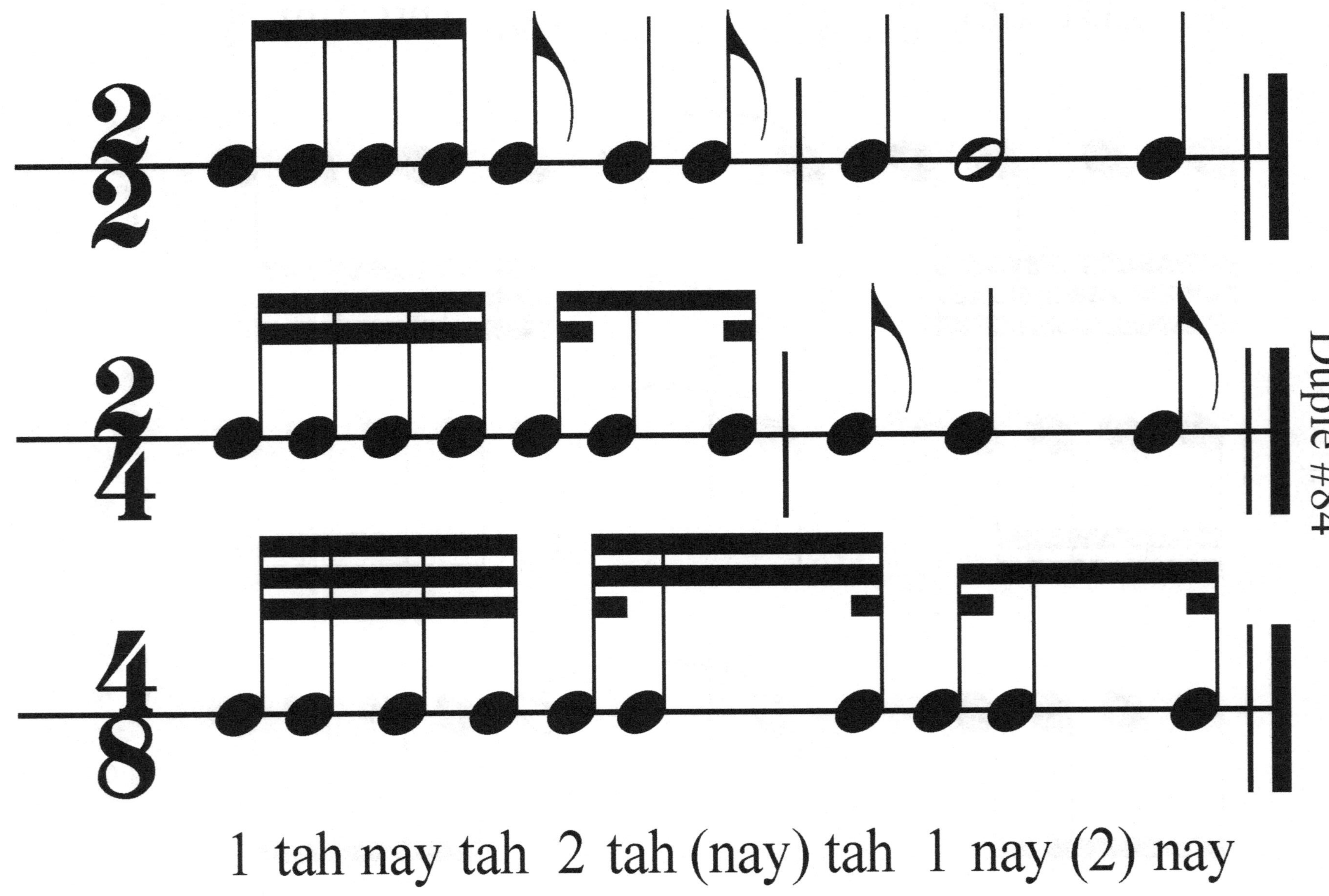
1 tah nay tah 2 tah (nay) tah 1 nay (2) nay

Duple #85

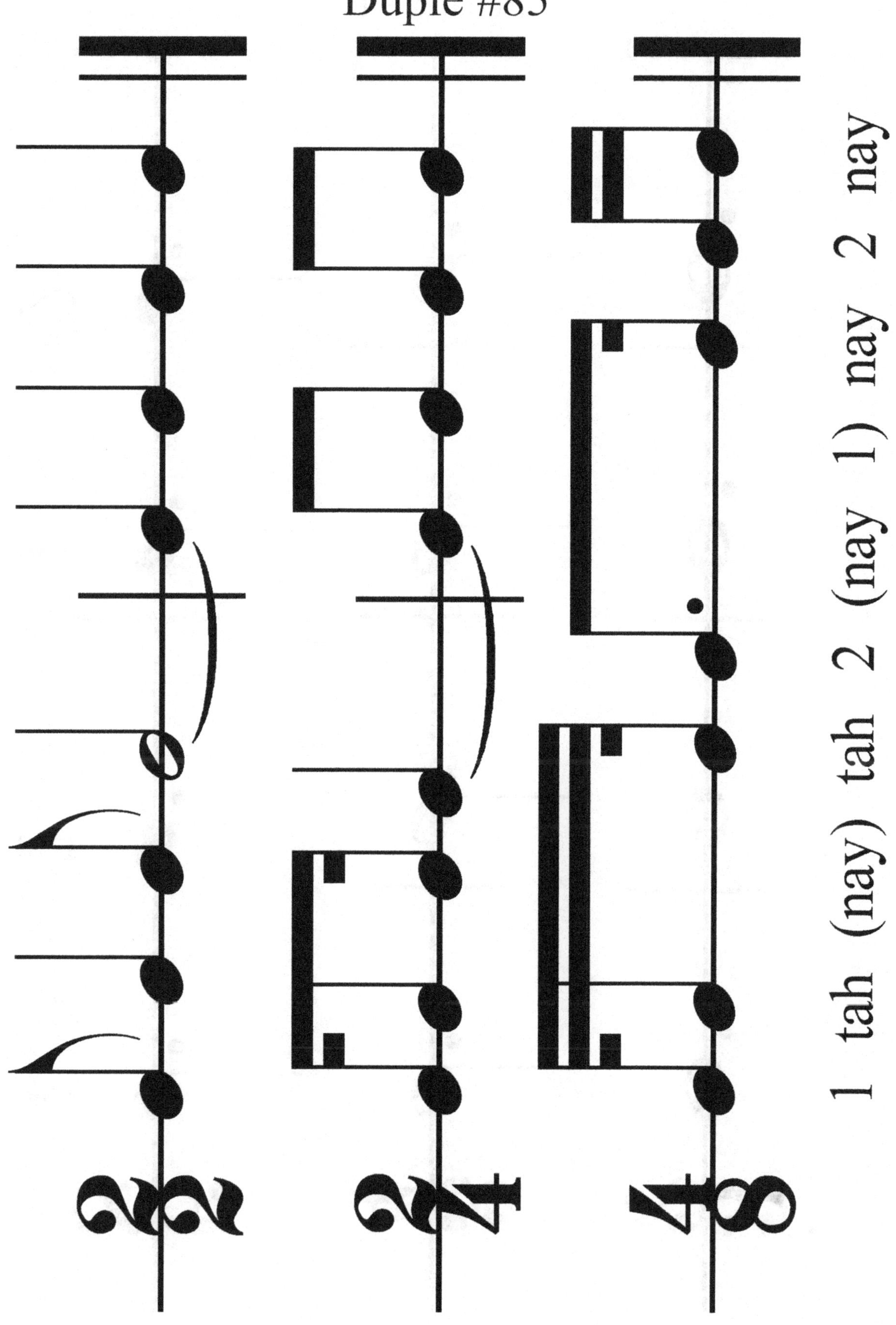
1 tah (nay) tah 2 (nay 1) nay 2 nay

Triple #1

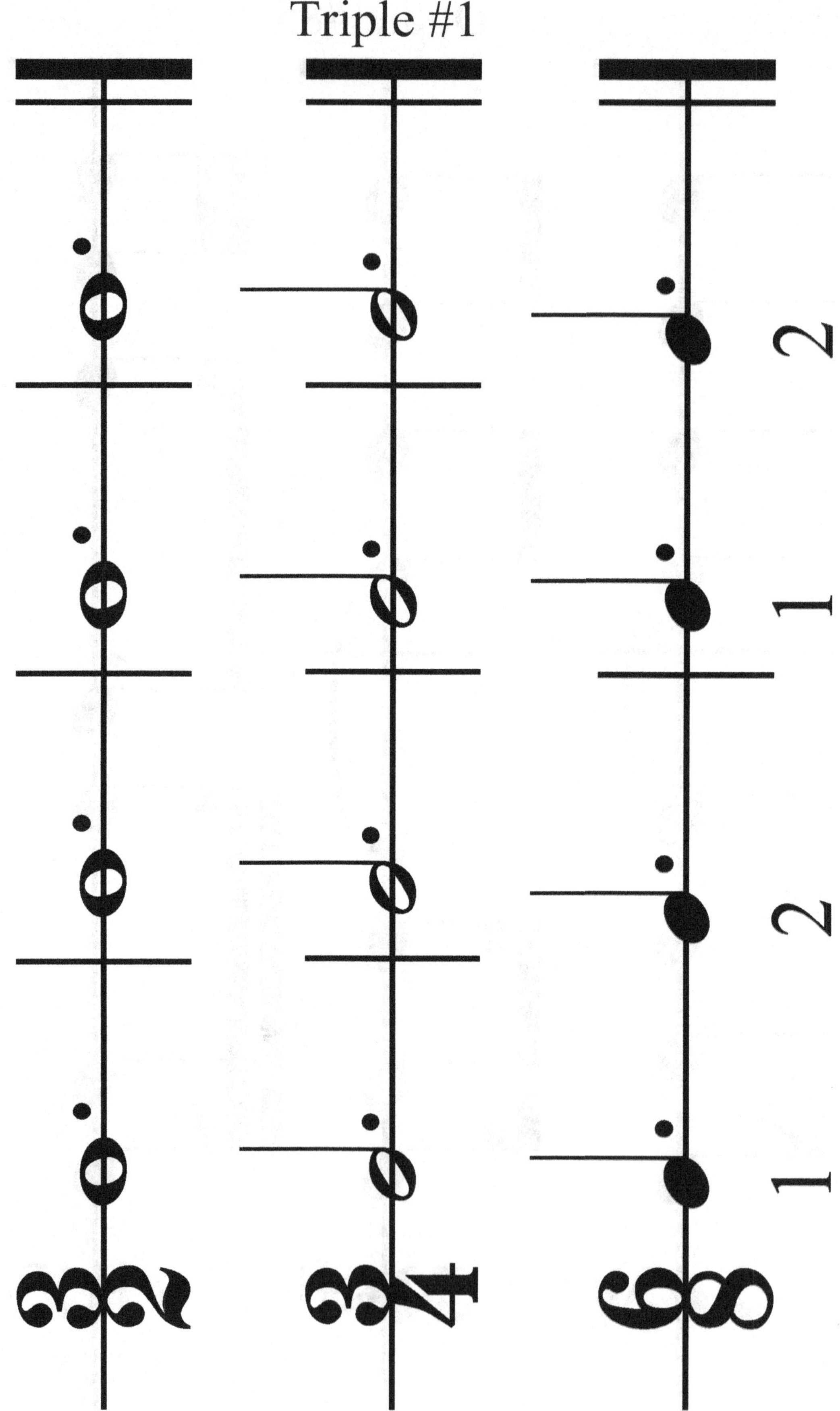

Triple #2

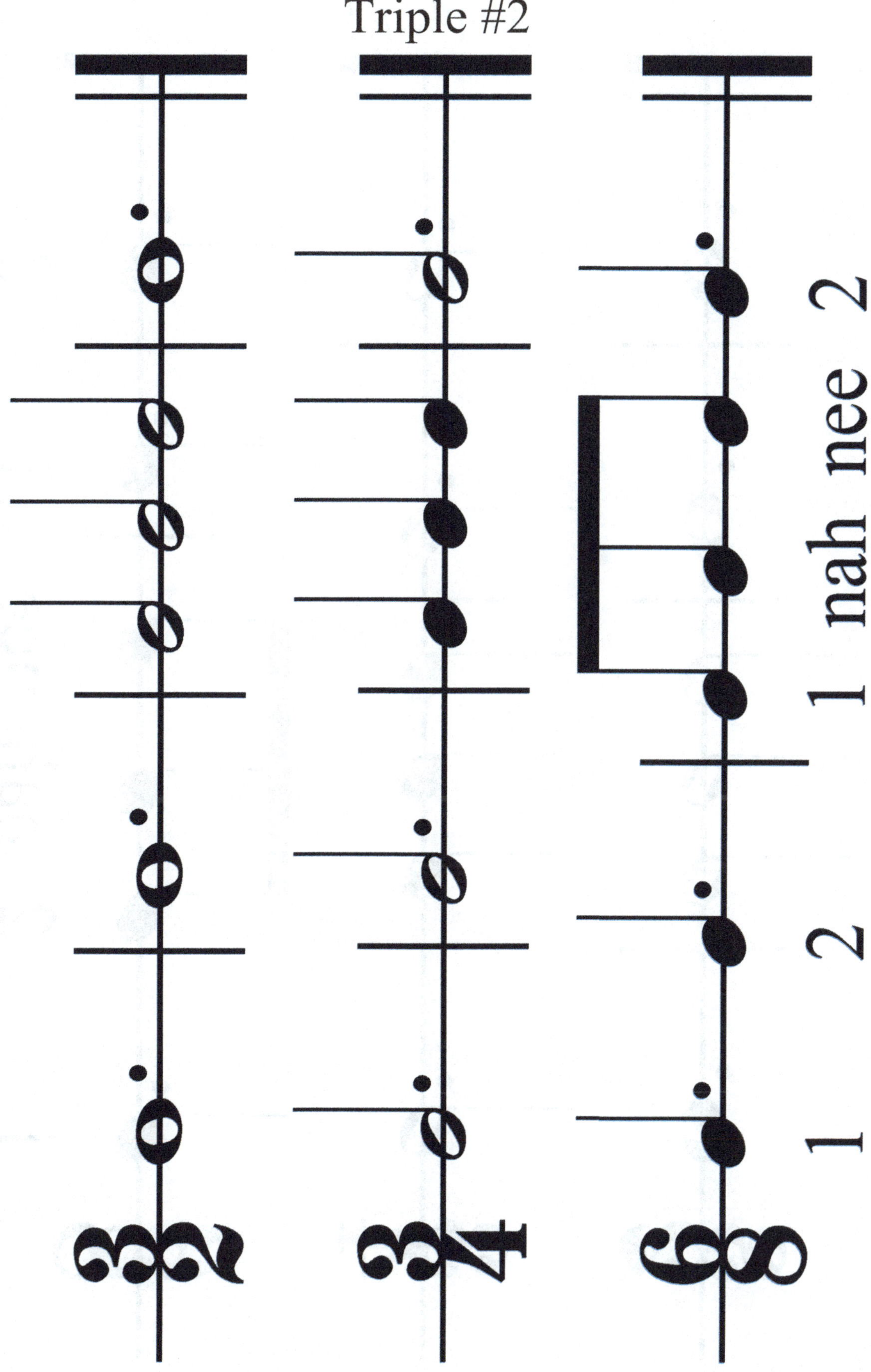

Triple #3

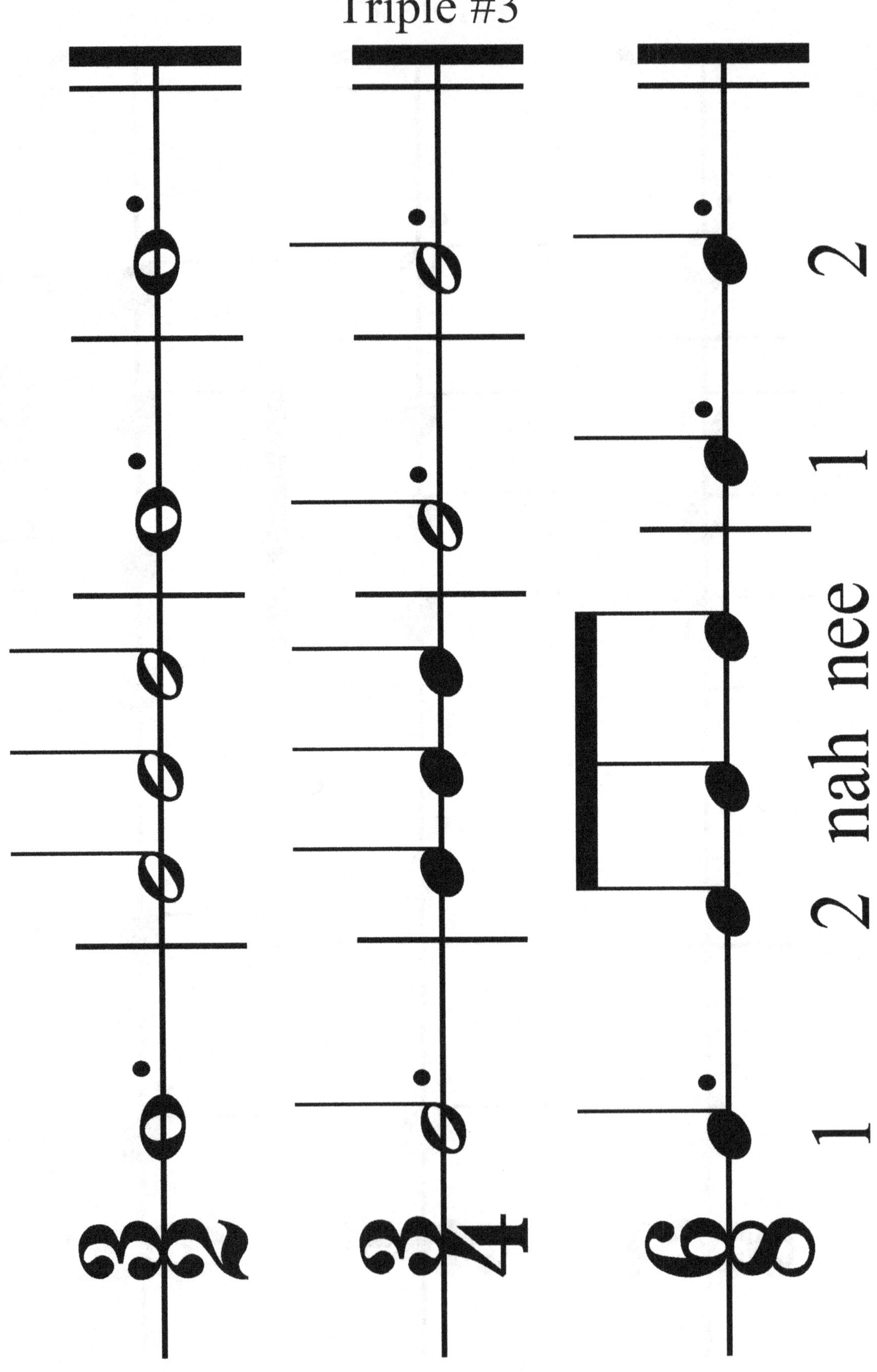

Triple #4

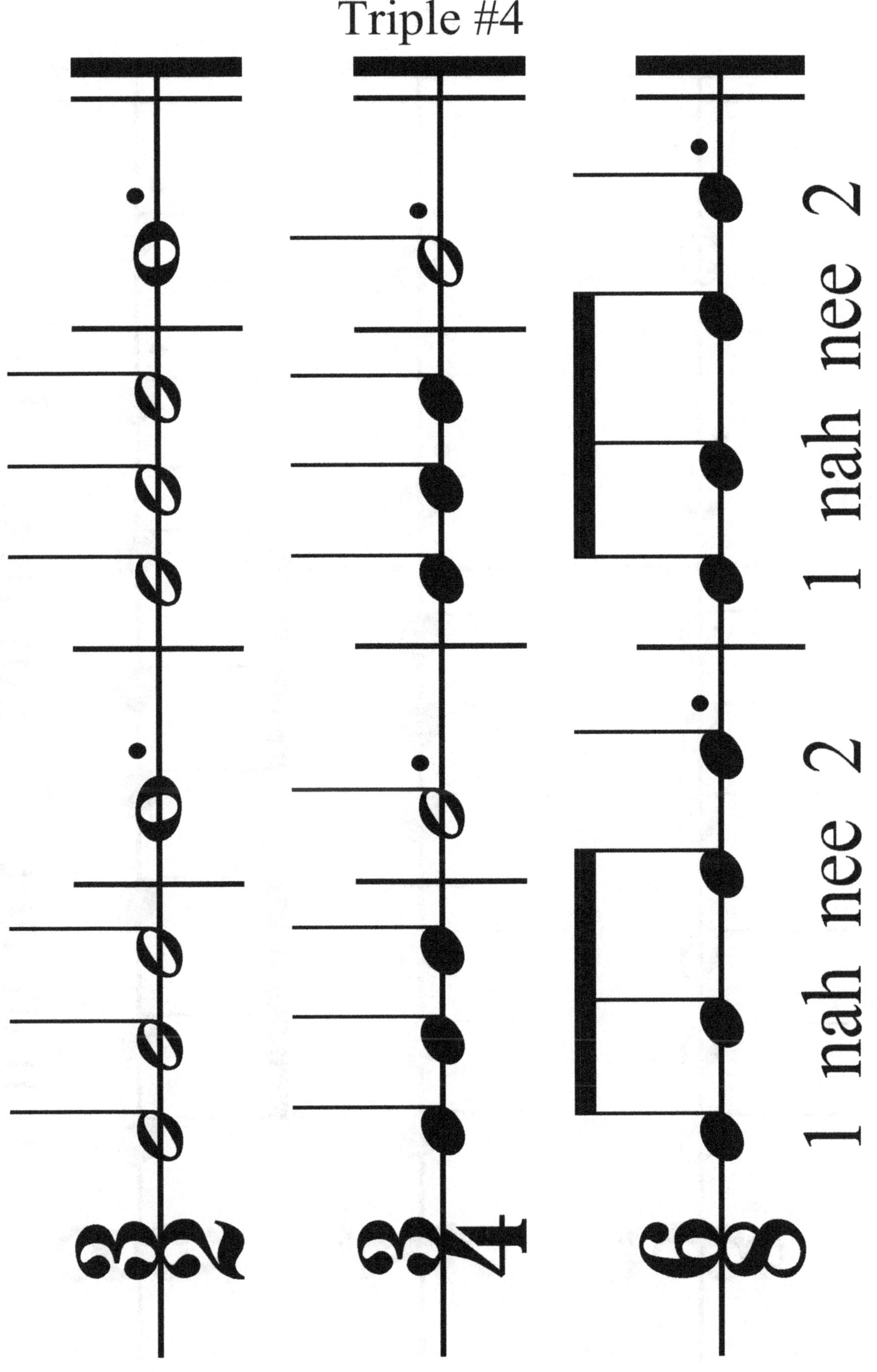

Triple #5

Triple #6

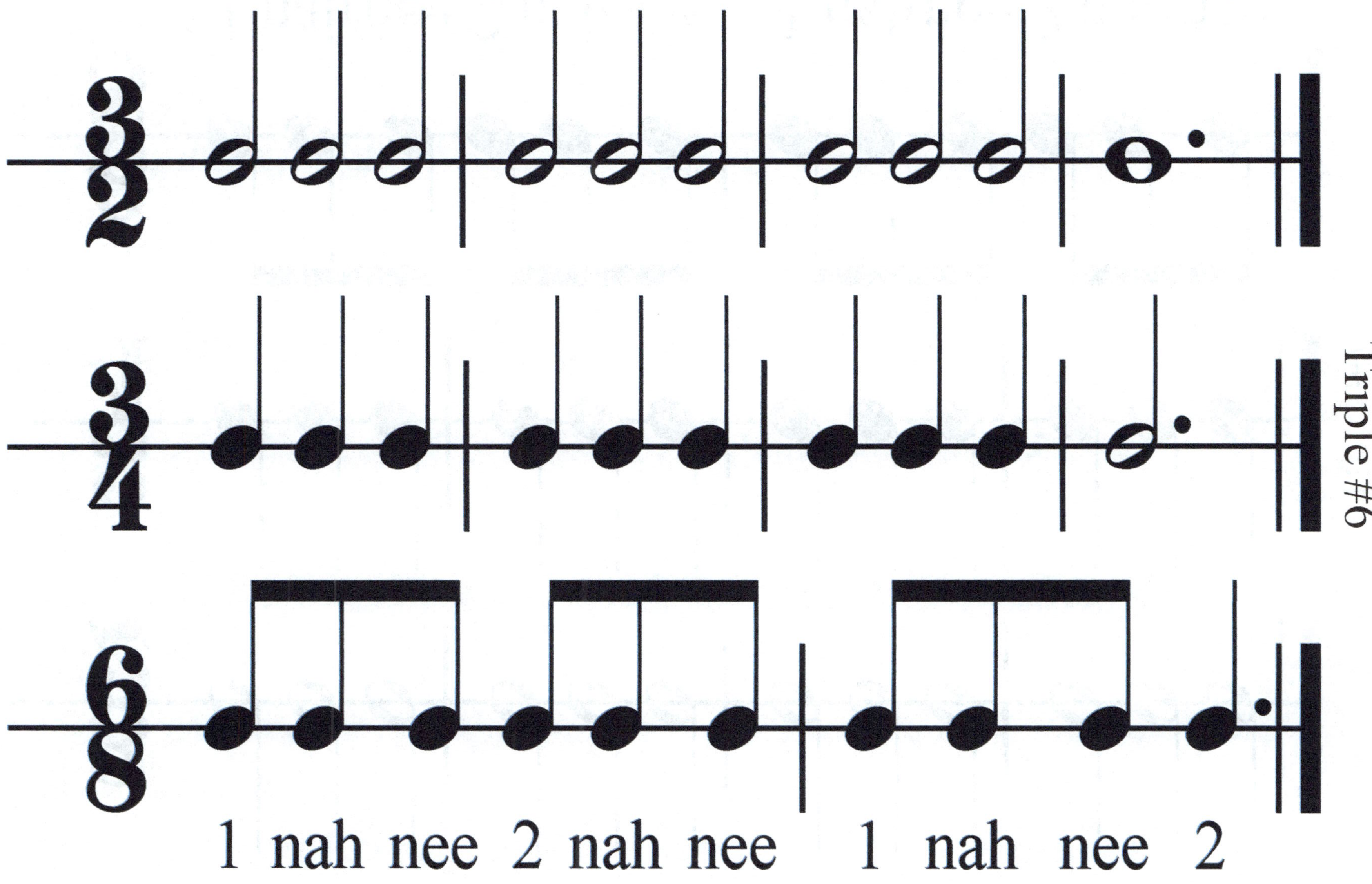
1 nah nee 2 nah nee 1 nah nee 2

Triple #7

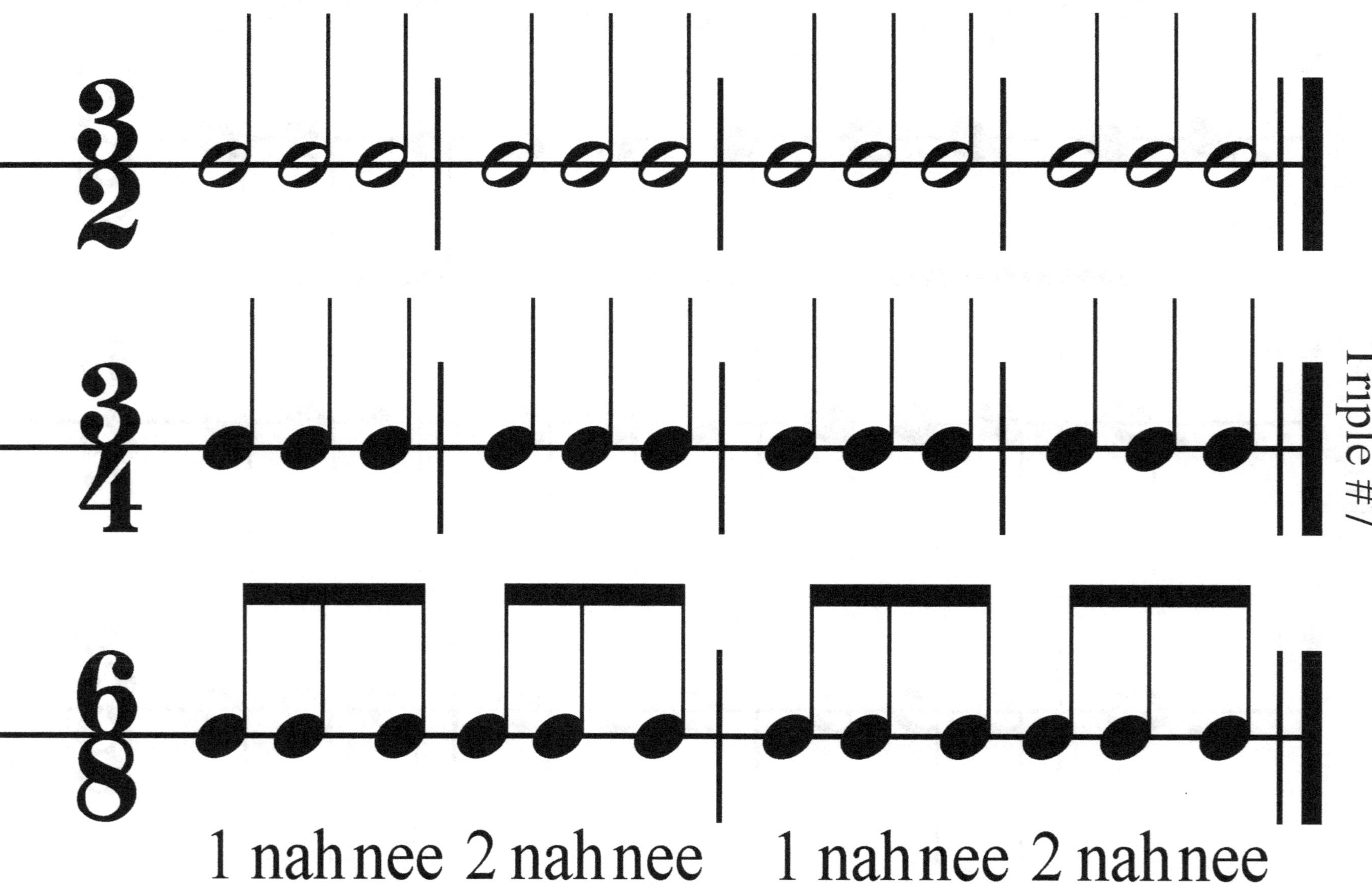
1 nahnee 2 nahnee
1 nahnee 2 nahnee

Triple #8

Triple #9

Triple #10

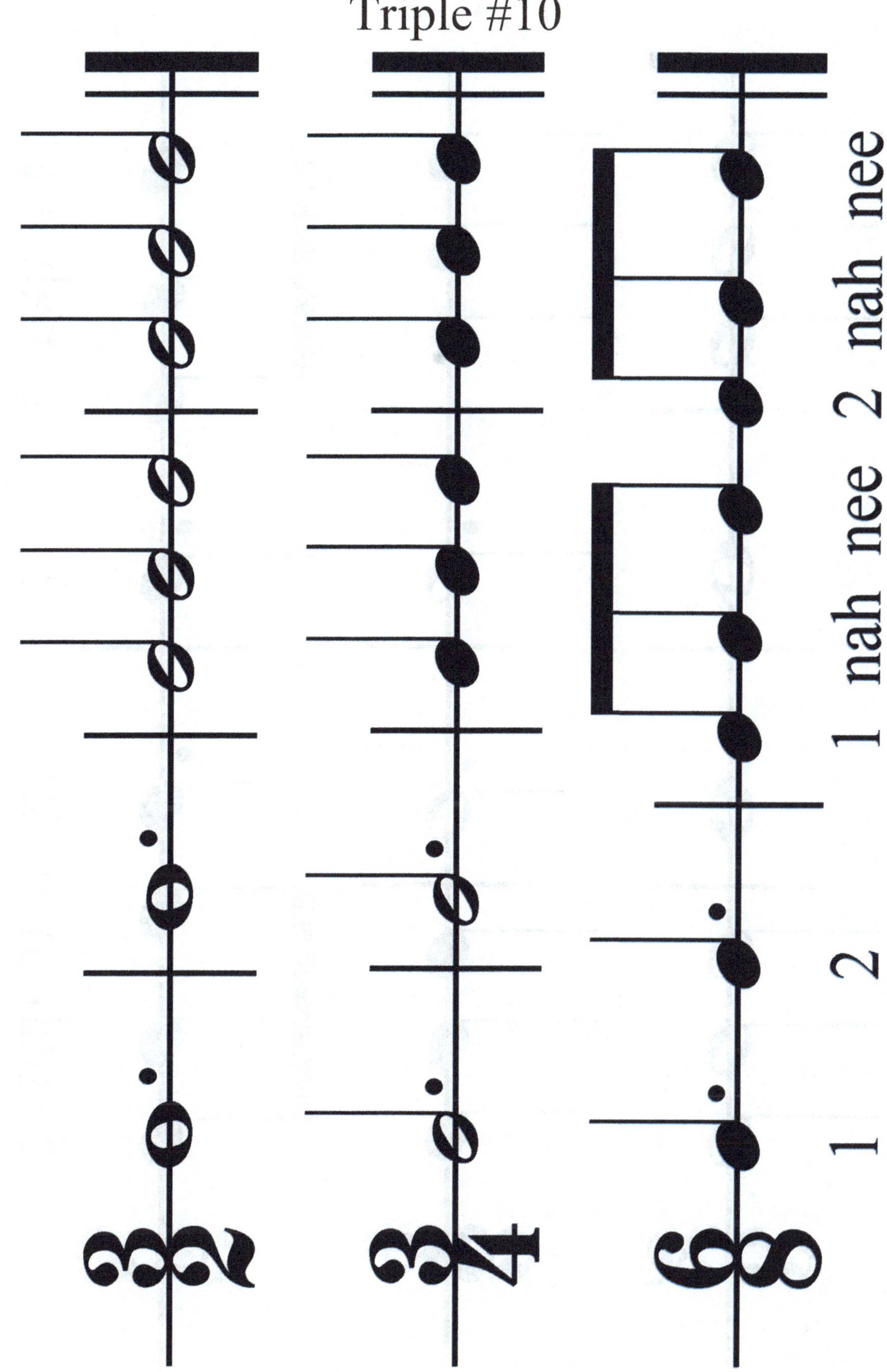
1 2 1 nah nee 2 nah nee

Triple #11

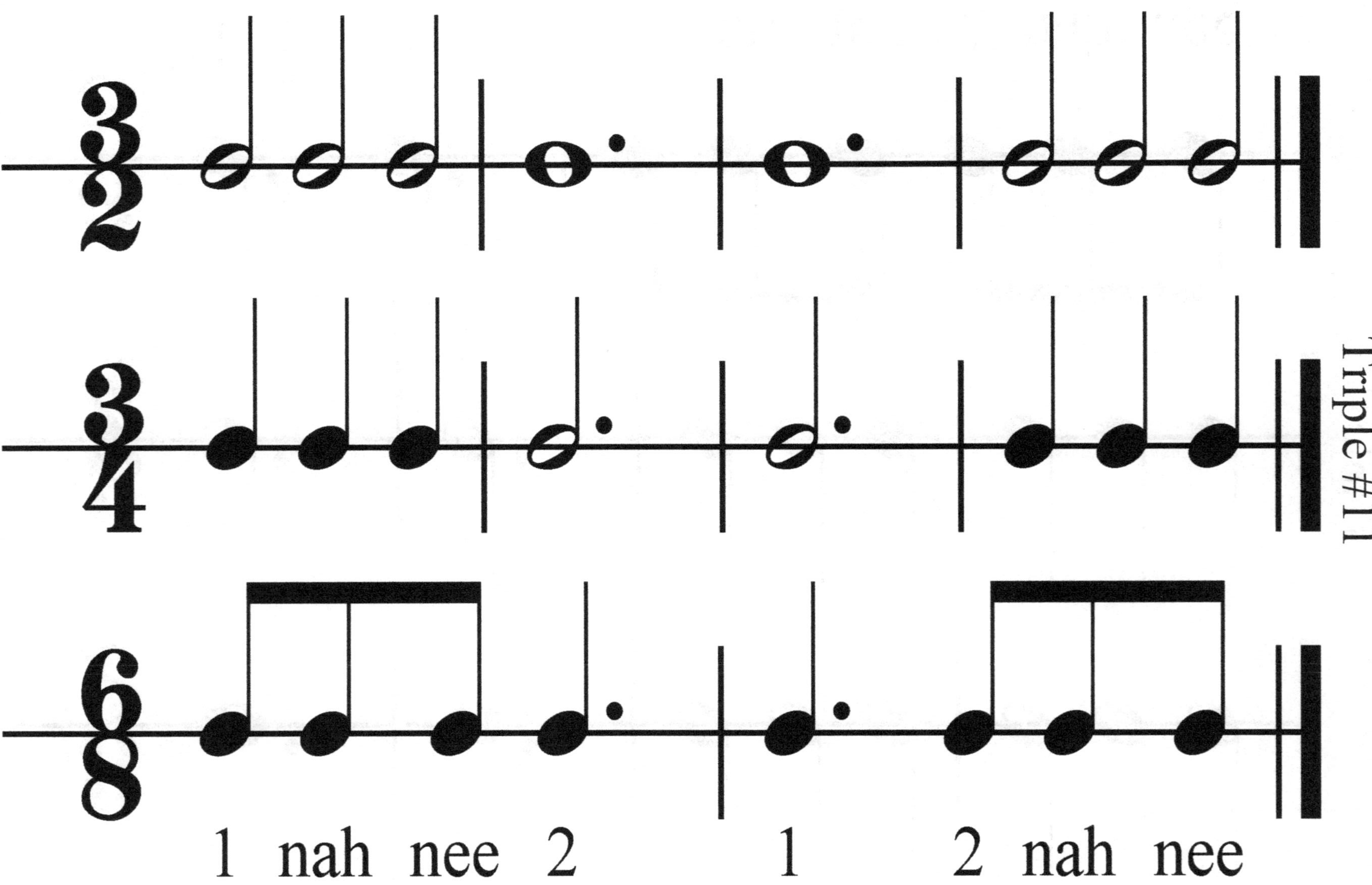
1 nah nee 2
1
2 nah nee

Triple #1a

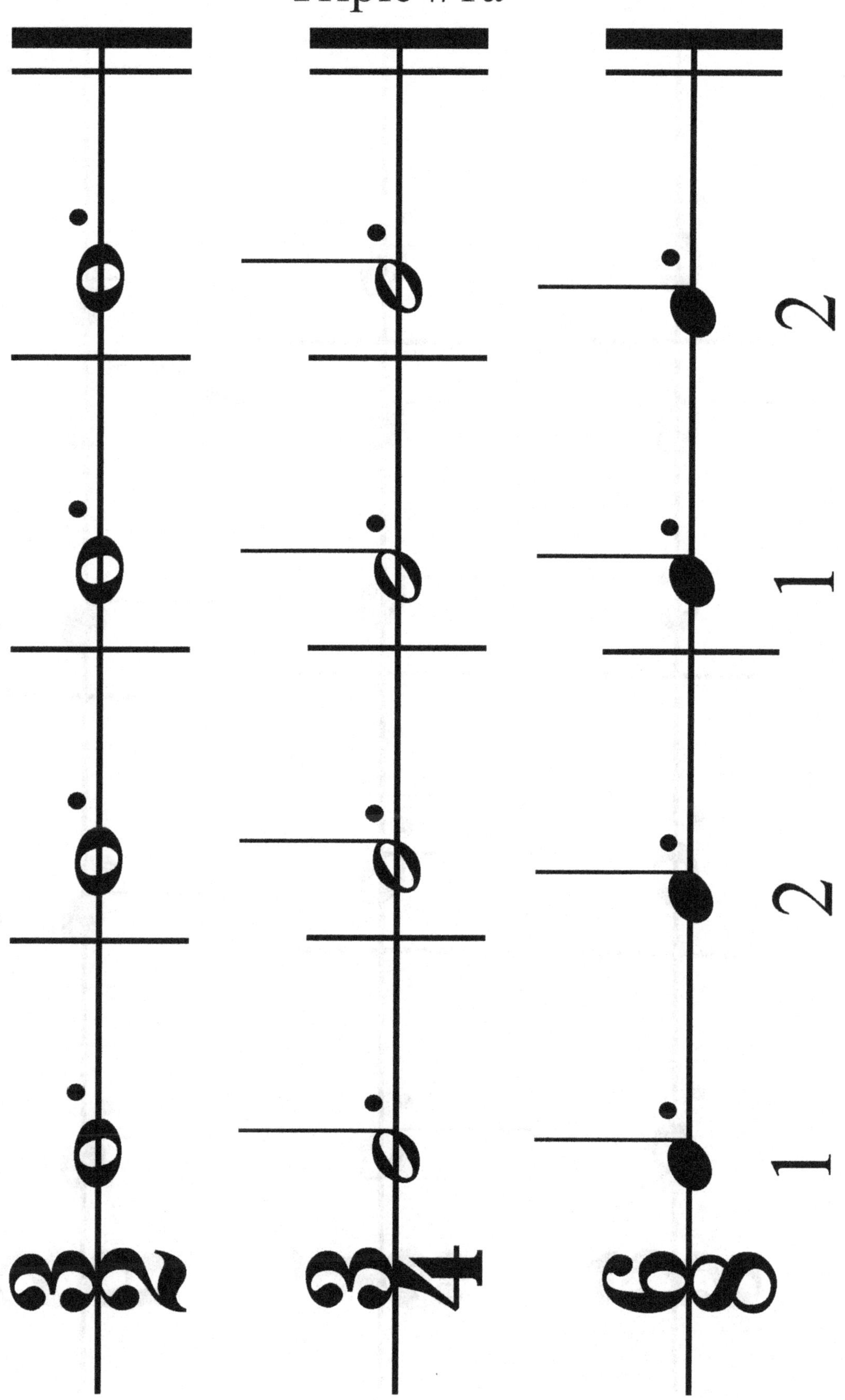

Triple #2a

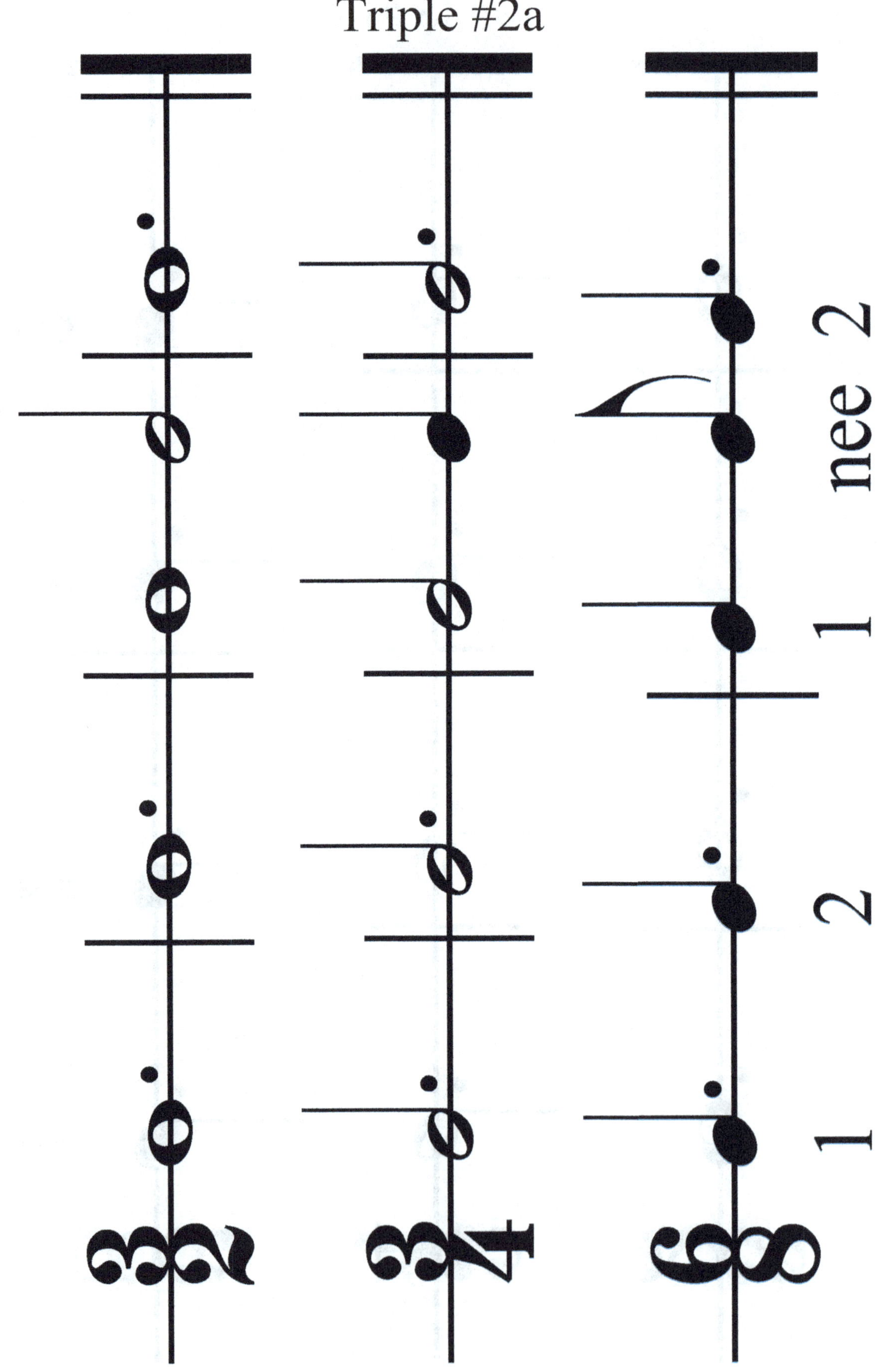

Triple #3a

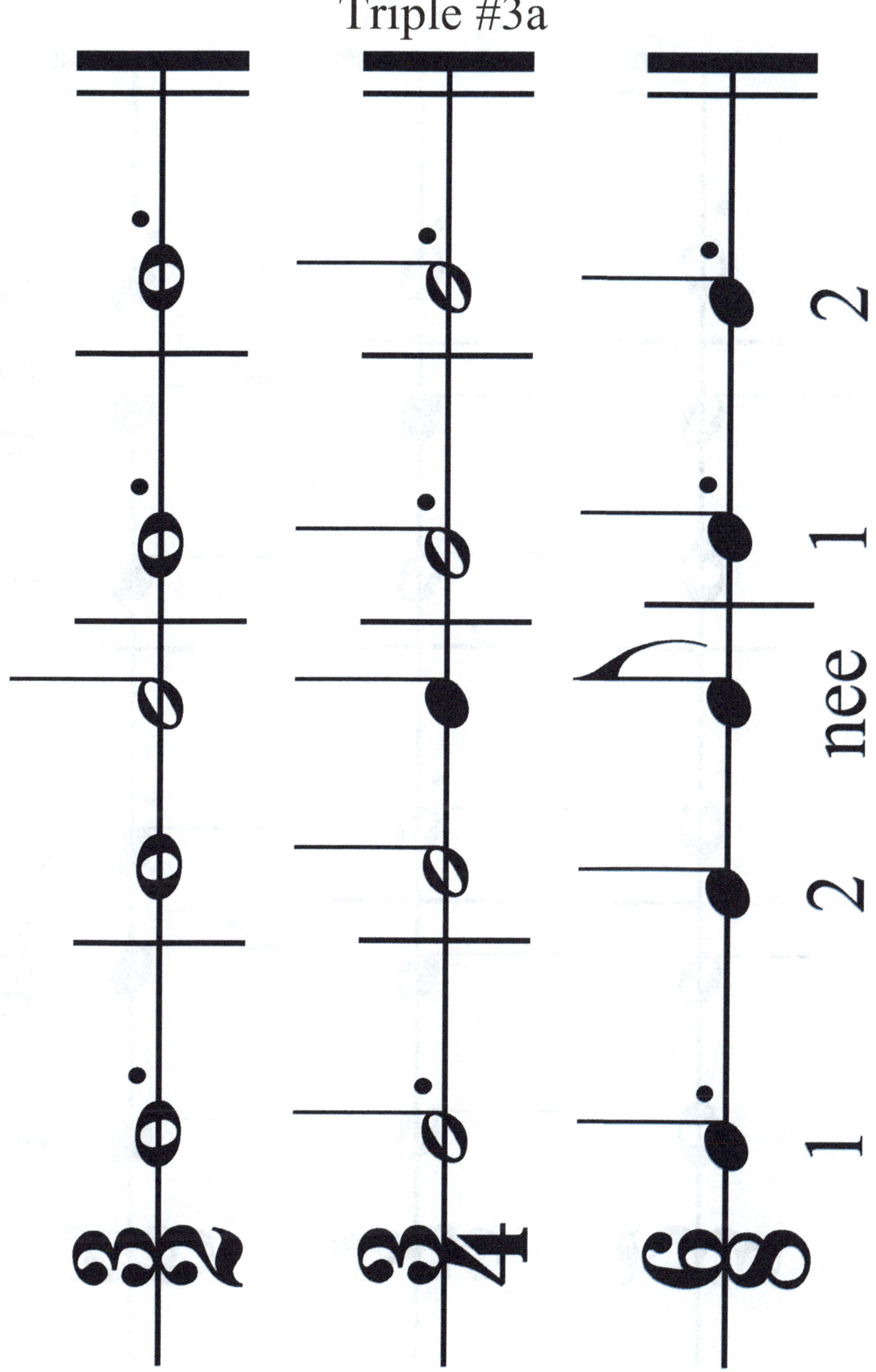

Triple #4a

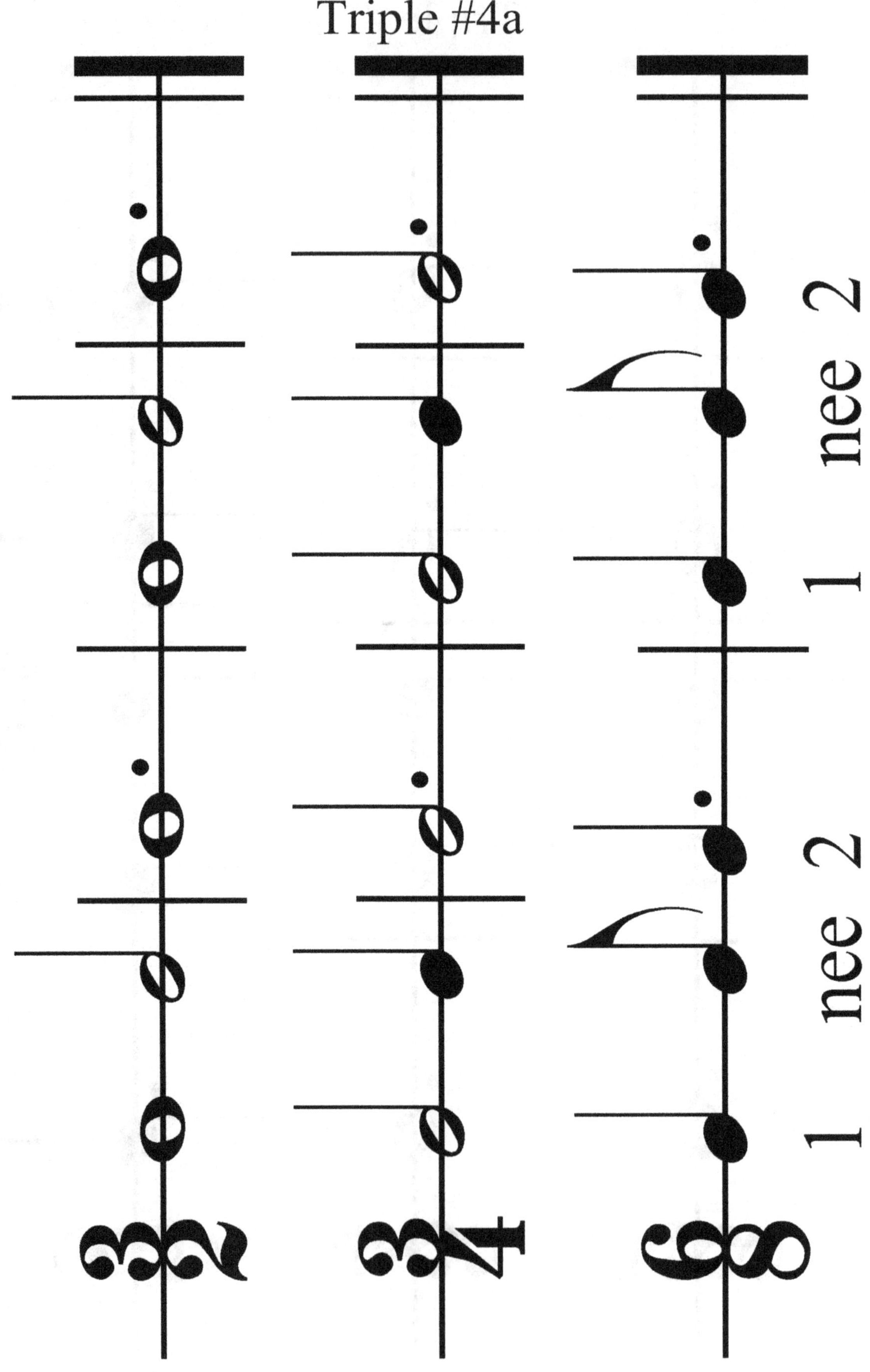

Triple #5a

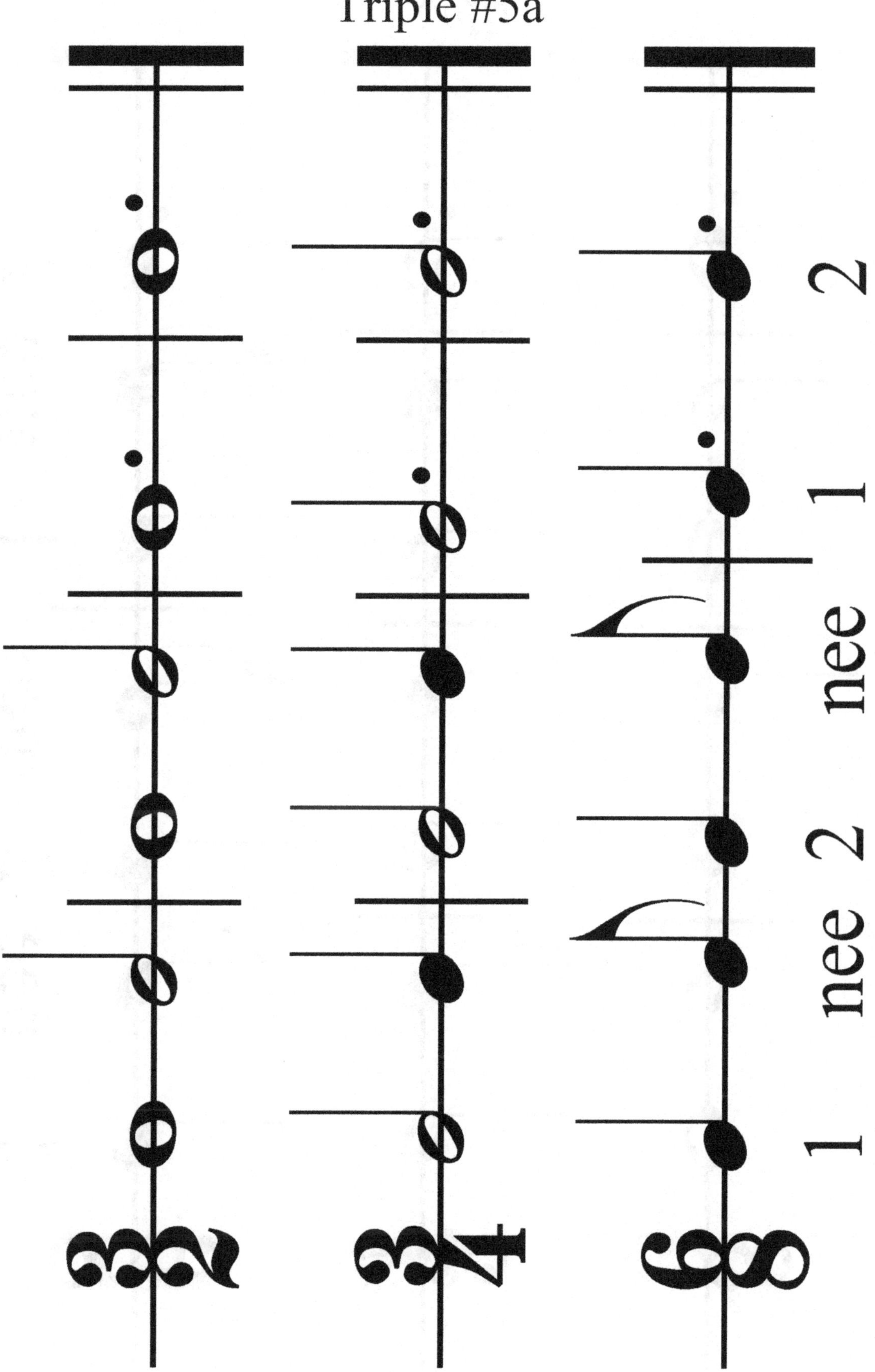

Triple #6a

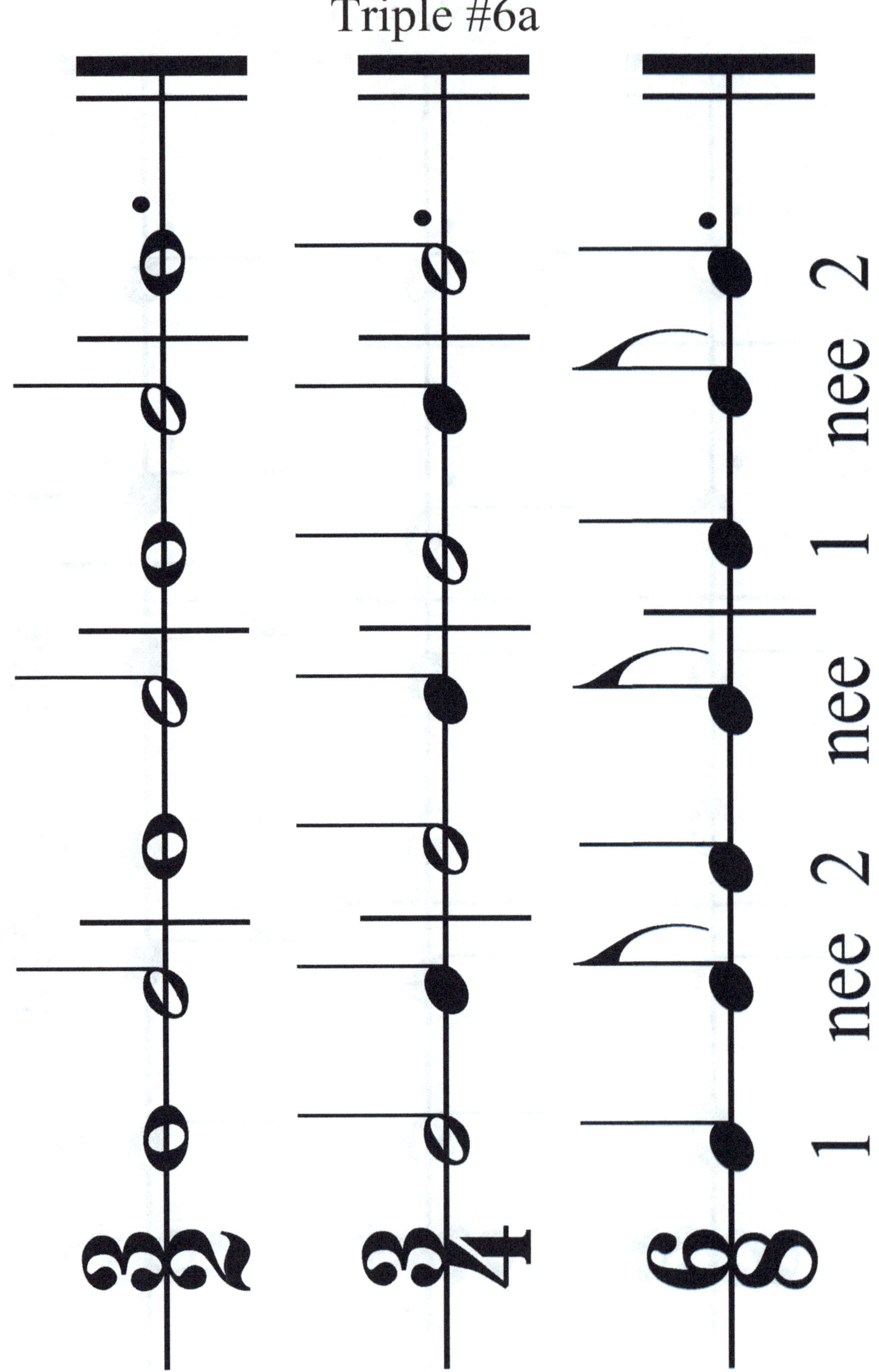
1 nee 2 nee 1 nee 2

Triple #7a

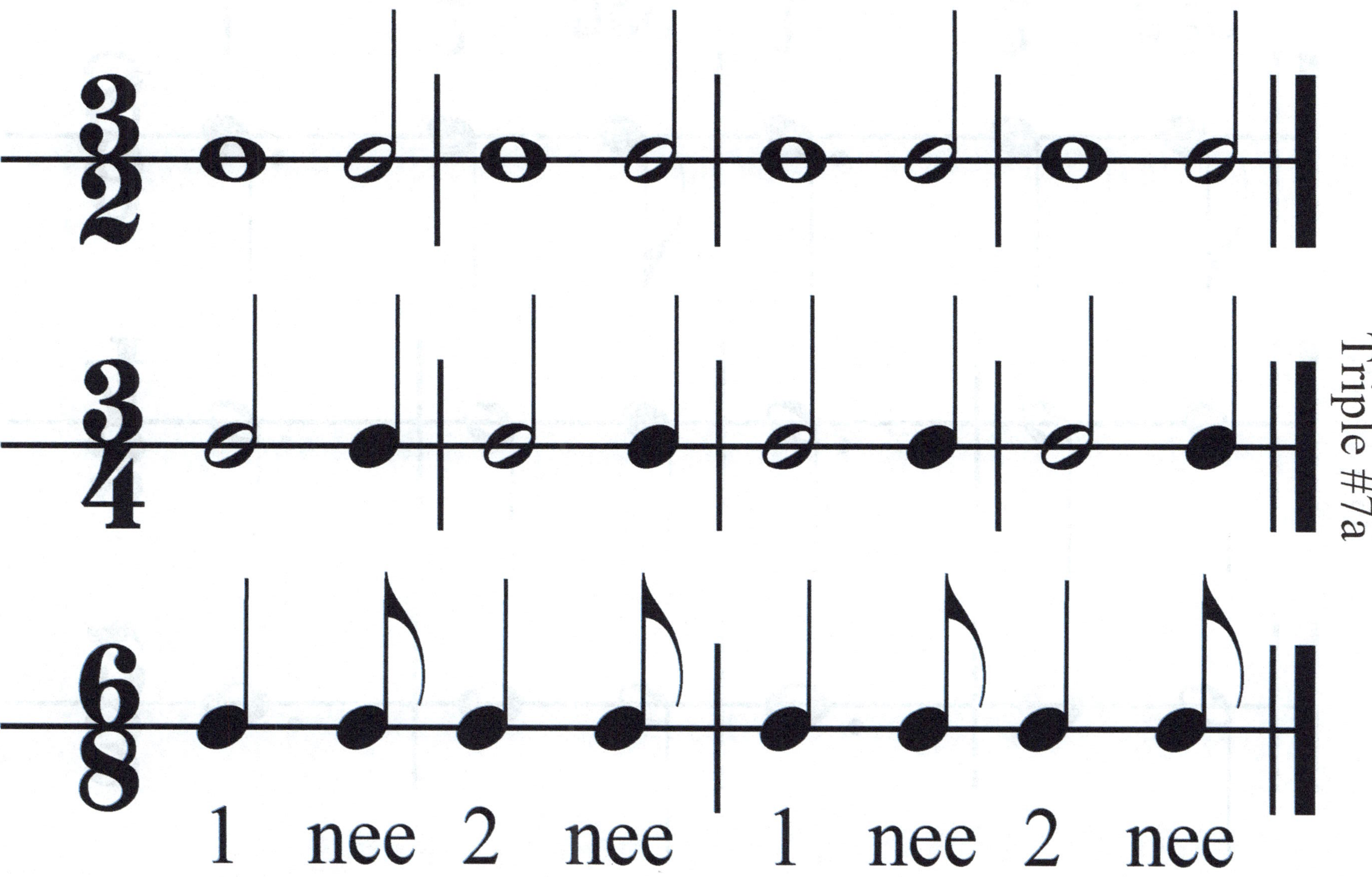

Triple #8a

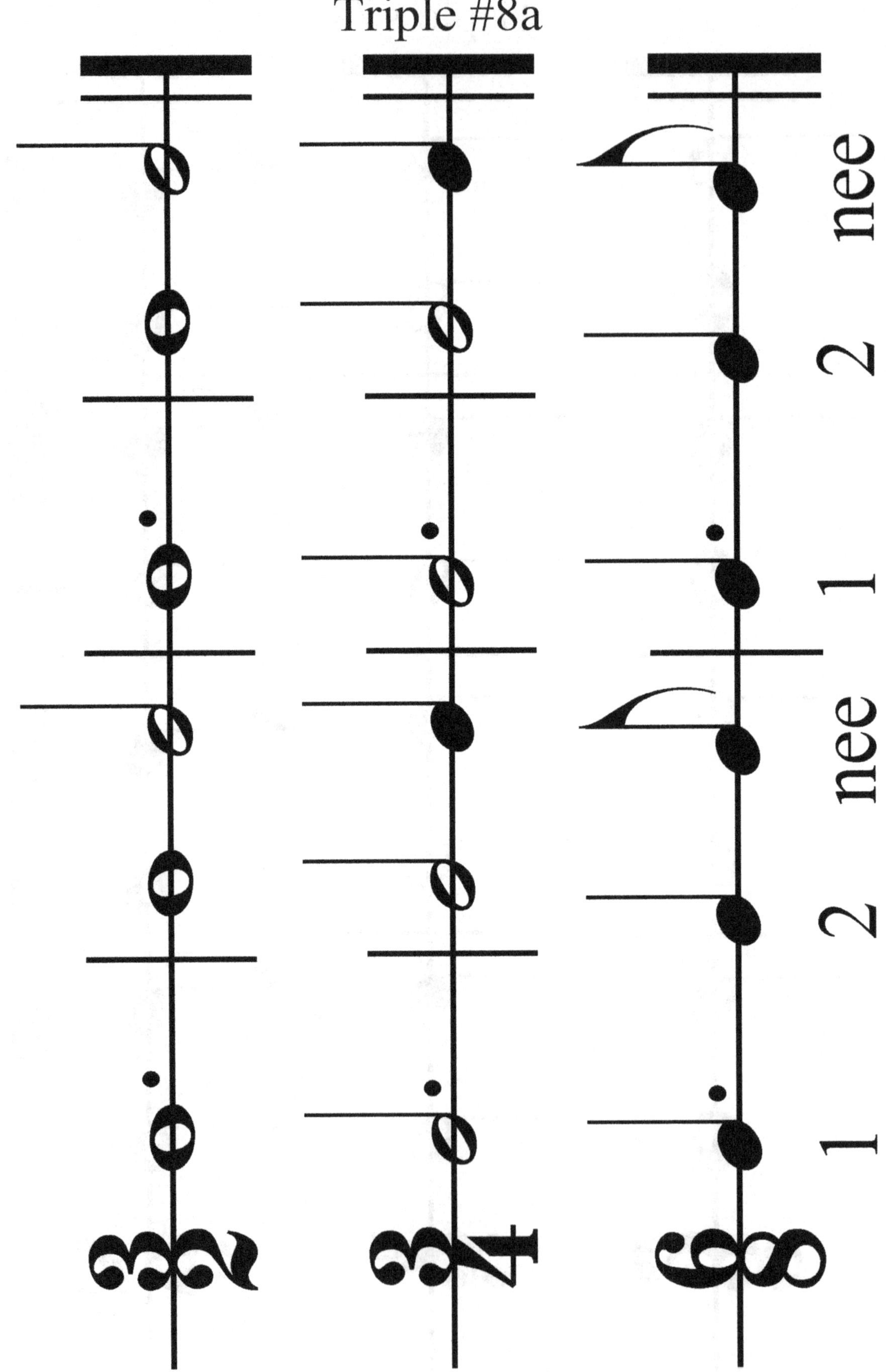

Triple #9a

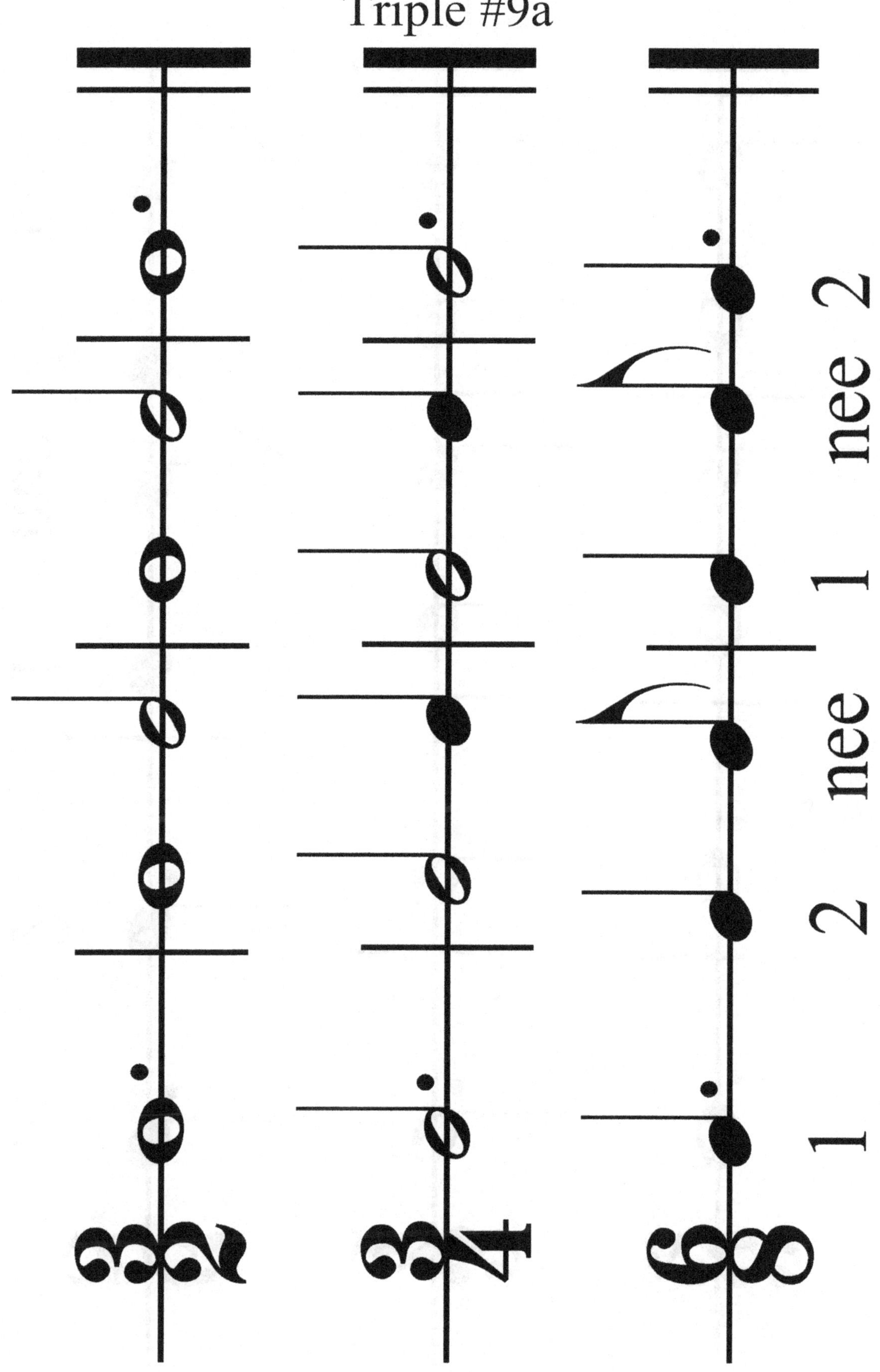

Triple #10a

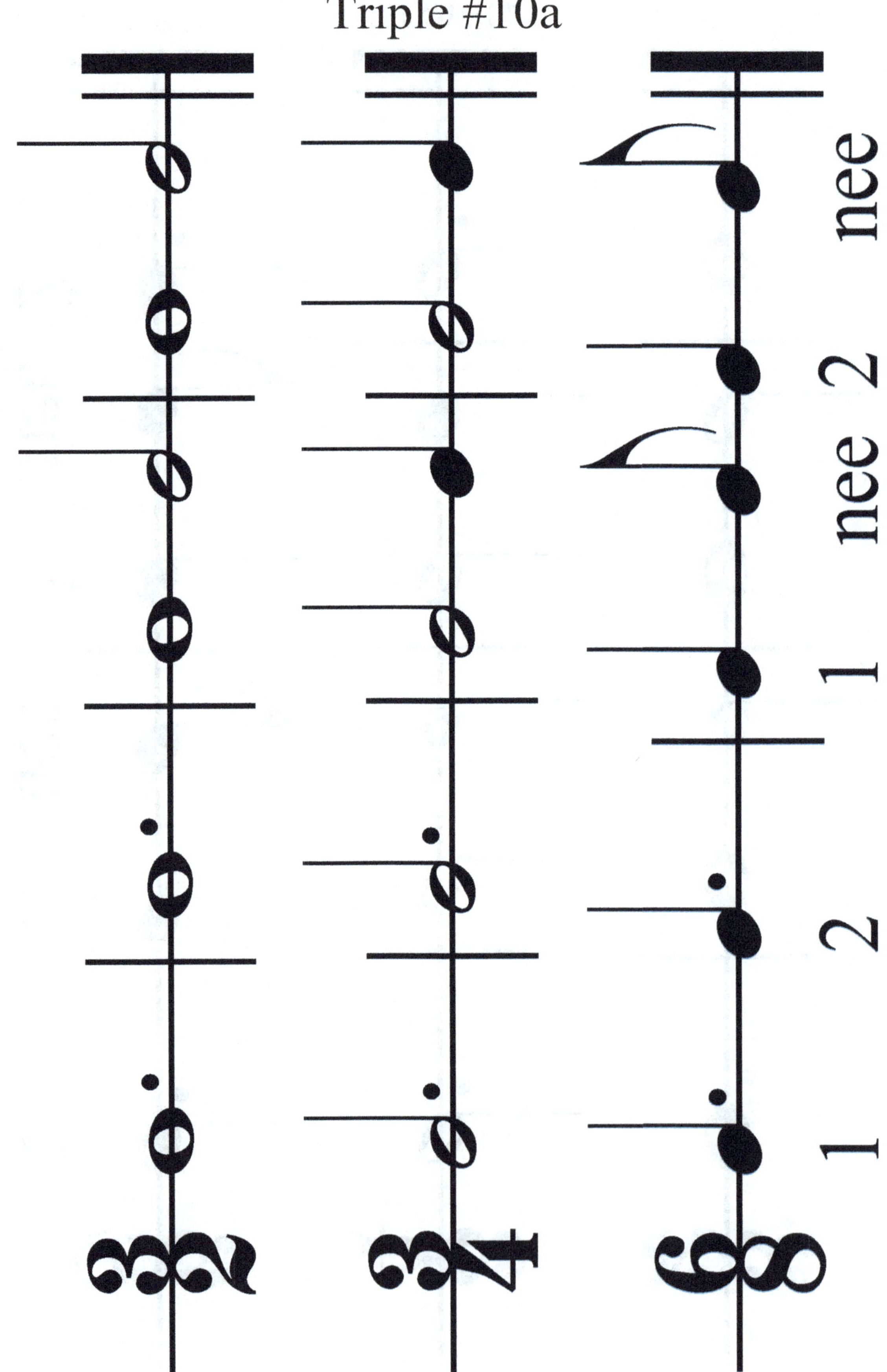

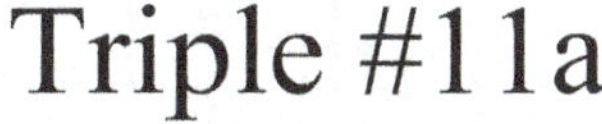

Triple #11a

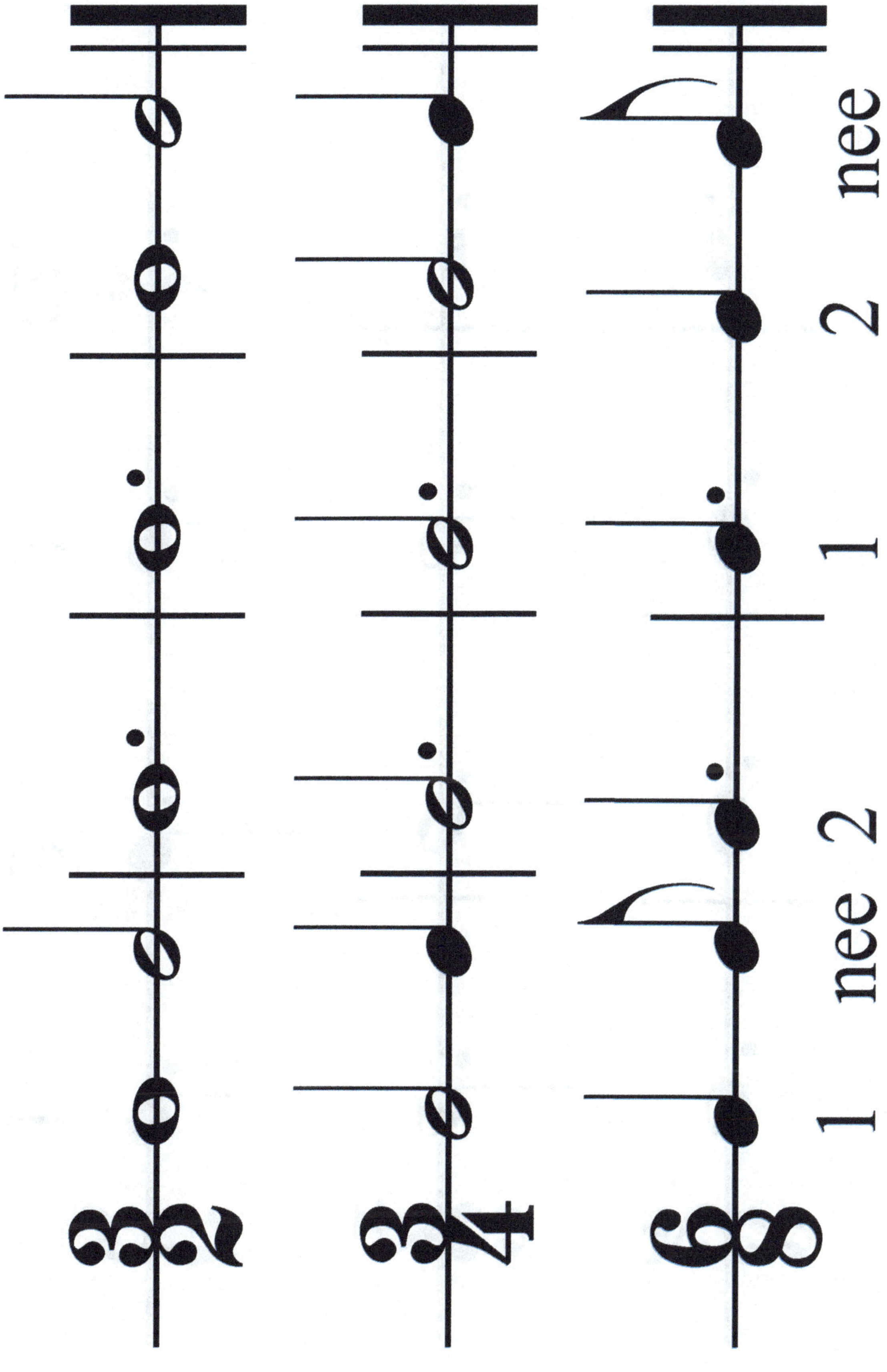

1 nee 2 1 2 nee

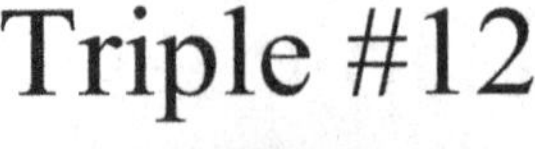

Triple #12

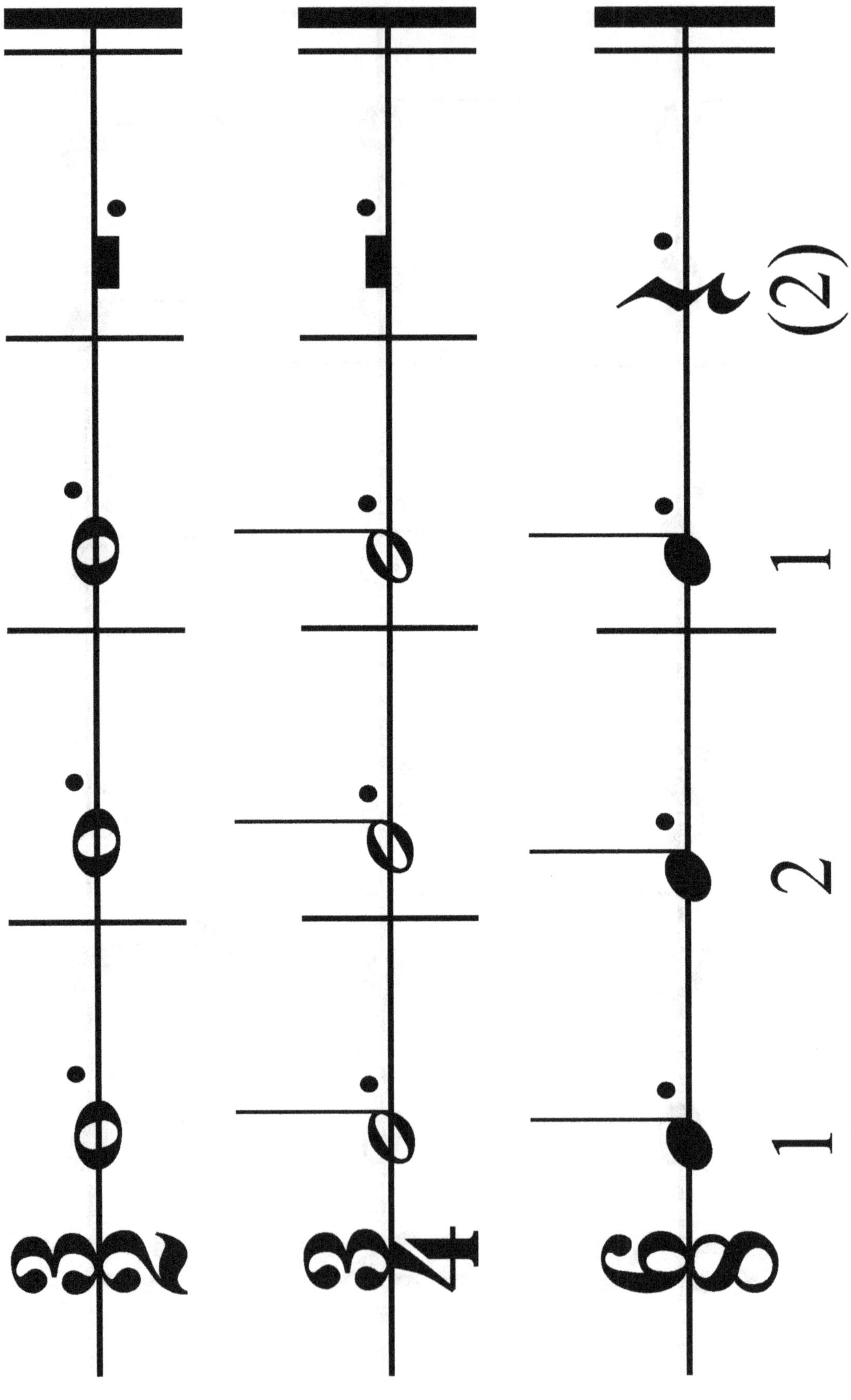

Triple #13

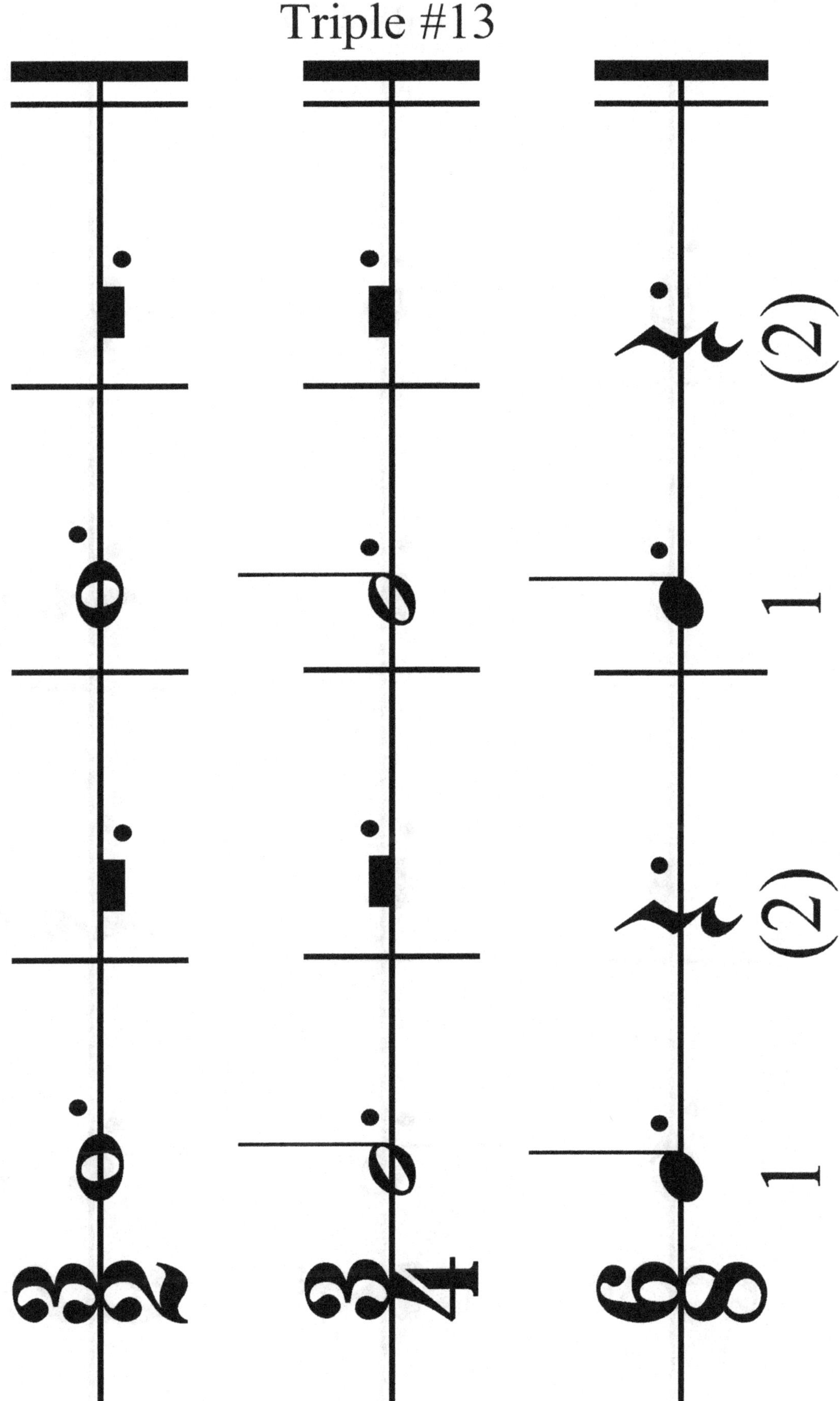

Triple #14

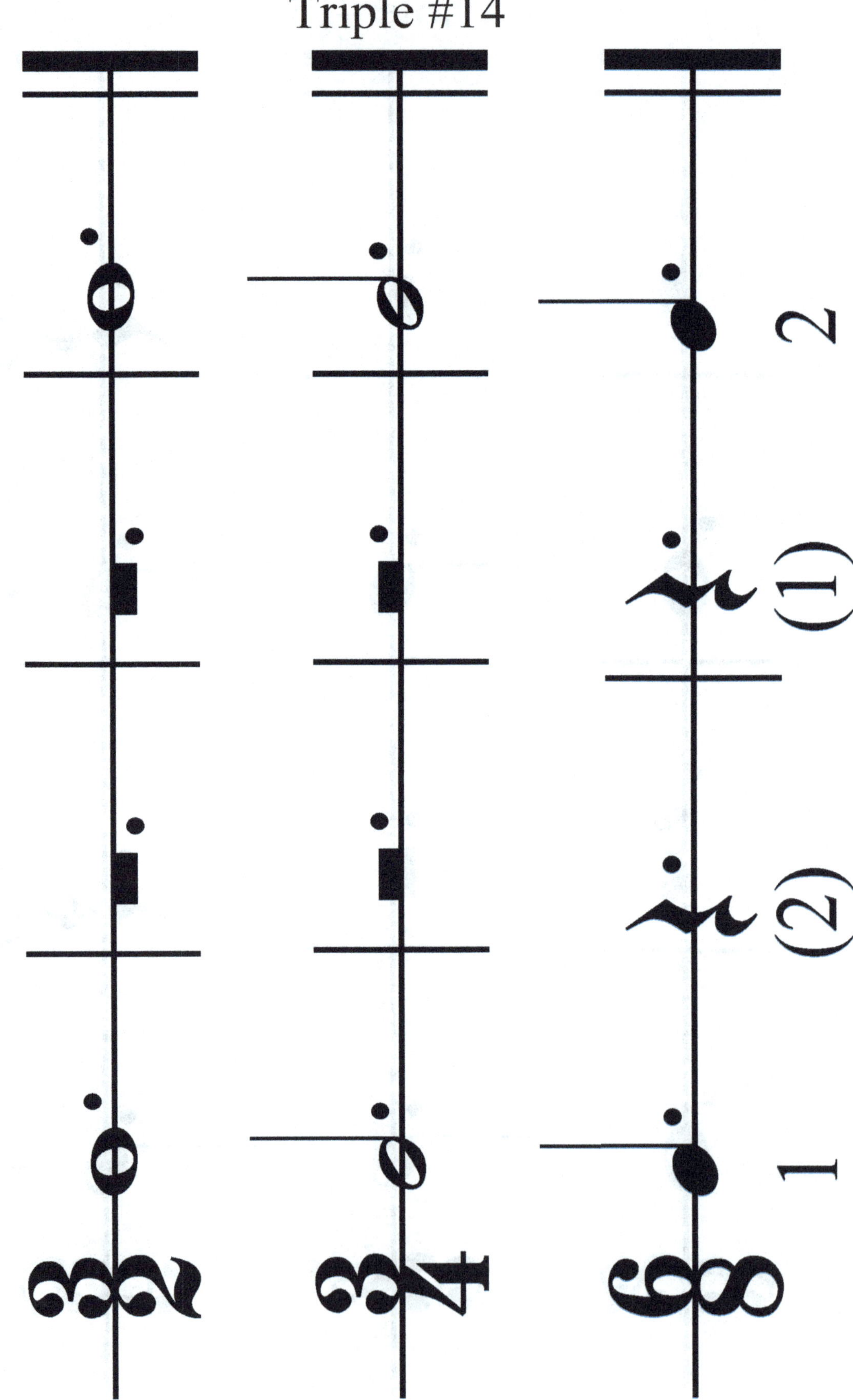

Triple #15

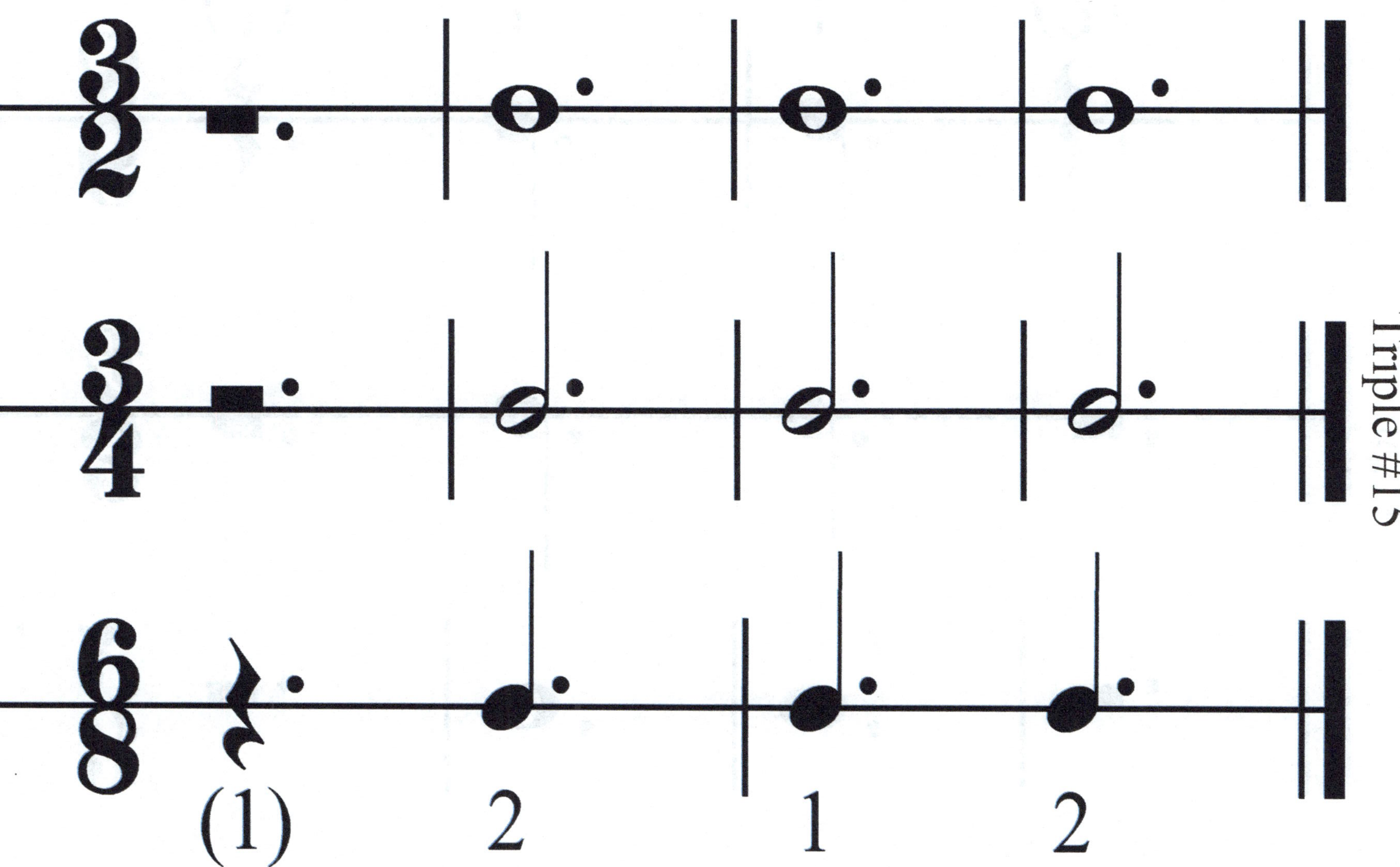

Triple #16

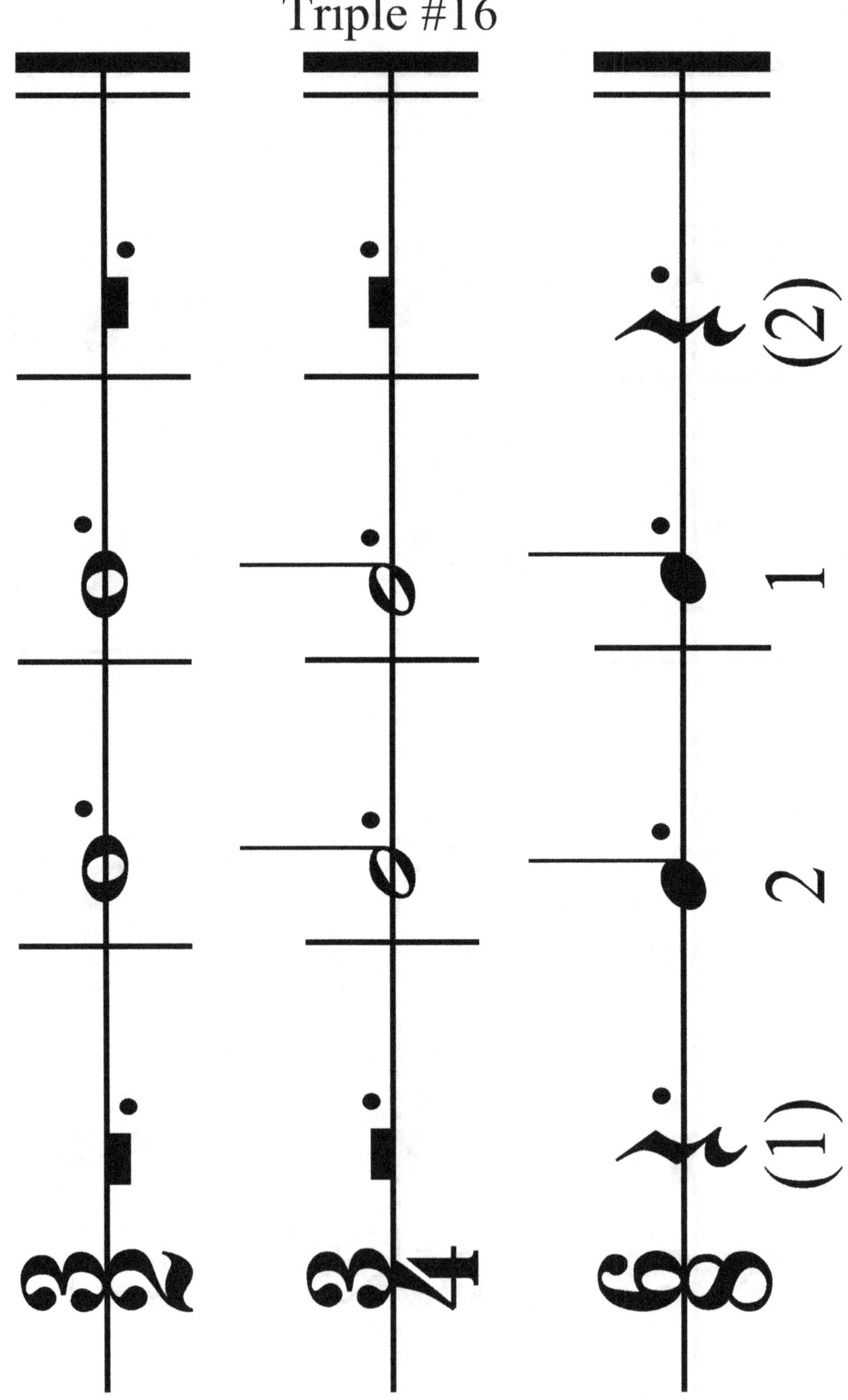

Triple #17

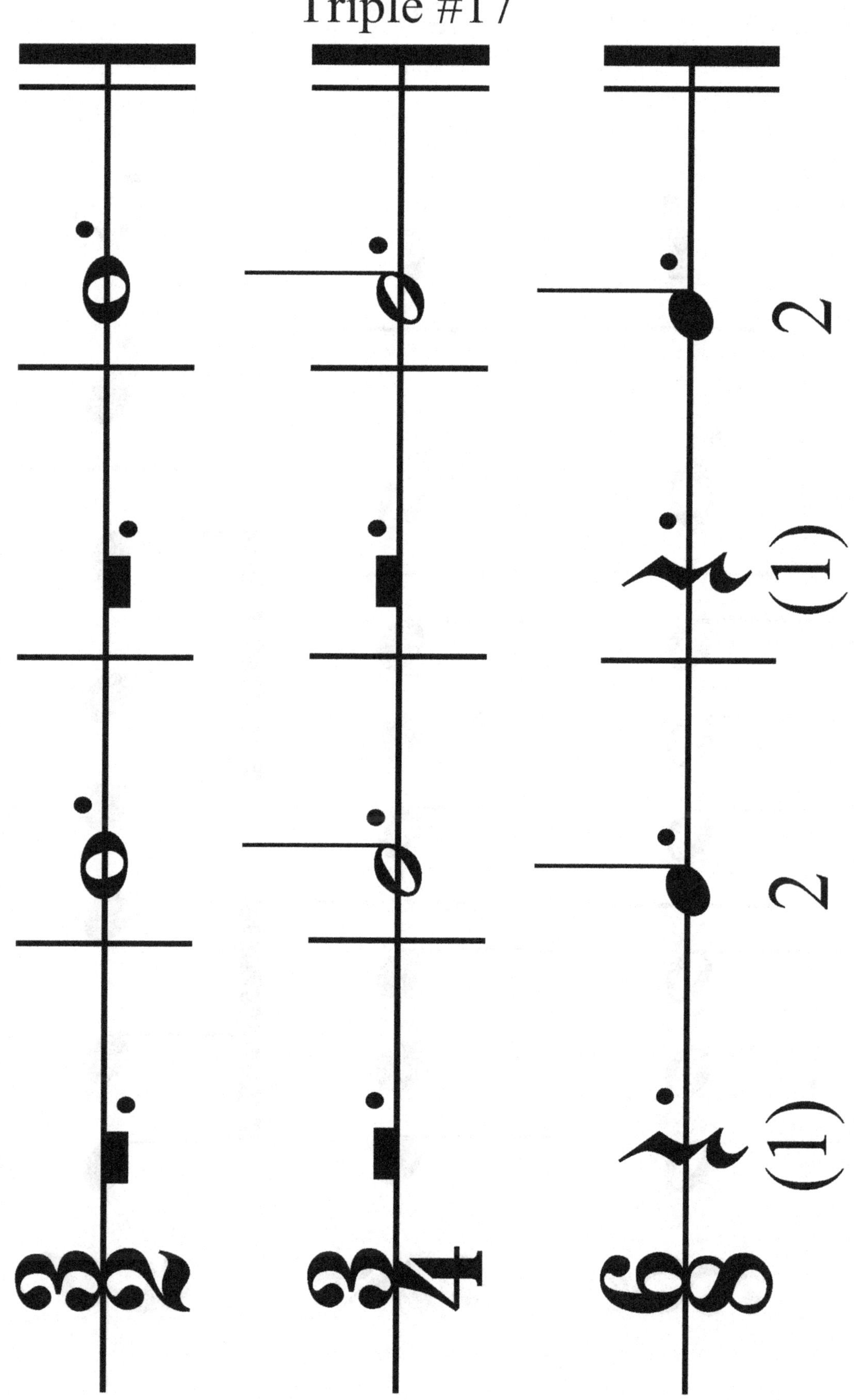

Triple #18

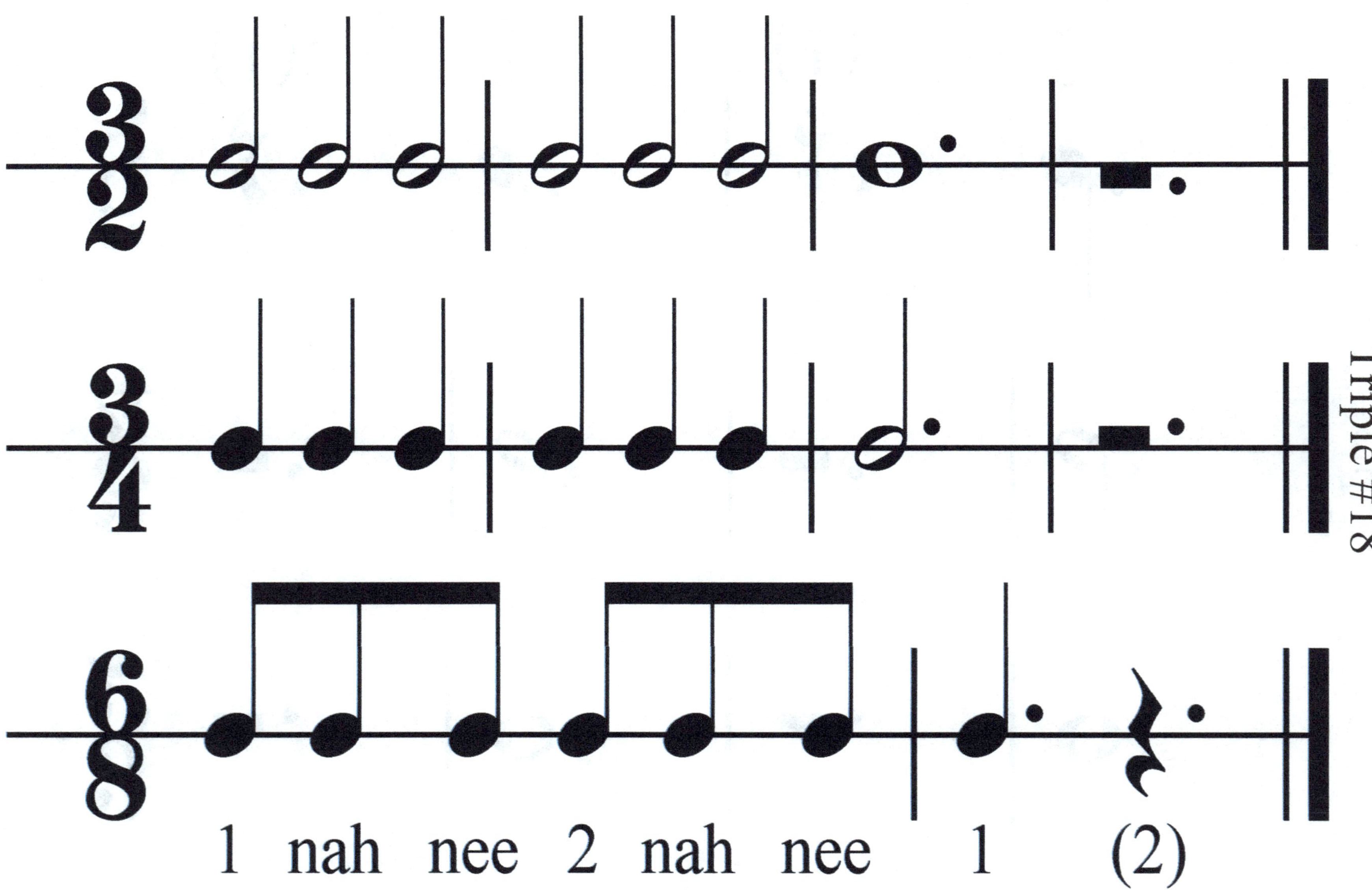

Triple #19

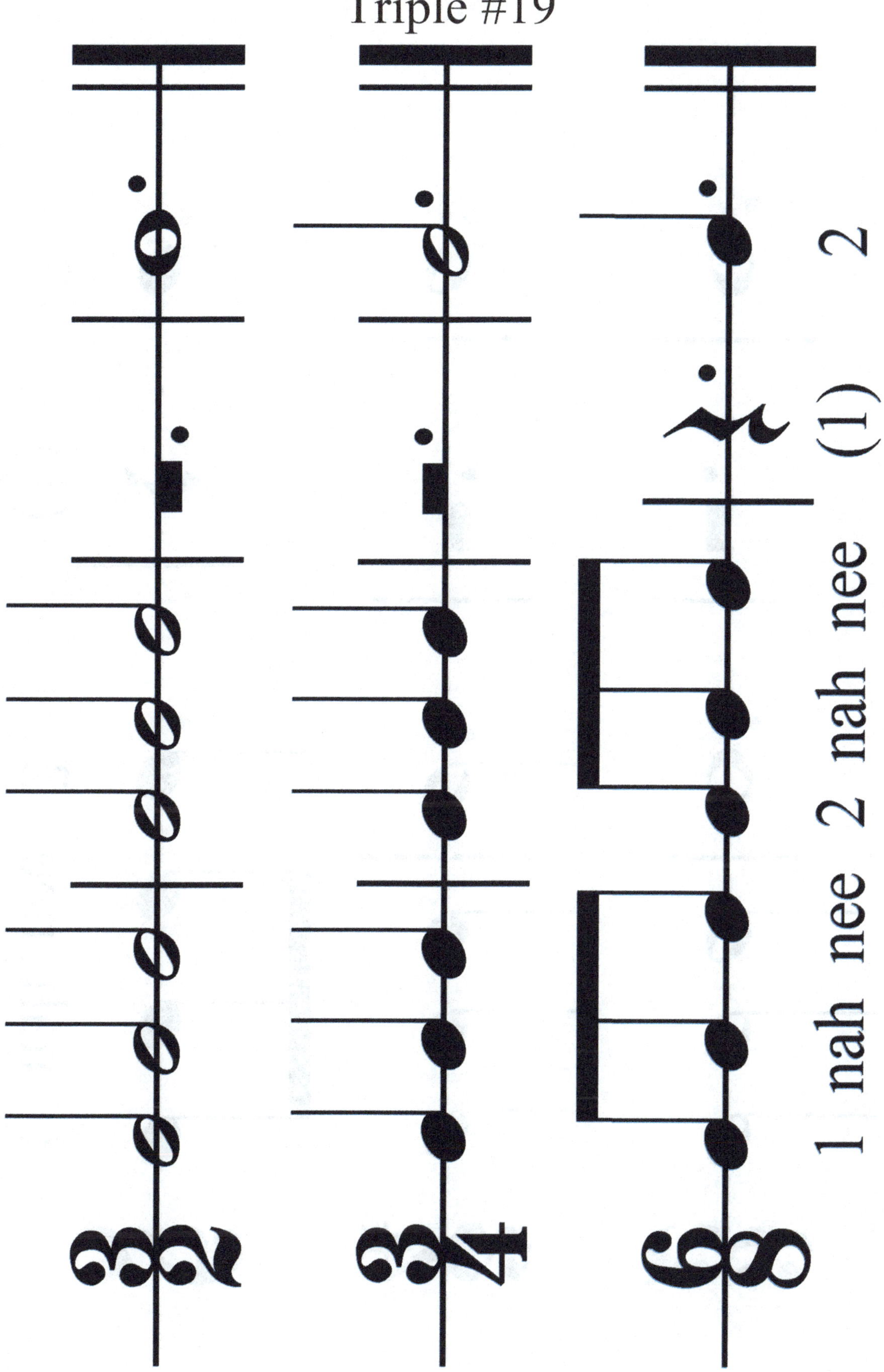

Triple #20

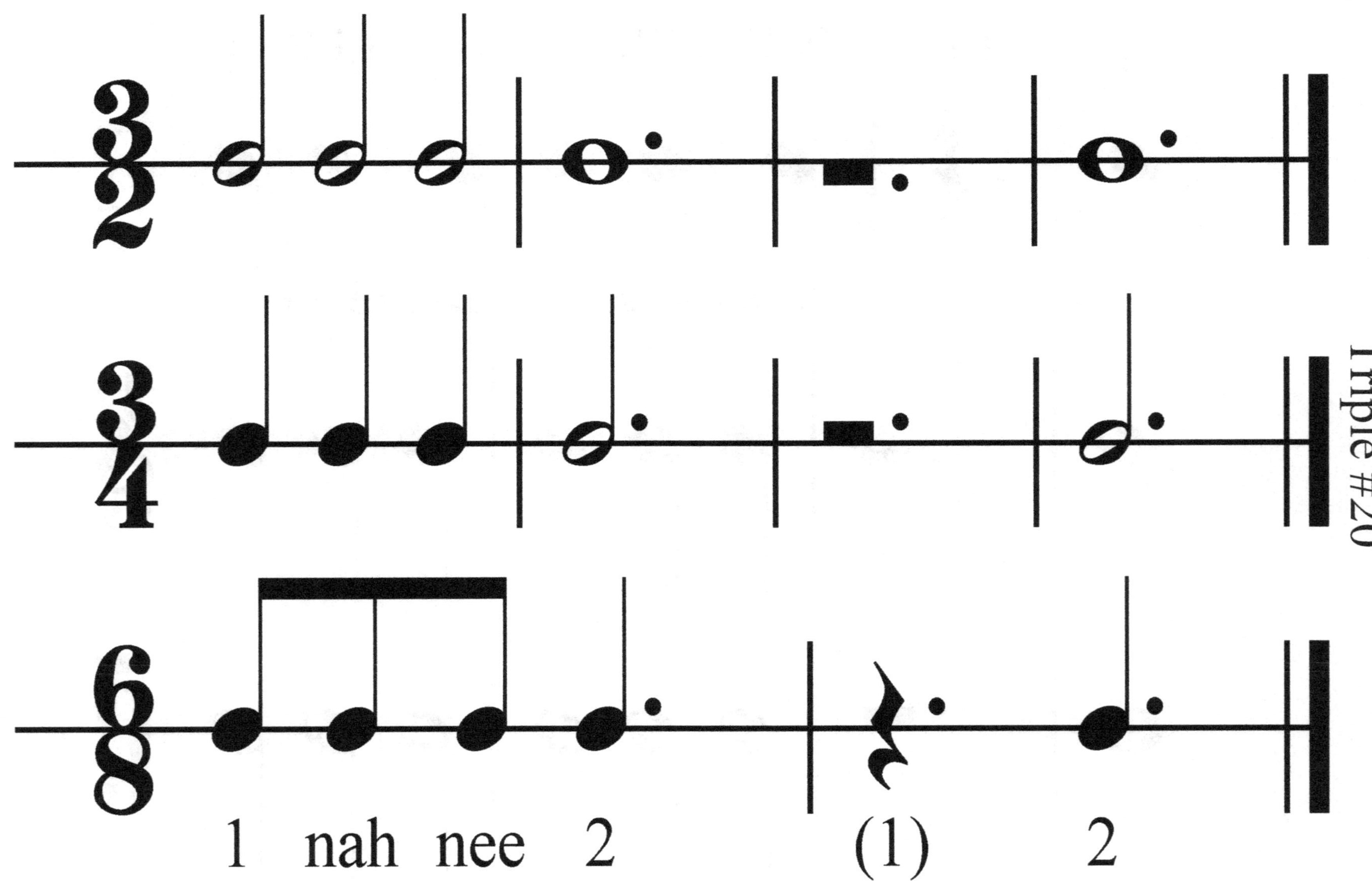

Triple #21

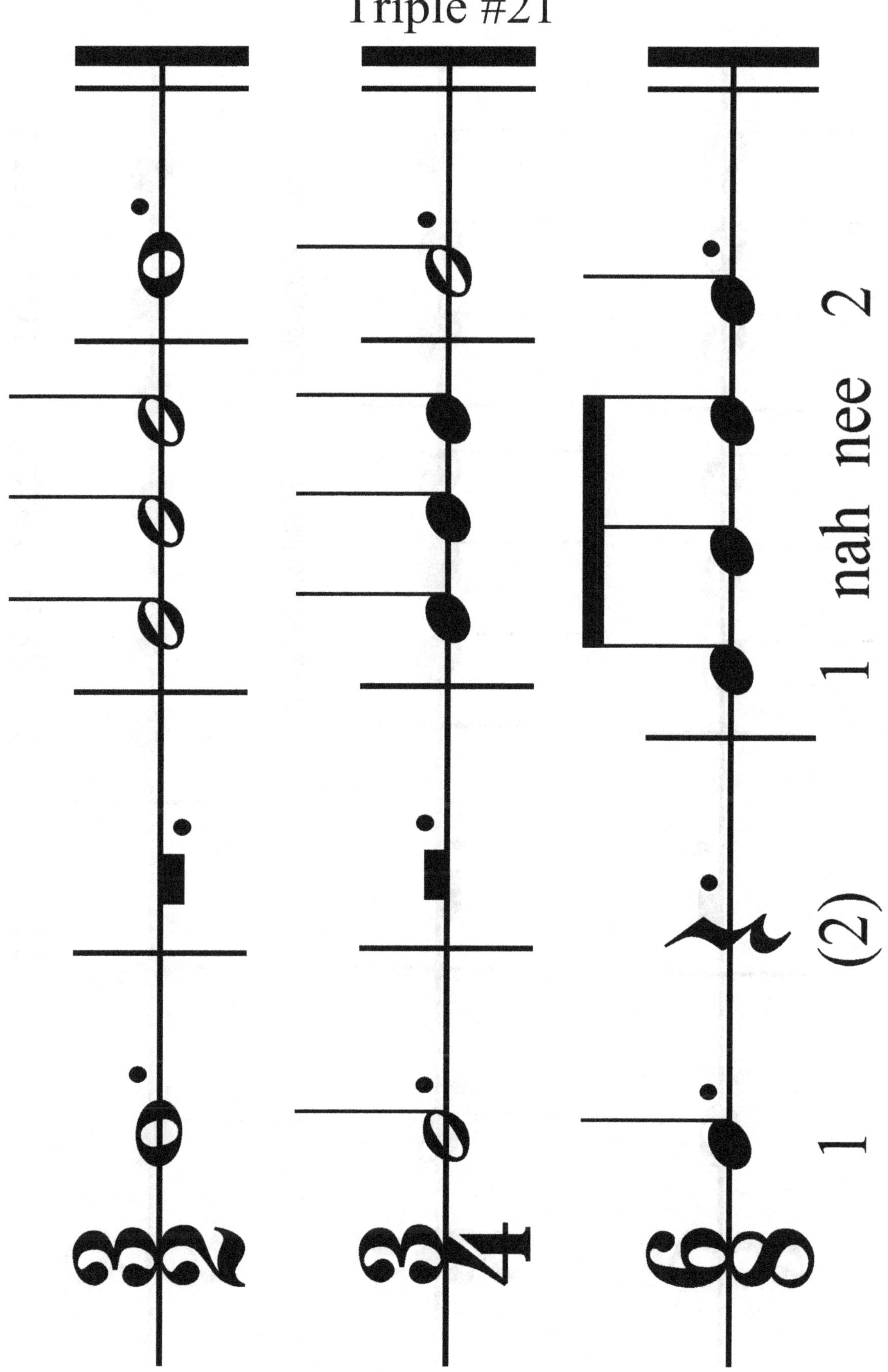

Triple #22

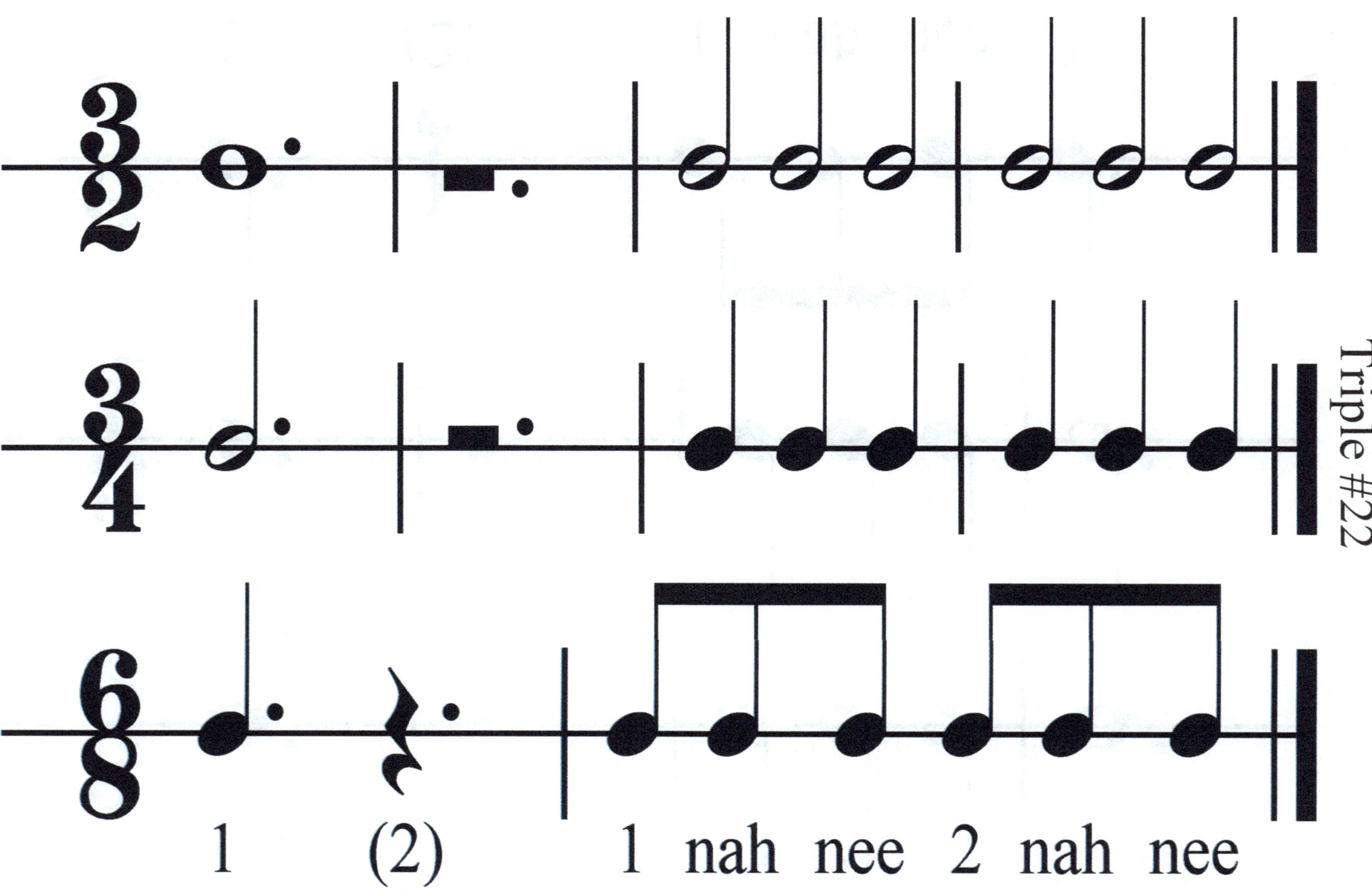

Triple #23

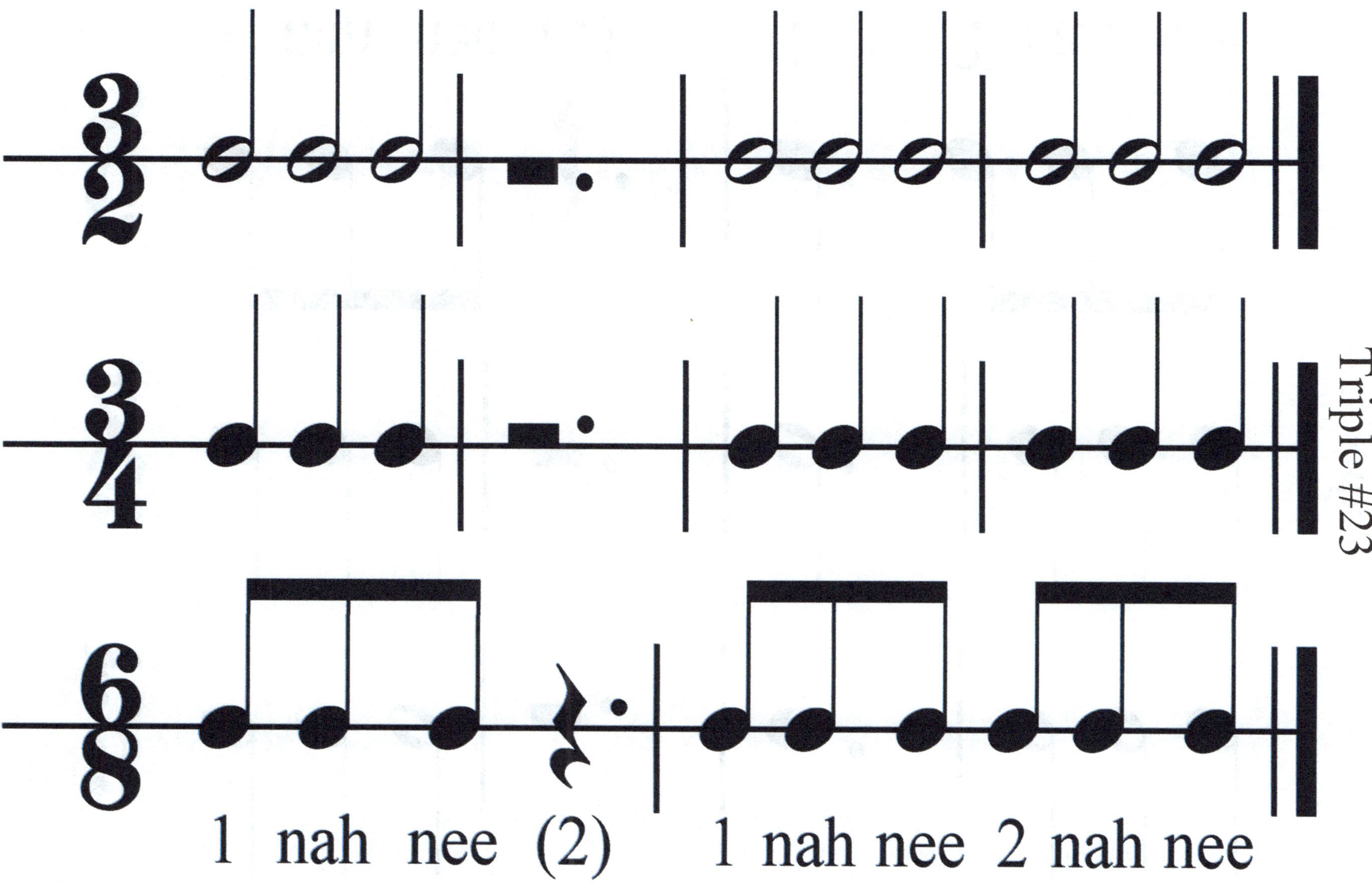

Triple #24

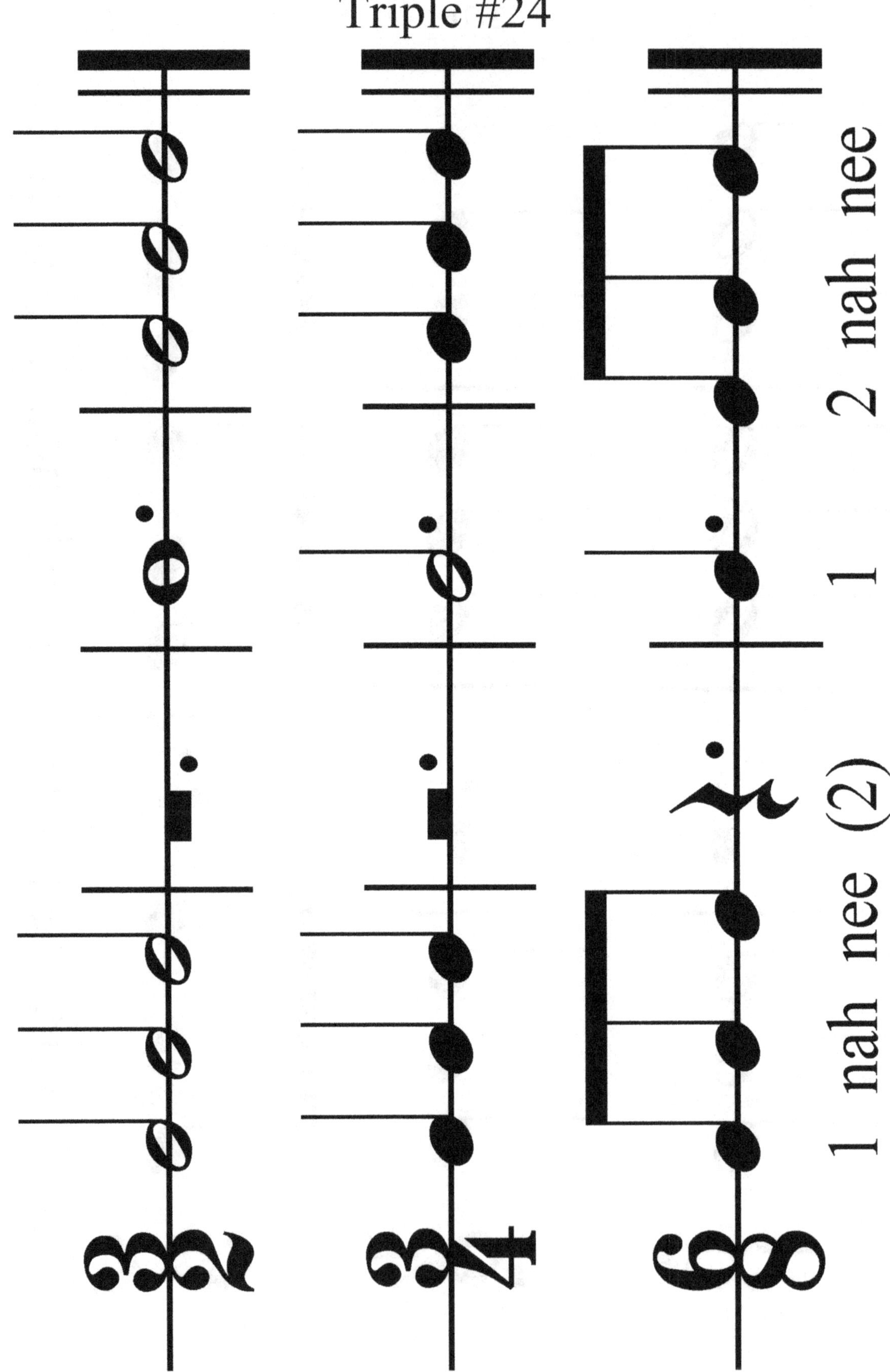

Triple #25

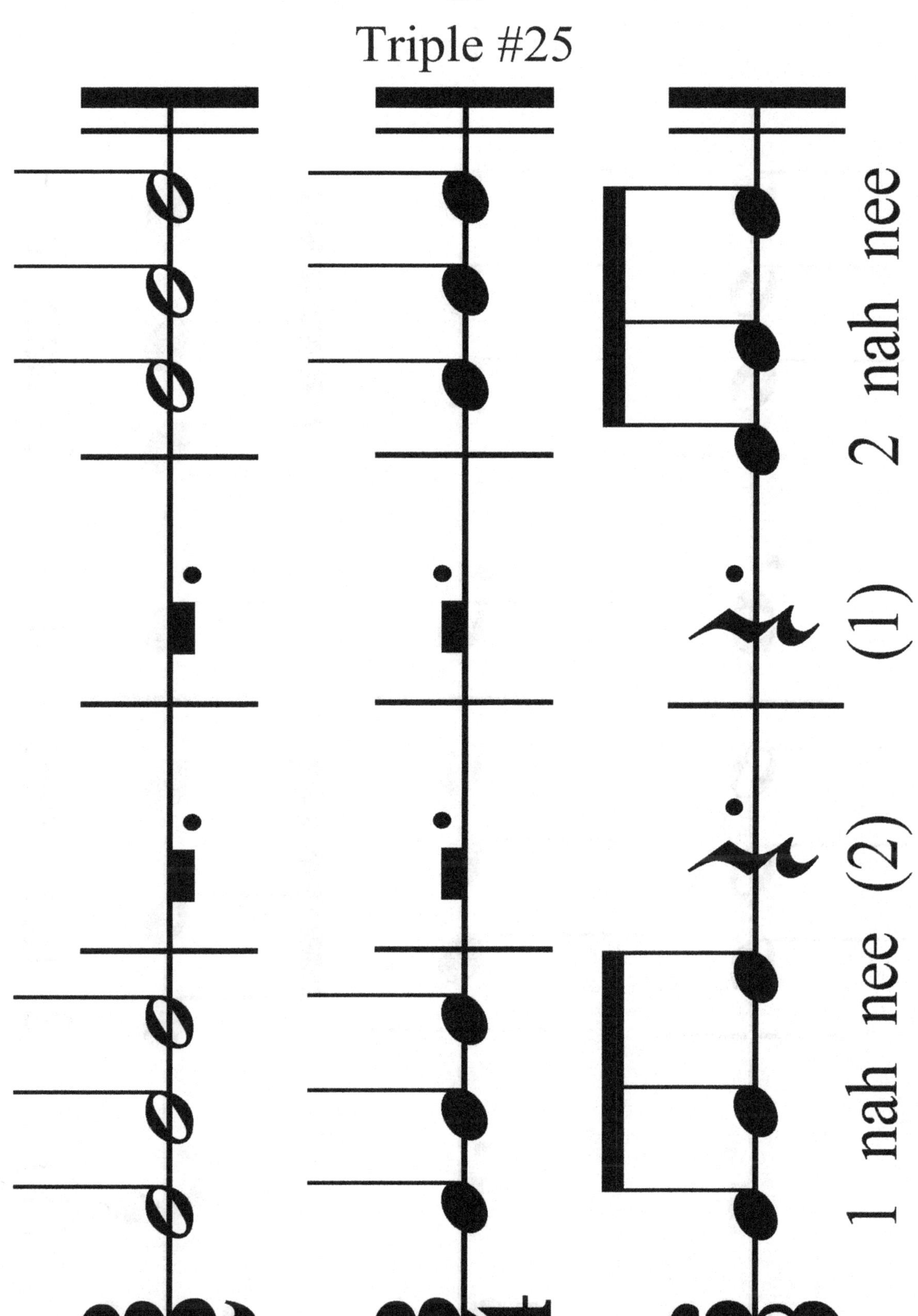

Triple #26

Triple #27

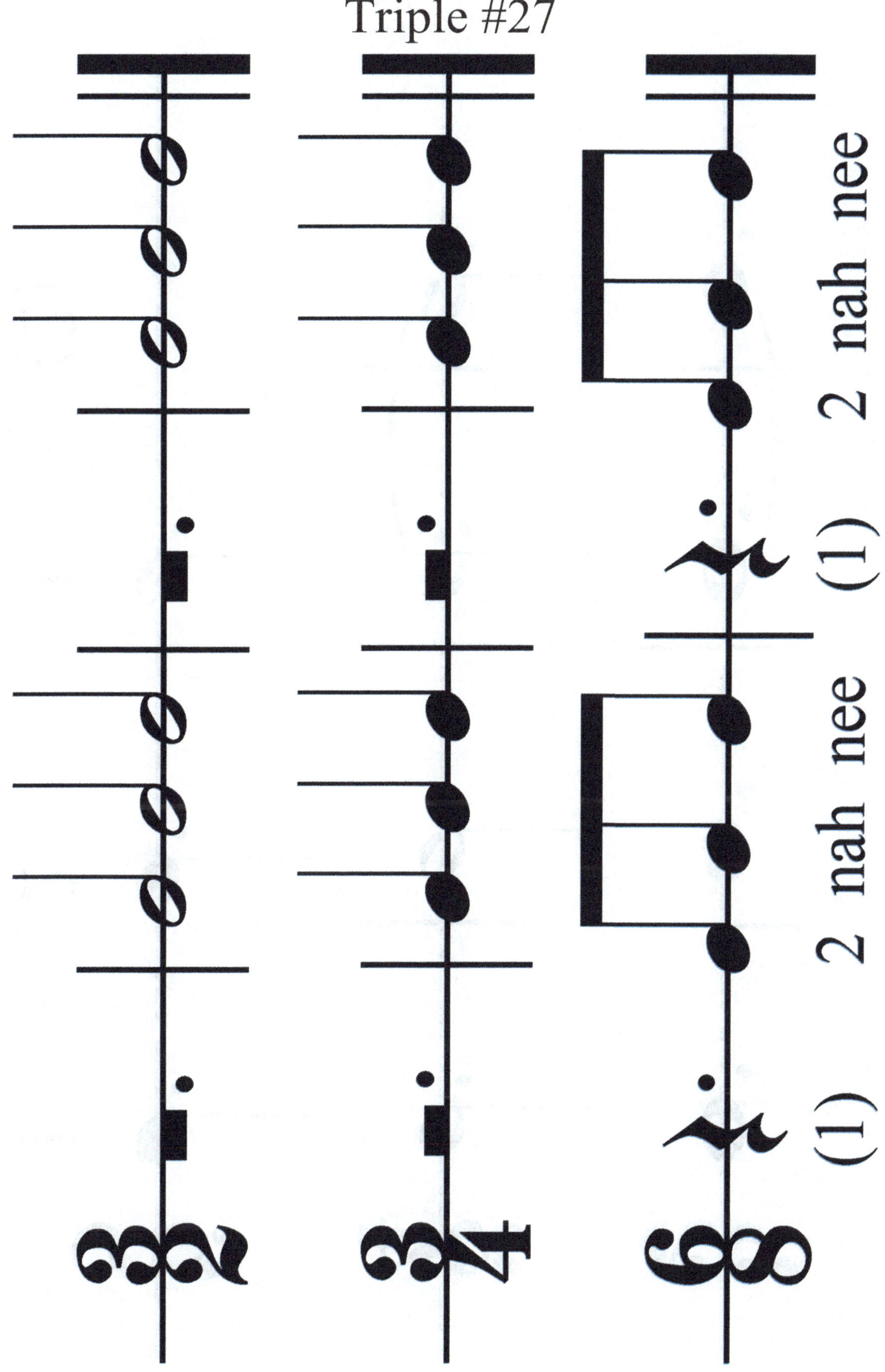

Triple #28

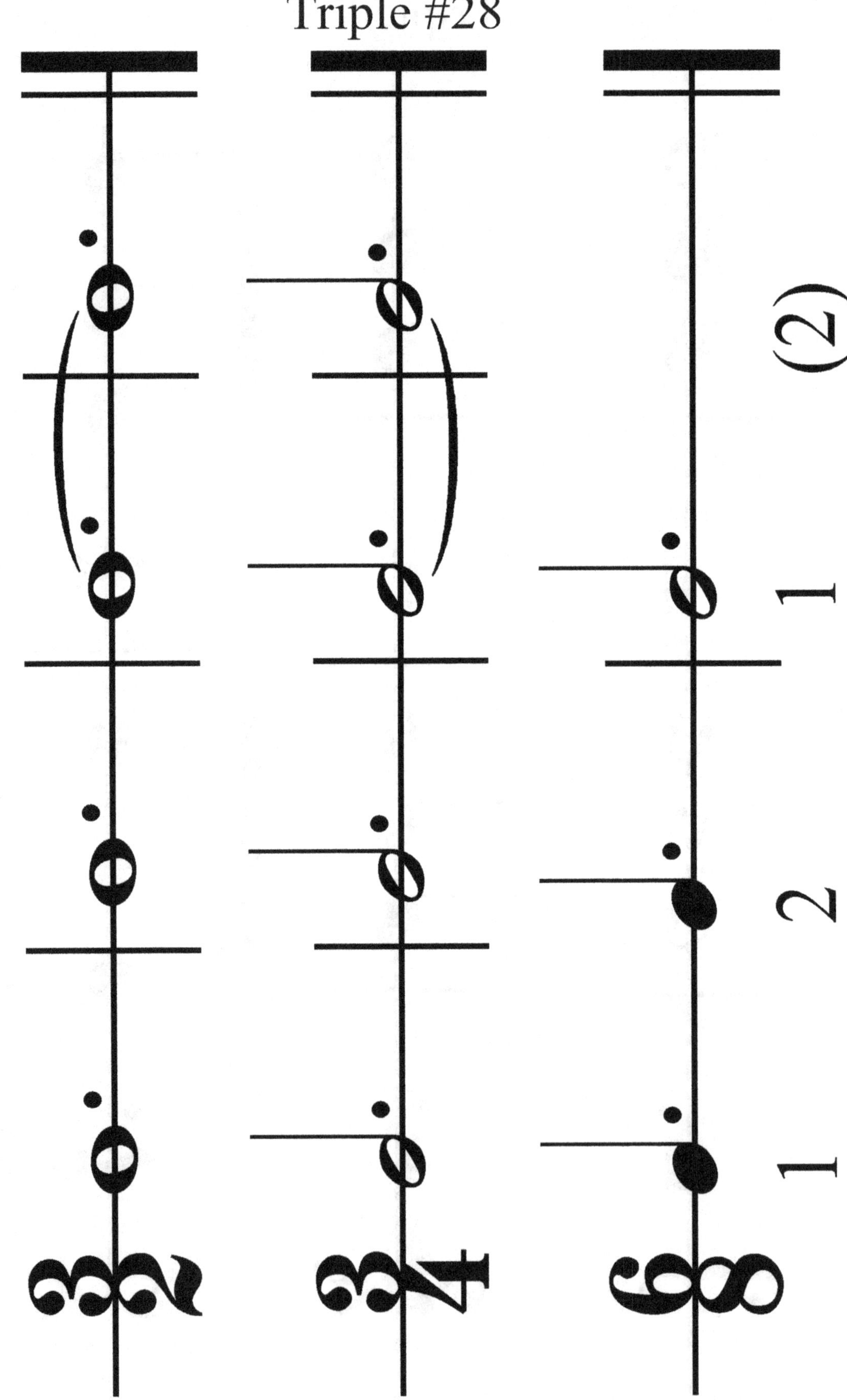

Triple #29

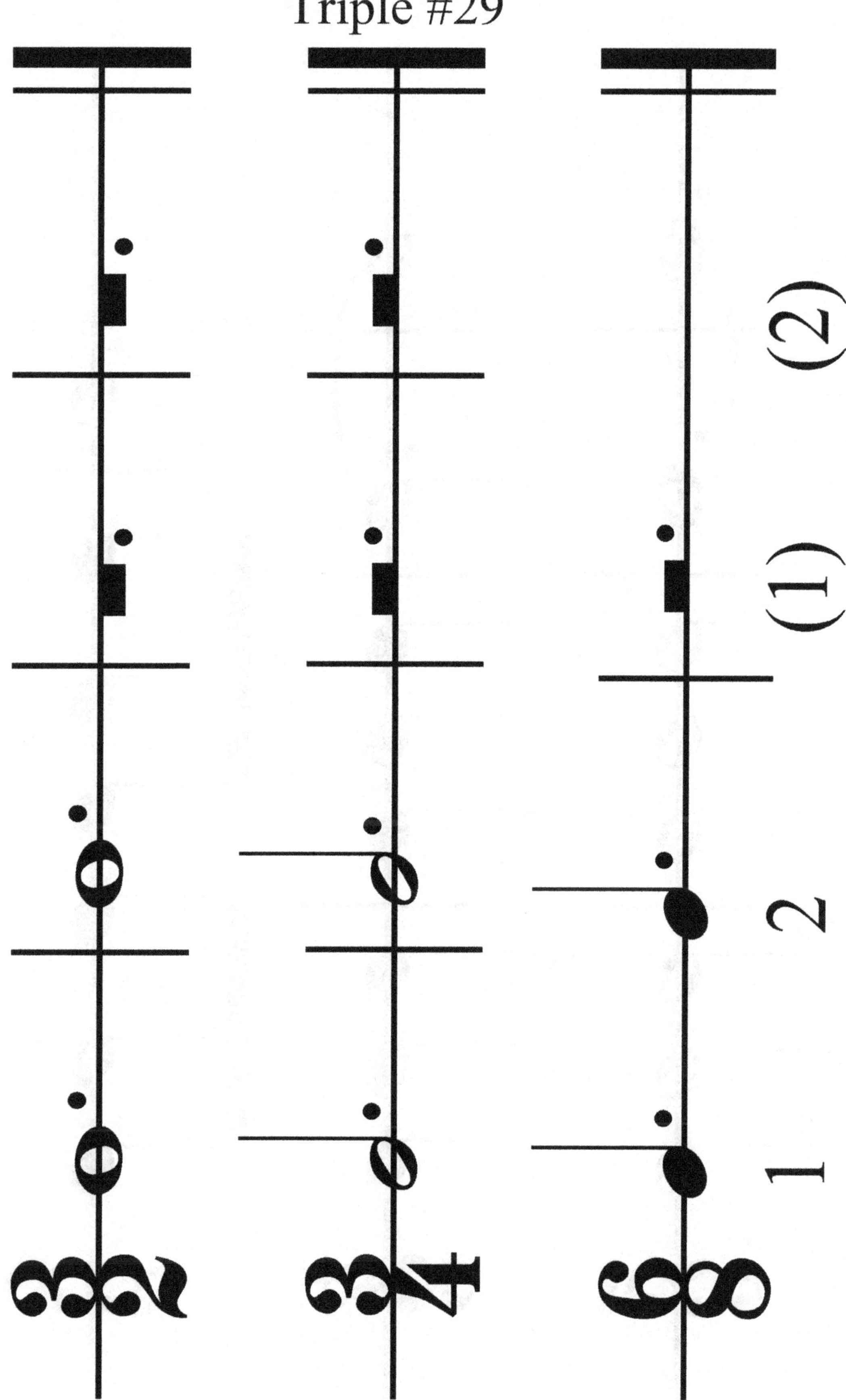

Triple #30

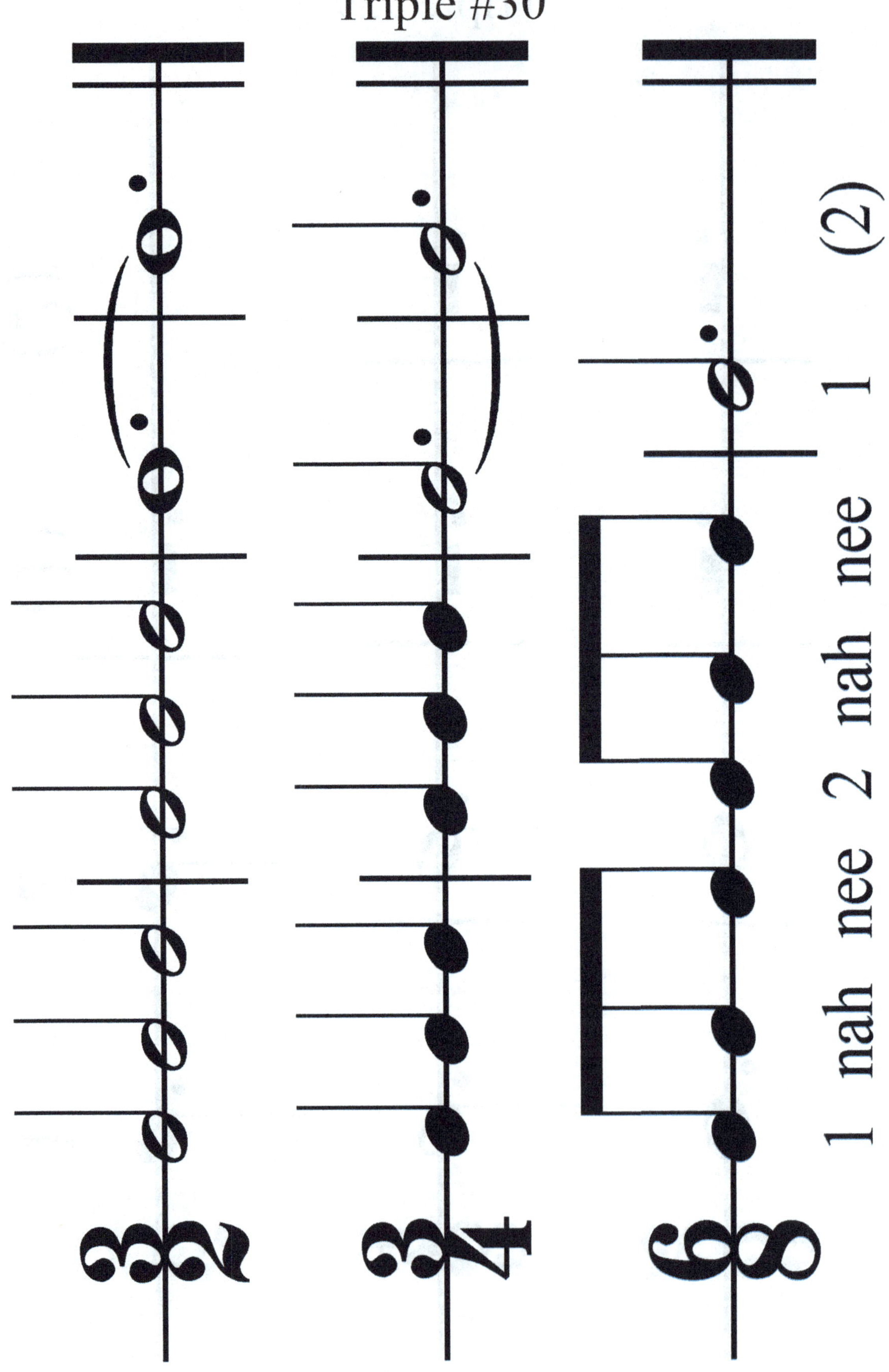
3/2
3/4
6/8
1 nah nee 2 nah nee 1 (2)

Triple #31

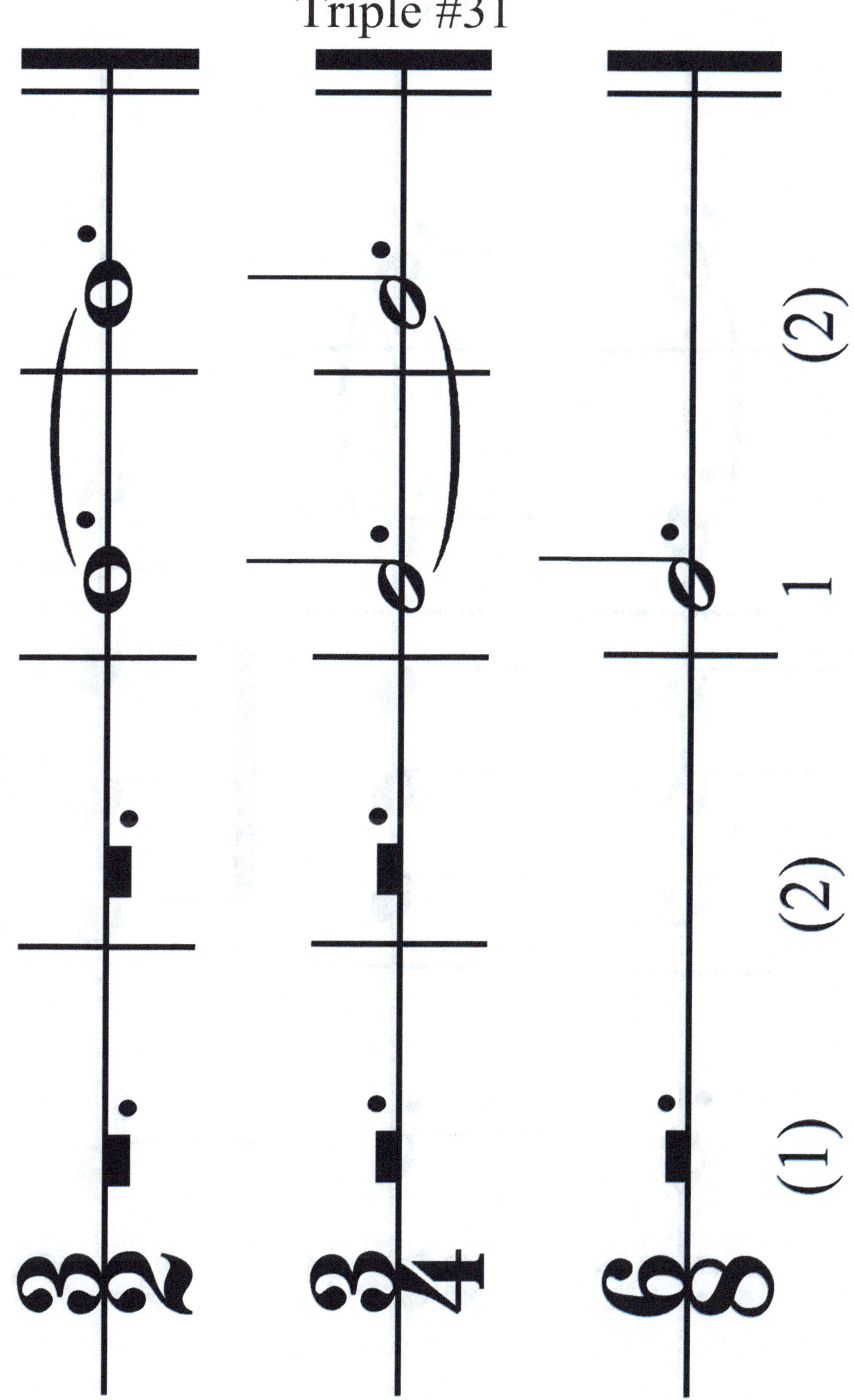

Triple #32

Triple #33

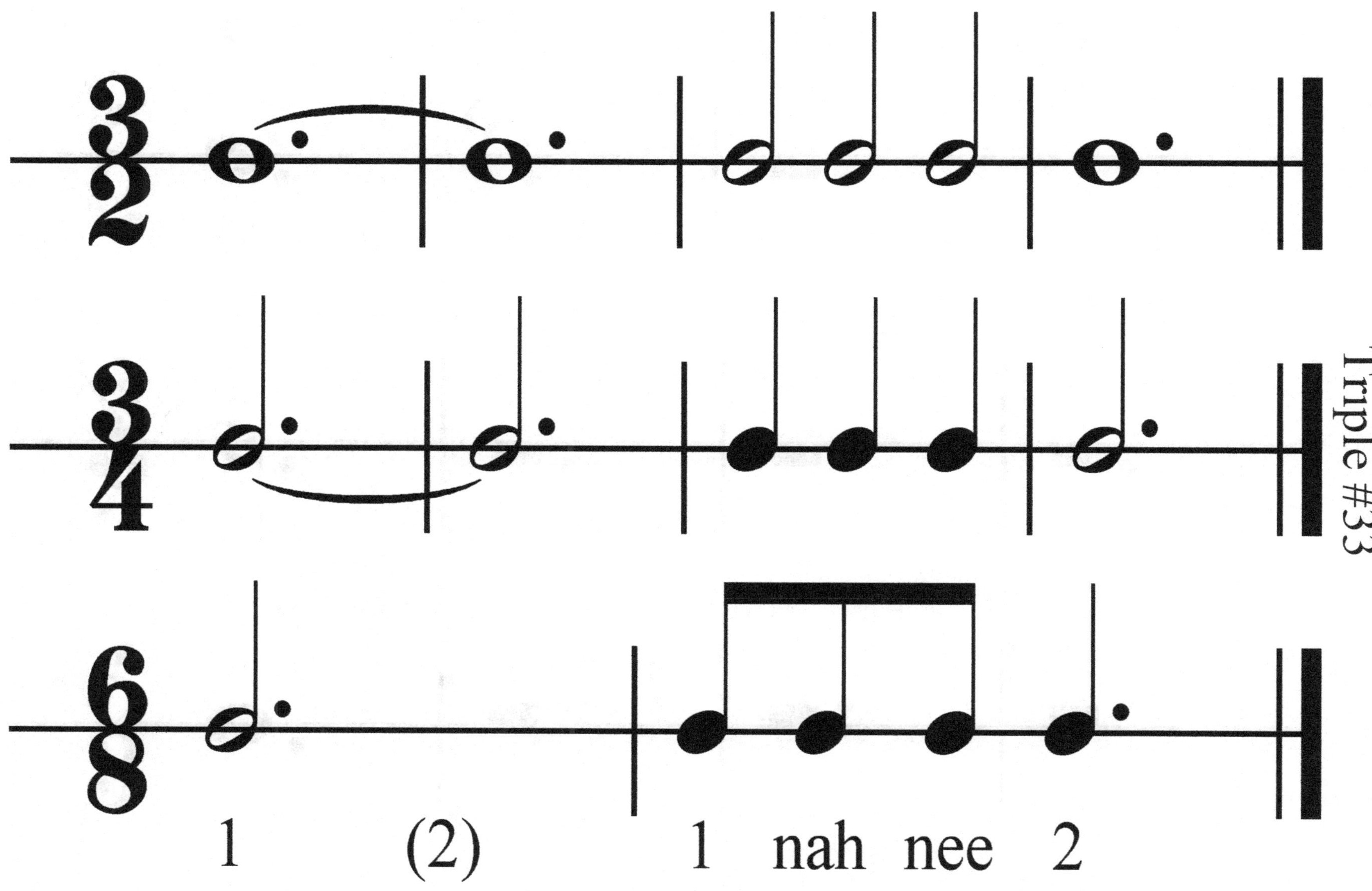

Triple #34

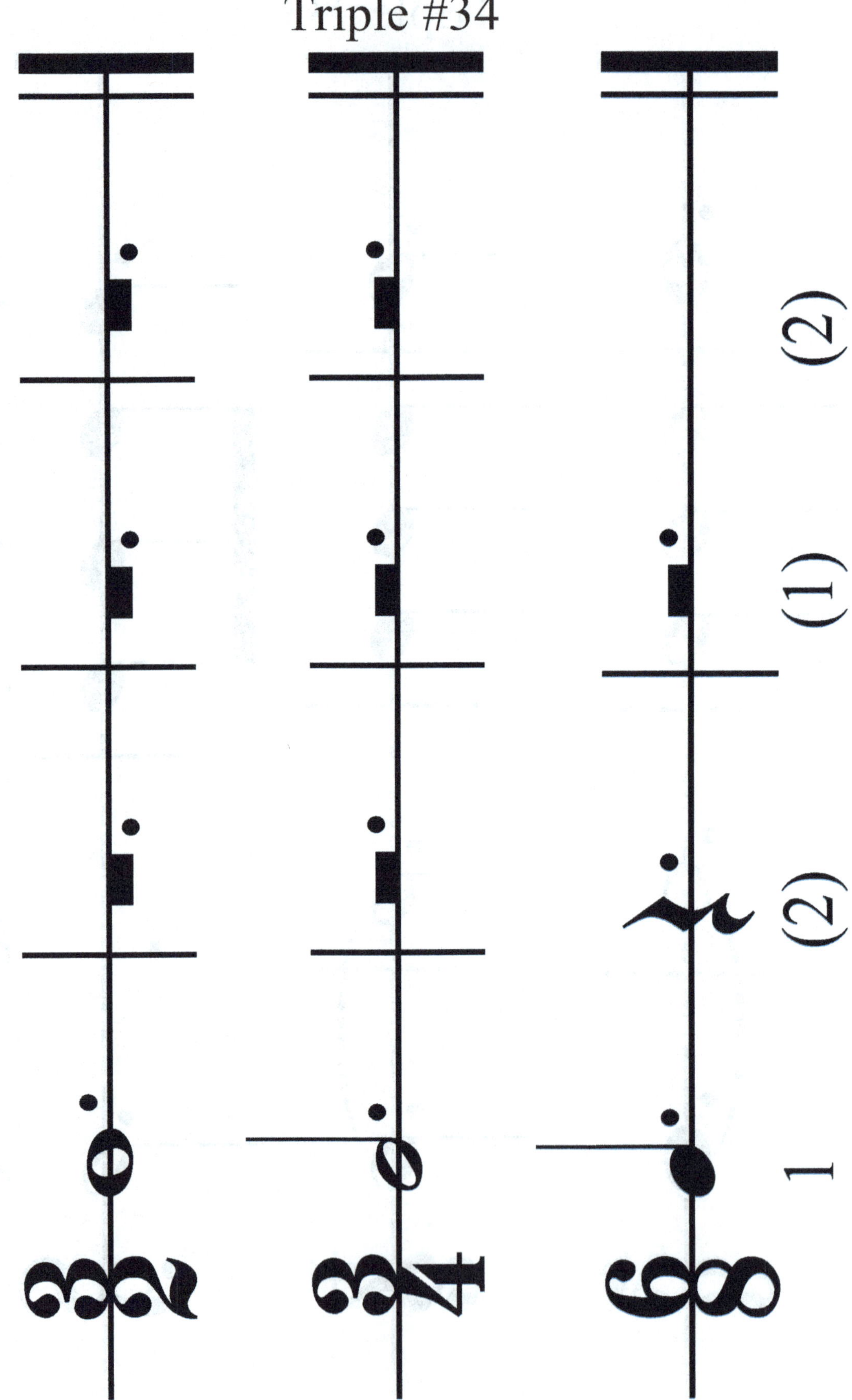

Triple #35

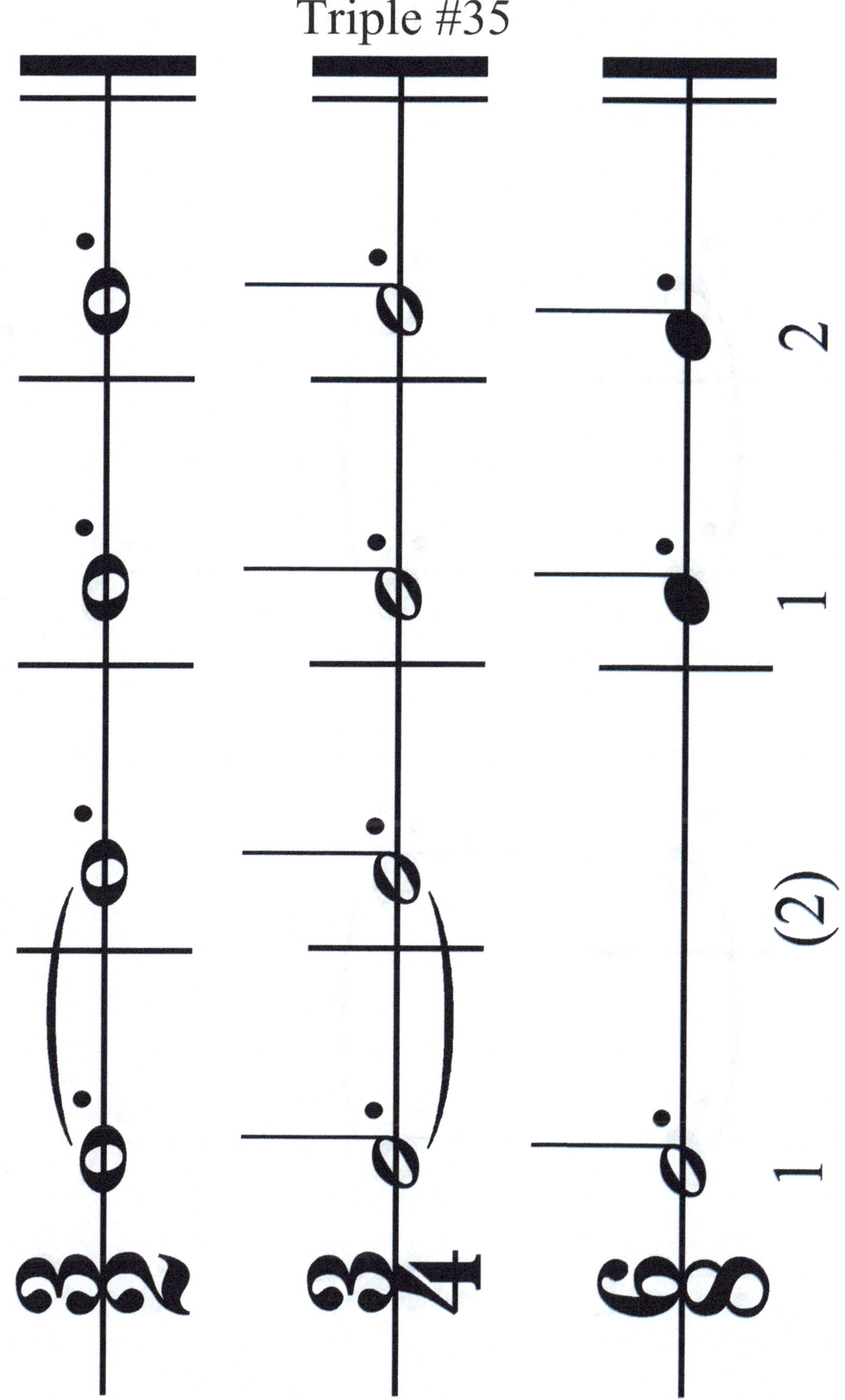

Triple #36

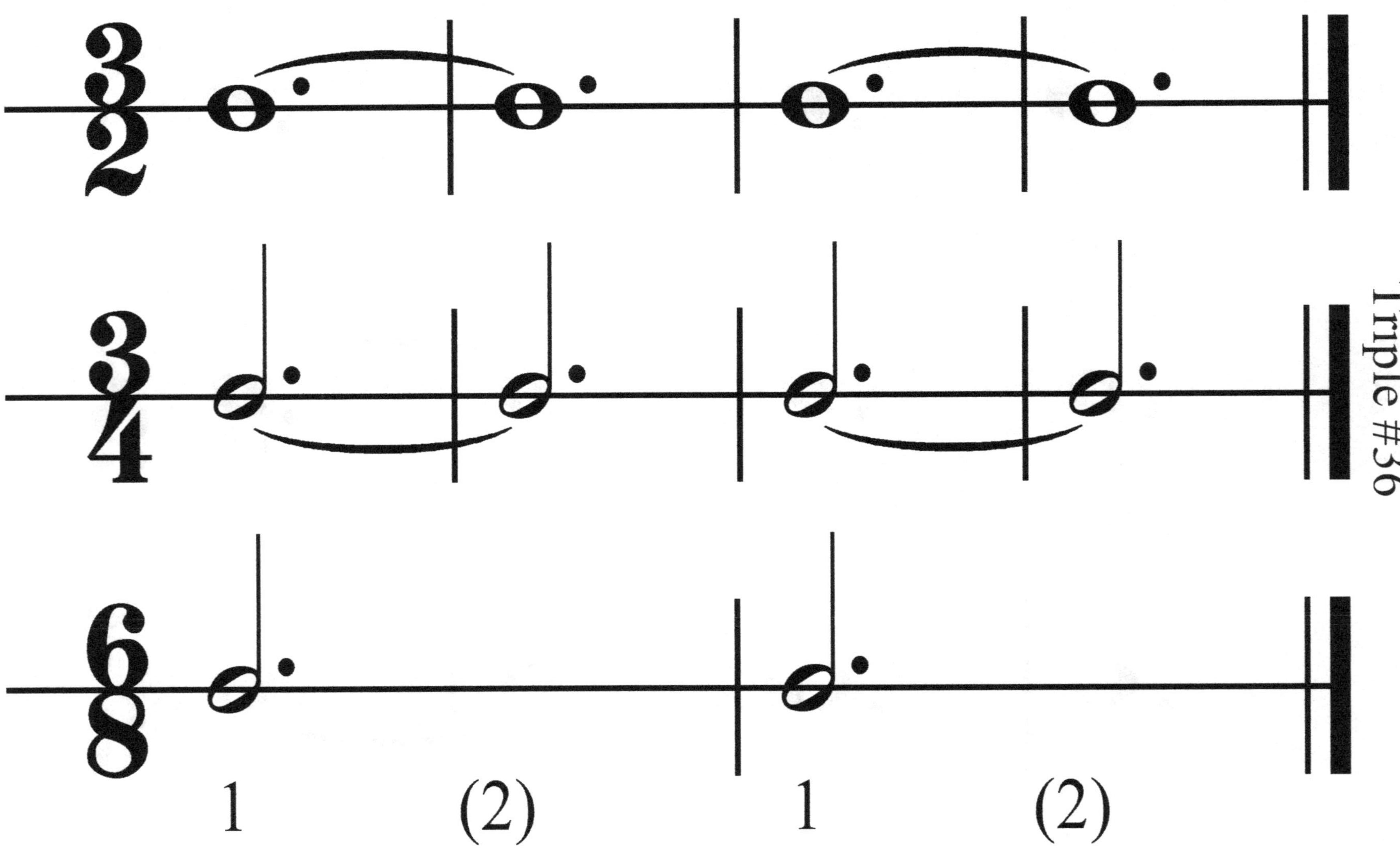

Triple #37

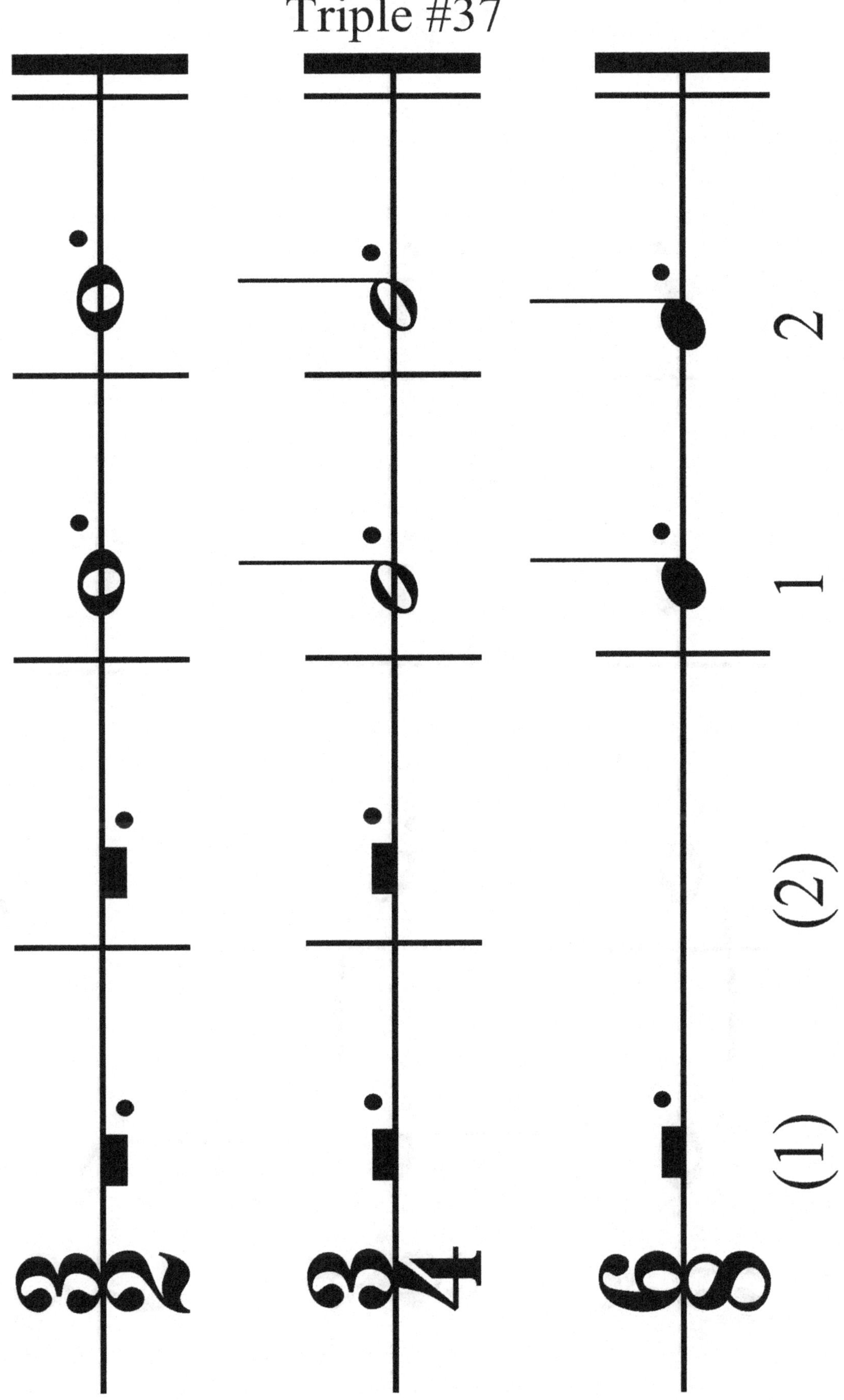

Triple #38

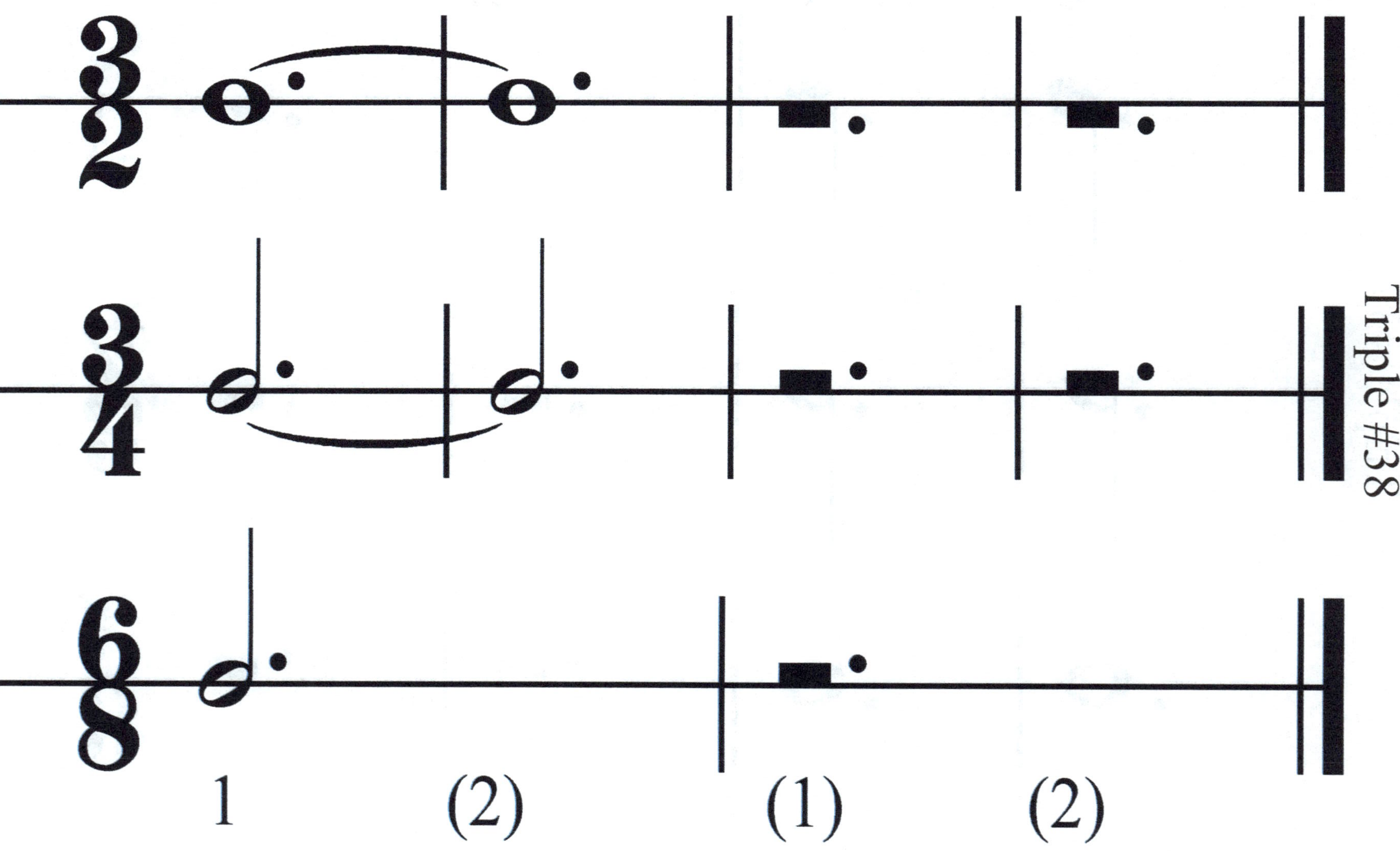

Triple #39

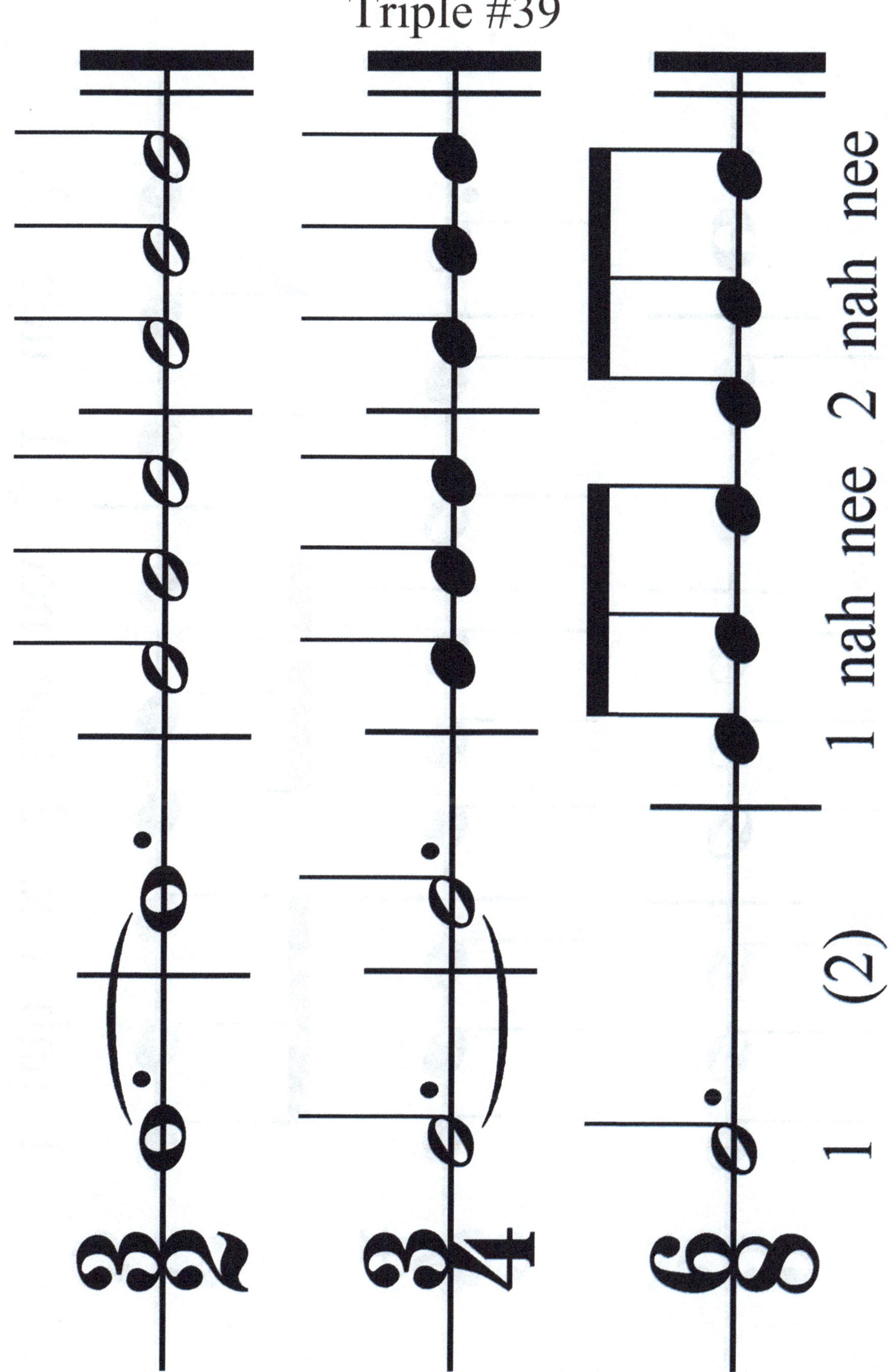
1 (2)
1 nah nee 2 nah nee

Triple #6b

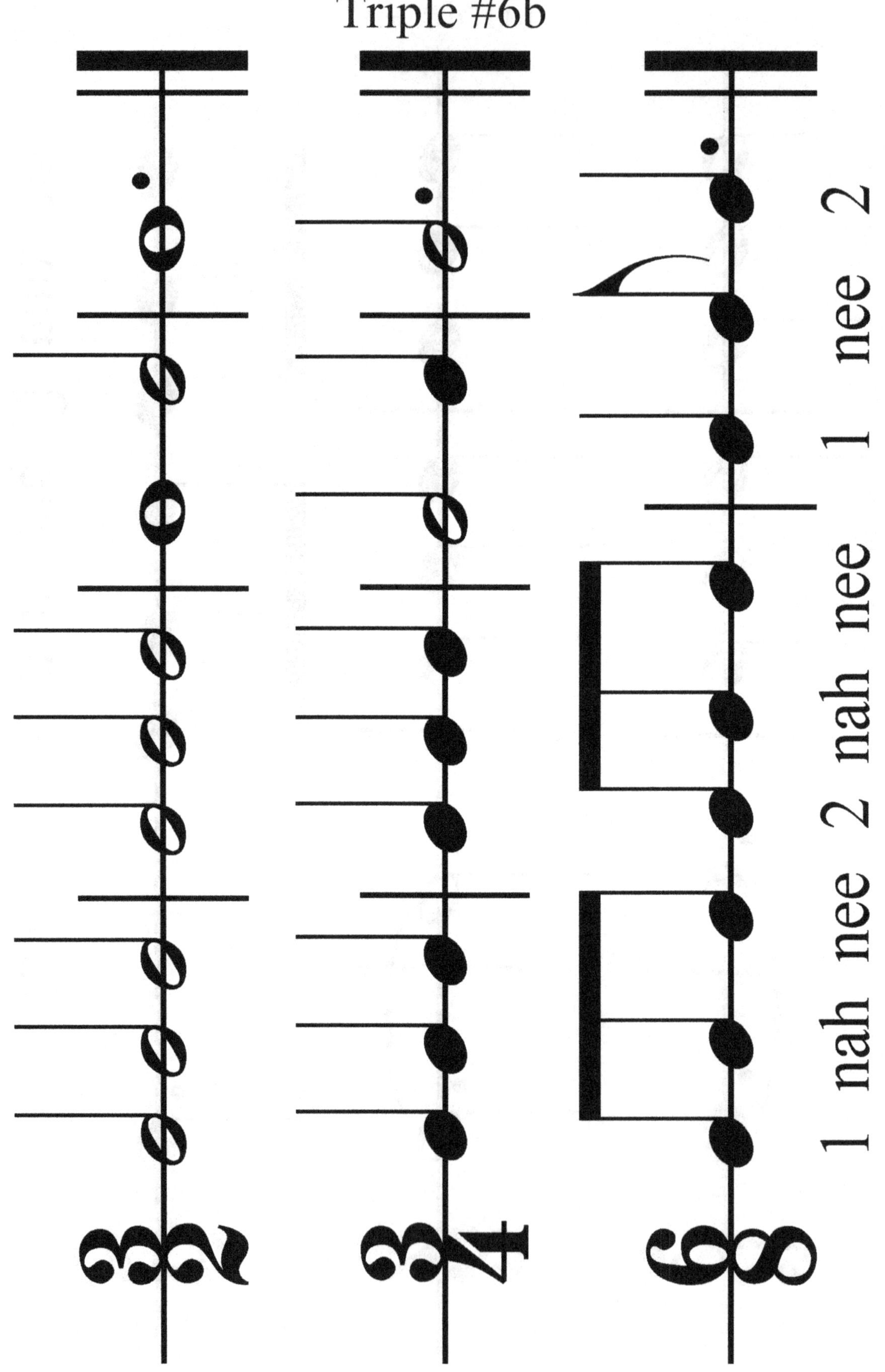

Triple #4b

Triple #7b

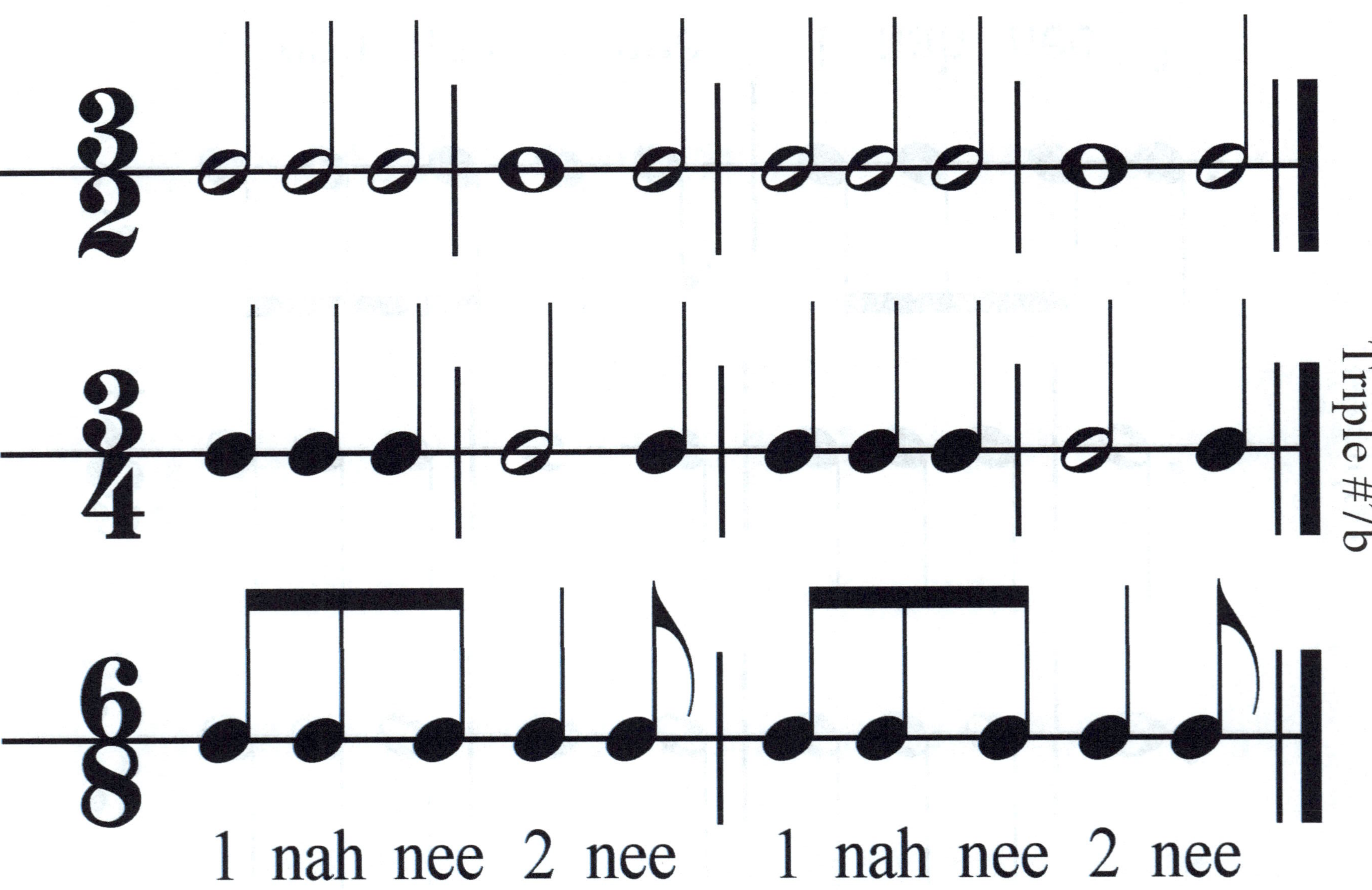
1 nah nee 2 nee 1 nah nee 2 nee

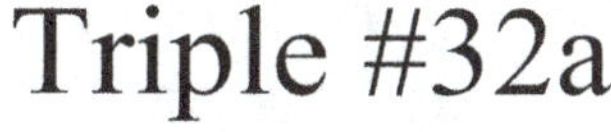

Triple #32a

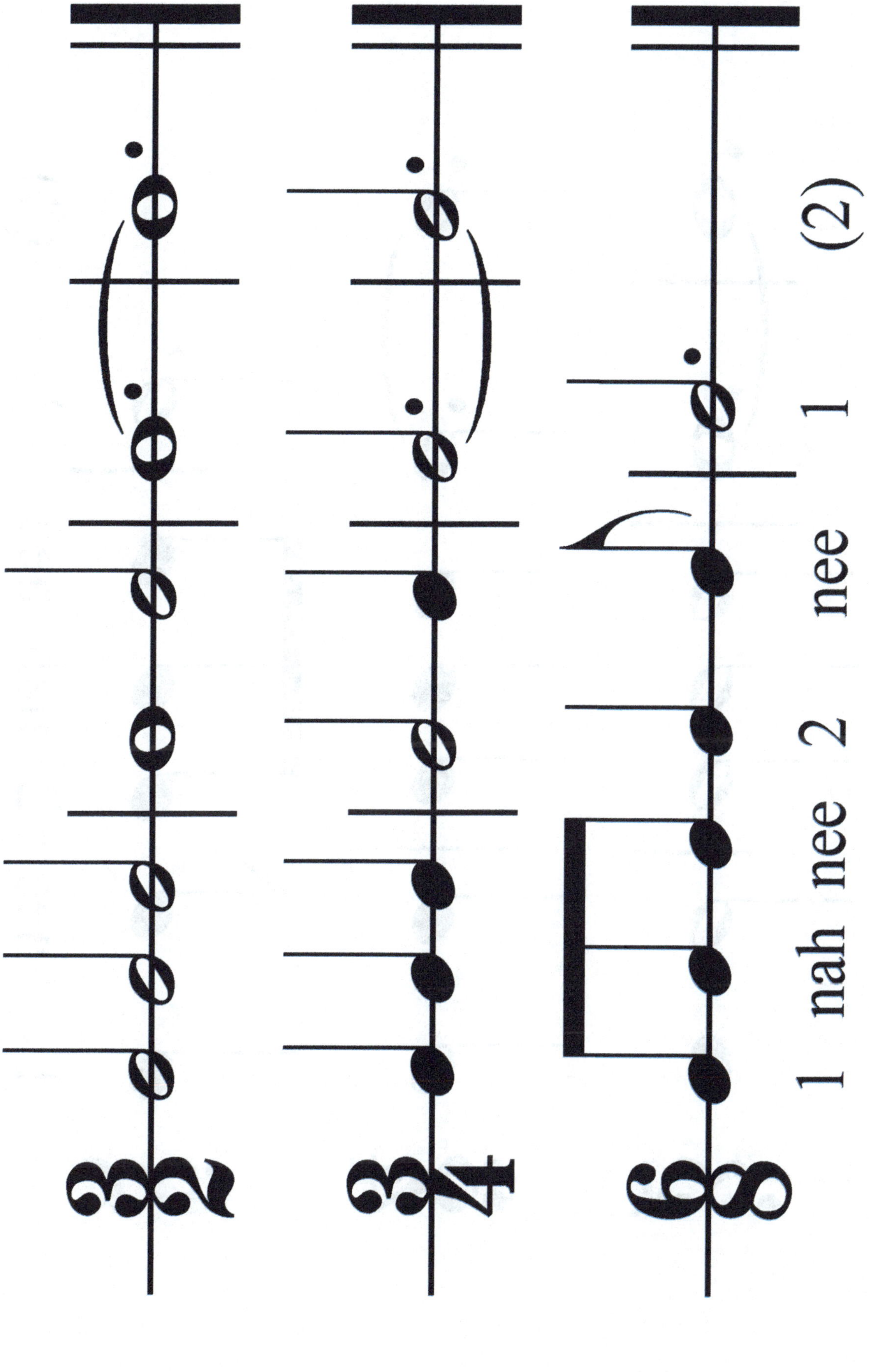

1 nah nee 2 nee 1 (2)

Triple #32b

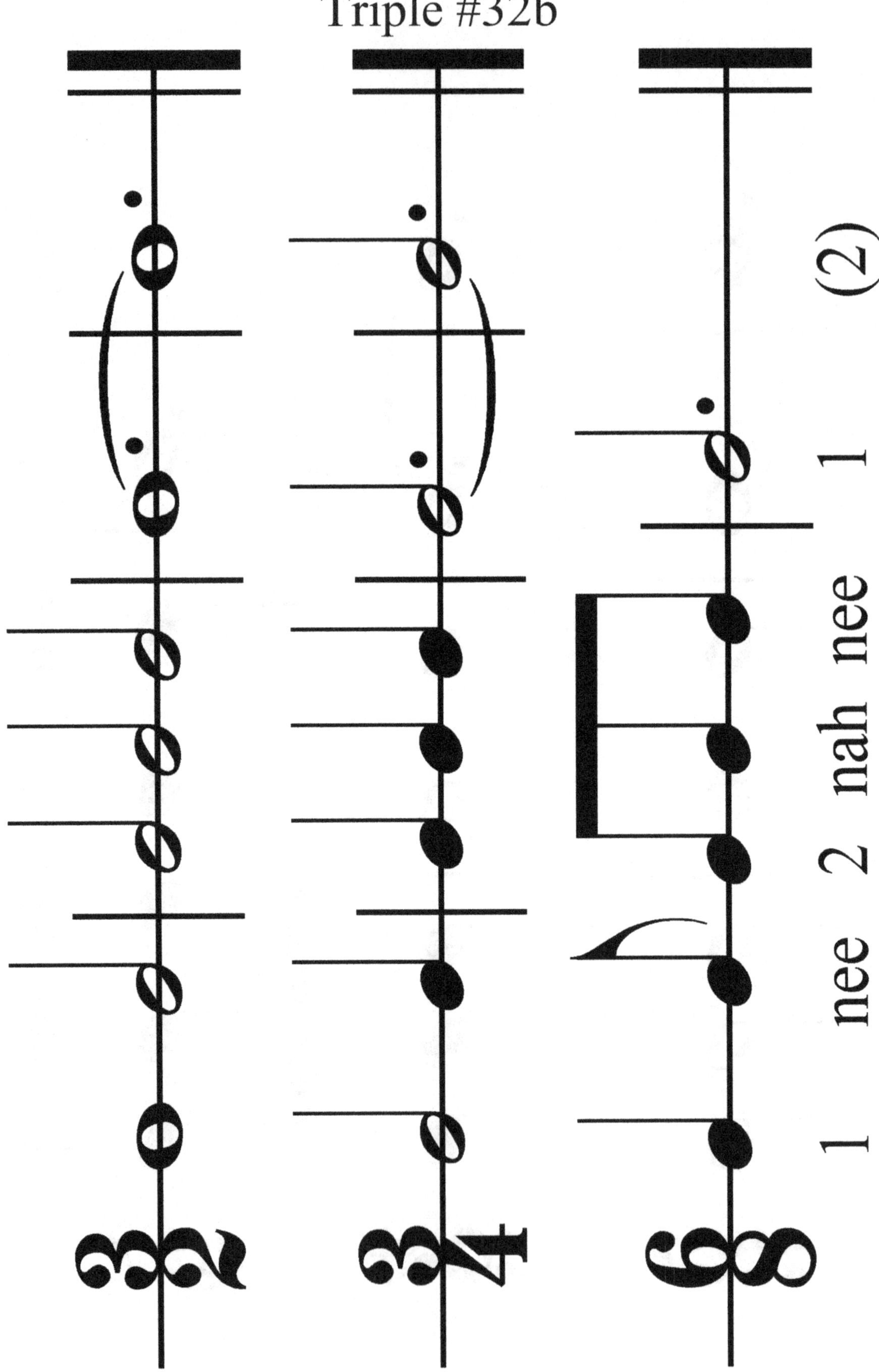

Triple #30a

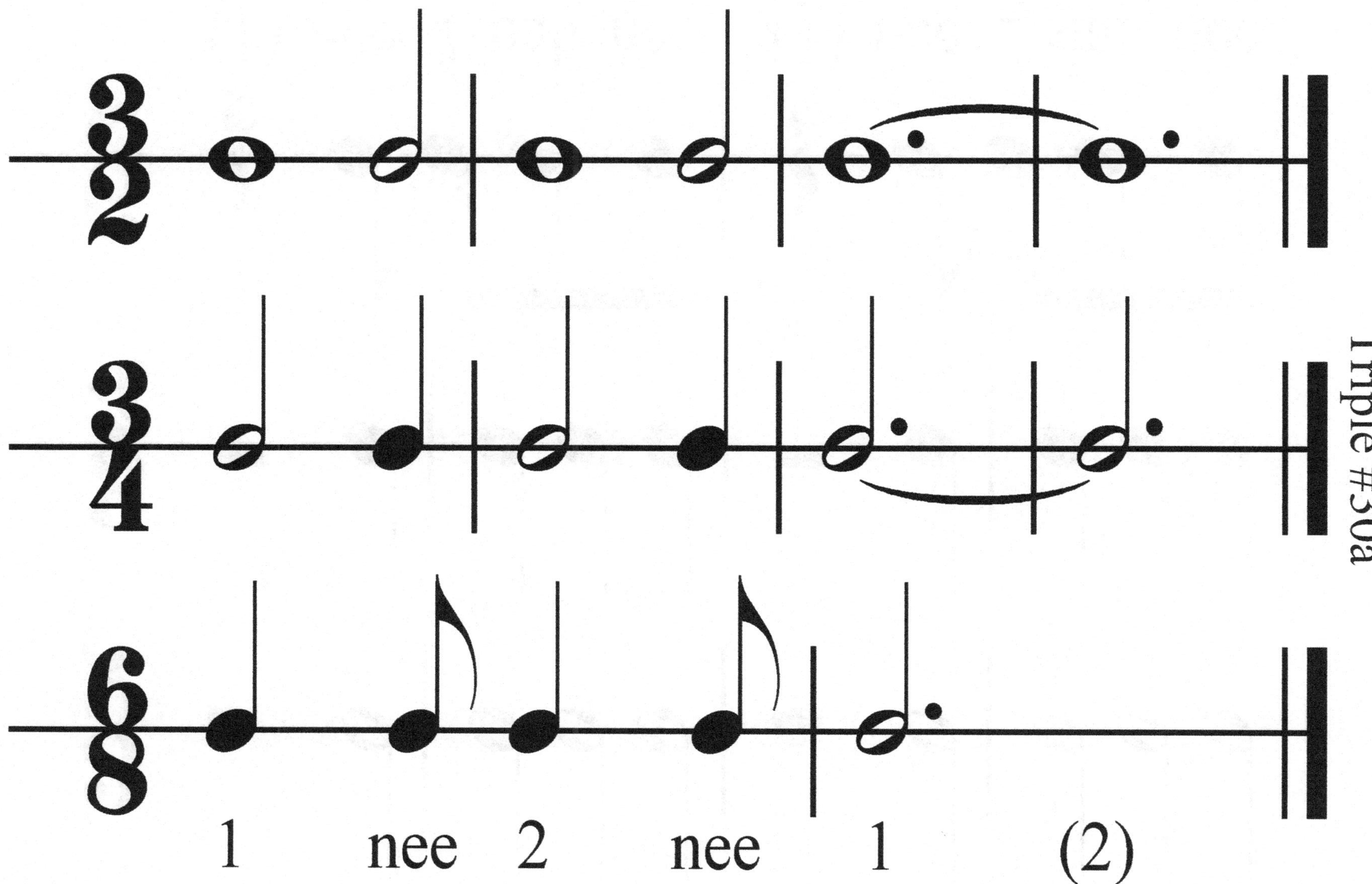

Triple #40

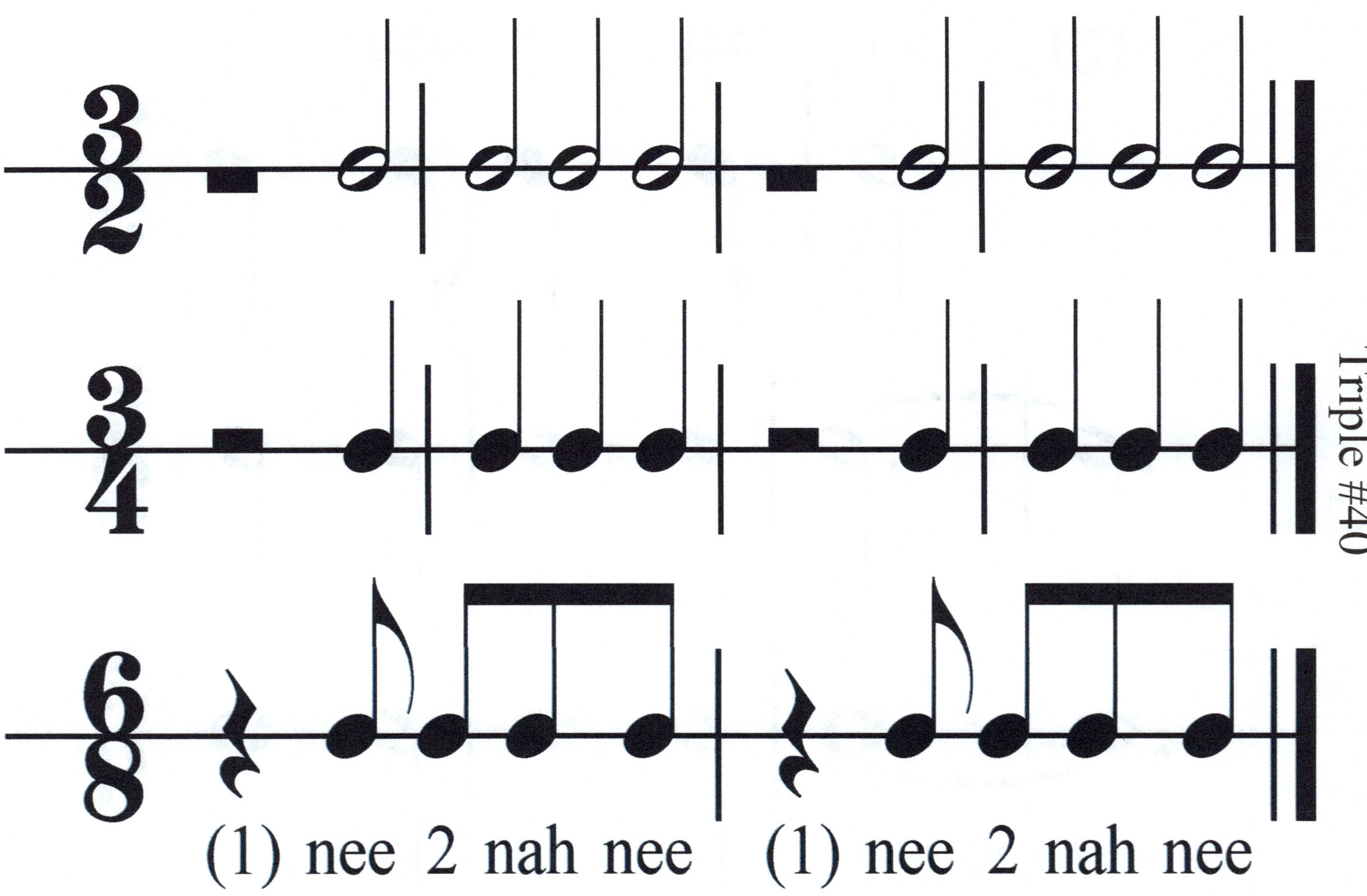

Triple #41

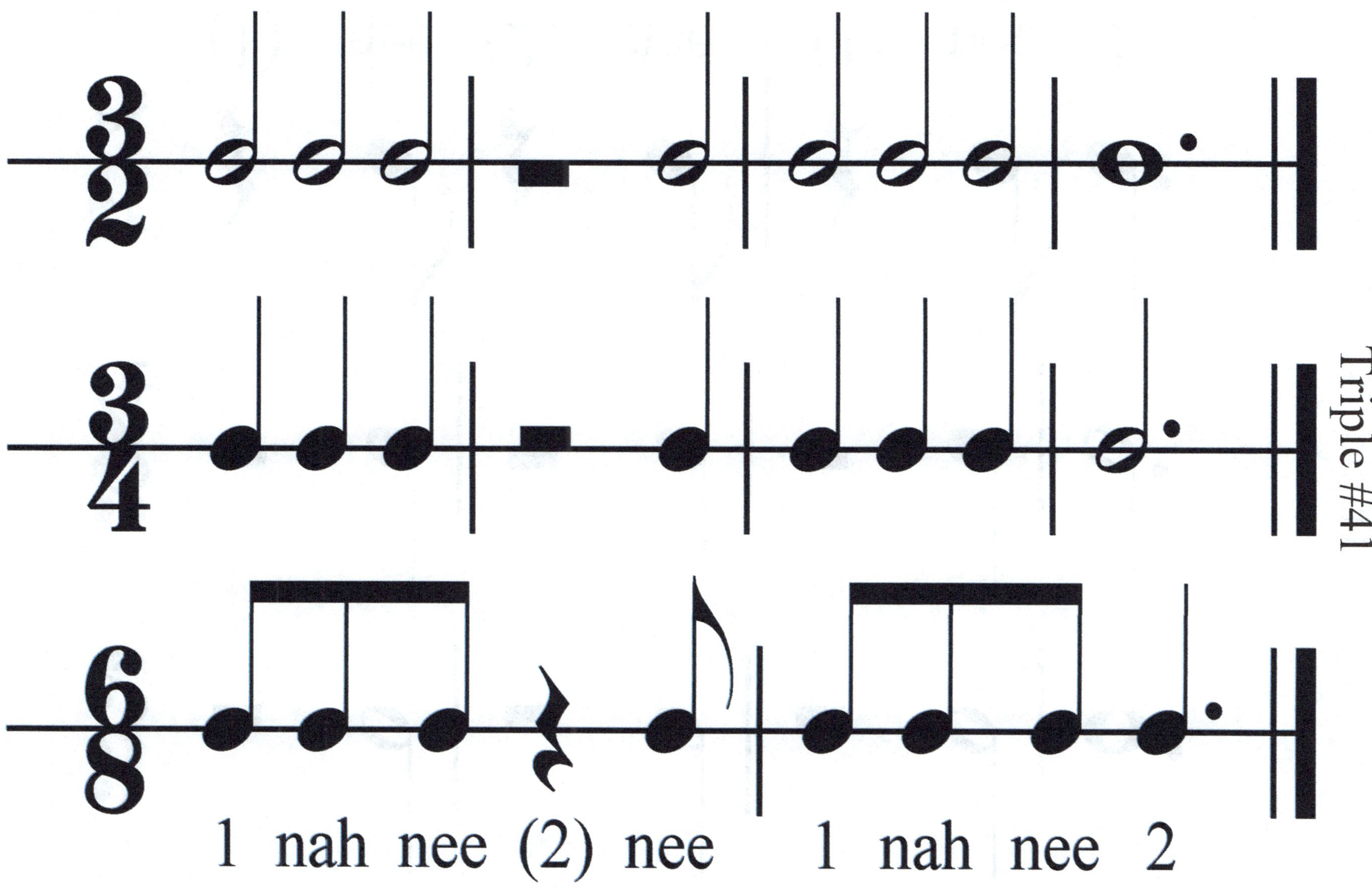

Triple #42

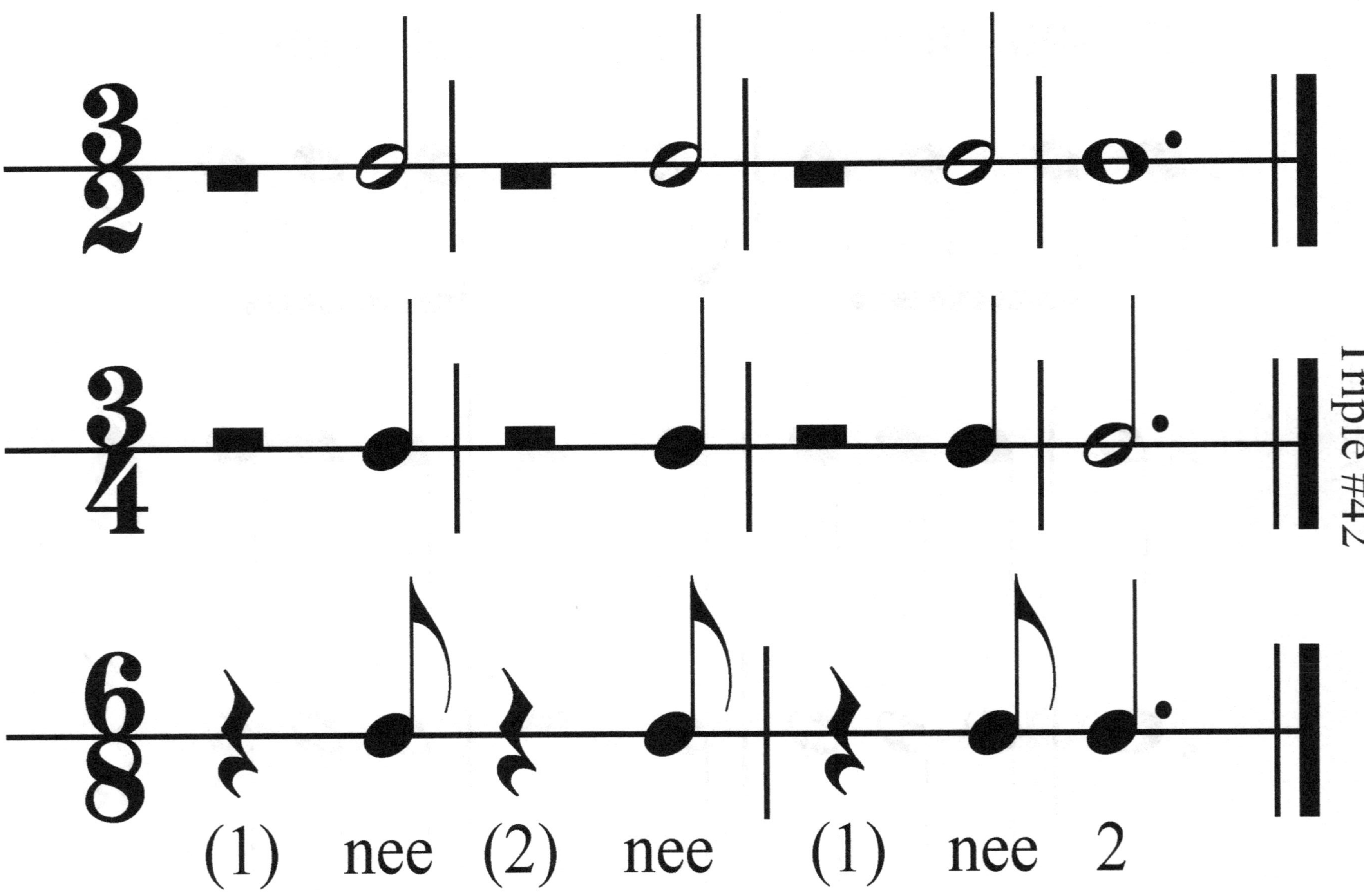

Triple #43

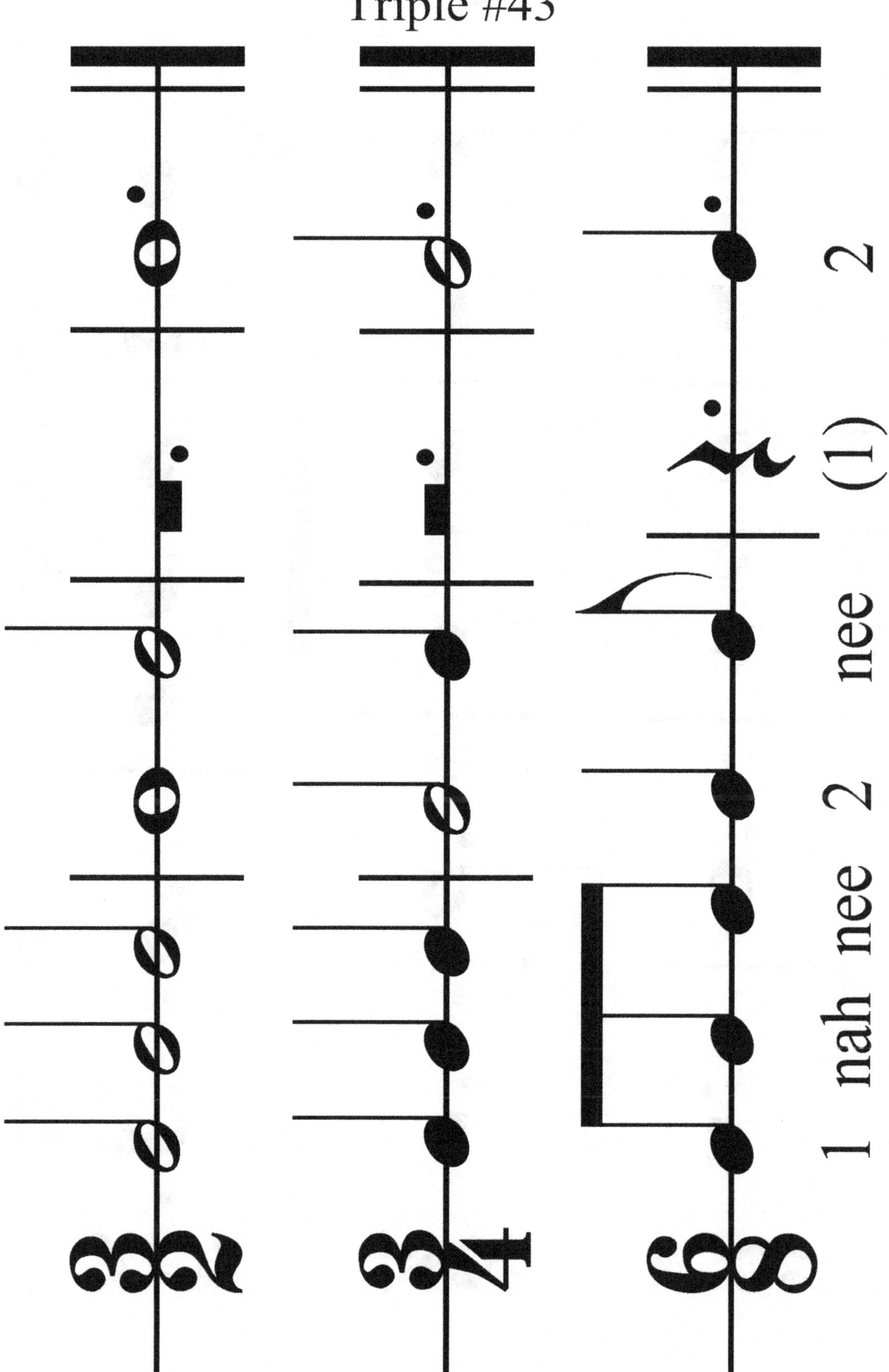

Triple #44

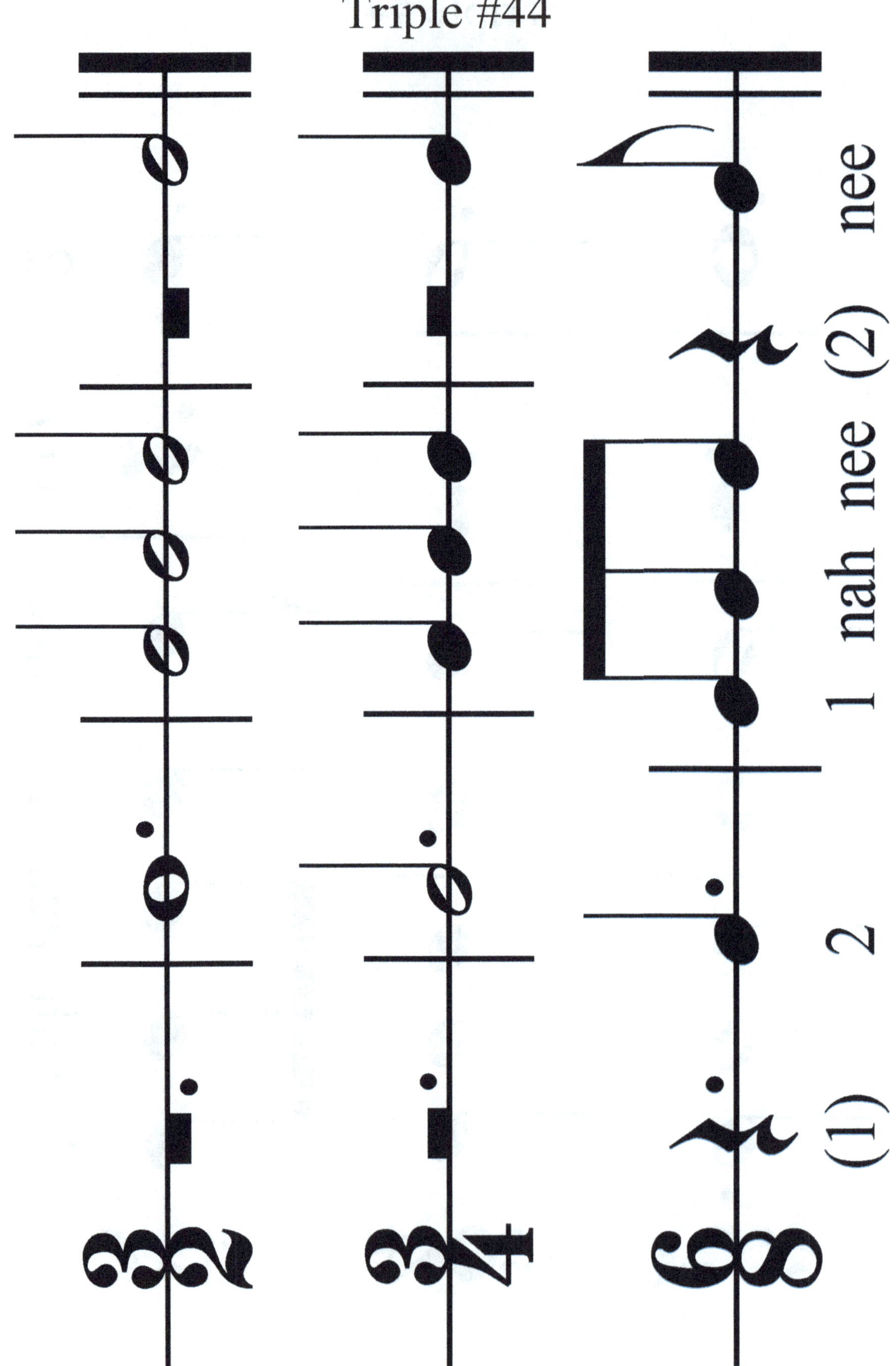

Triple #45

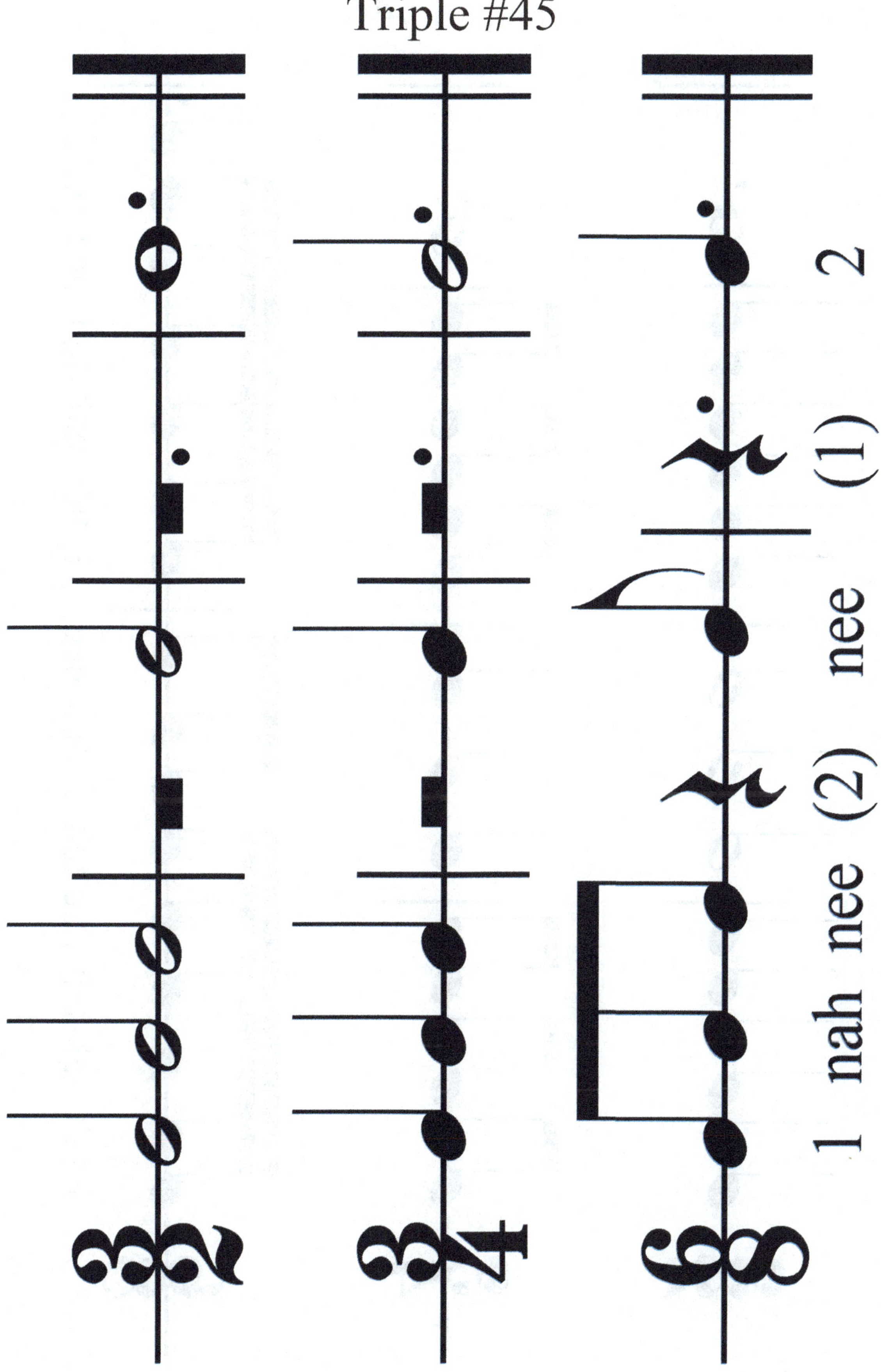
1 nah nee (2) nee (1) 2

Triple #46

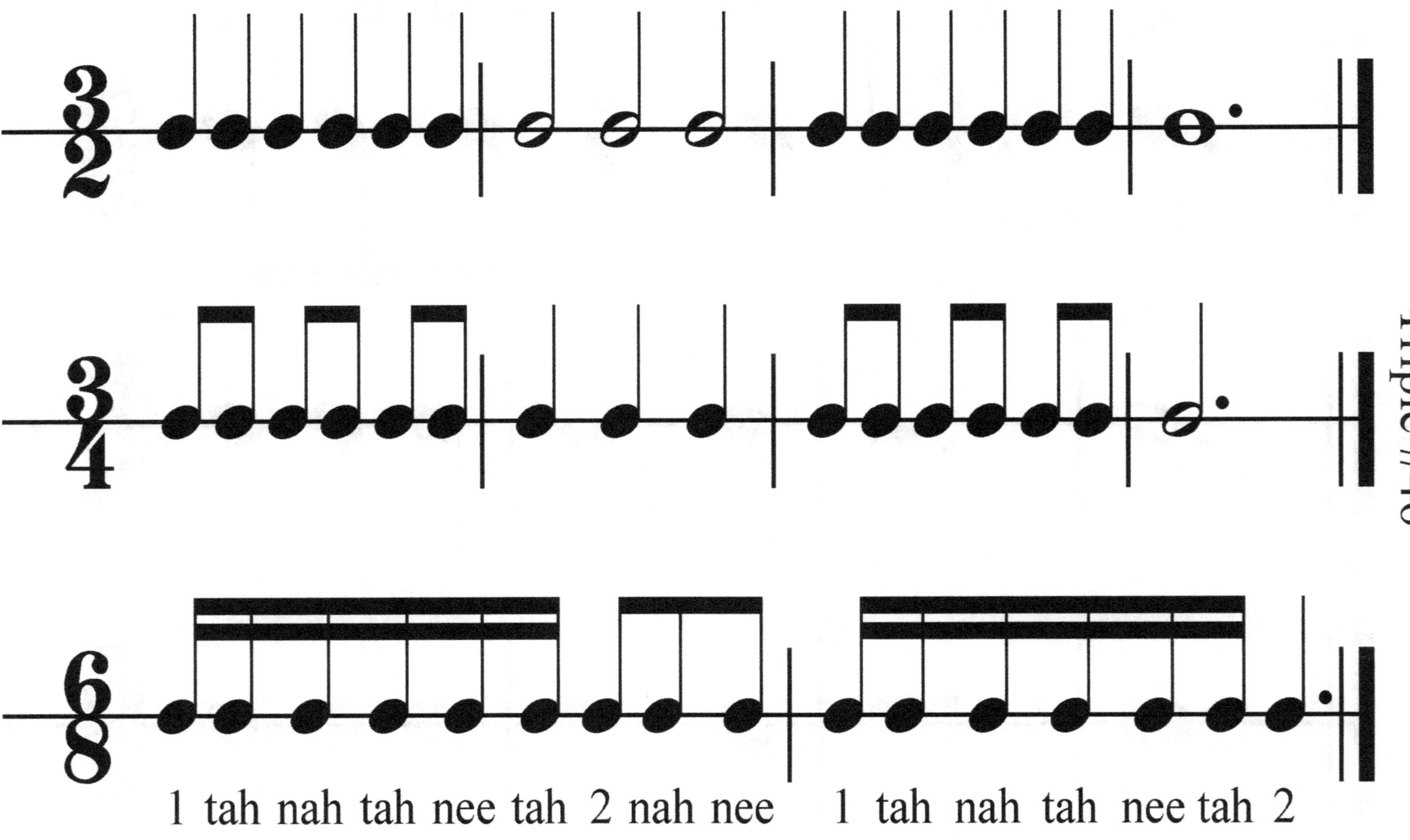
1 tah nah tah nee tah 2 nah nee 1 tah nah tah nee tah 2

Triple #47

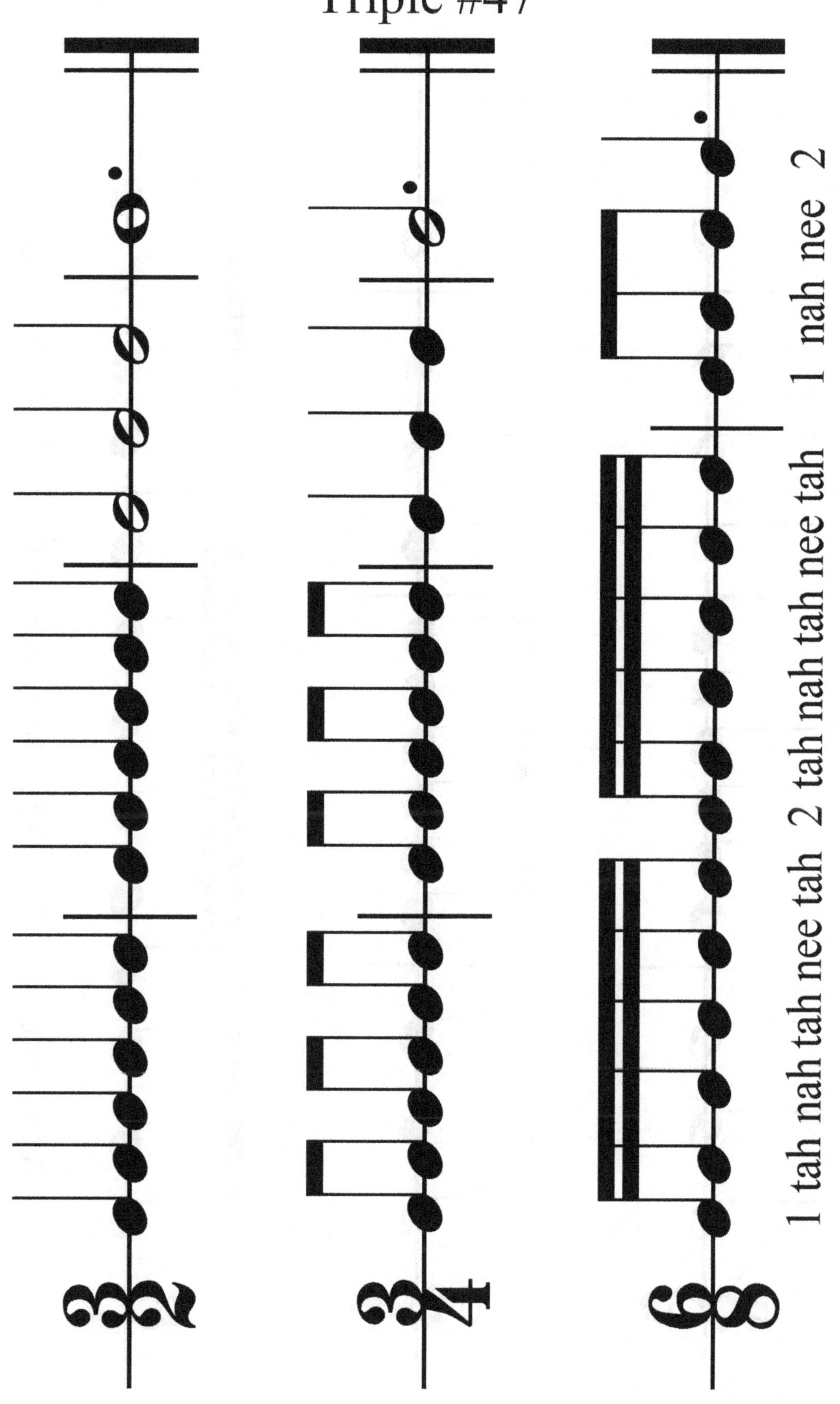
1 tah nah tah nee tah 2 tah nah tah nee tah 1 nah nee 2

Triple #48

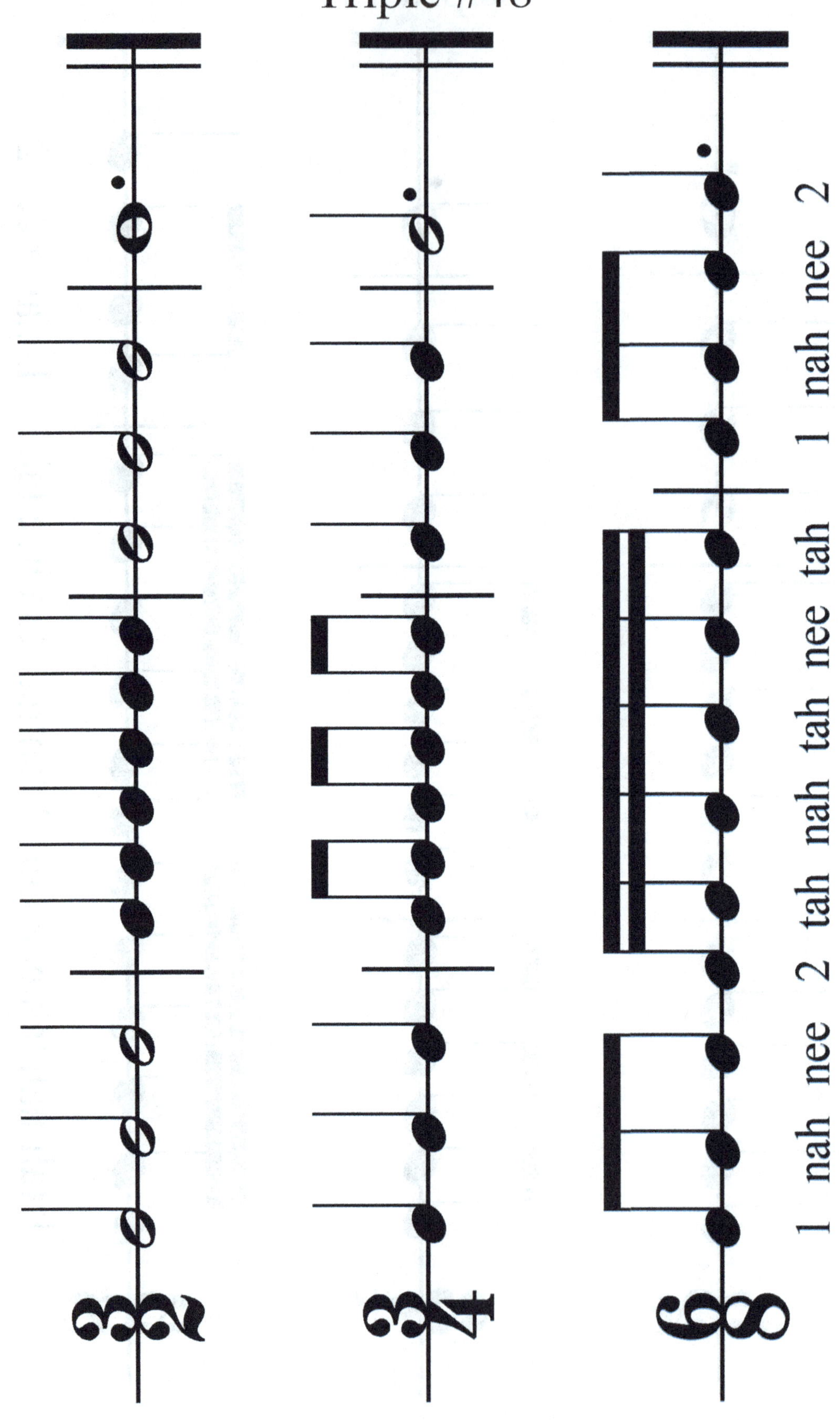

Triple #49

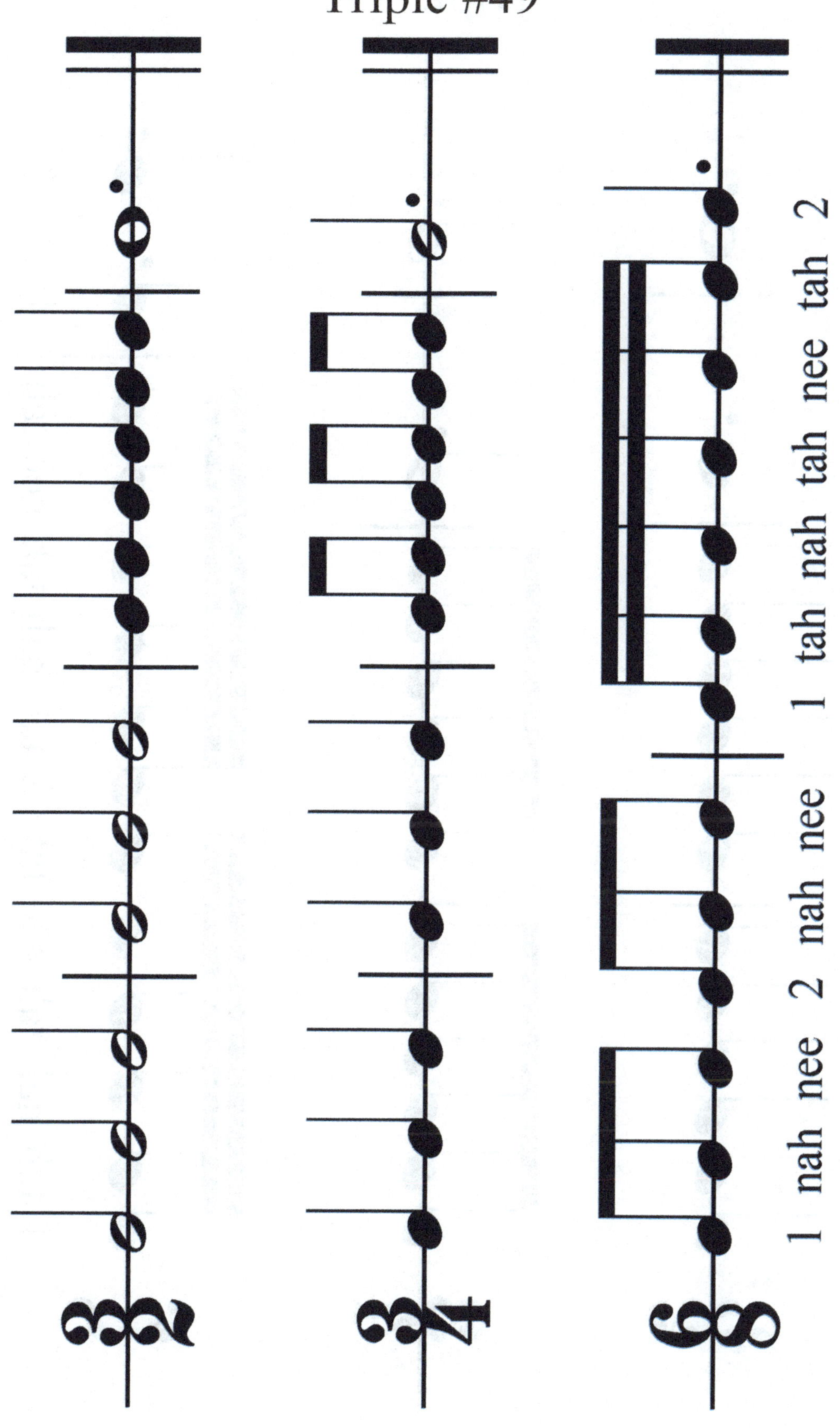

Triple #50

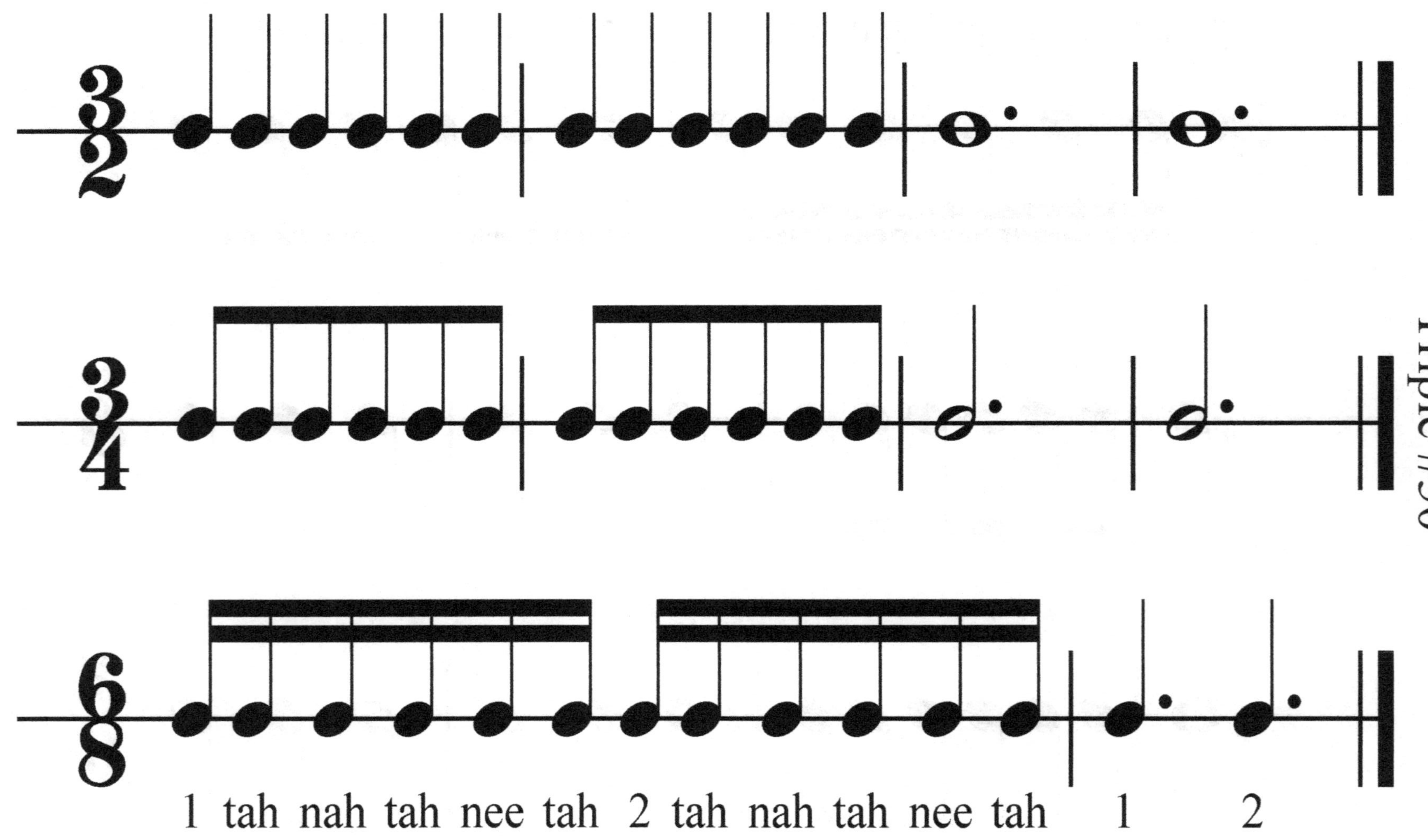
1 tah nah tah nee tah 2 tah nah tah nee tah 1 2

Triple #51

1 tahnahtahneetah 2 tahnahtahneetah 1 tah nah tah nee tah 2

Triple #52

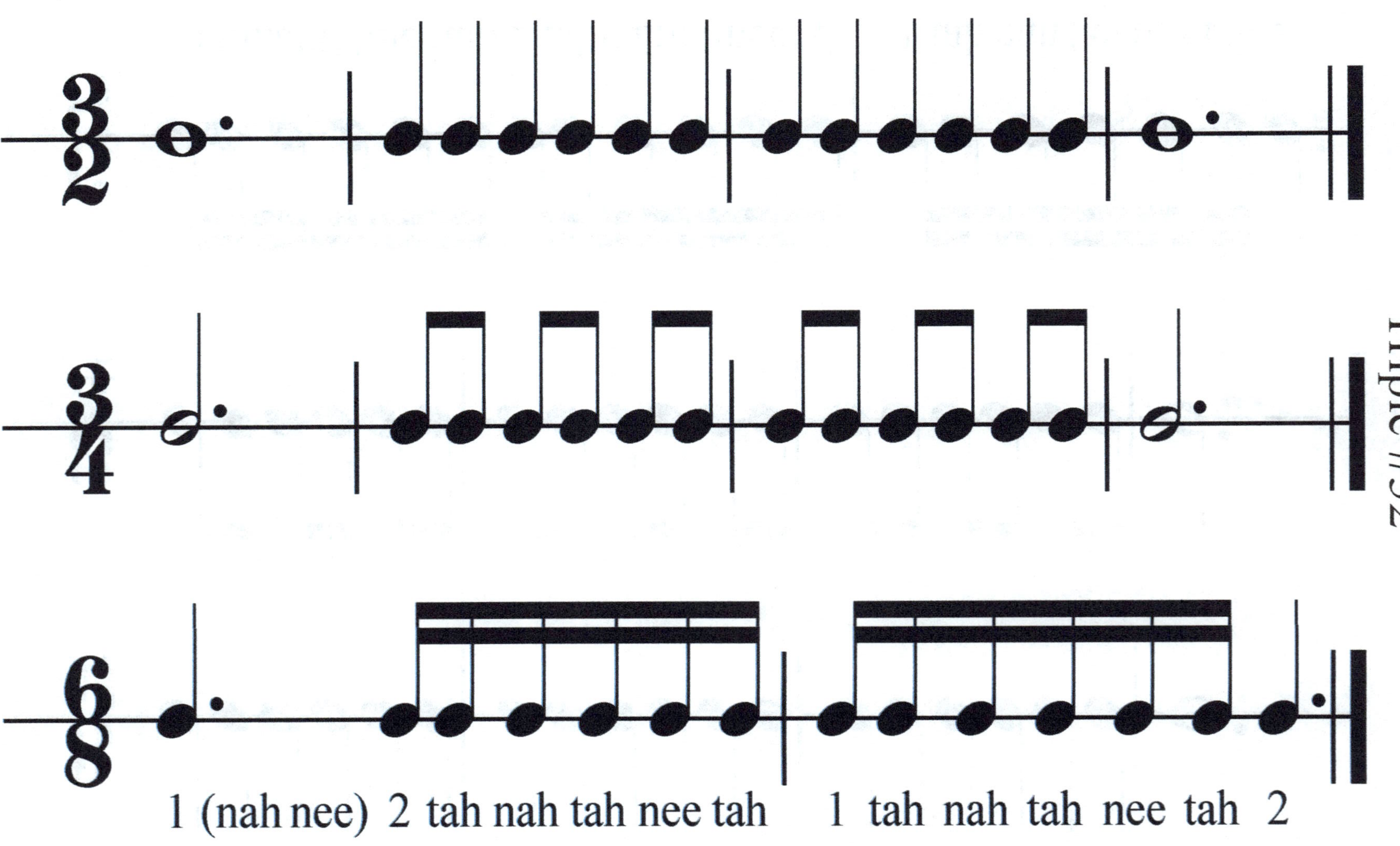
1 (nah nee) 2 tah nah tah nee tah 1 tah nah tah nee tah 2

Triple #53

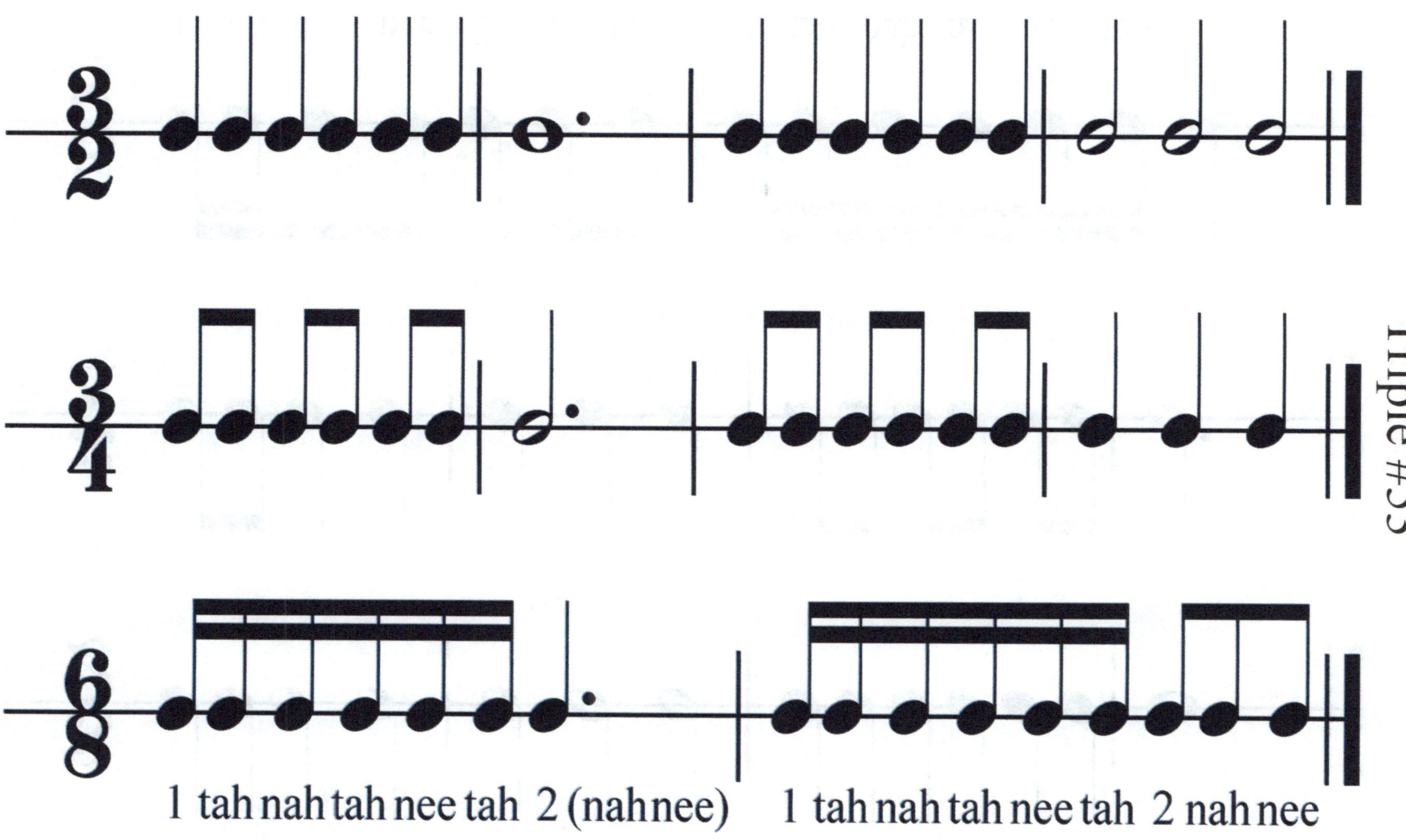
3
2
3
4
6
8
1 tah nah tah nee tah 2 (nahnee)
1 tah nah tah nee tah 2 nahnee

Triple #54

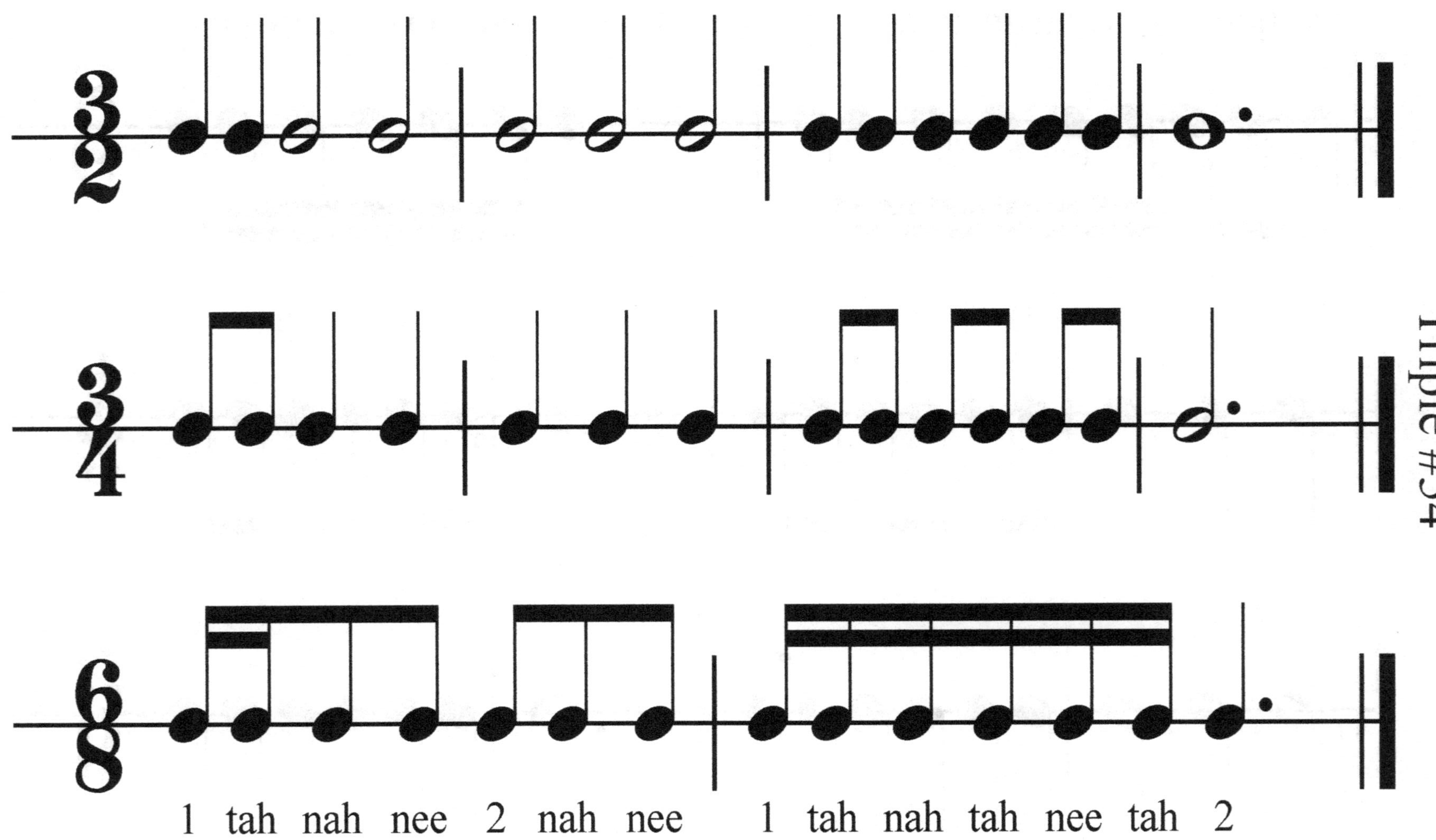

Triple #55

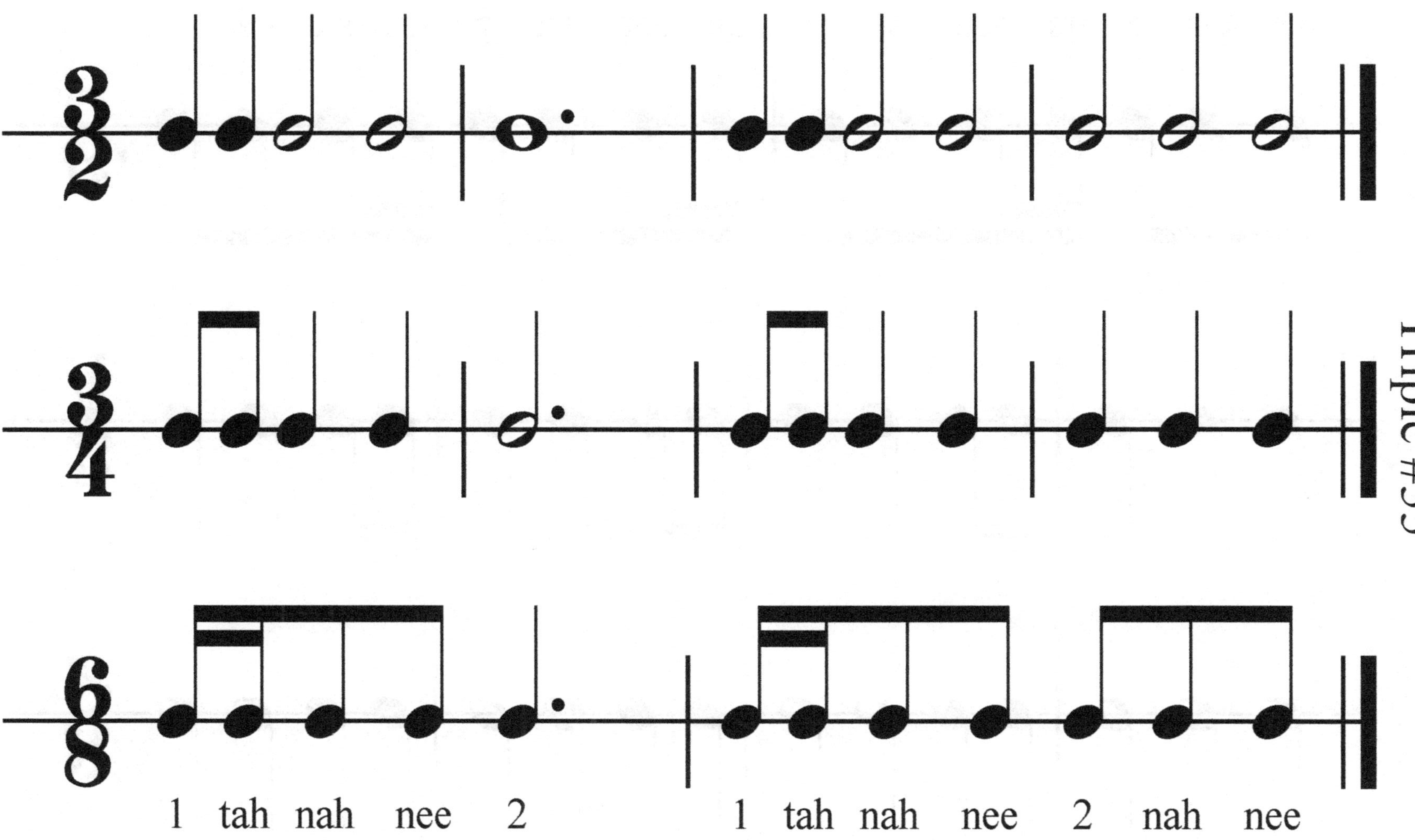
1 tah nah nee 2
1 tah nah nee 2 nah nee

Triple #56

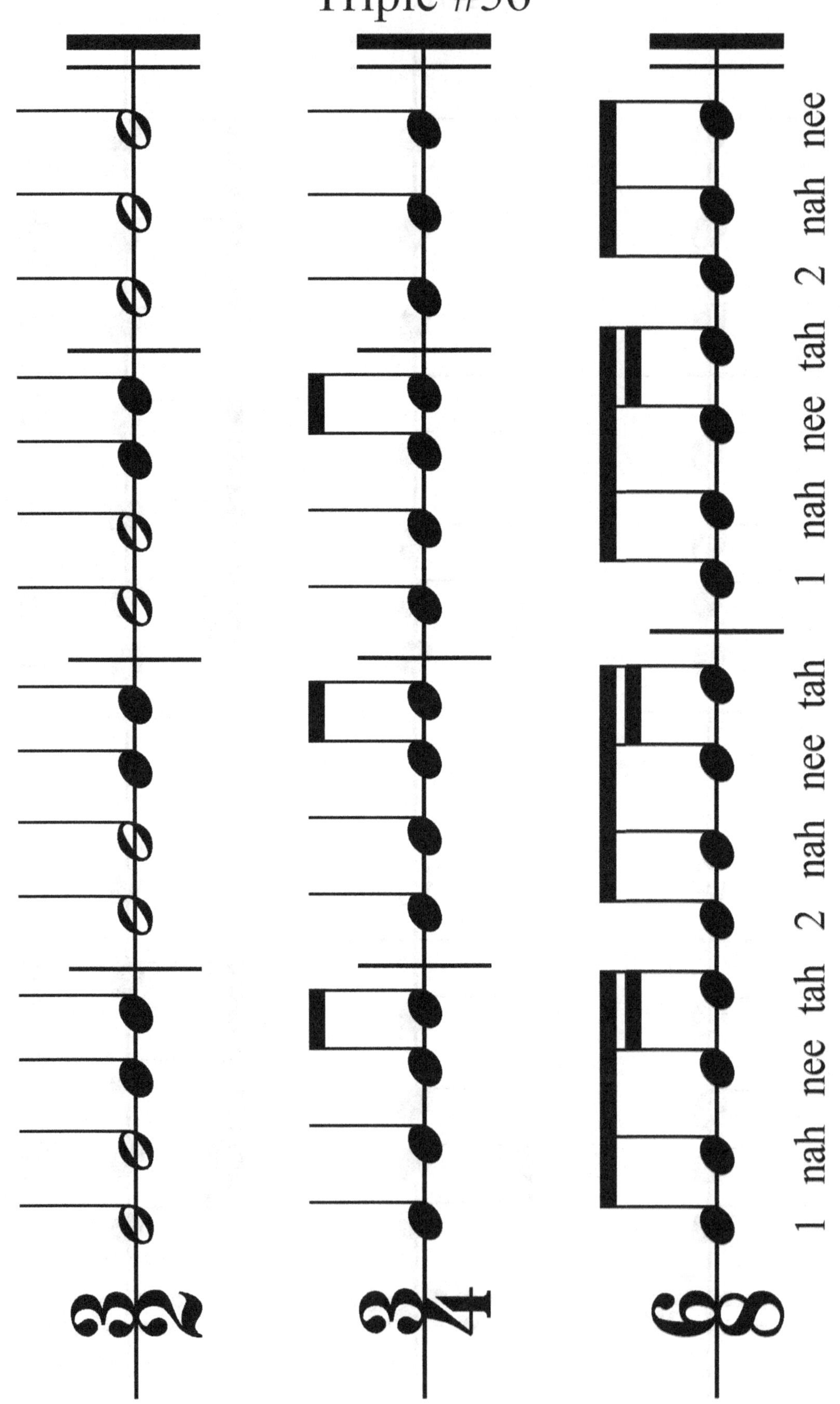
1 nah nee tah 2 nah nee tah 1 nah nee tah 2 nah nee

Triple #57

Triple #58

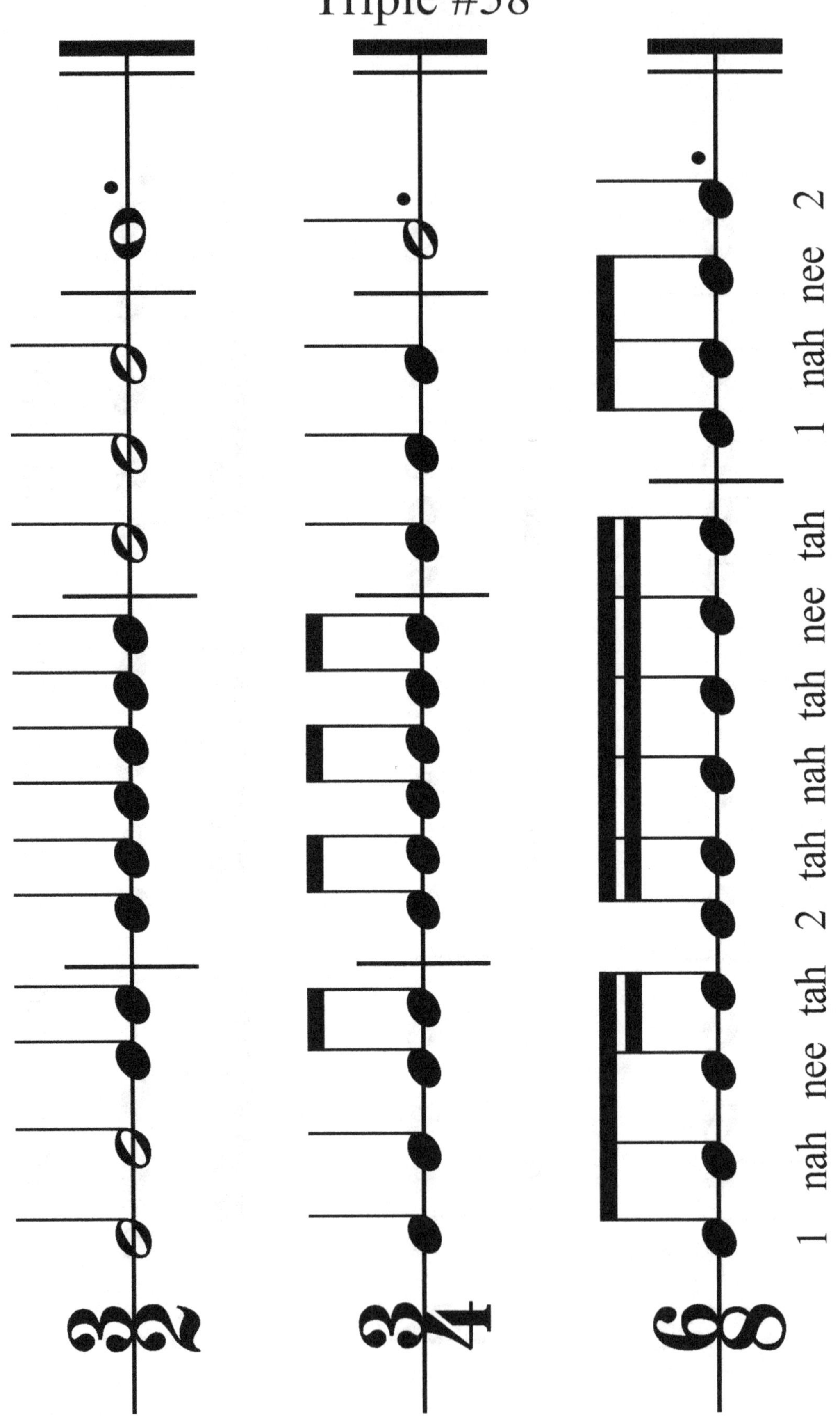

1 nah nee tah 2 tah nah tah nee tah 1 nah nee 2

Triple #59

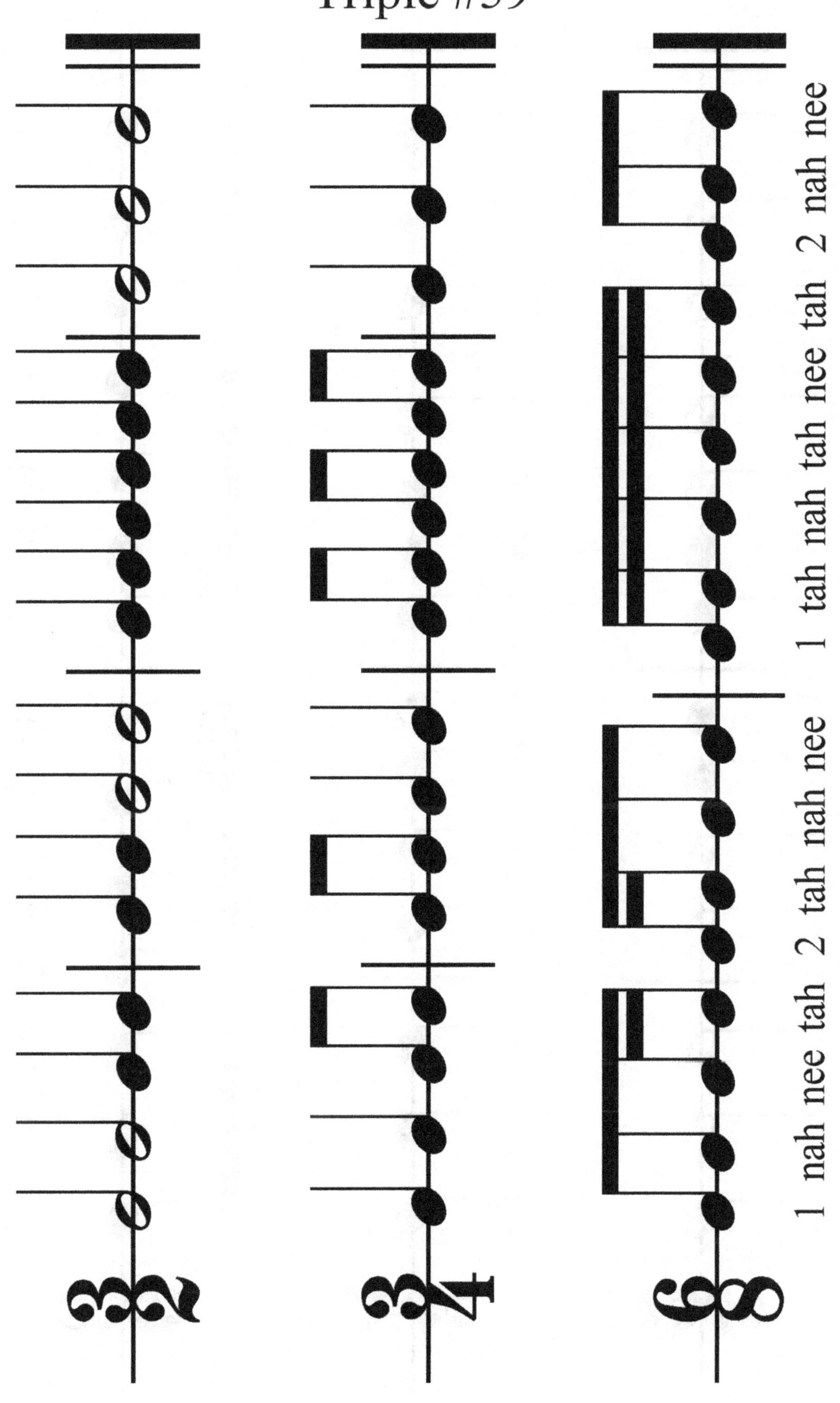

Triple #60

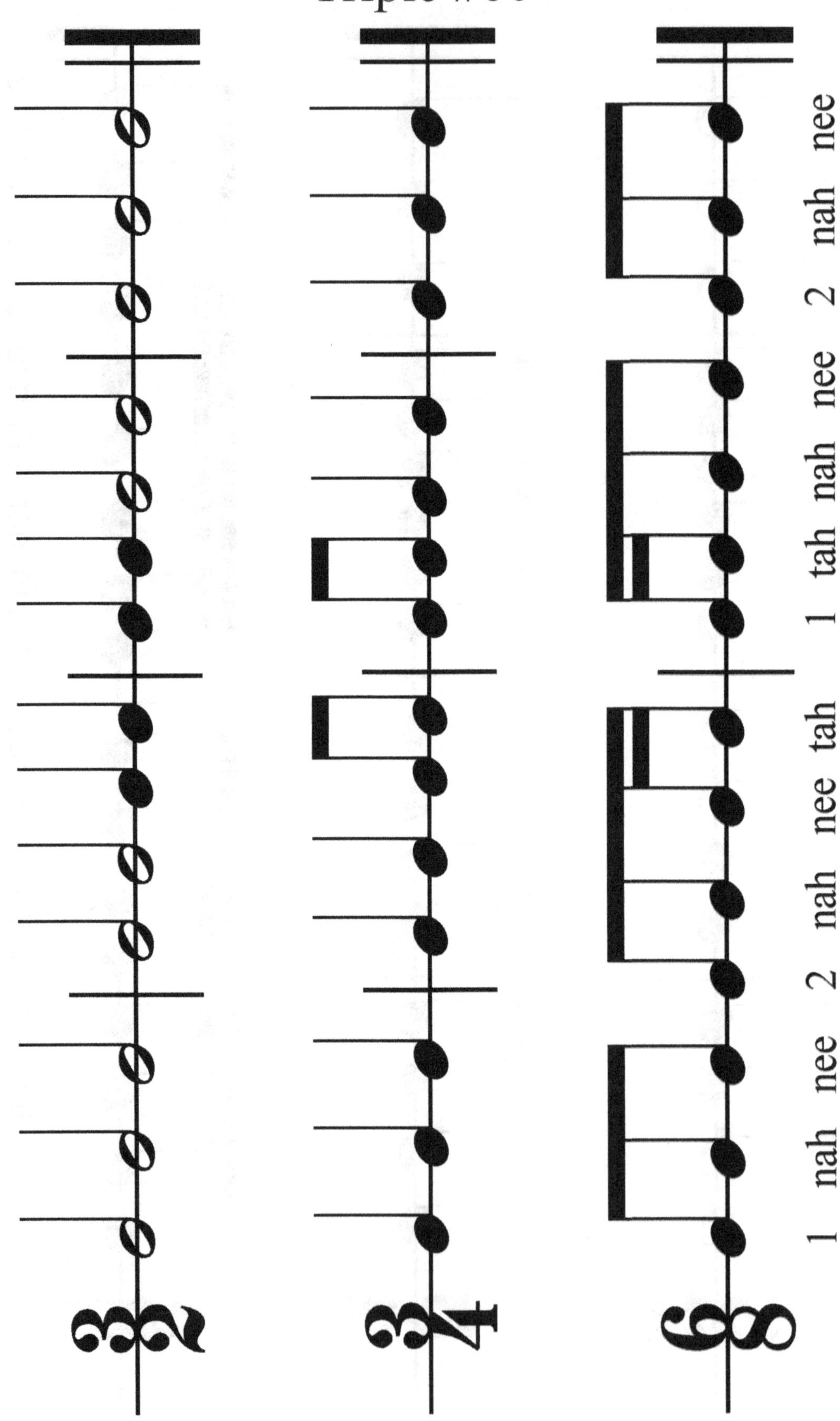
1 nah nee 2 nah nee tah 1 tah nah nee 2 nah nee

Triple #61

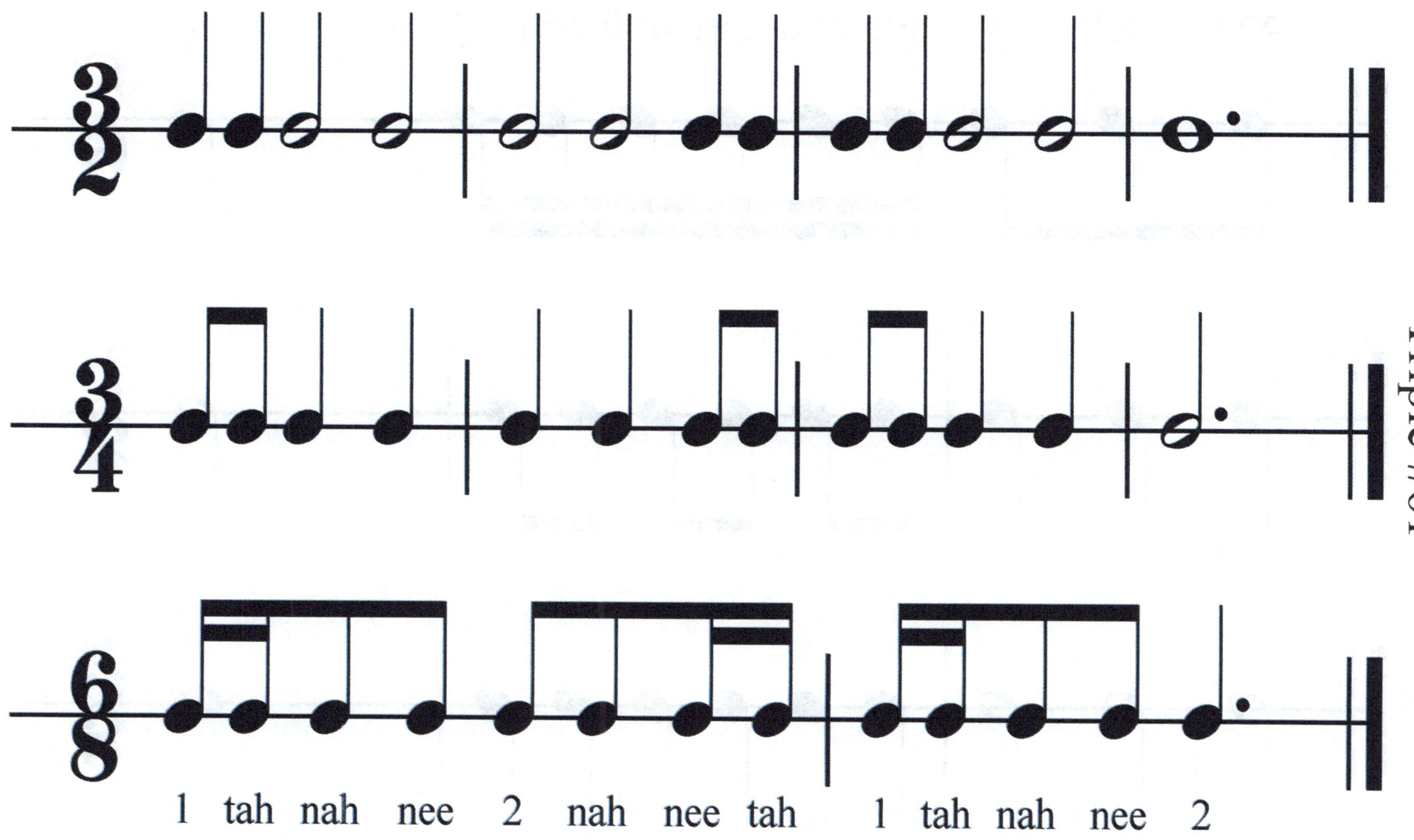
1 tah nah nee 2 nah nee tah 1 tah nah nee 2

Triple #62

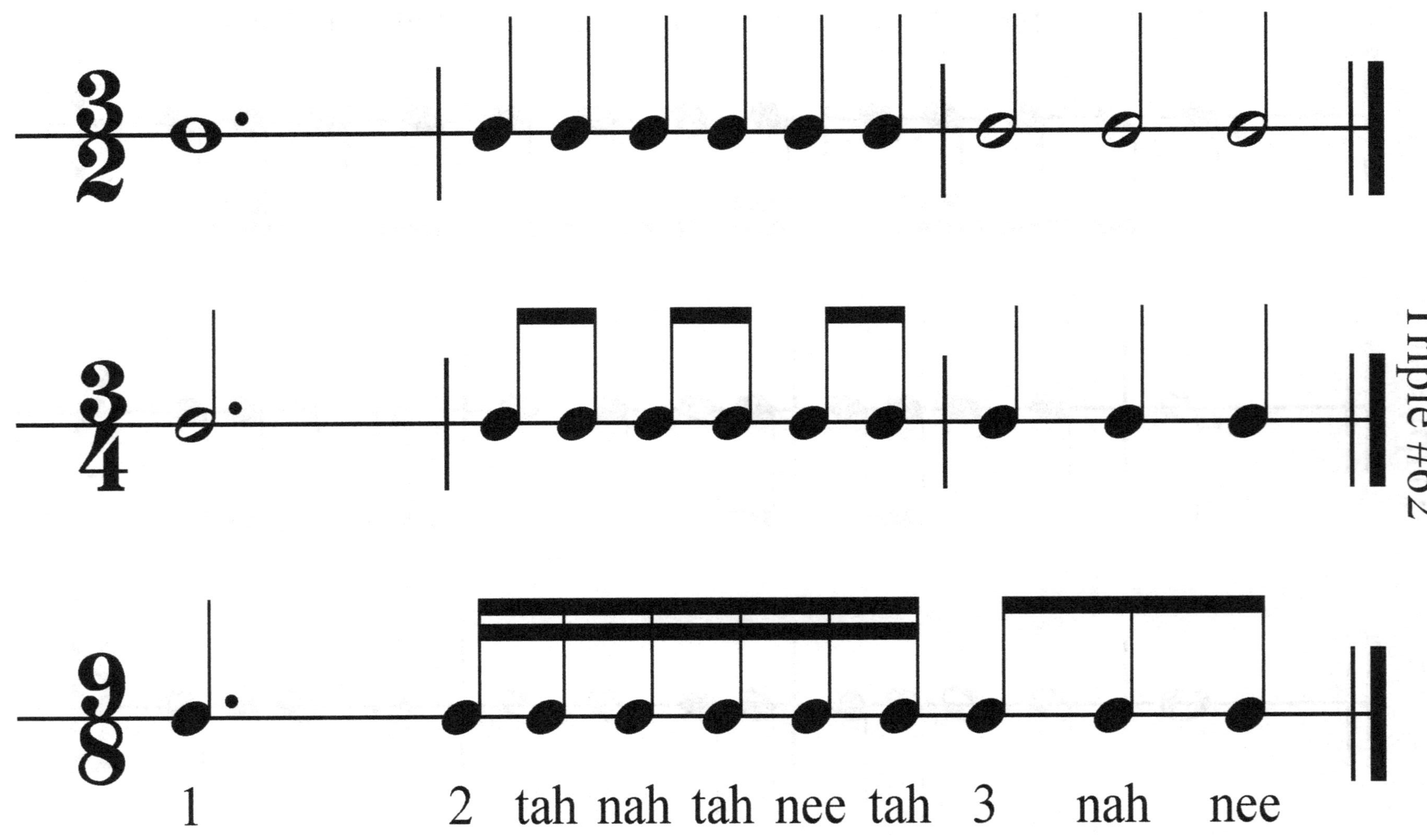
1 2 tah nah tah nee tah 3 nah nee

Triple #63

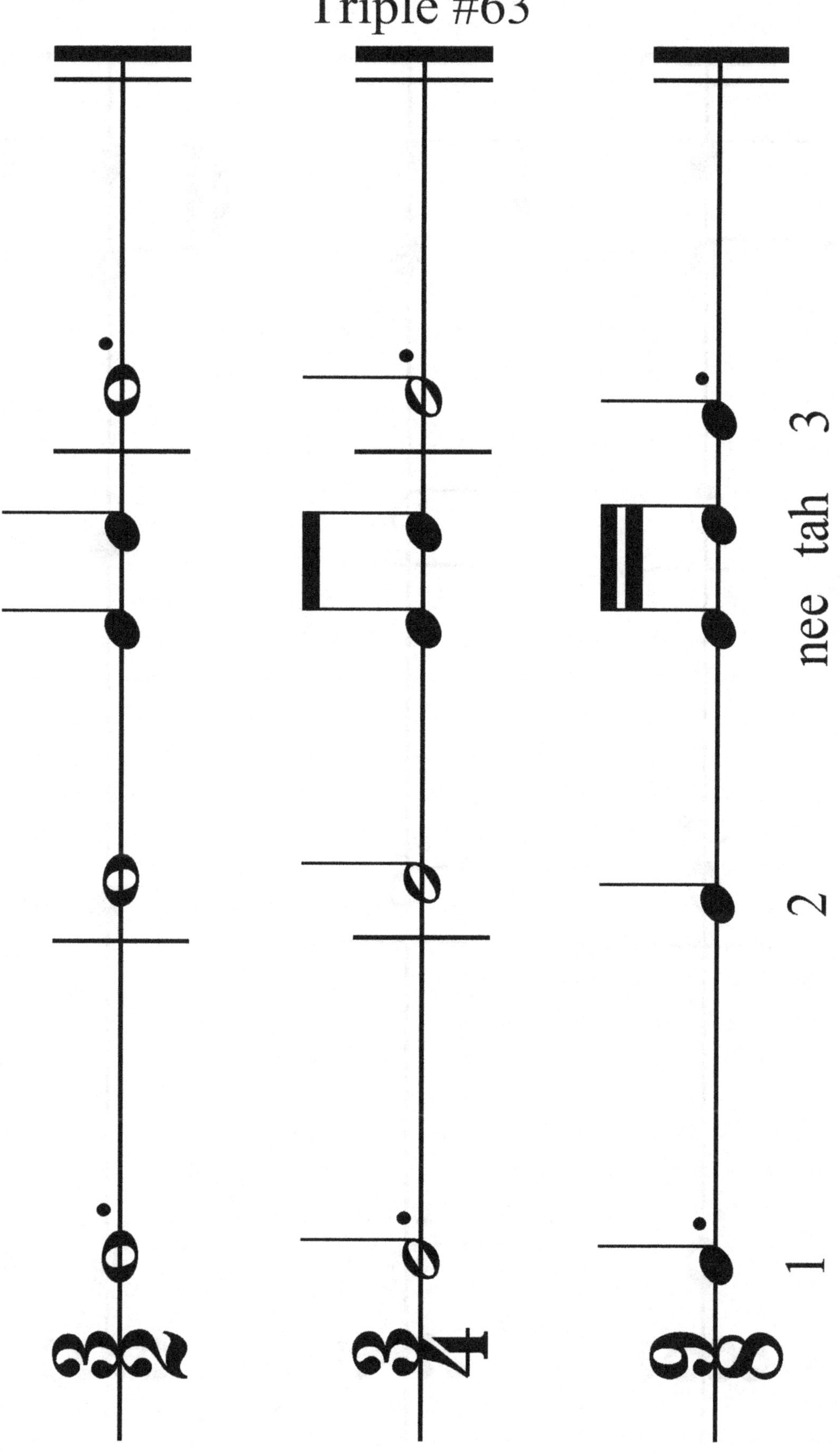

Triple #64

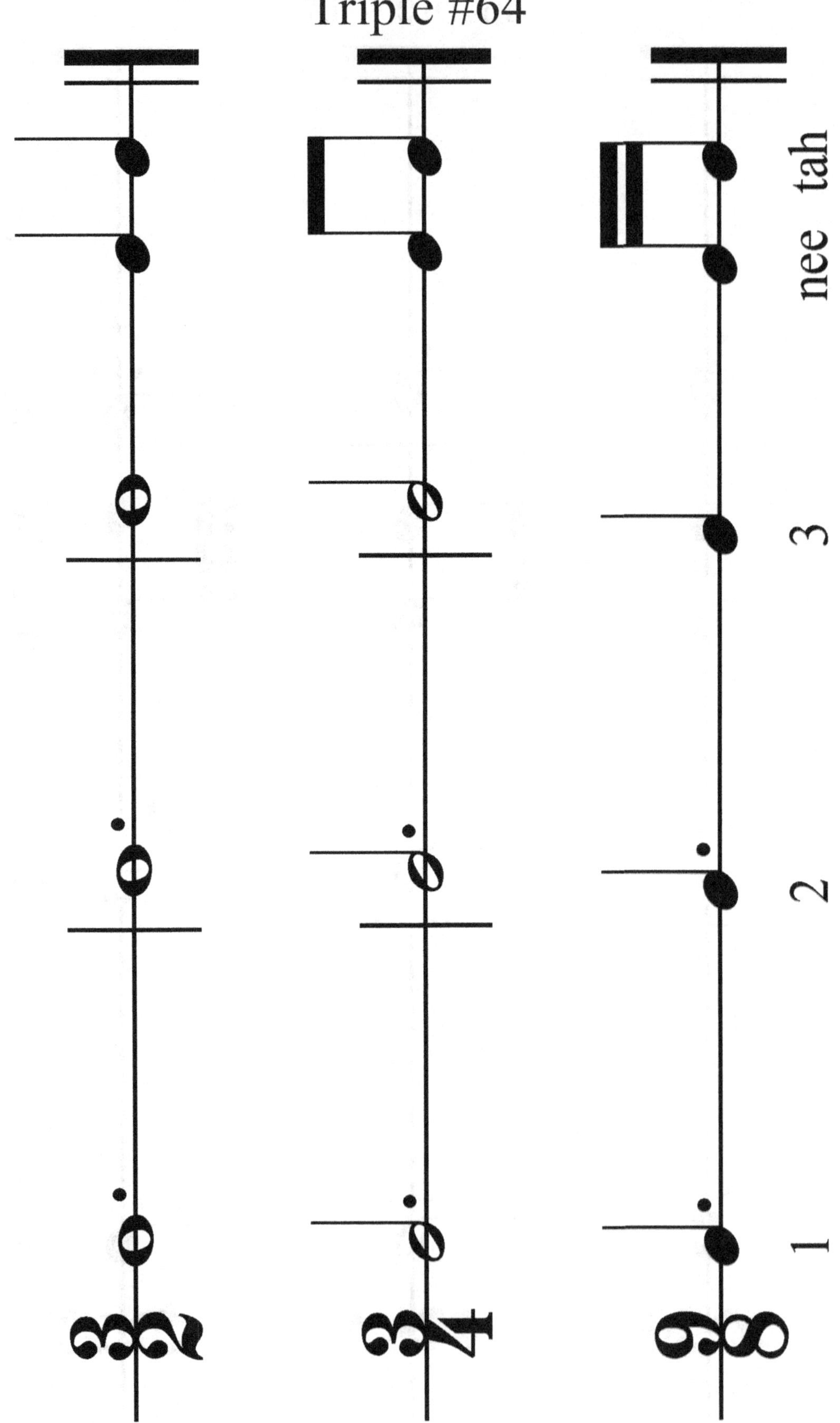

Triple #65

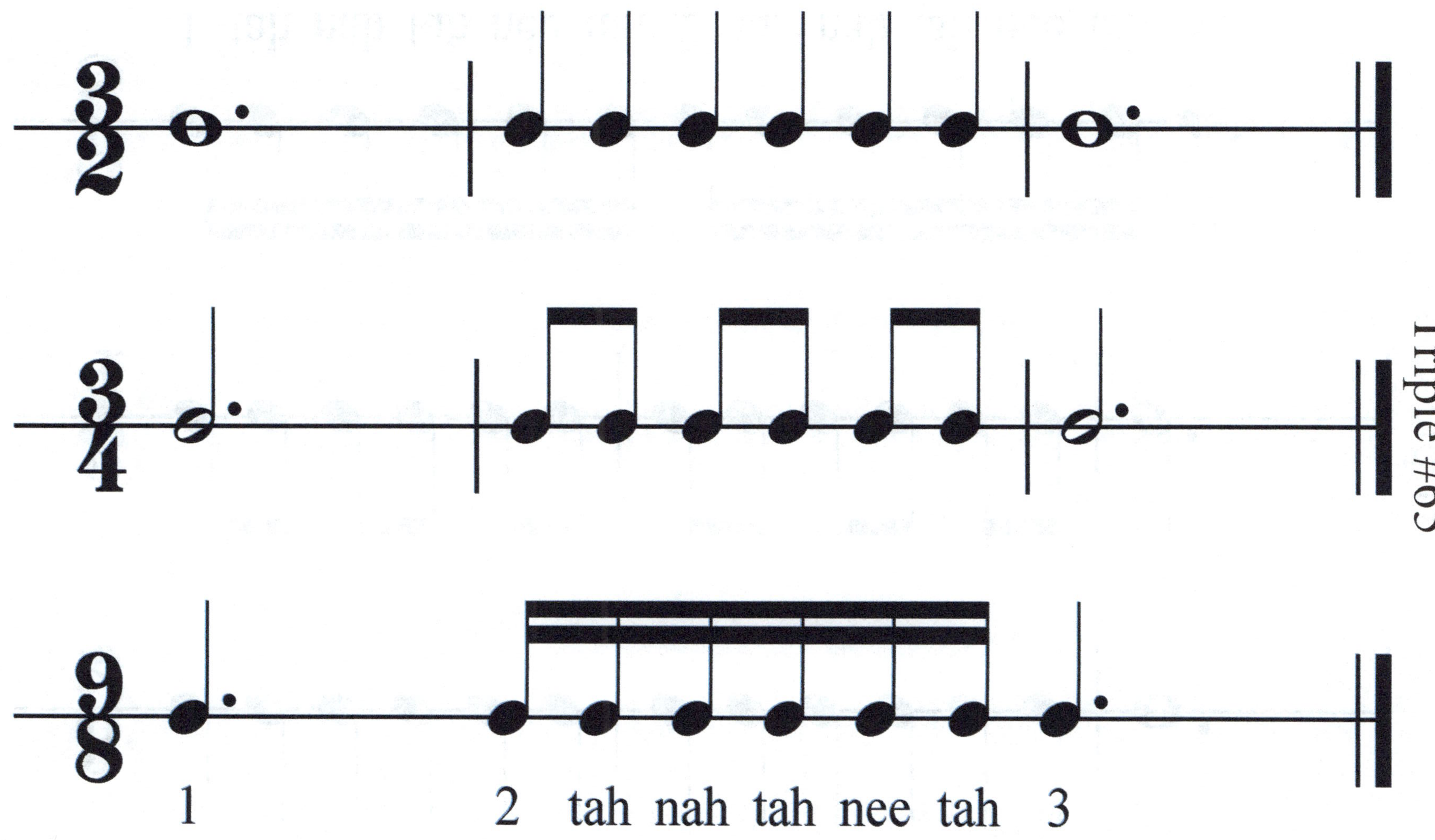
1
2 tah nah tah nee tah 3

Triple #66

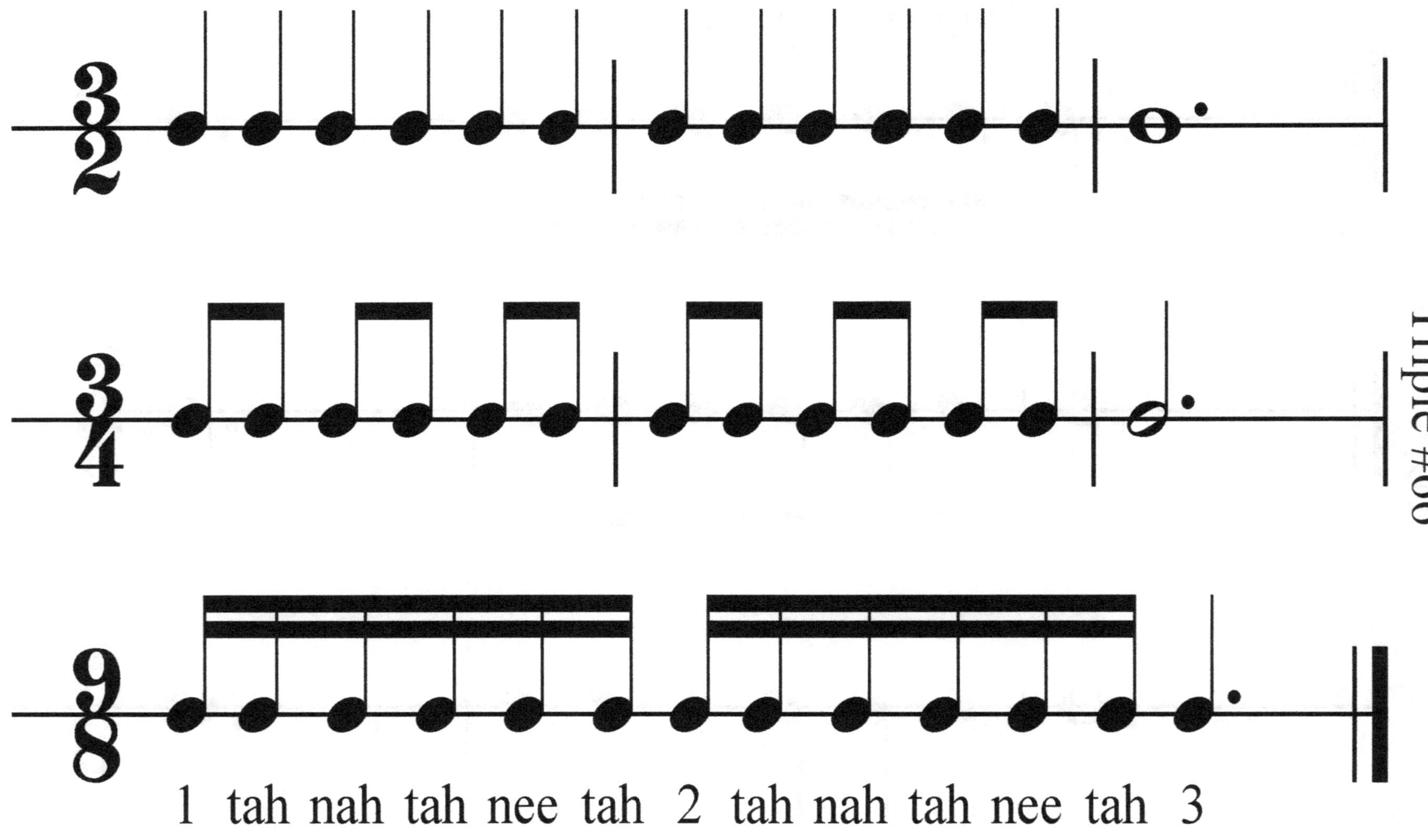
1 tah nah tah nee tah 2 tah nah tah nee tah 3

Triple #67

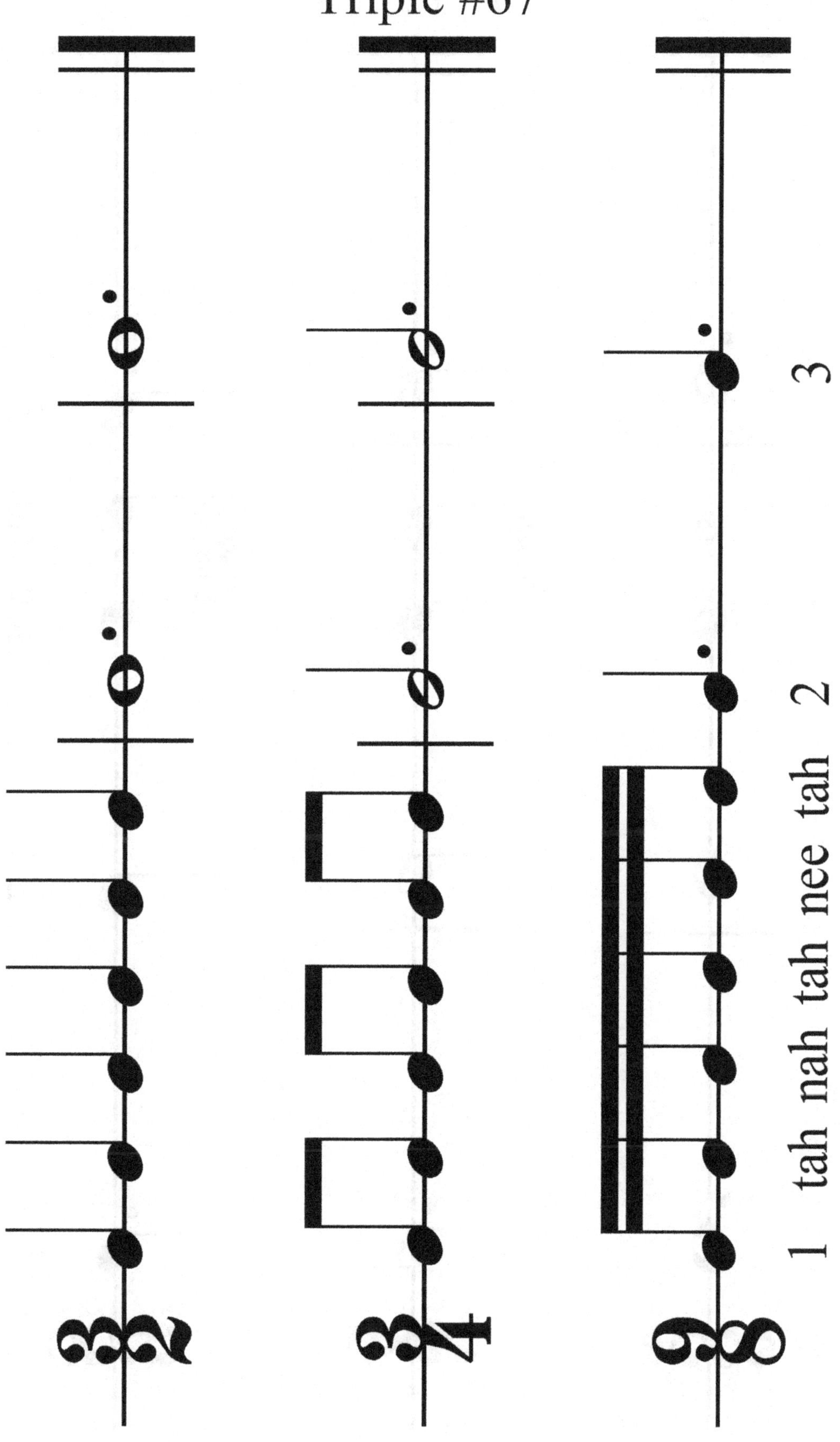

Triple #68

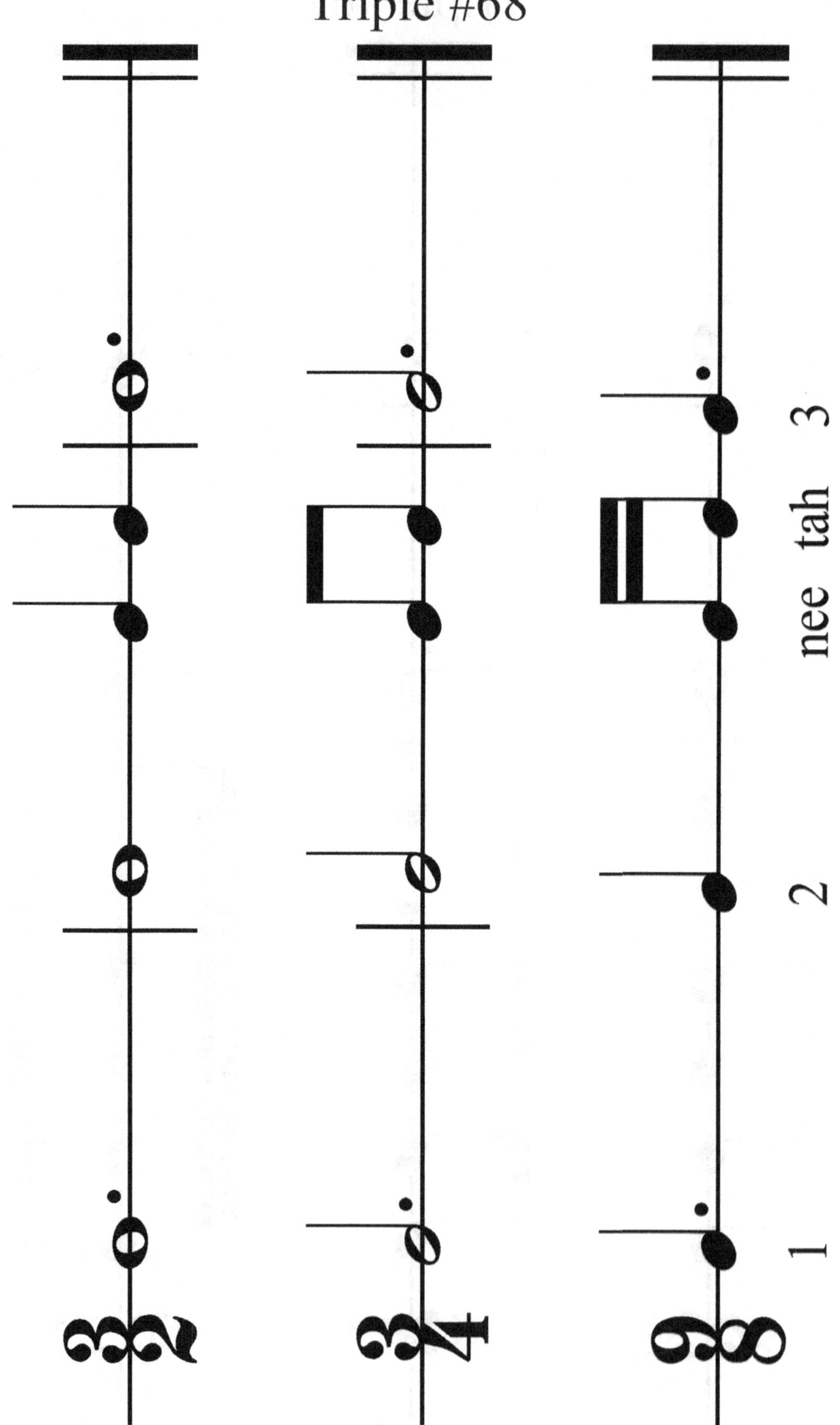

Triple #69

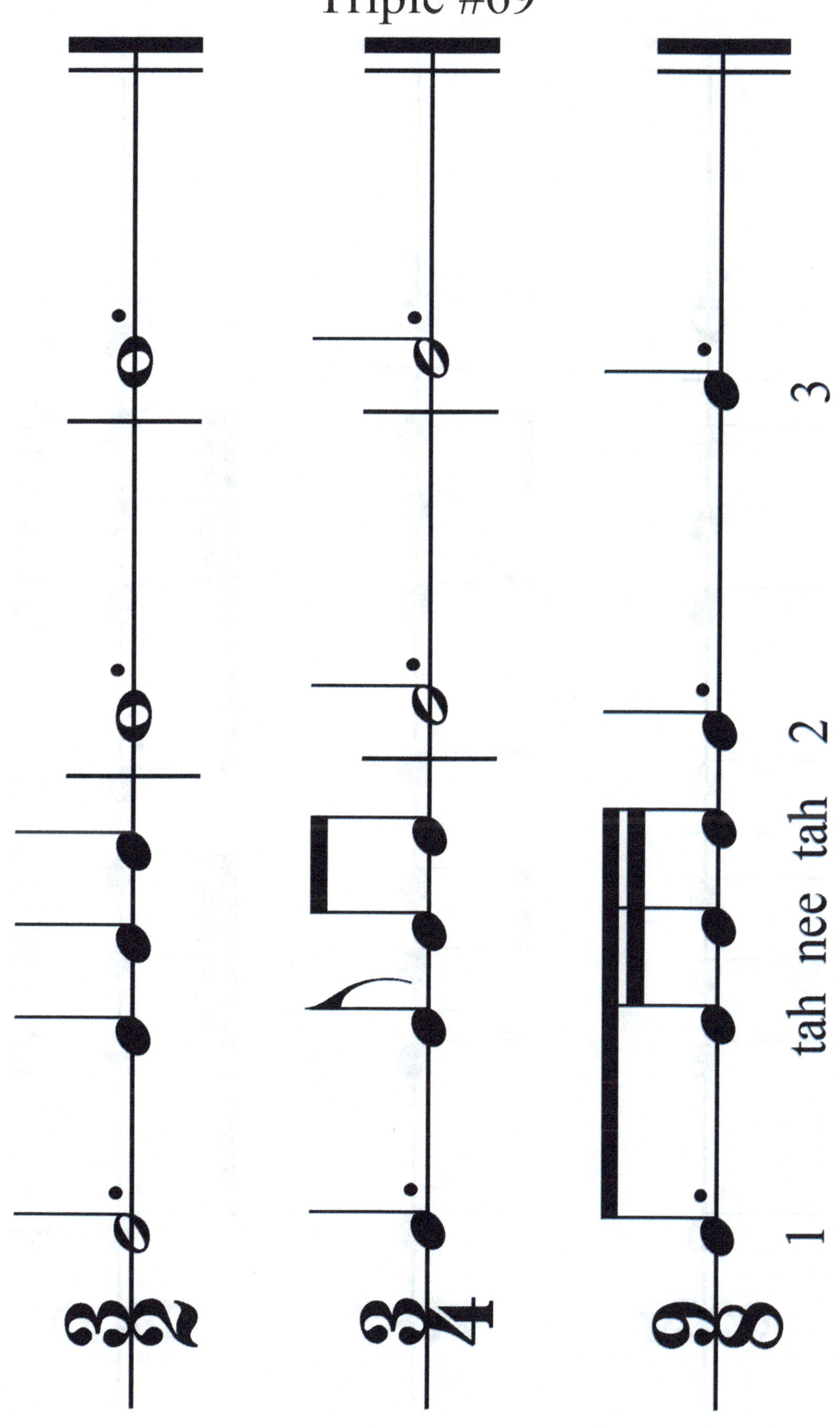

Triple #70

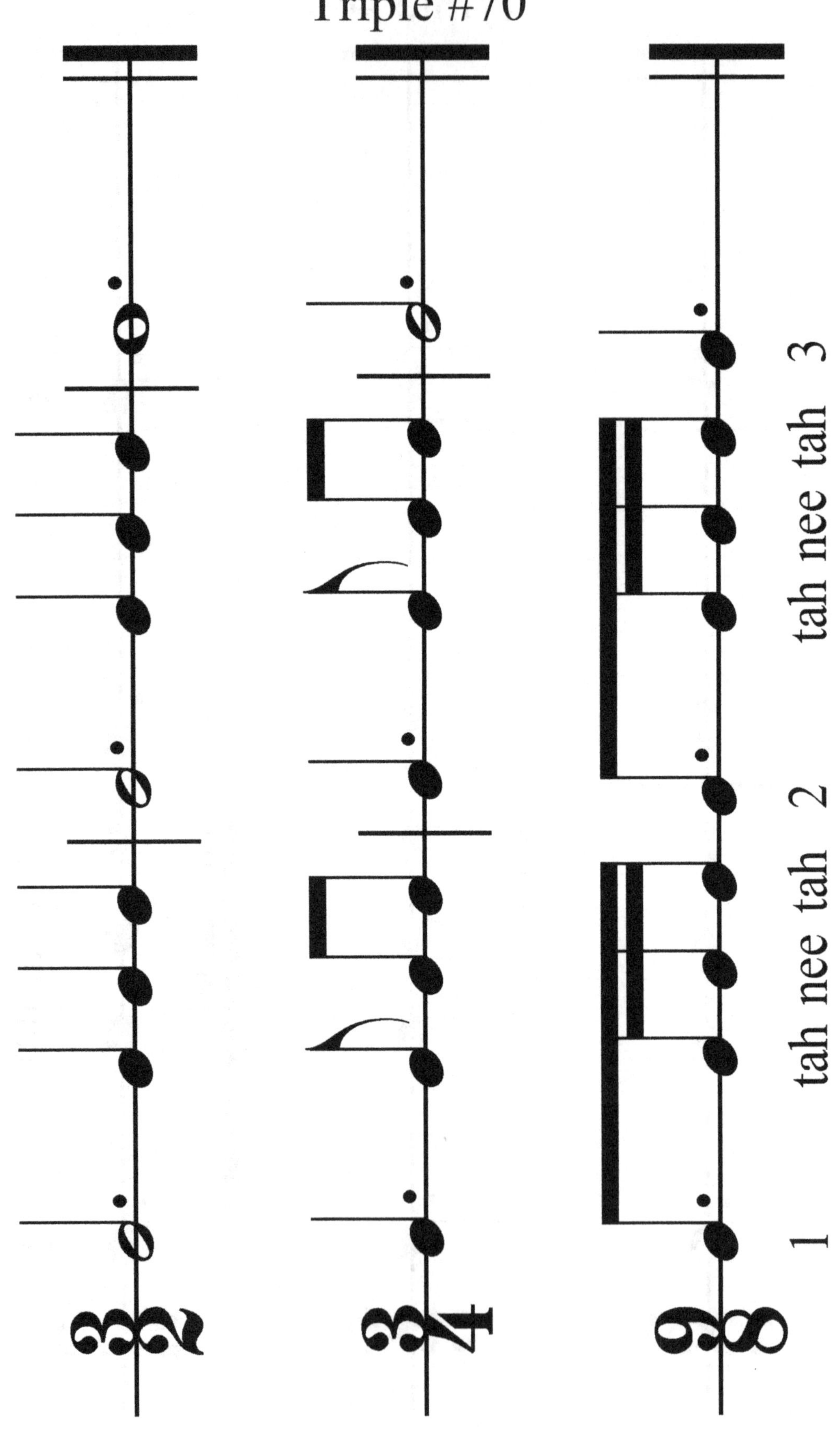

Triple #71

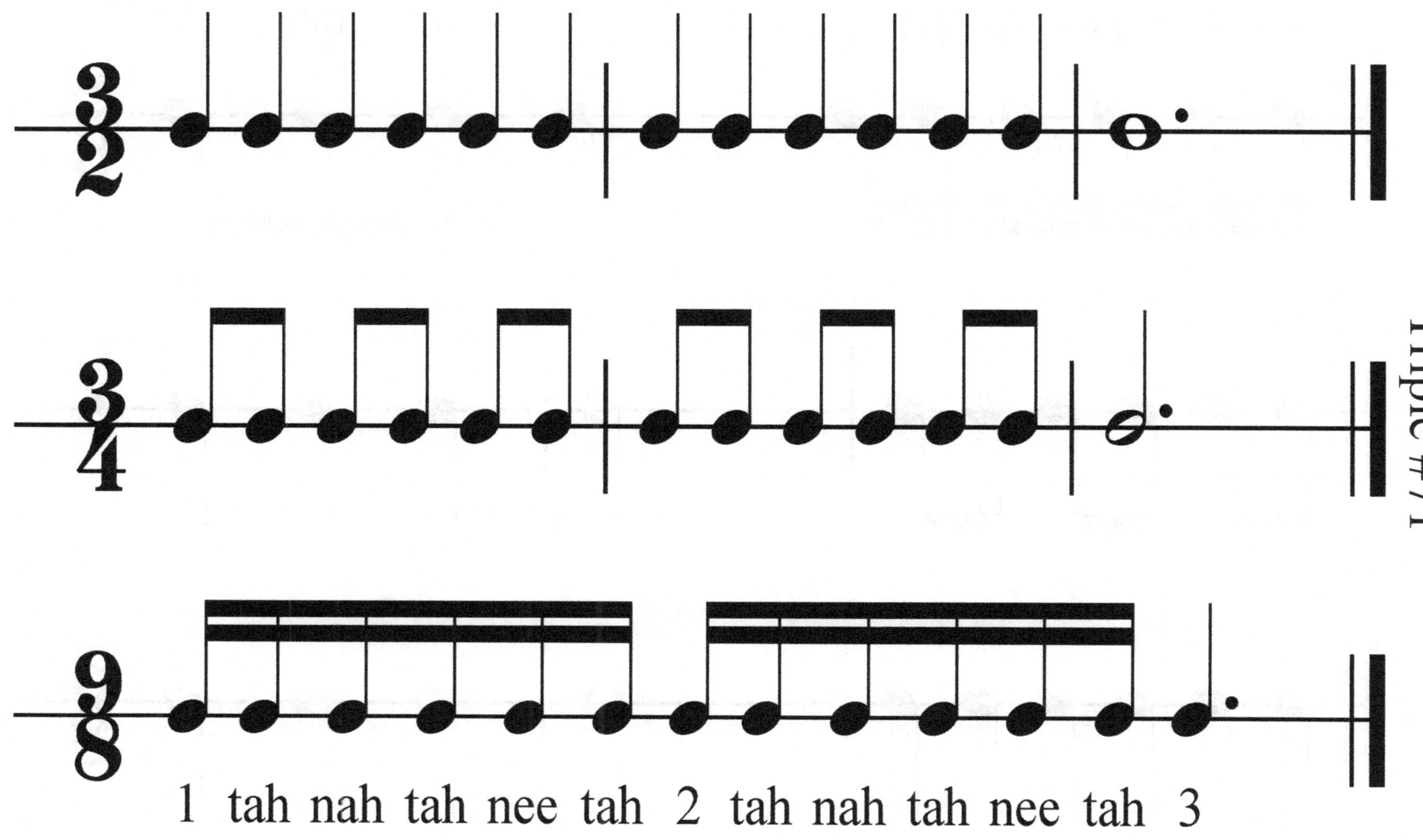
3/2
3/4
9/8
1 tah nah tah nee tah 2 tah nah tah nee tah 3

Triple #72

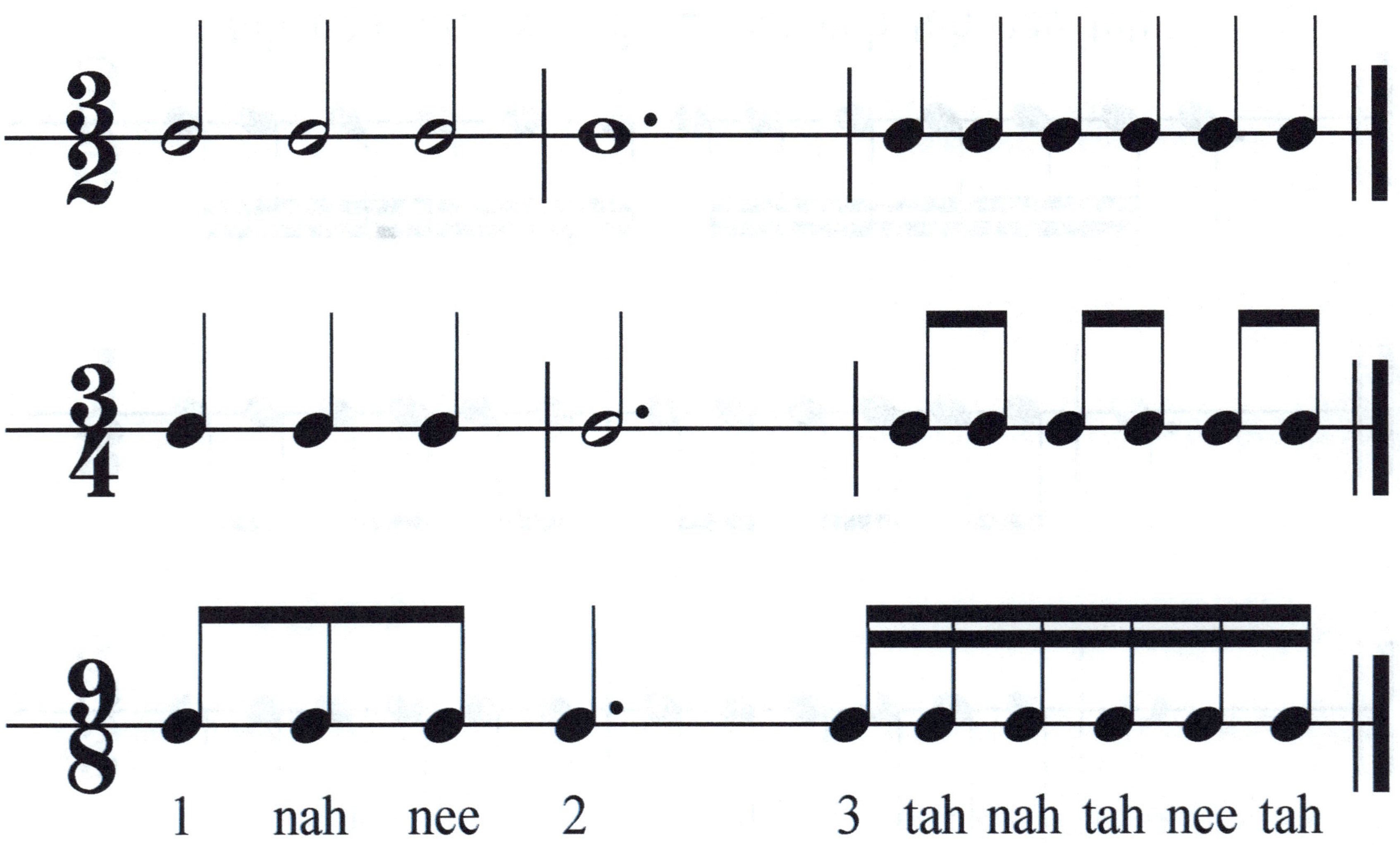
3/2
3/4
9/8
1 nah nee 2 3 tah nah tah nee tah

Triple #73

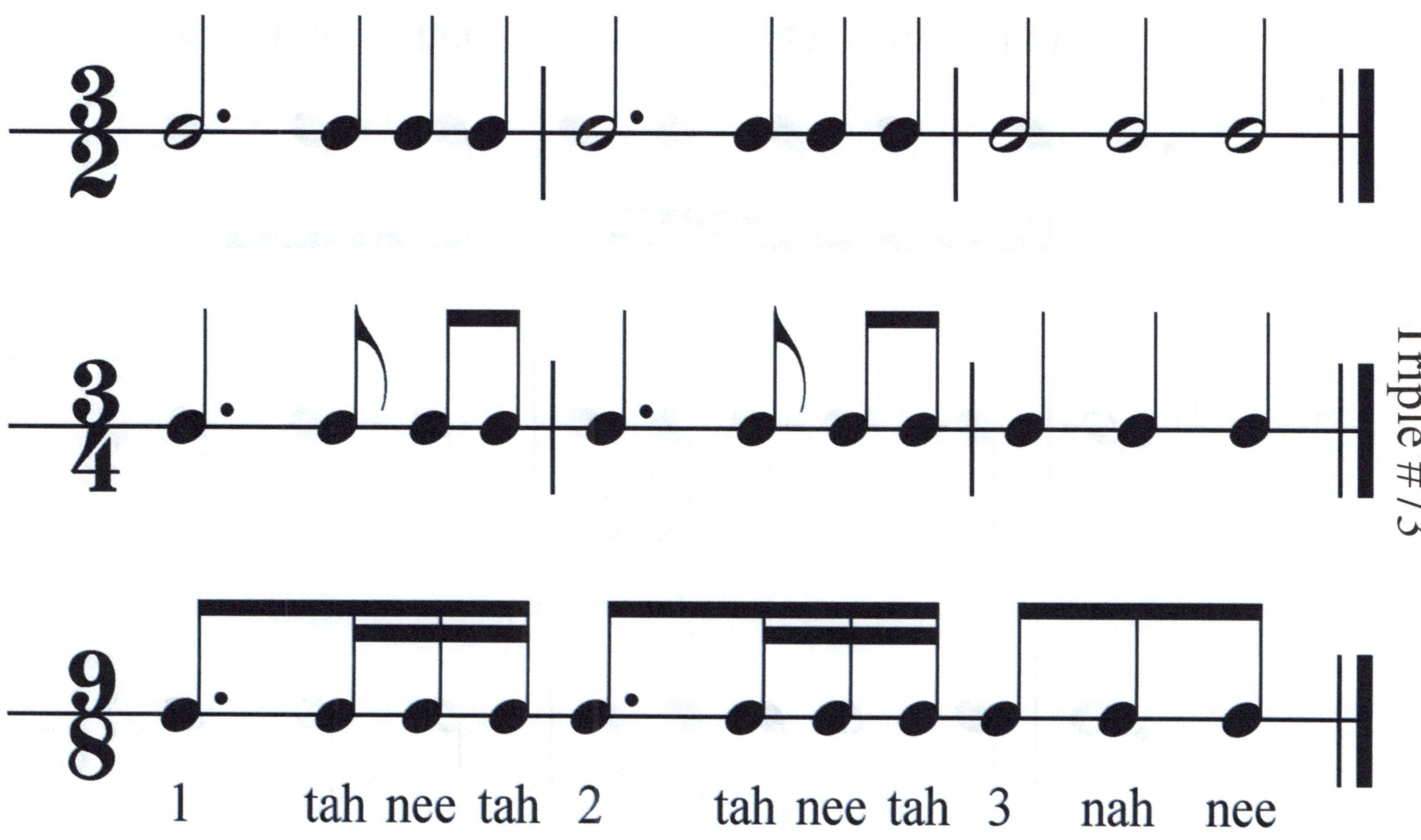
1 tah nee tah 2 tah nee tah 3 nah nee

Triple #74

Triple #75

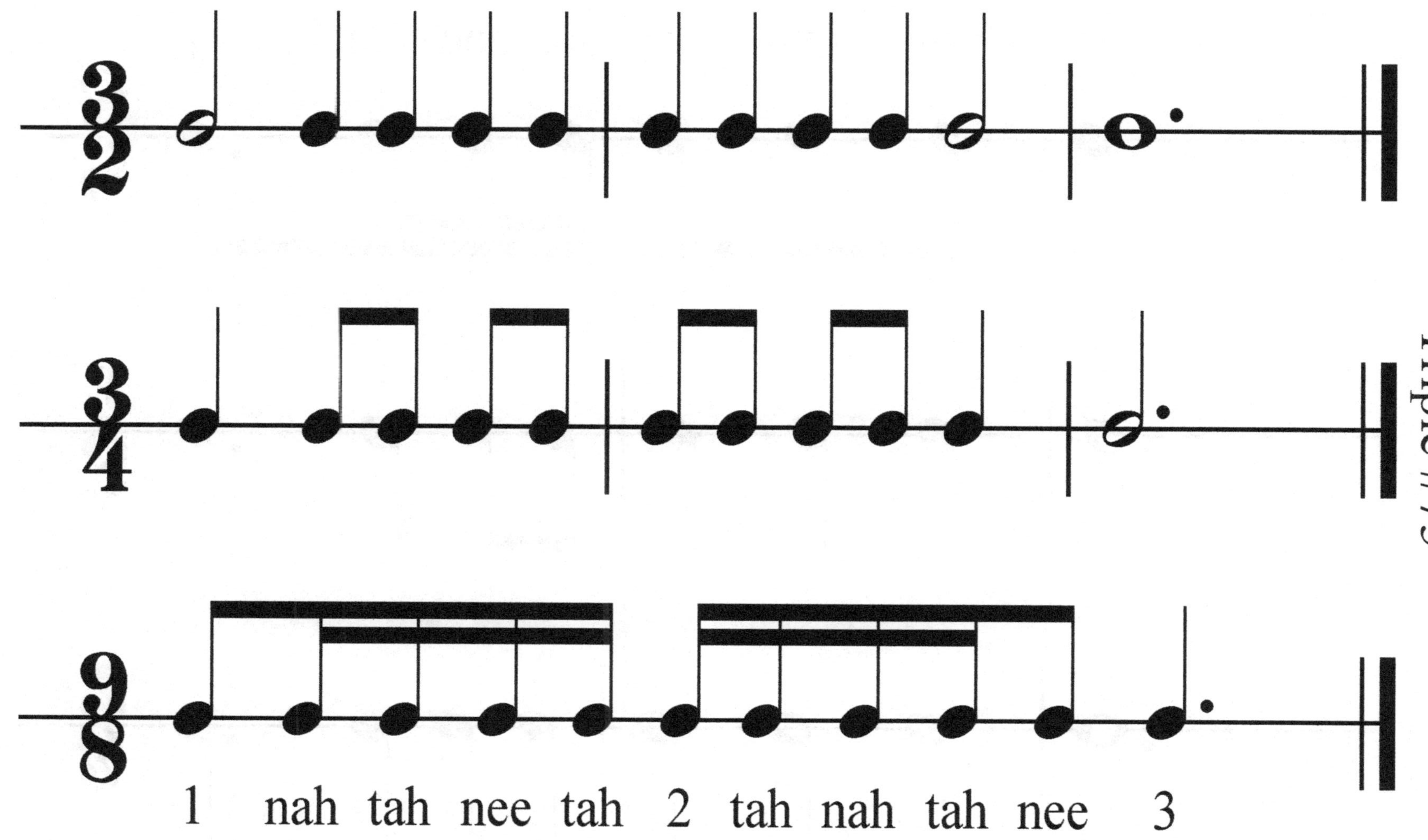

1 nah tah nee tah 2 tah nah tah nee 3

Triple #76

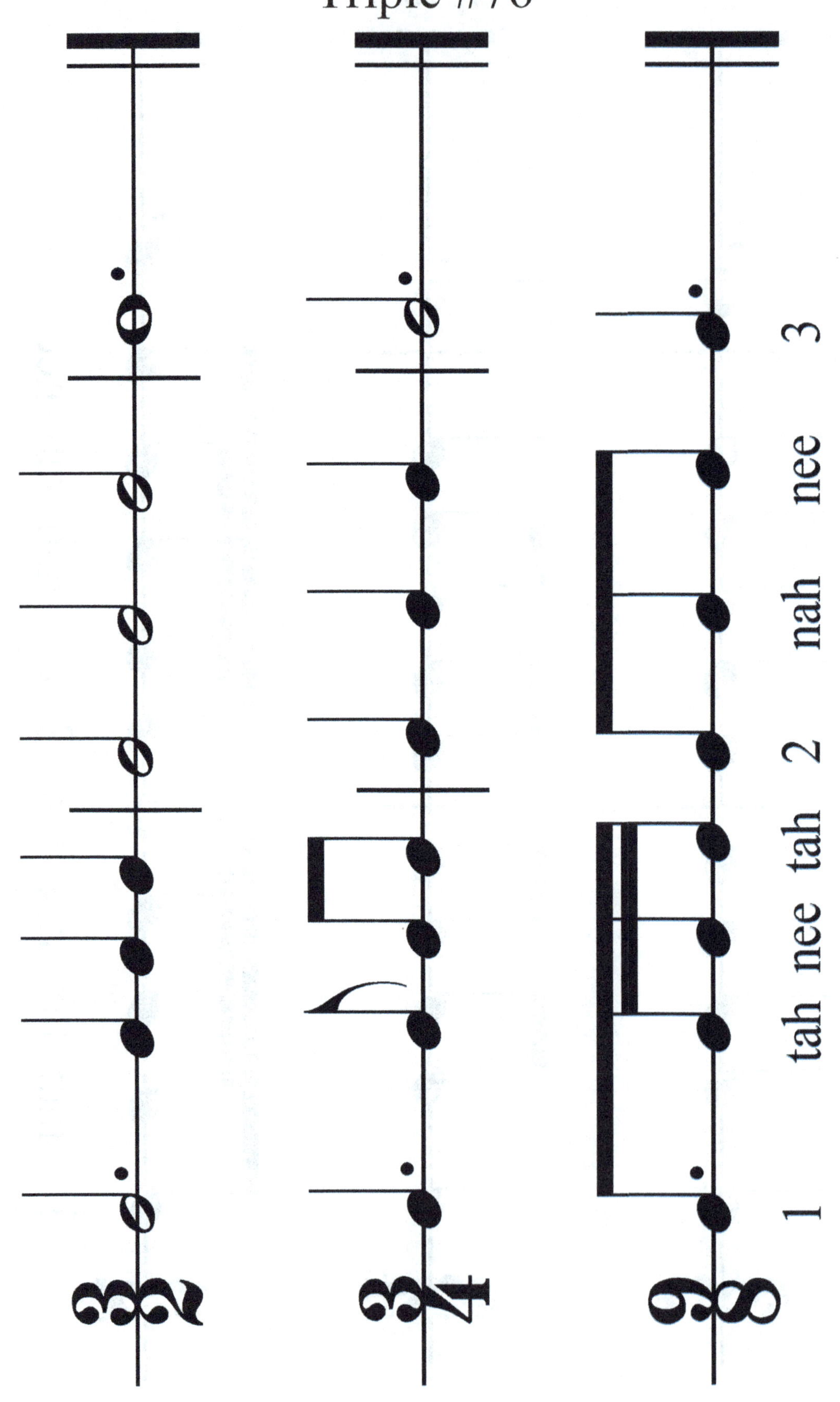
3/2
3/4
9/8
1 tah nee tah 2 nah nee 3

Triple #77

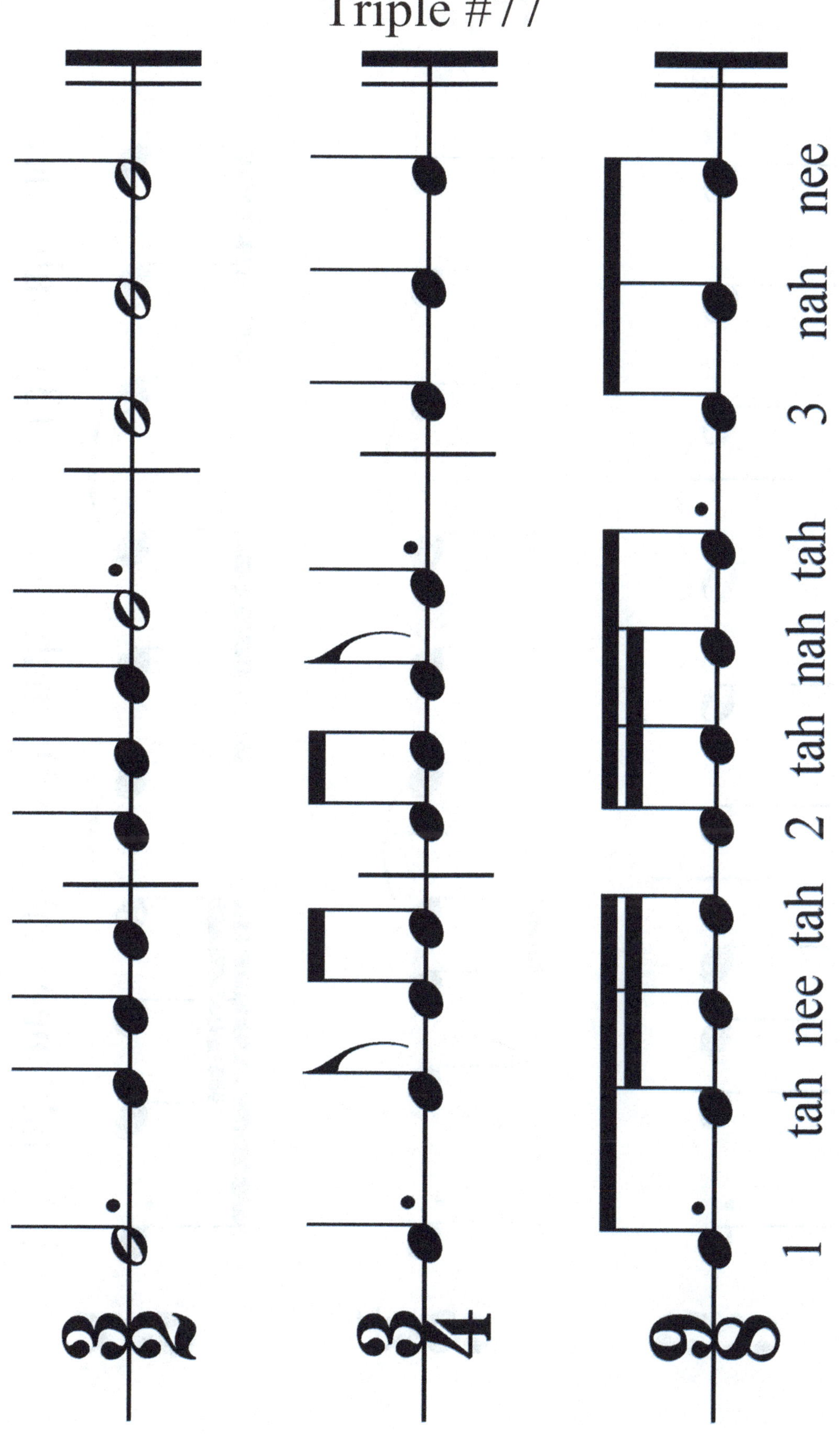

Triple #78

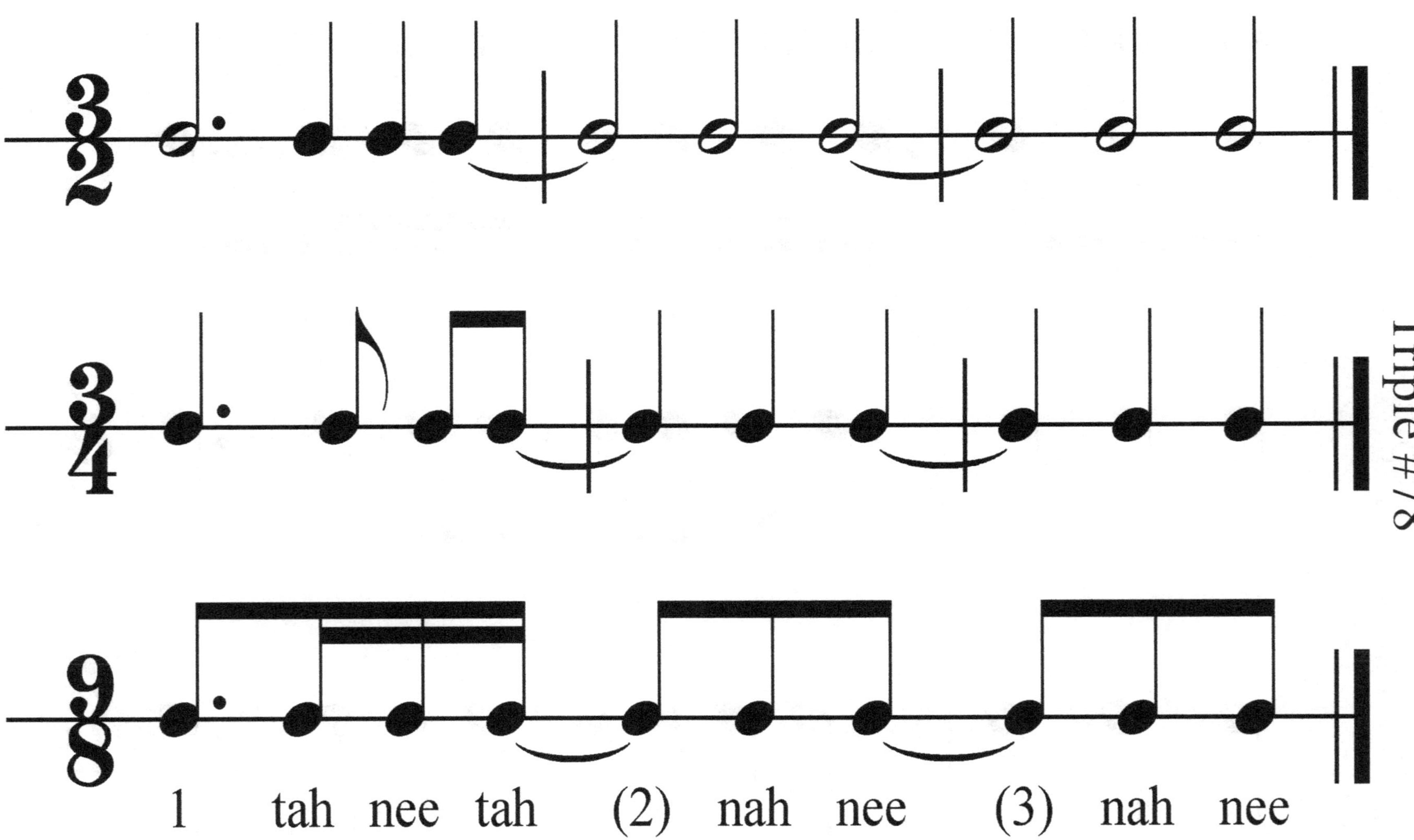
1 tah nee tah (2) nah nee (3) nah nee

Triple #79

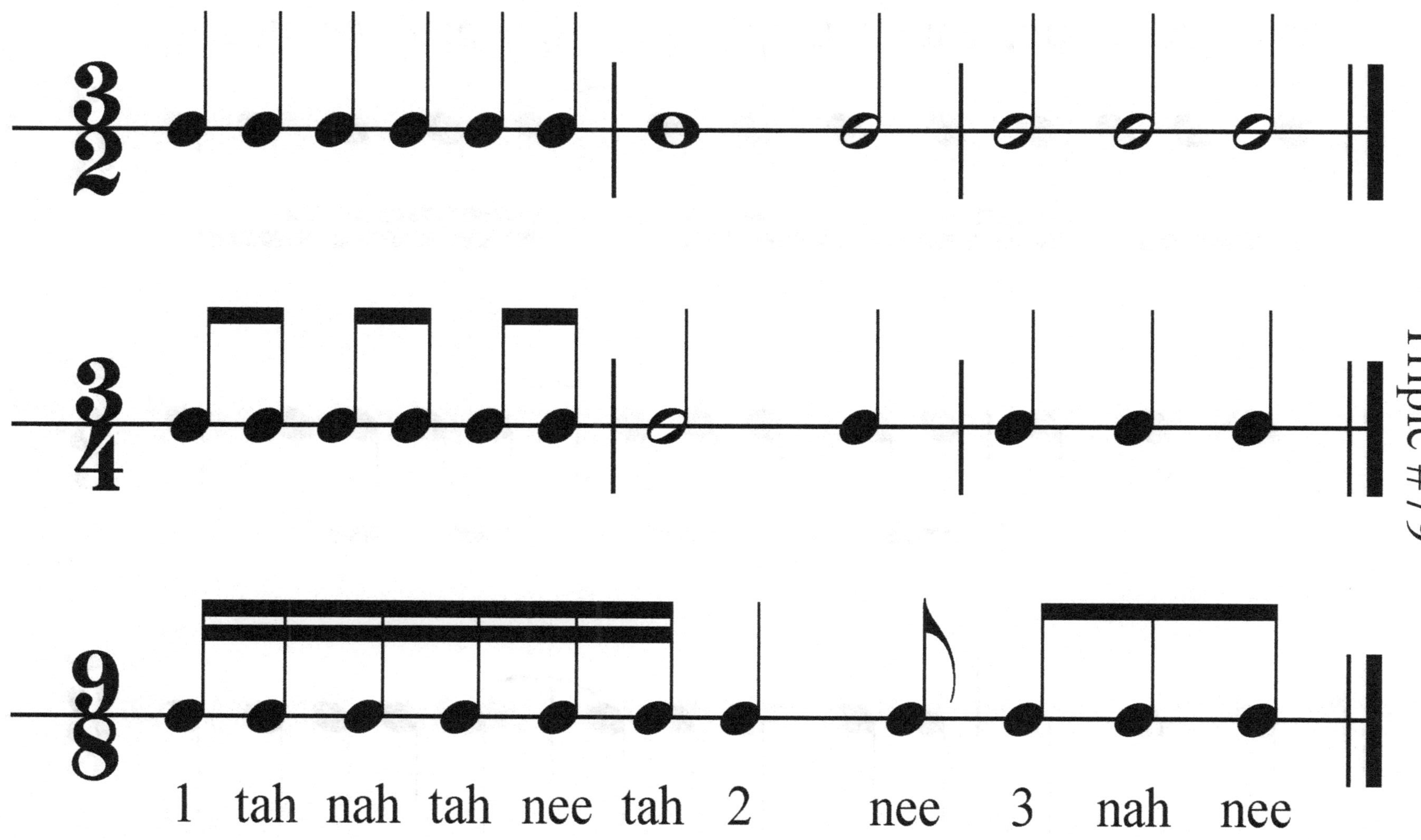
1 tah nah tah nee tah 2 nee 3 nah nee

Triple #80

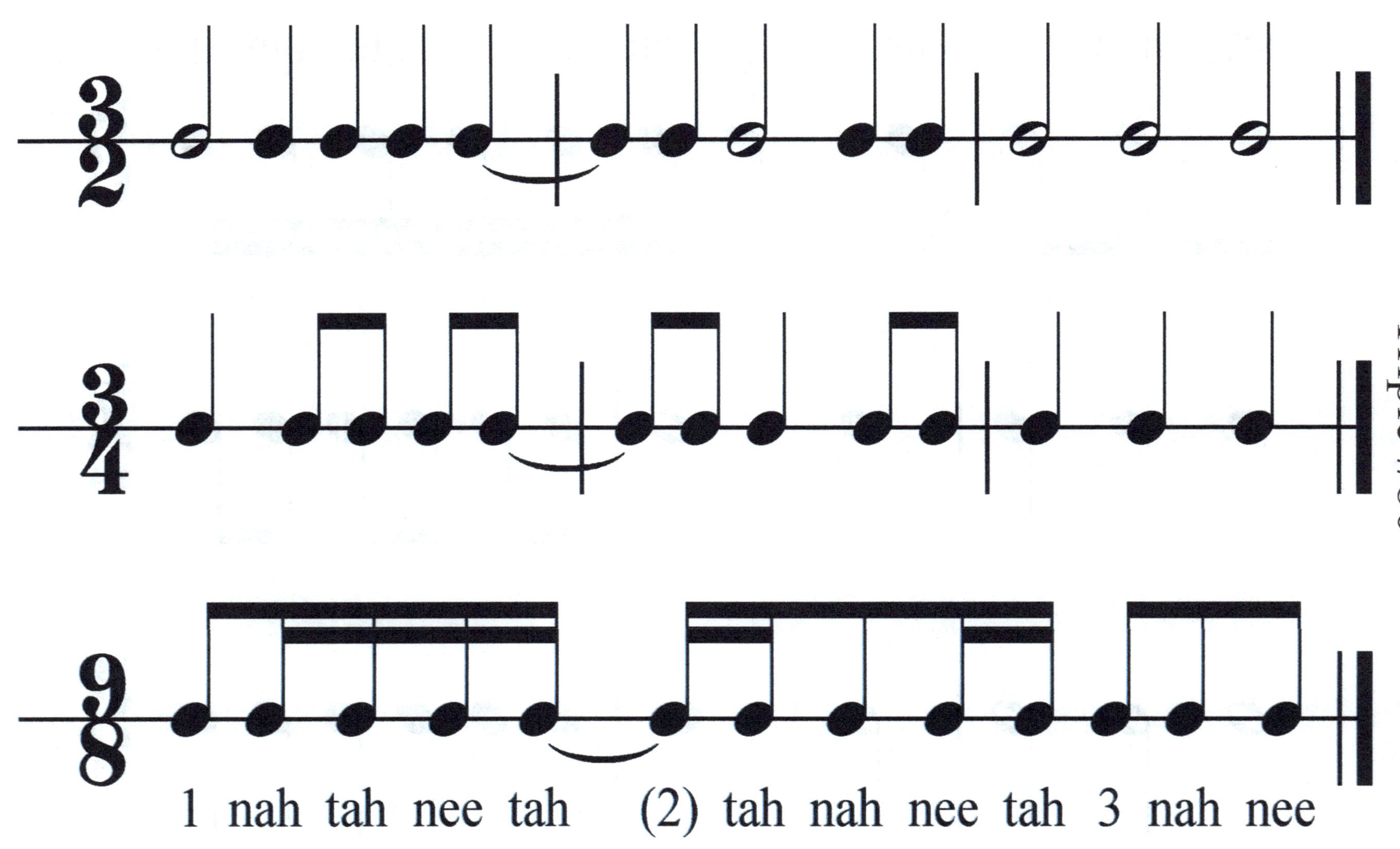
1 nah tah nee tah (2) tah nah nee tah 3 nah nee

Triple #81

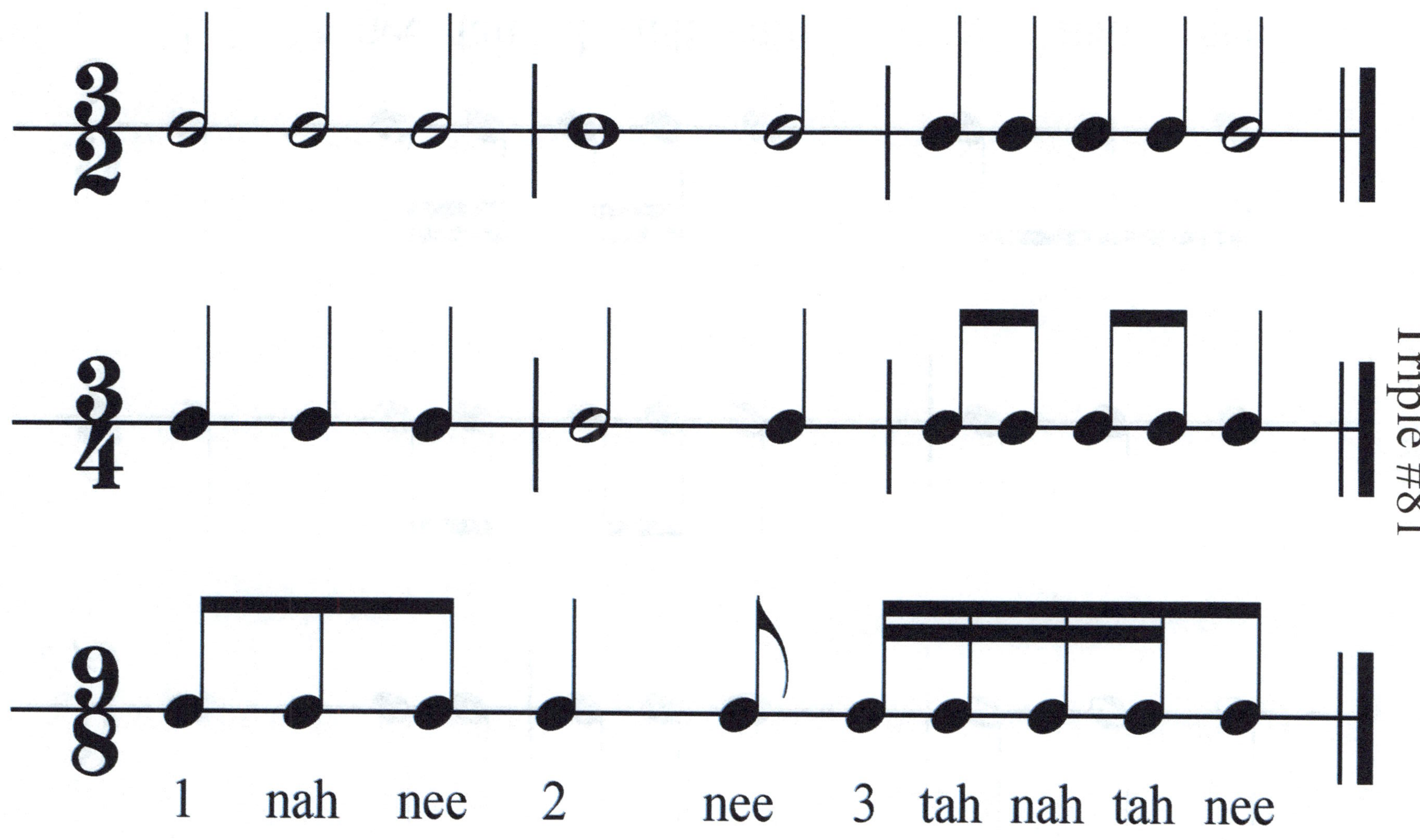
3/2
3/4
9/8
1 nah nee 2 nee 3 tah nah tah nee

Triple #82

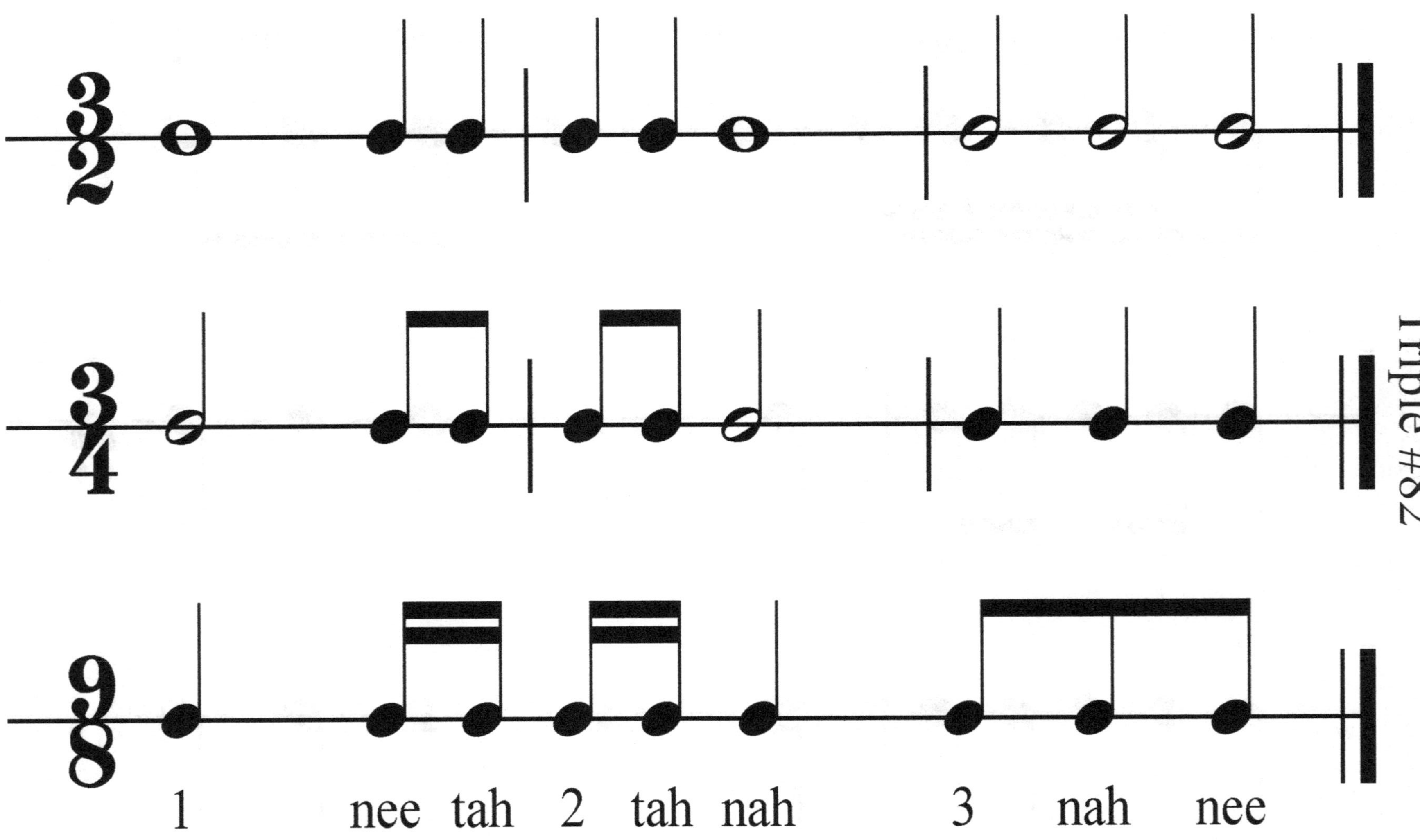
1 nee tah 2 tah nah 3 nah nee

Triple #83

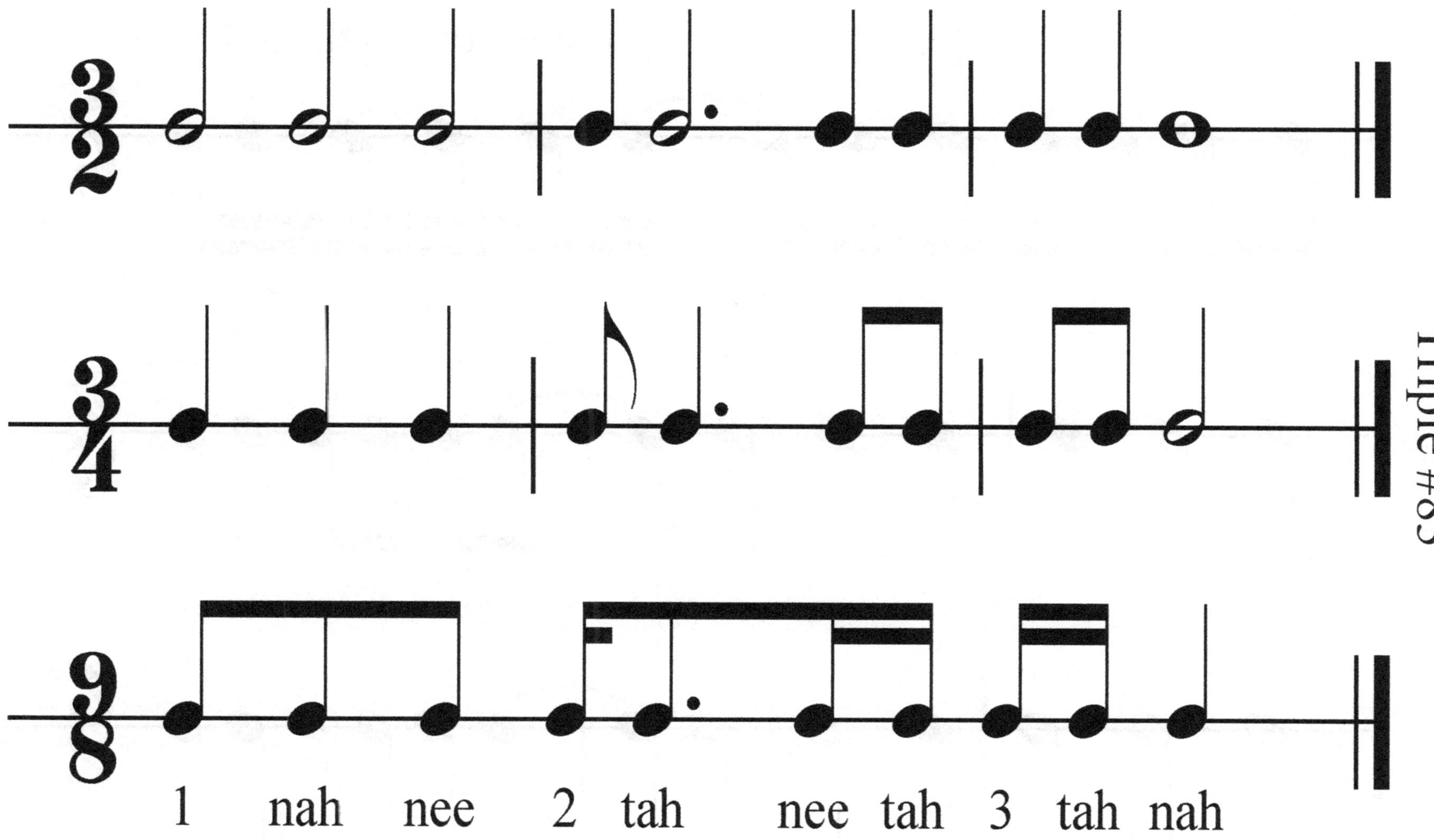
1 nah nee 2 tah nee tah 3 tah nah

Triple #84

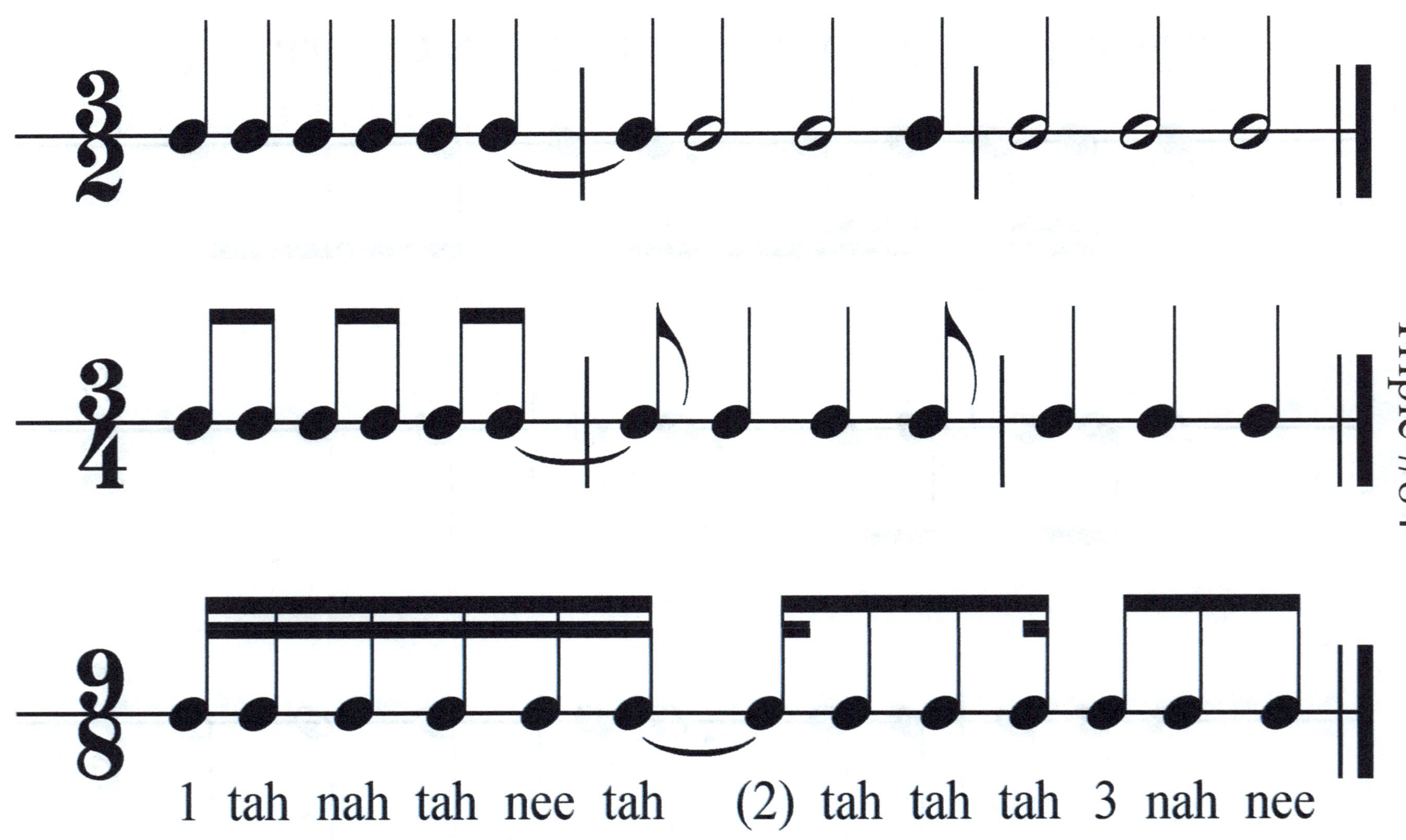
1 tah nah tah nee tah (2) tah tah tah tah 3 nah nee

Triple #85

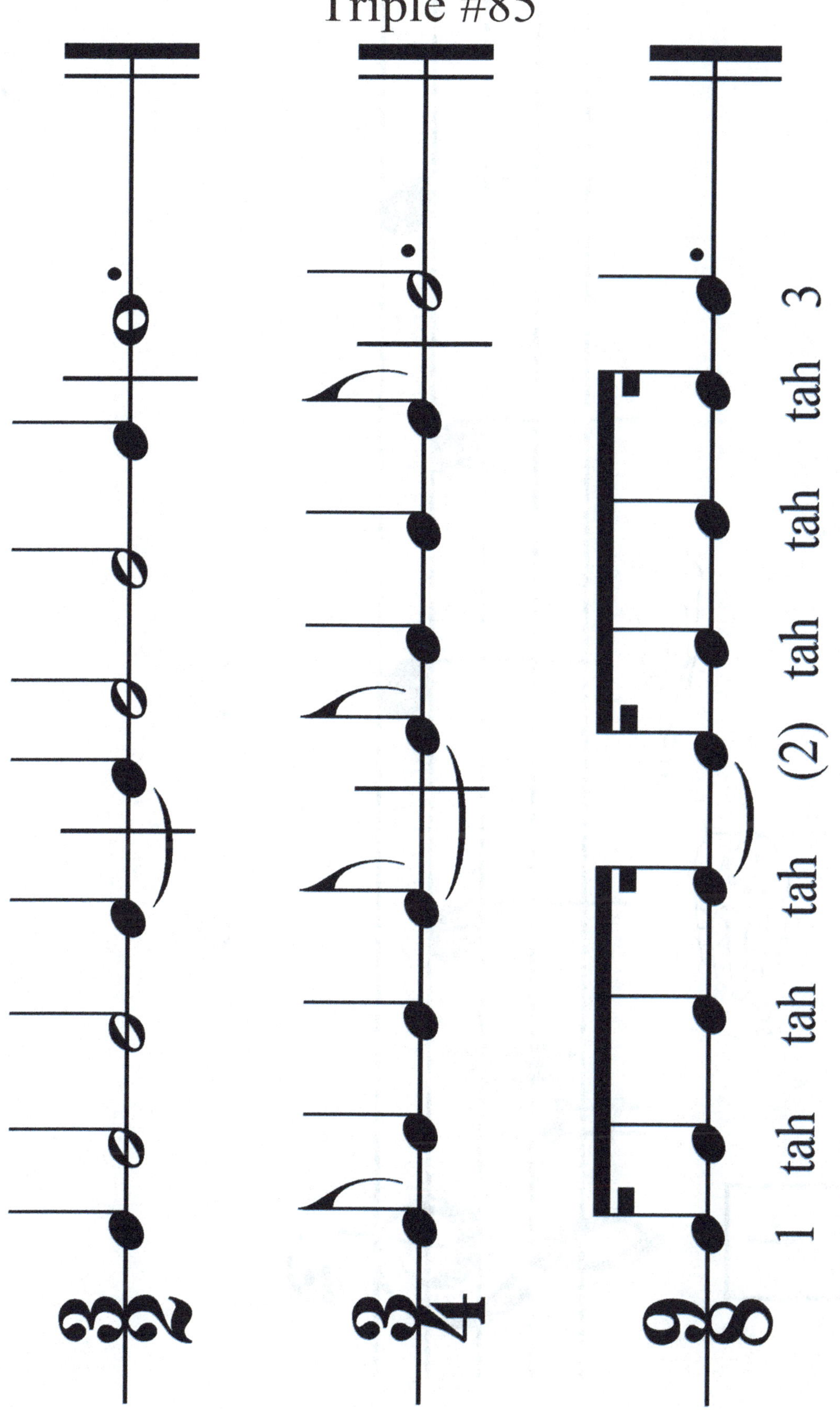

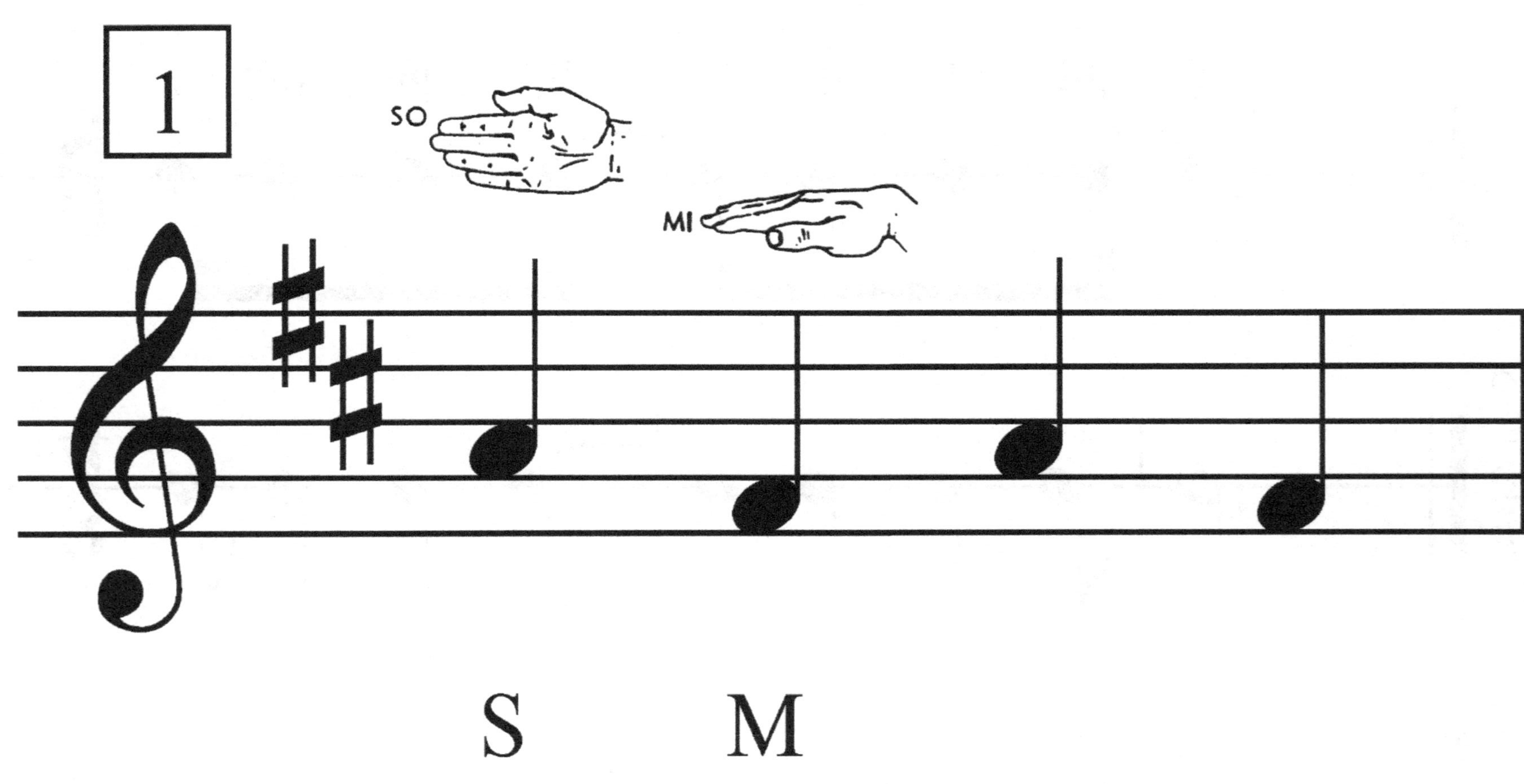

S-M

S-M

S-M

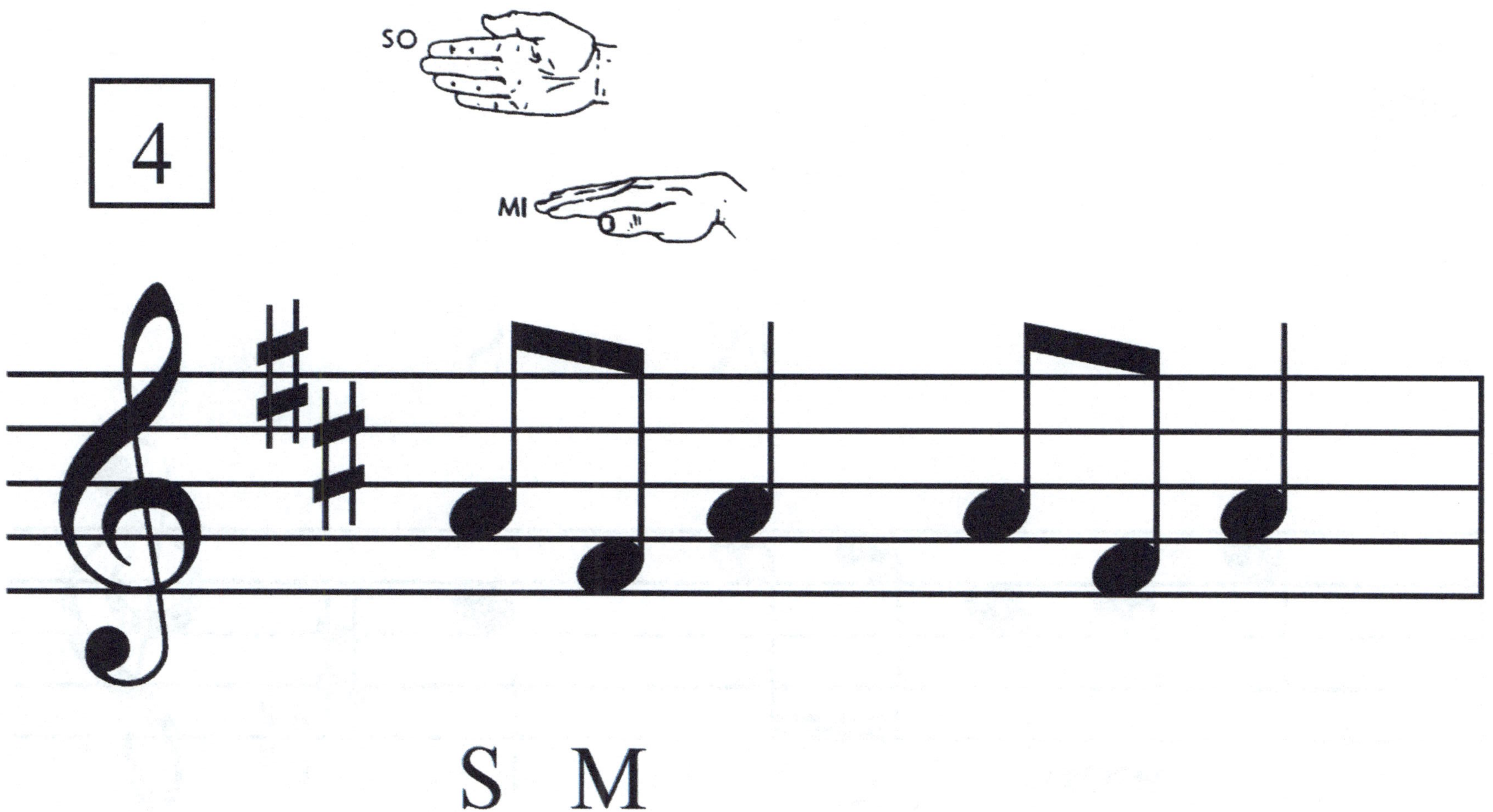

S-M

S M

S-M

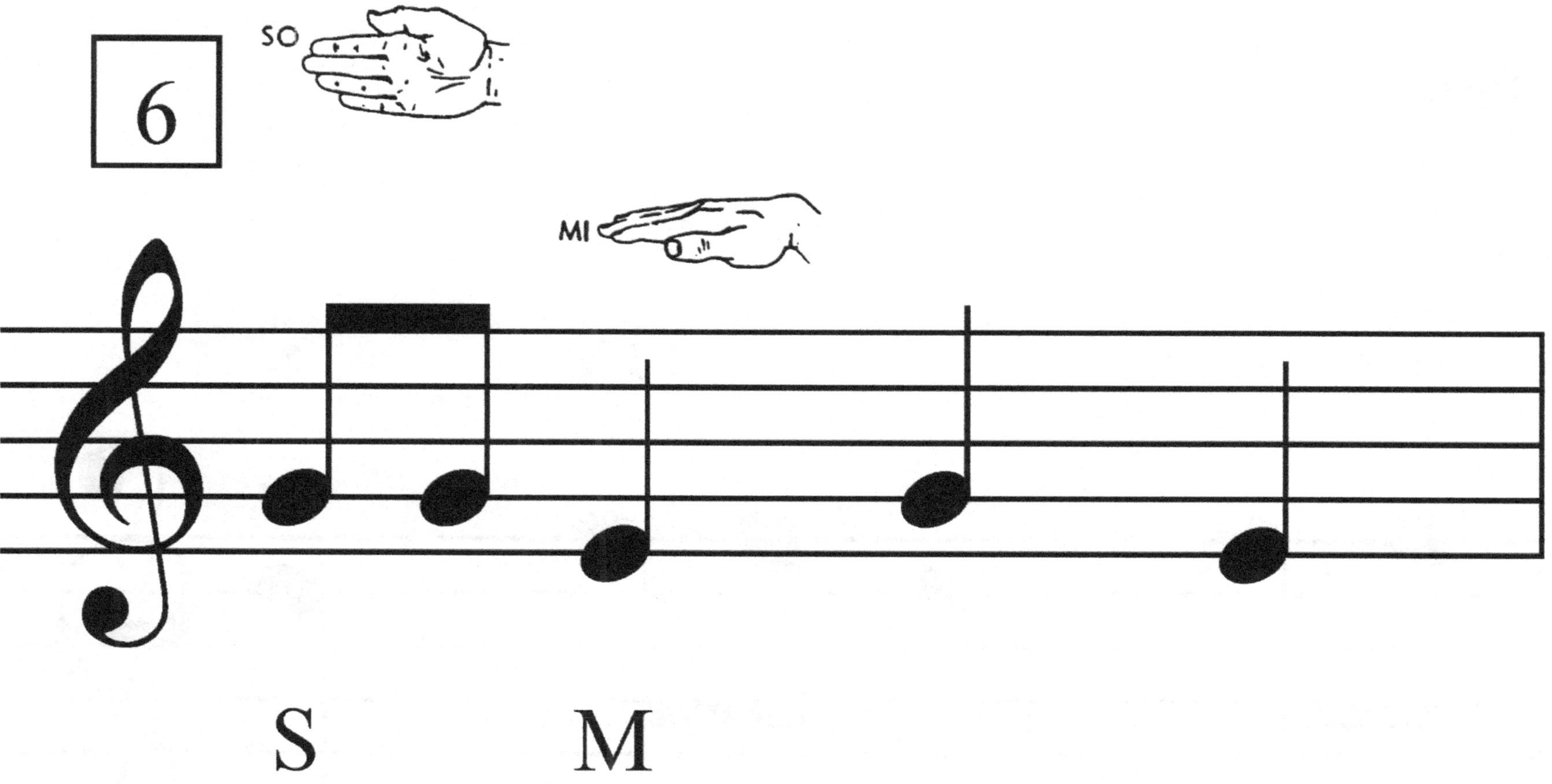

S-M

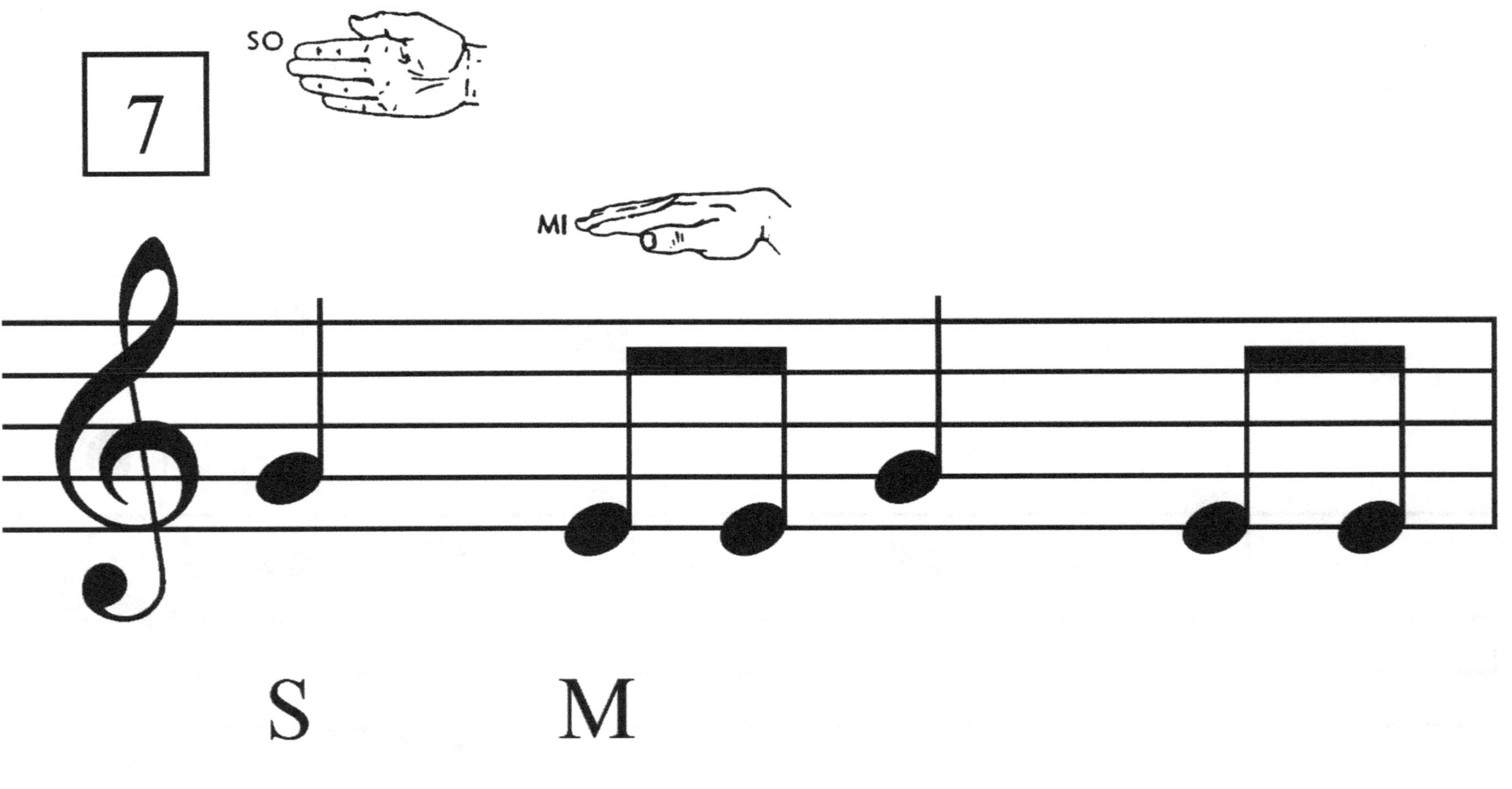

S-M

S-M

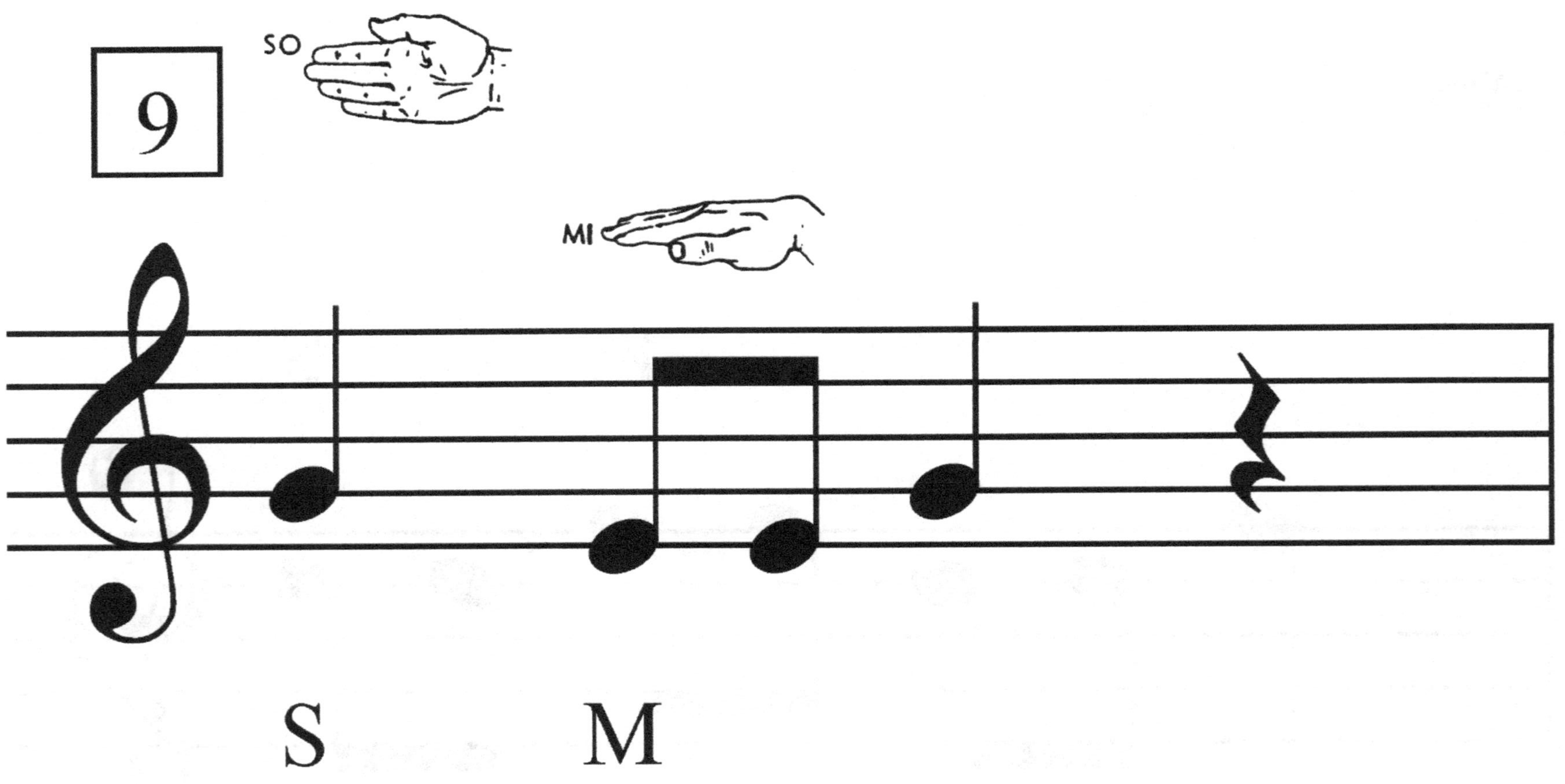

S-M

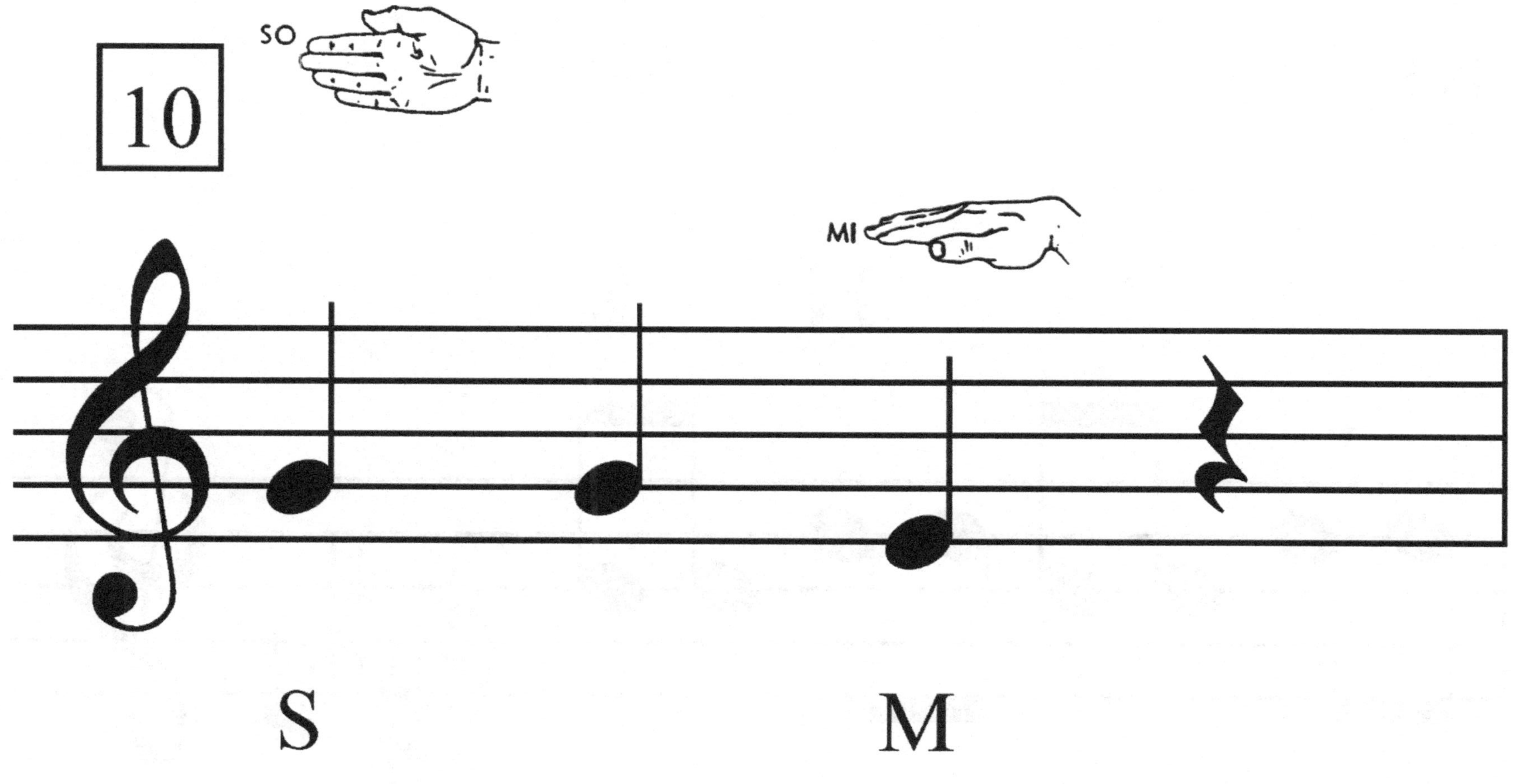

S-M

S-M

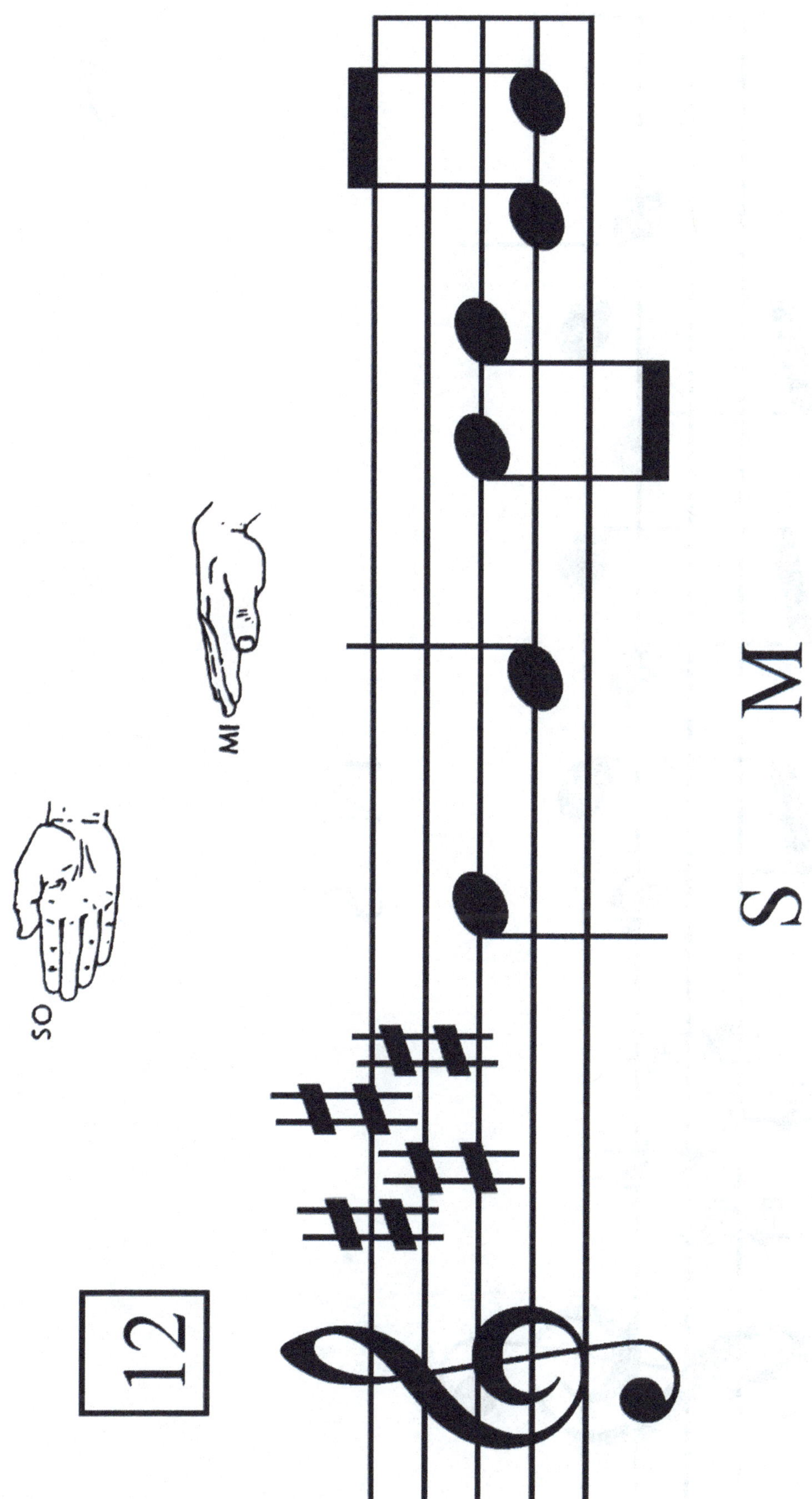

S-M

13

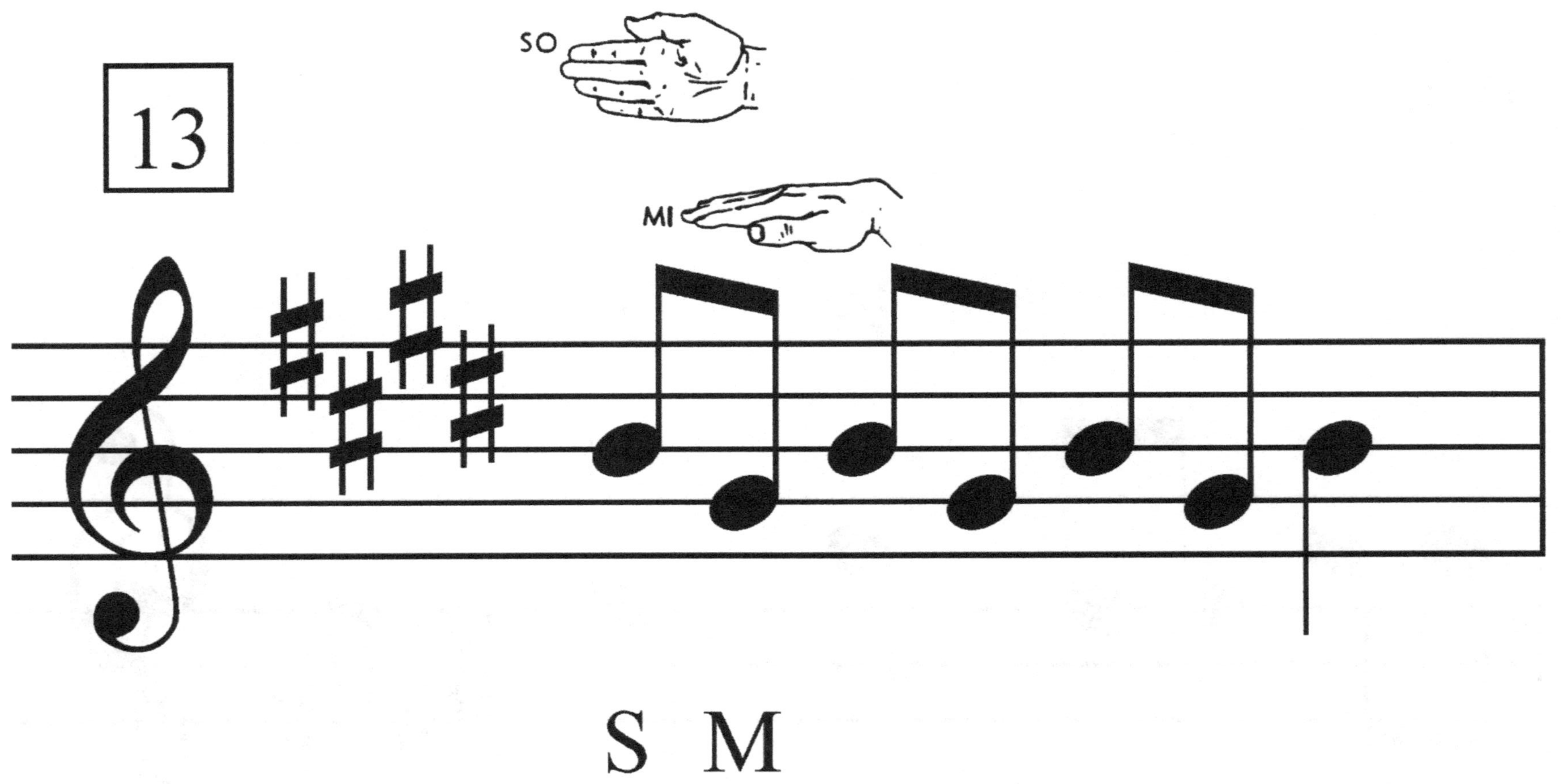

S M

S-M

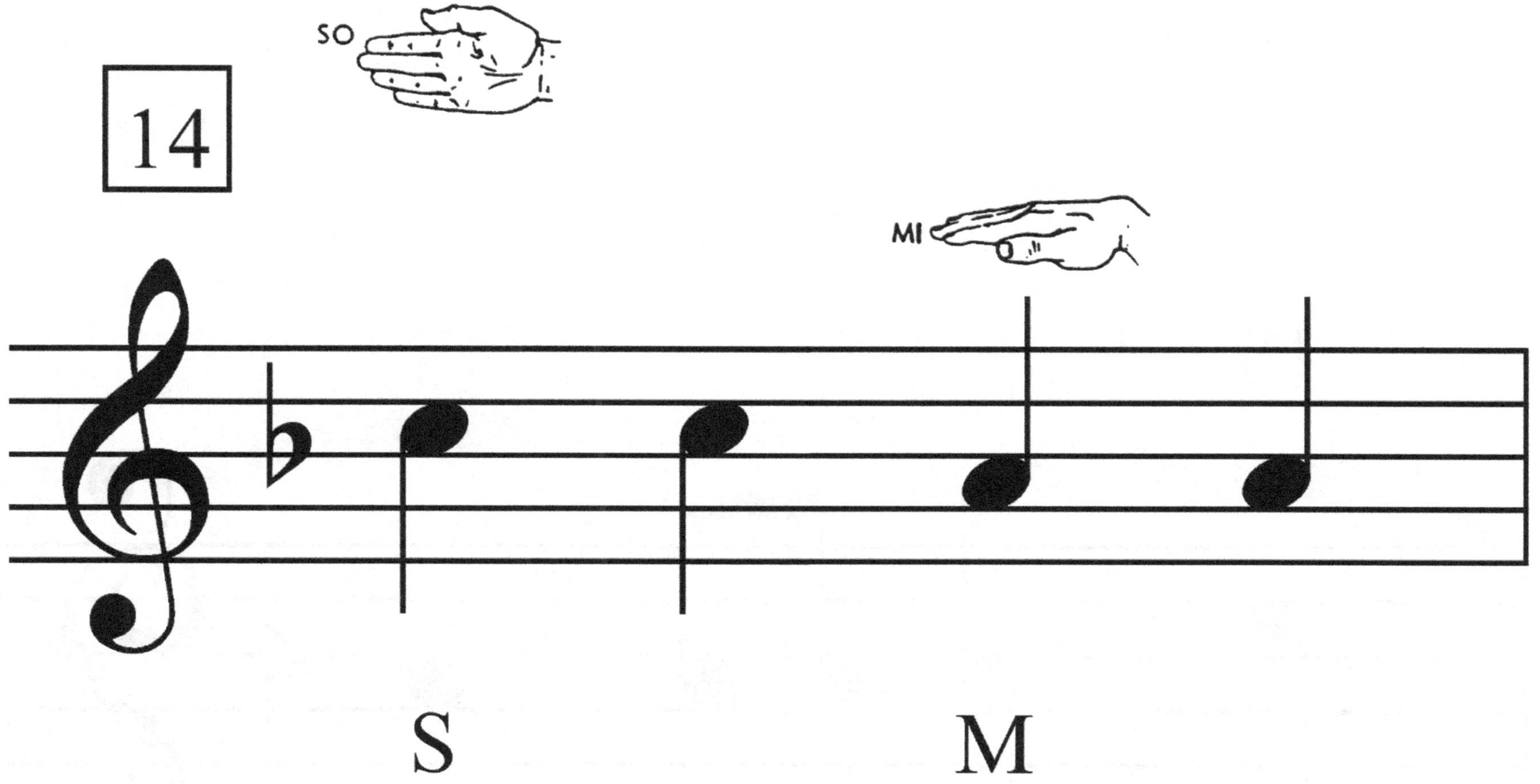

S-M

S-M

16

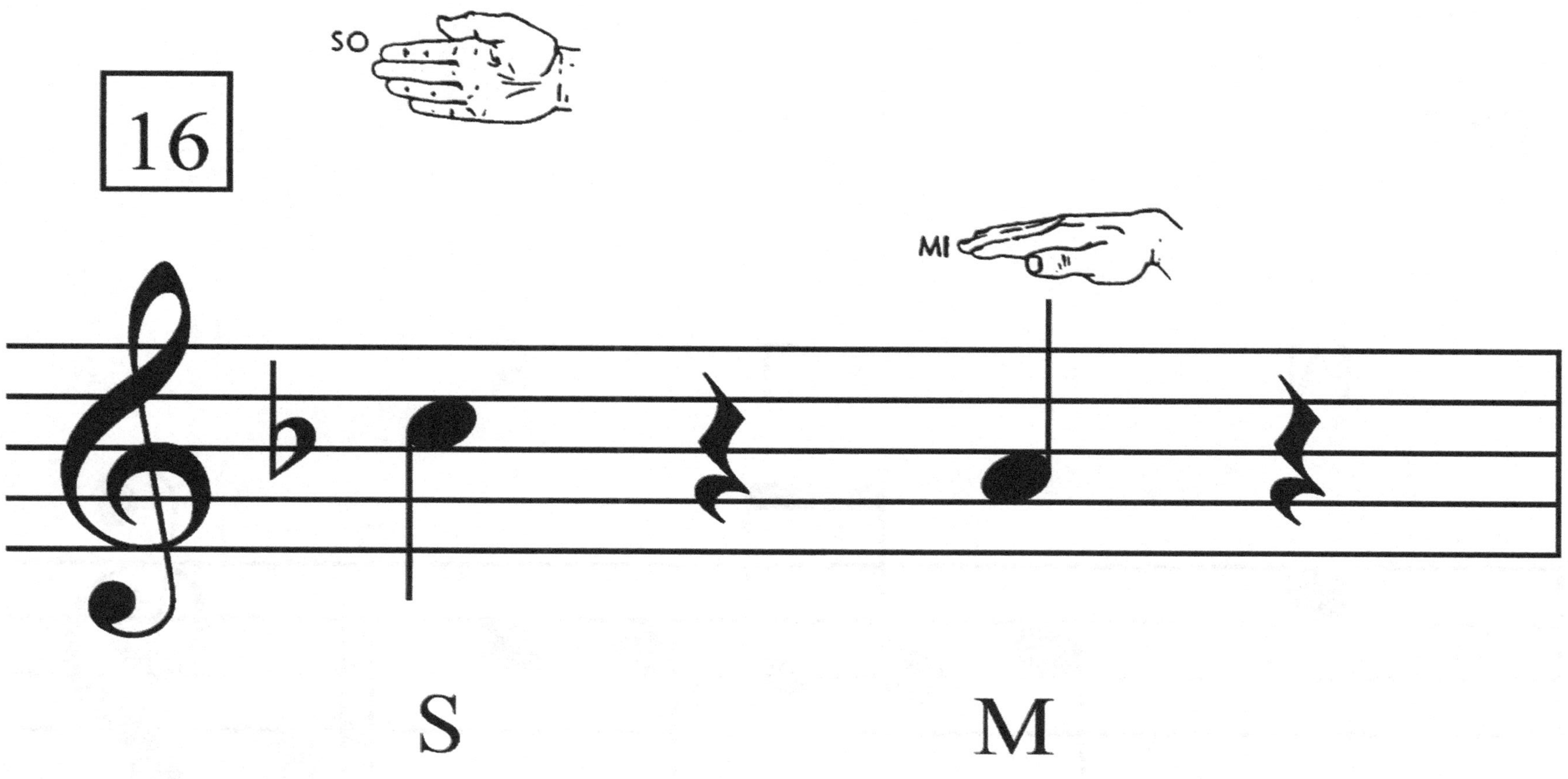

S M

S-M

17

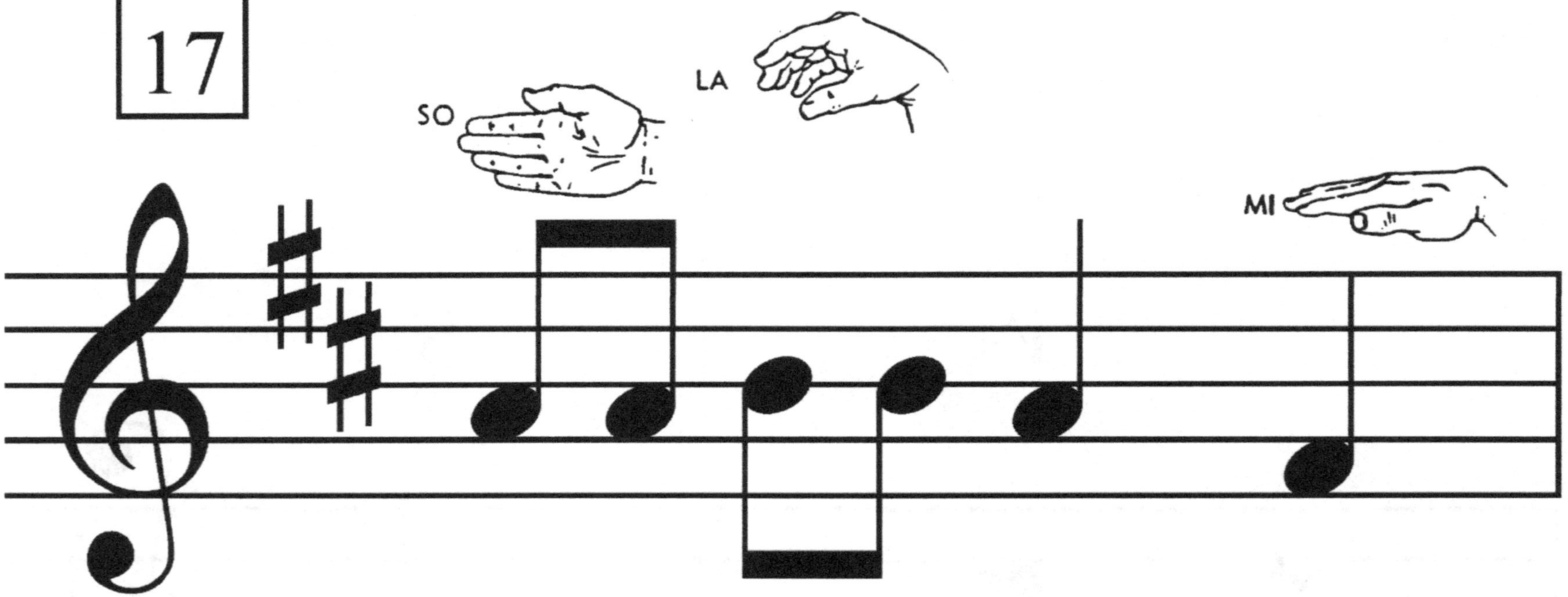

SO
LA
MI

S L M

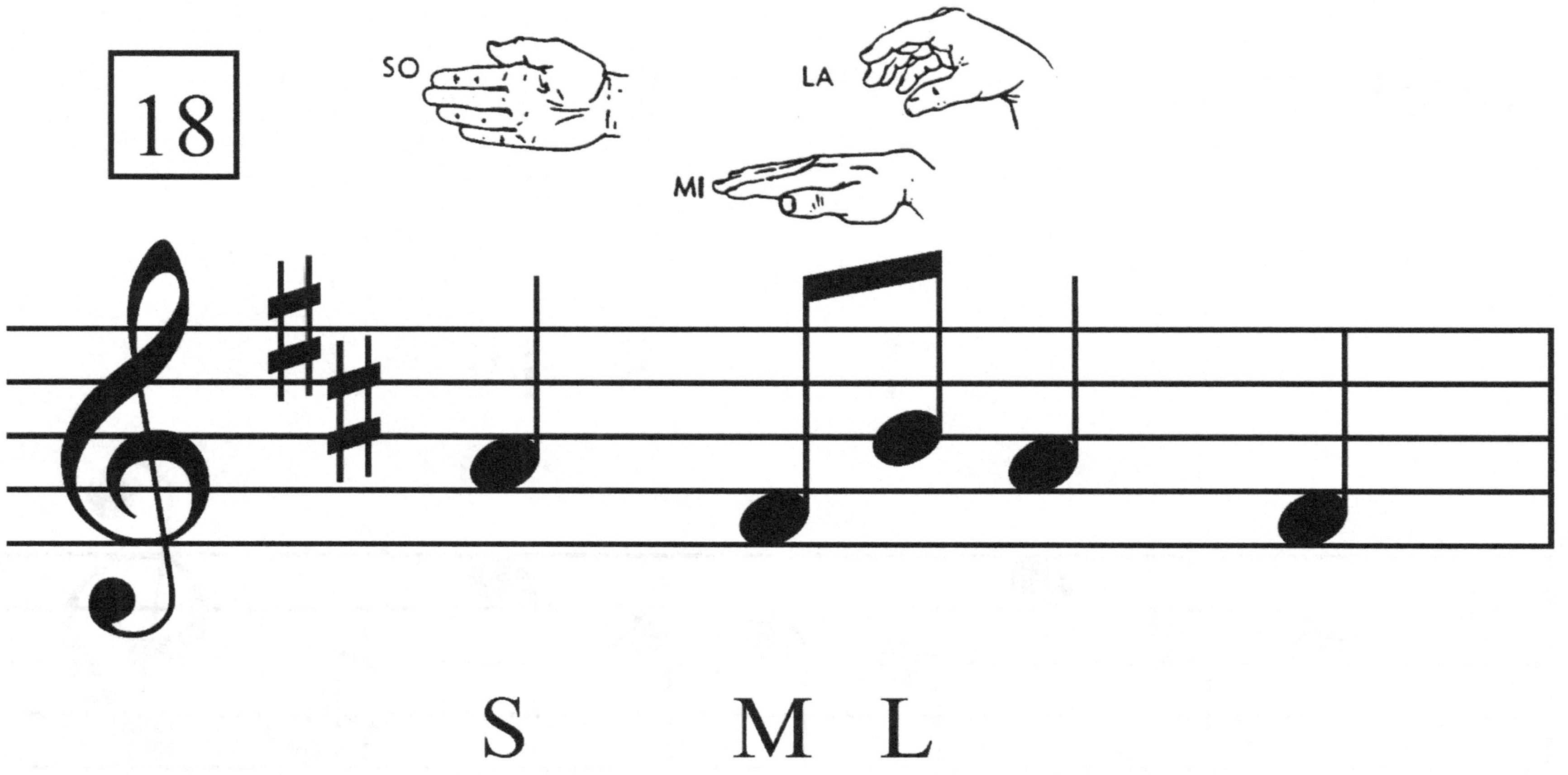

L-S-M

L-S-M

20

SO

LA

MI

S L M

21

S L M

L-S-M

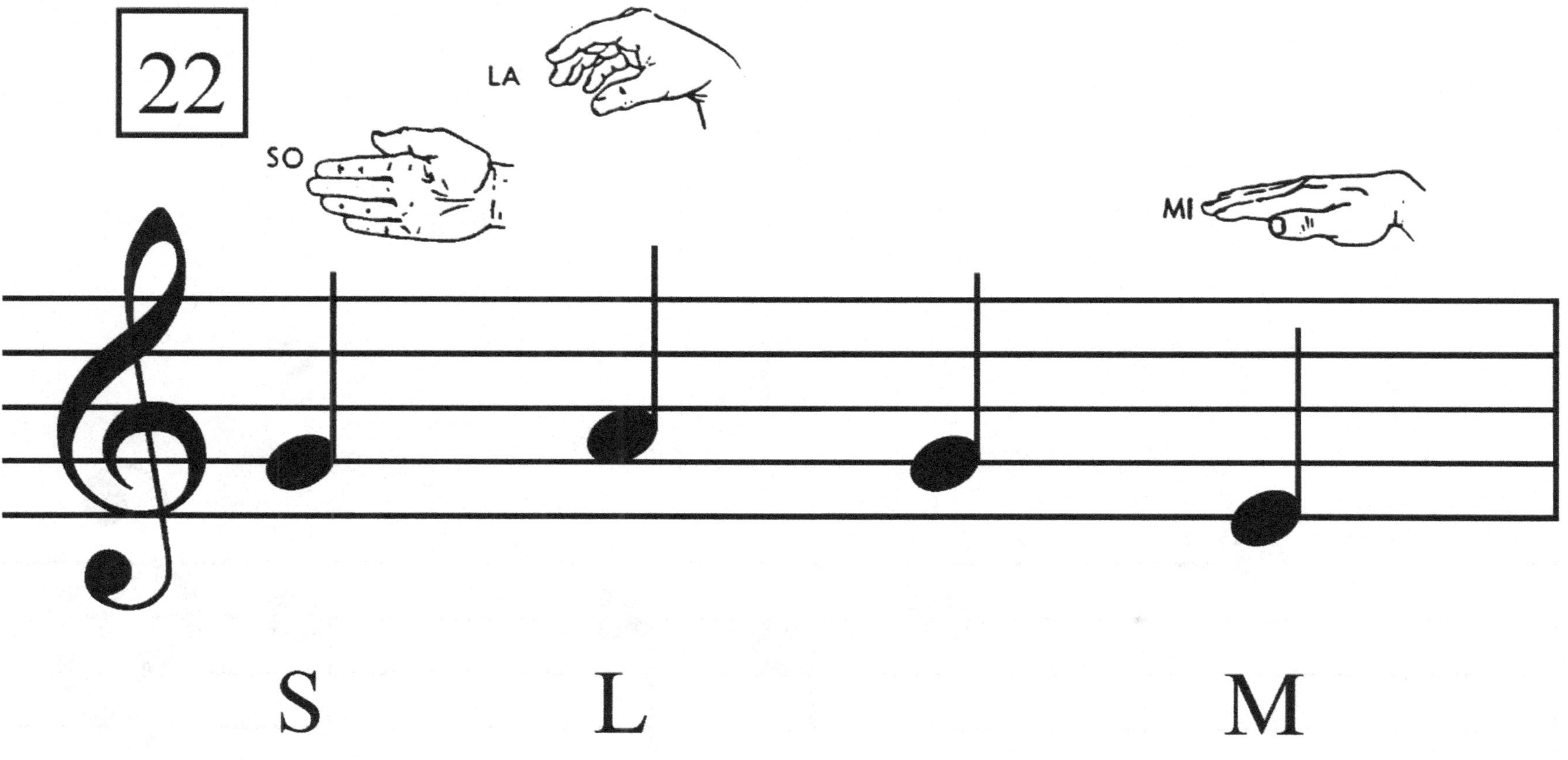

L-S-M

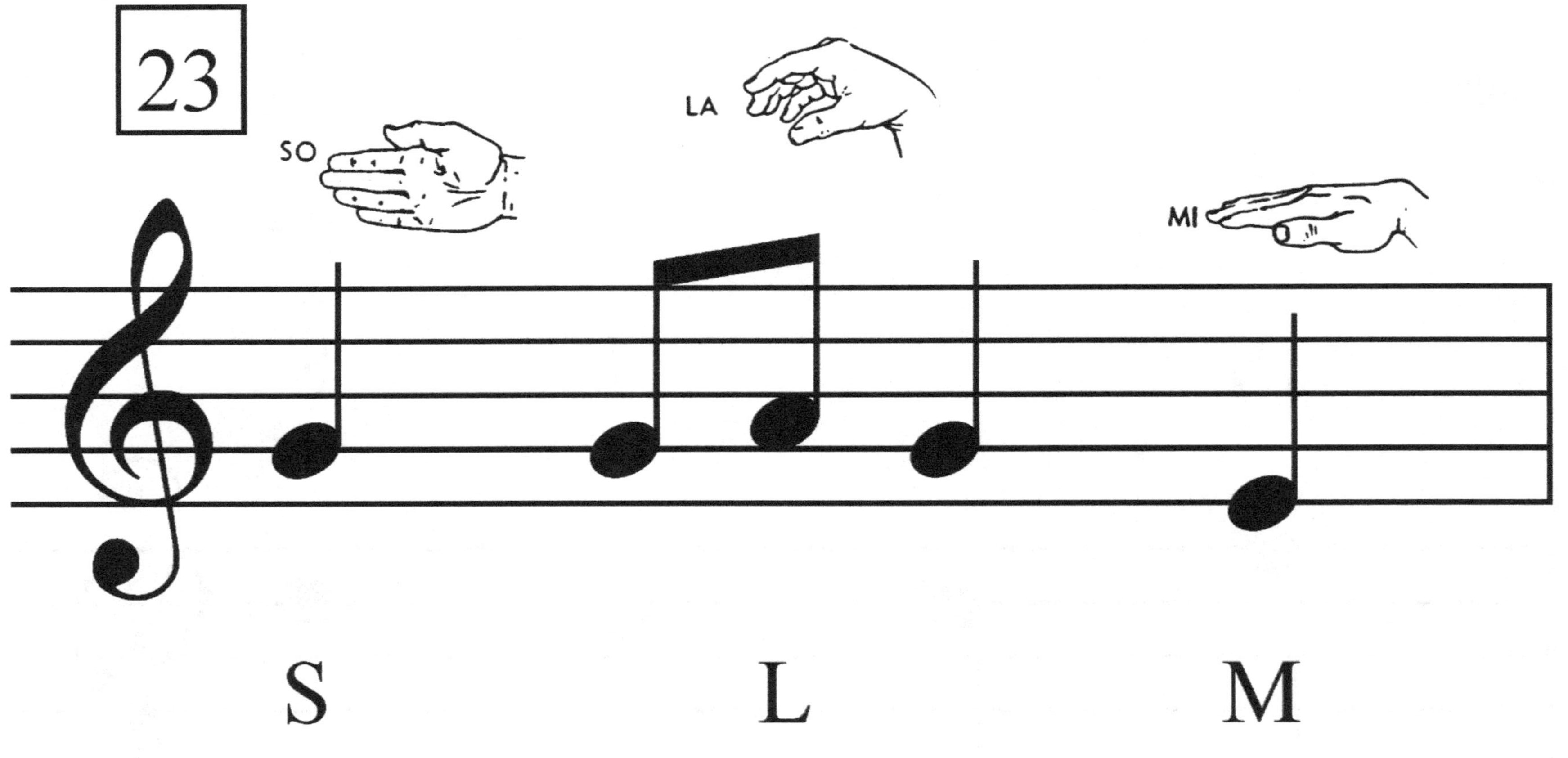

L-S-M

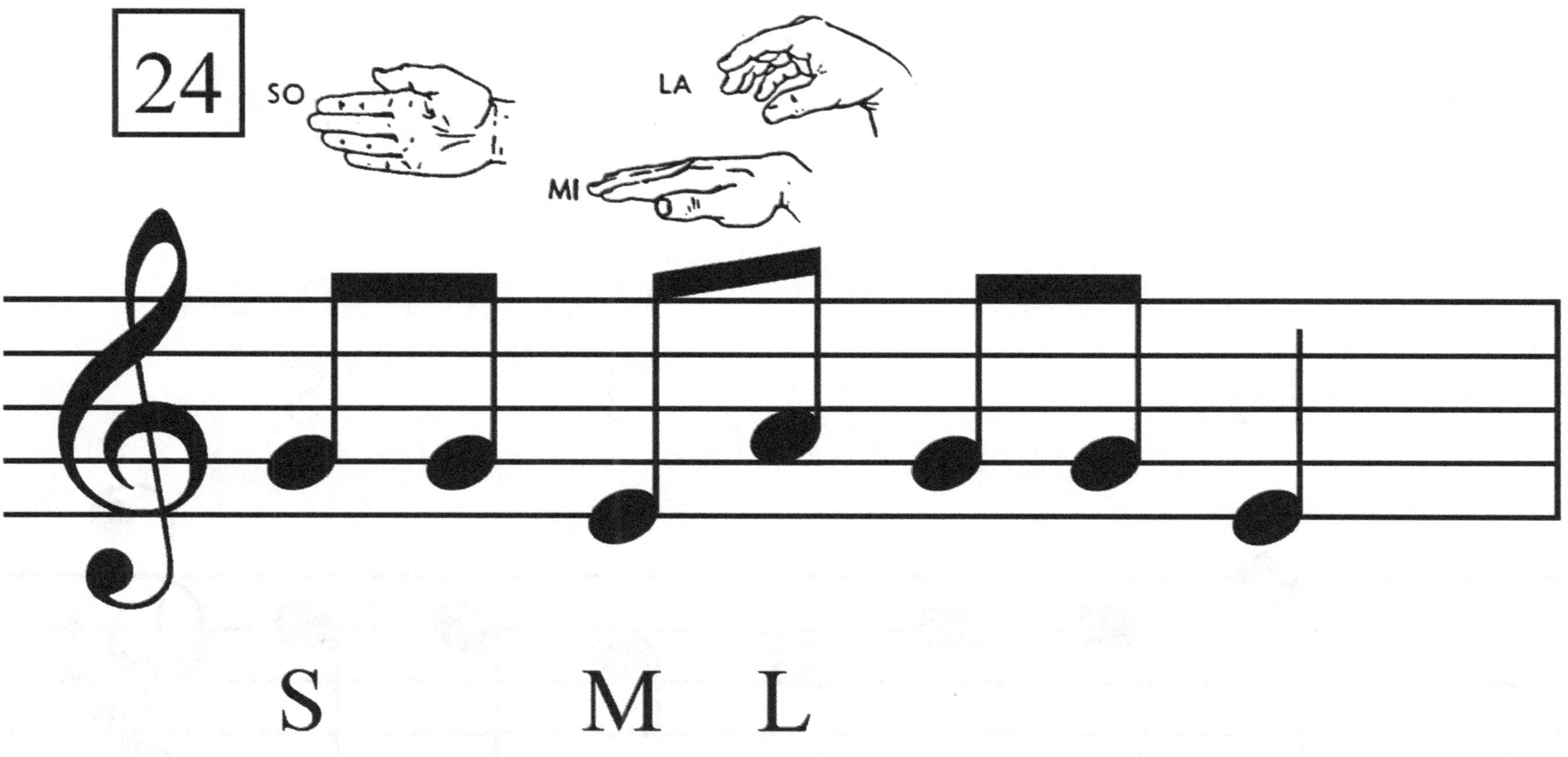

L-S-M

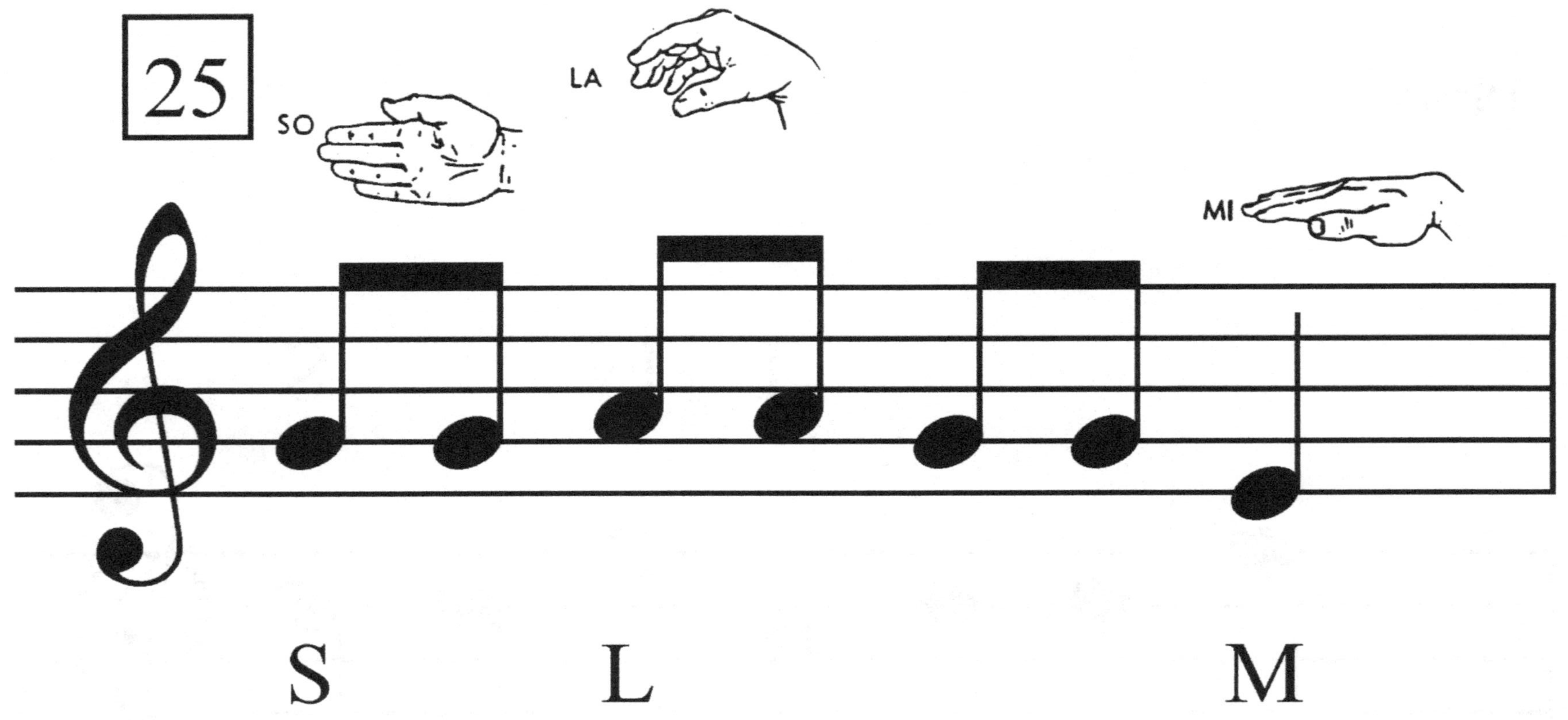

L-S-M

S M L

L-S-M

L-S-M

L-S-M

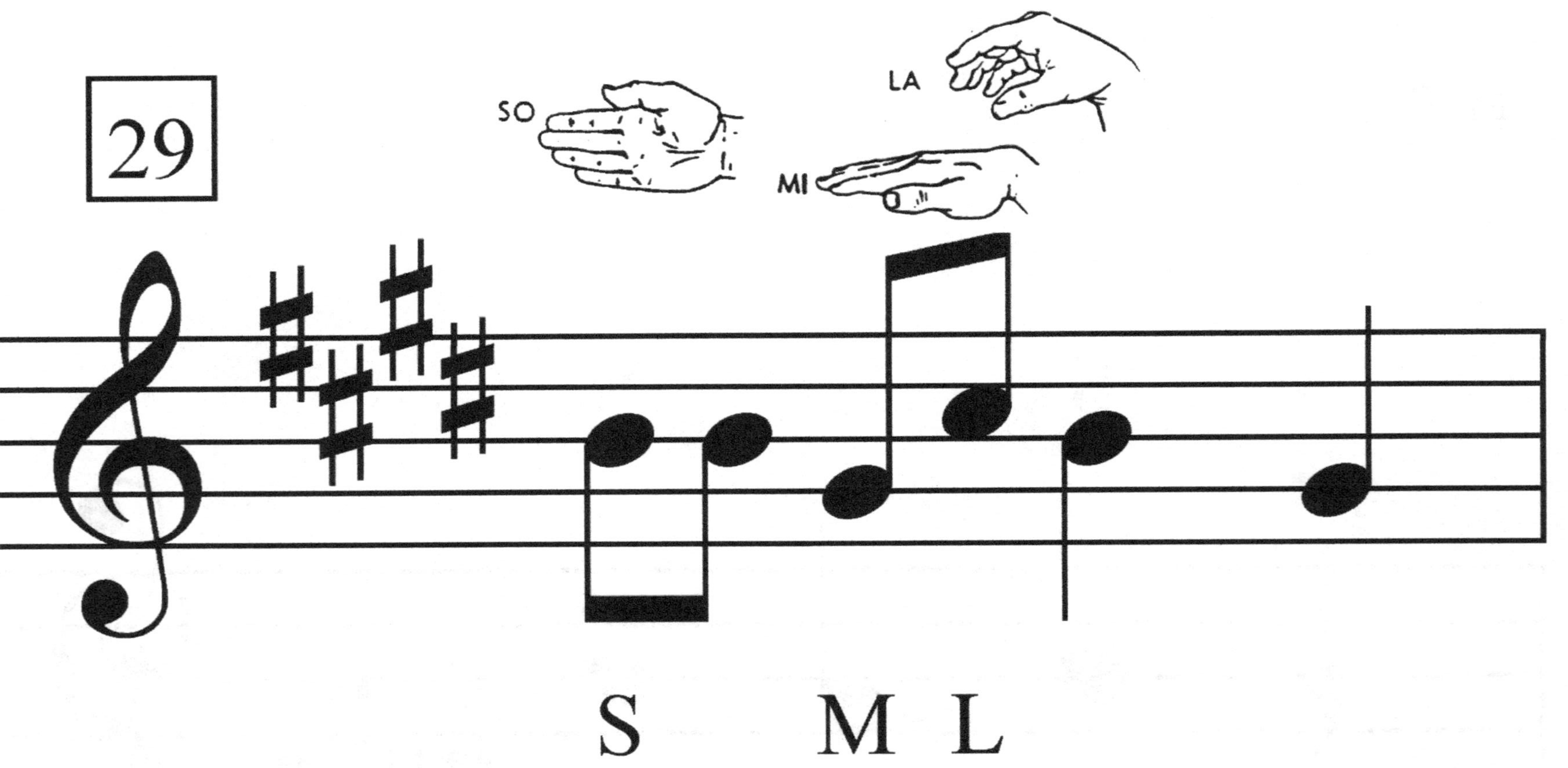

L-S-M

L-S-M

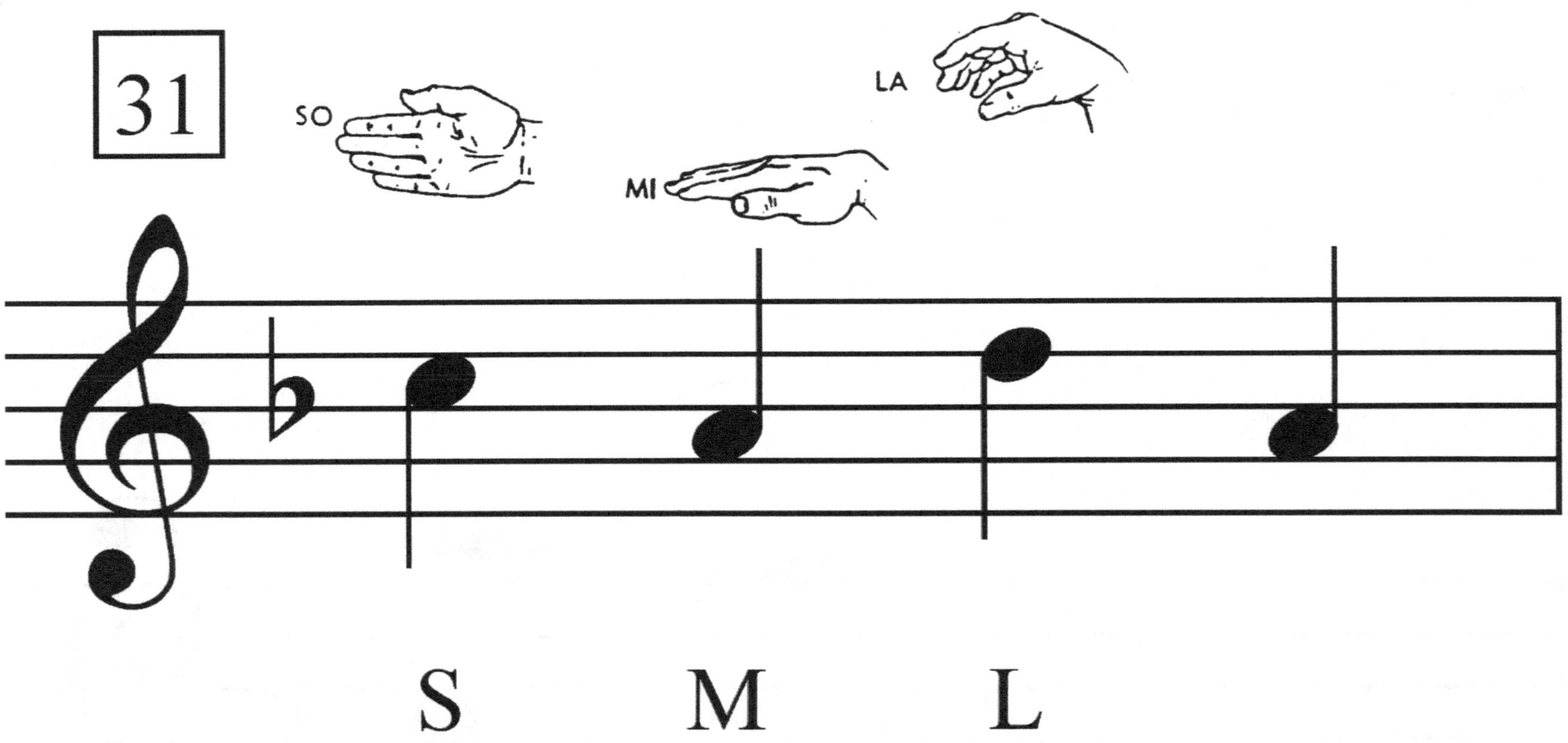

L-S-M

32

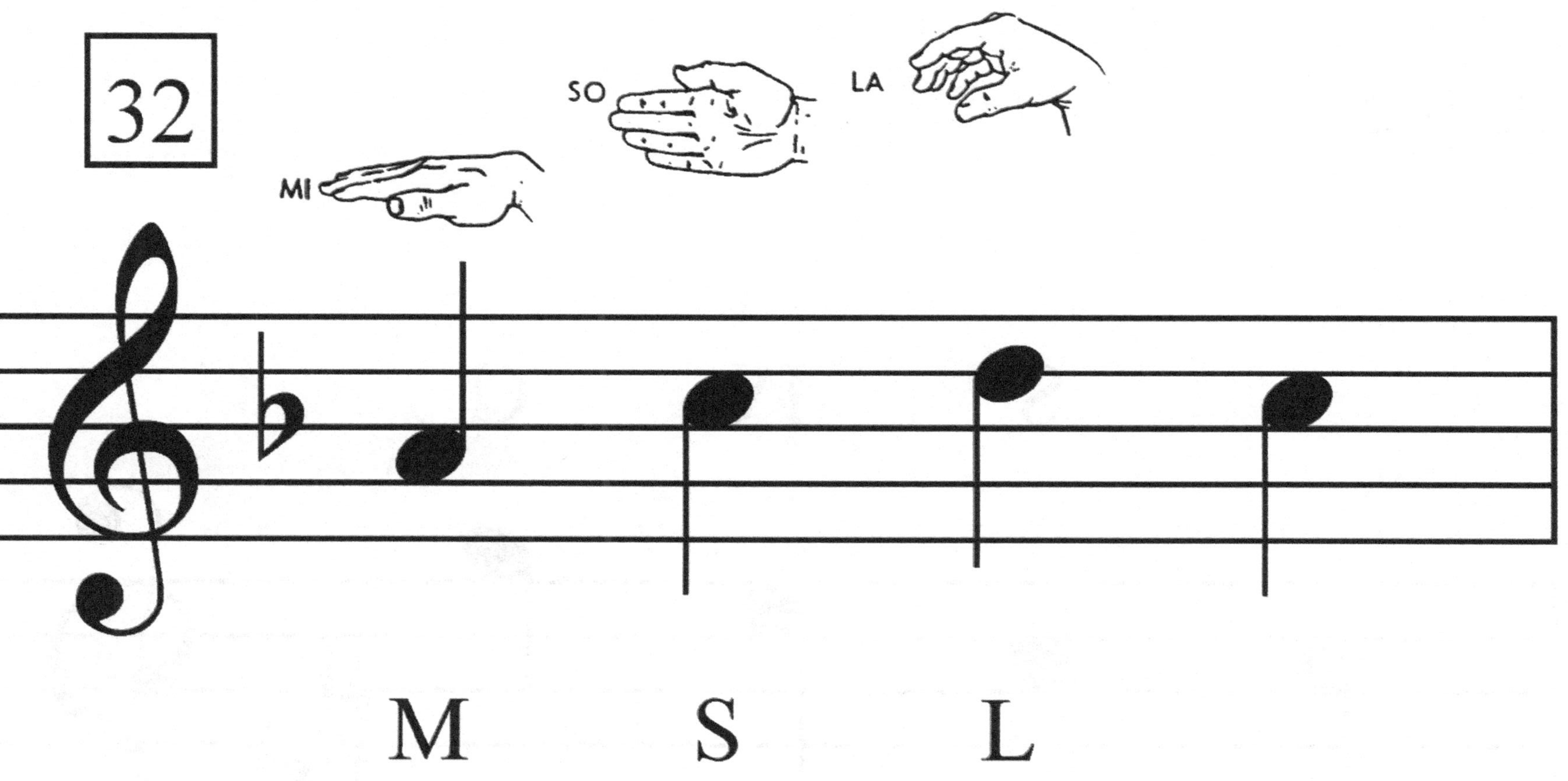

M S L

L-S-M

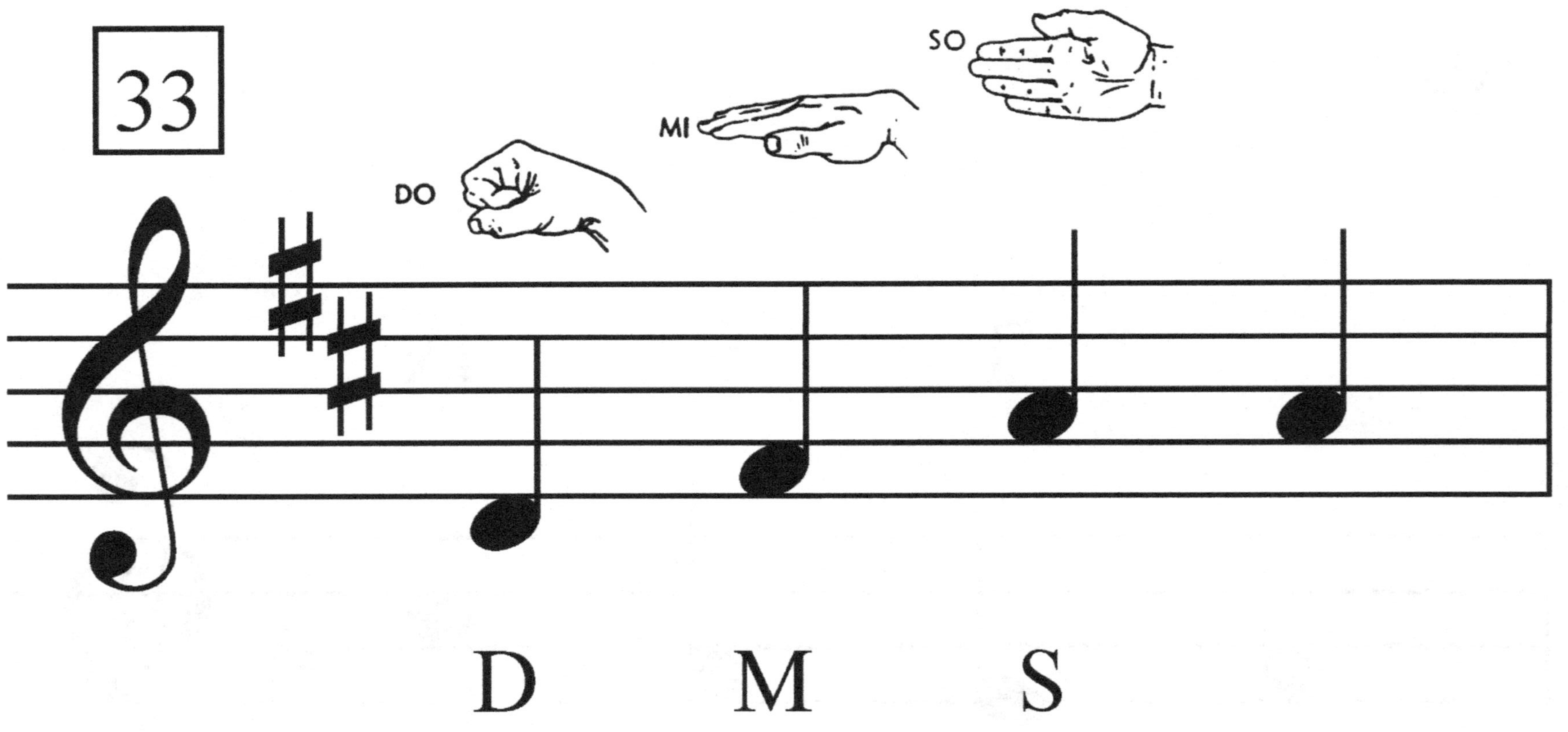

S-M-D

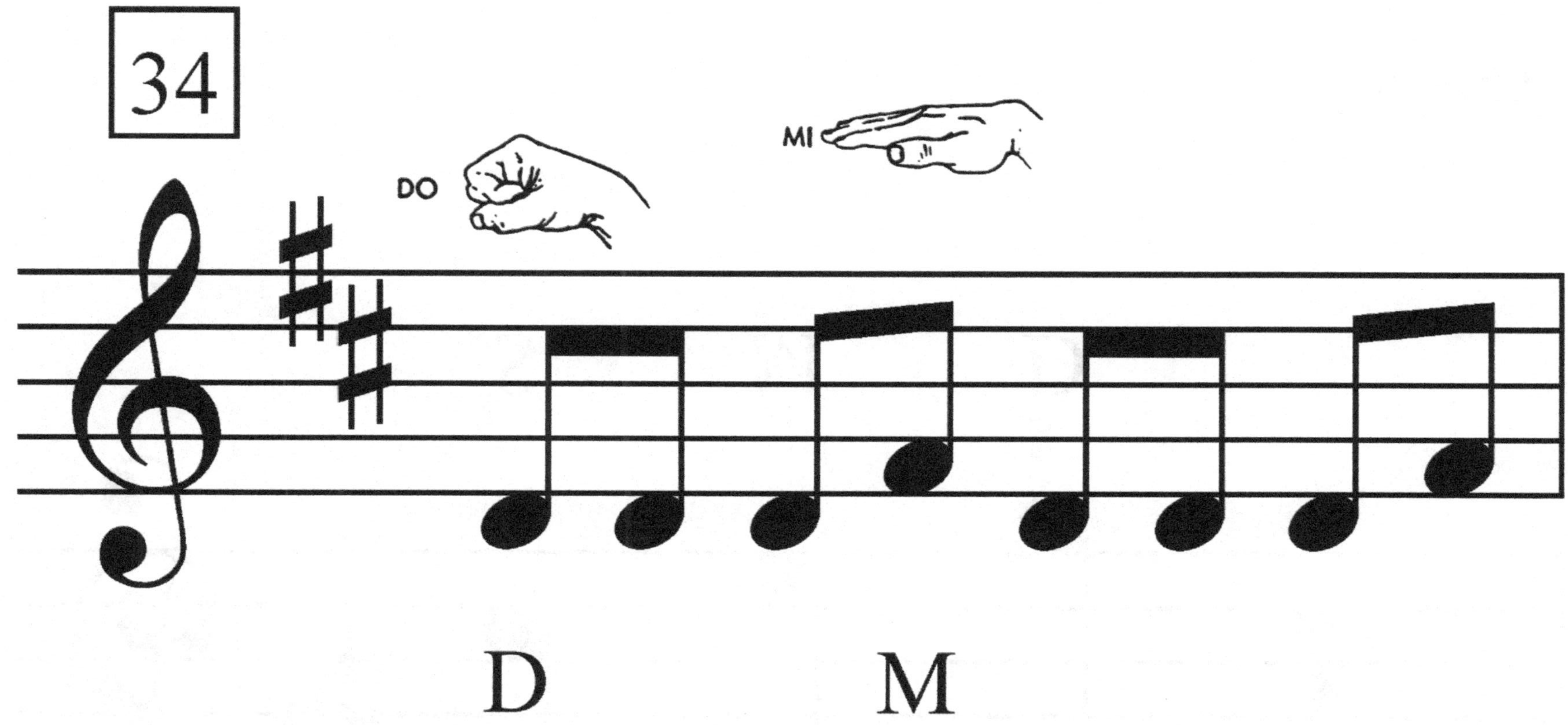

S-M-D

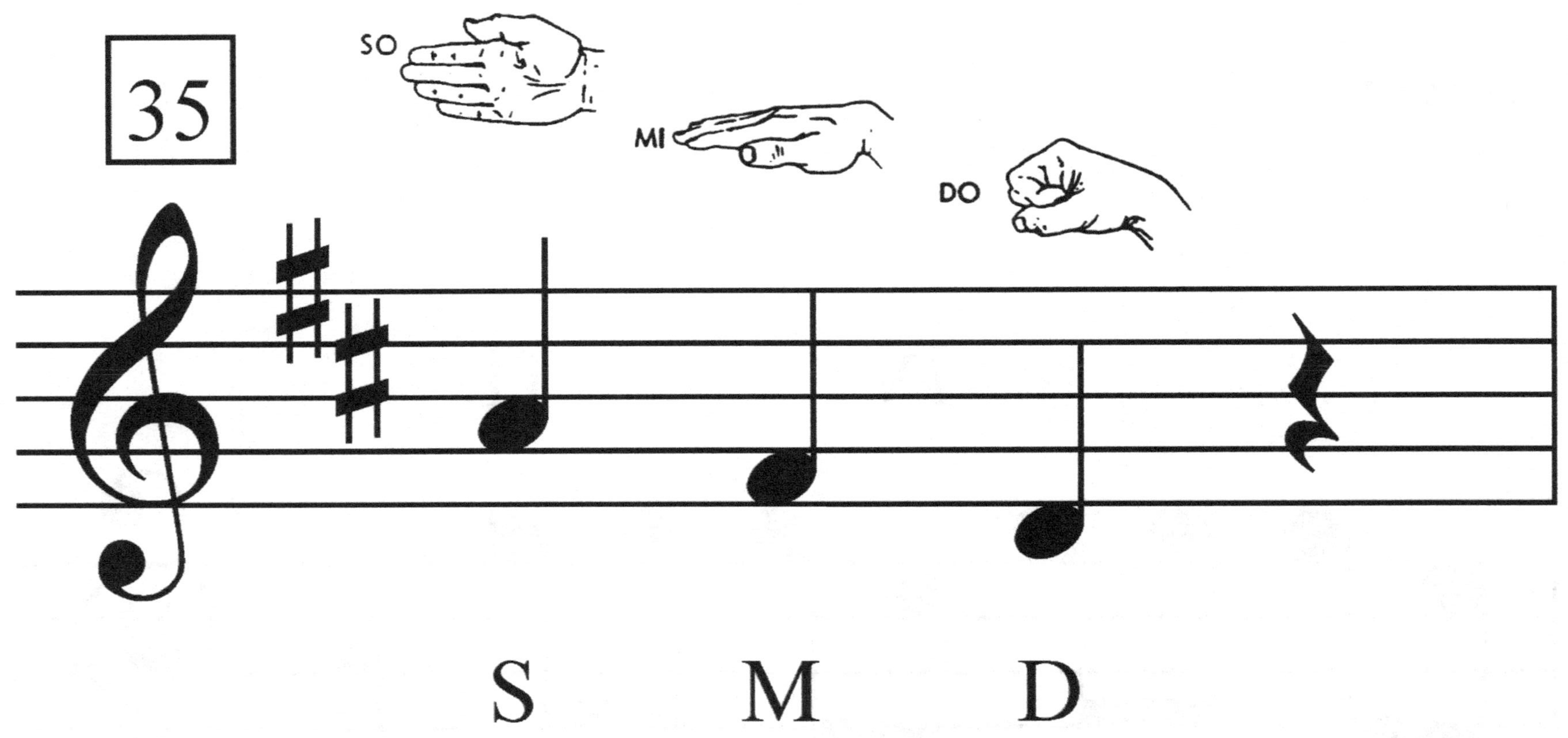
35
SO
MI
DO
S
M
D

S-M-D

S-M-D

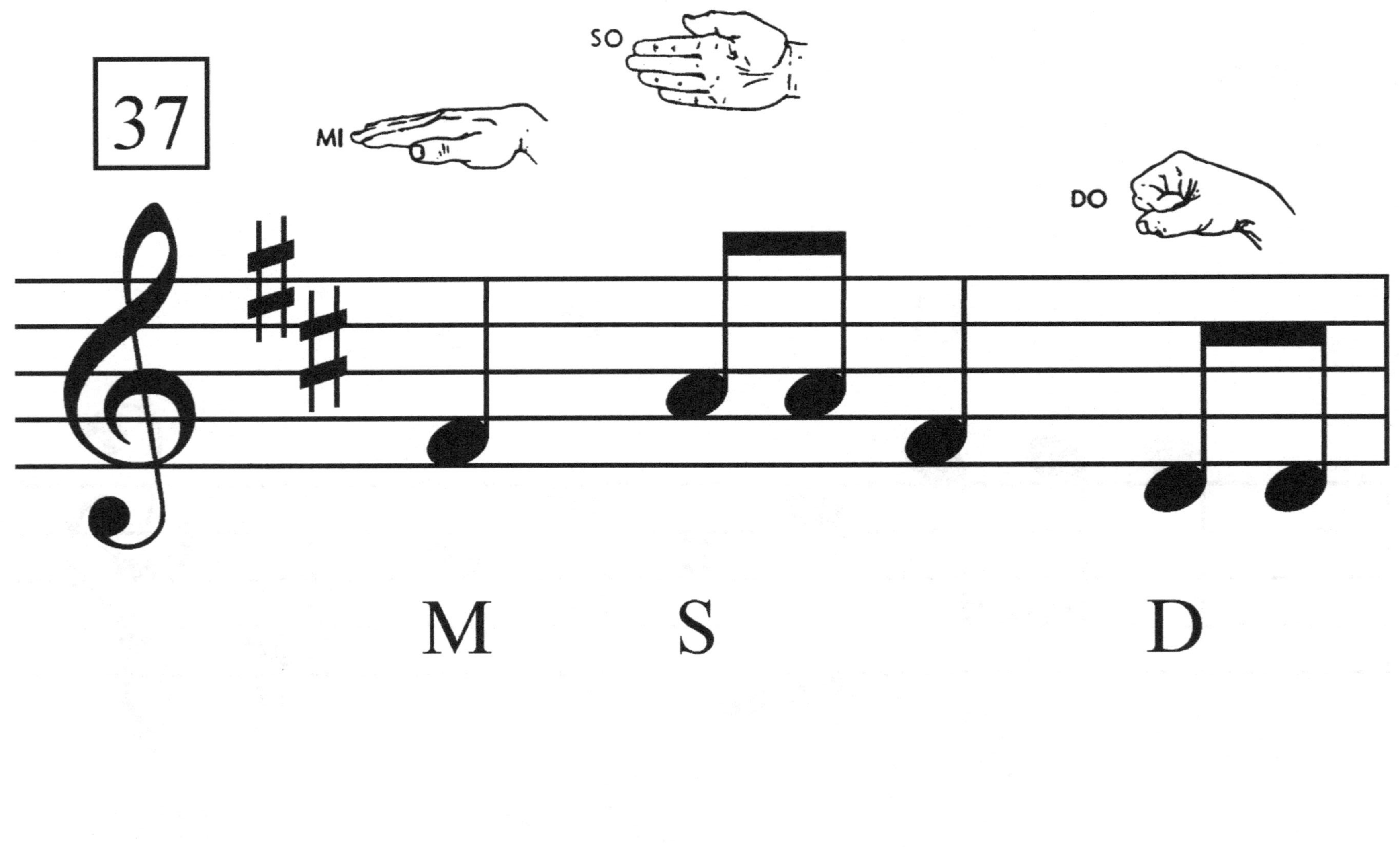

S-M-D

S-M-D

S-M-D

S-M-D

S-M-D

42

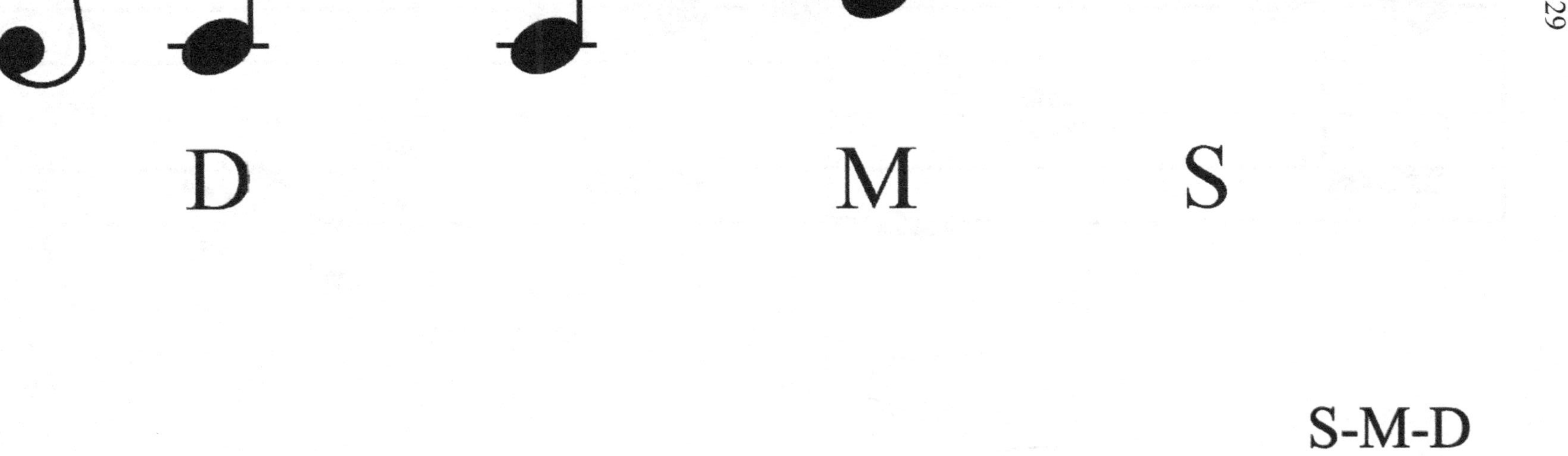

S-M-D

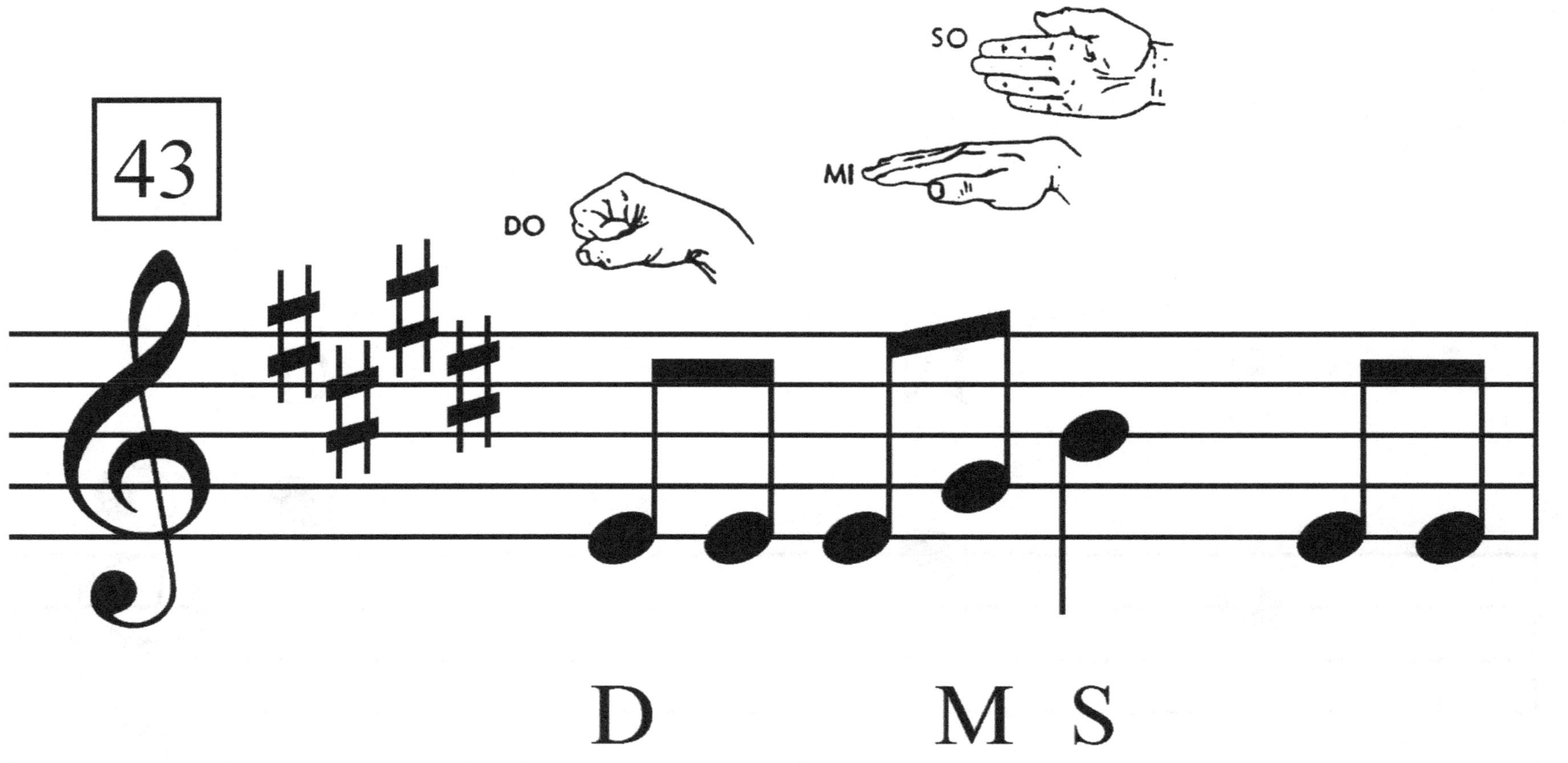

S-M-D

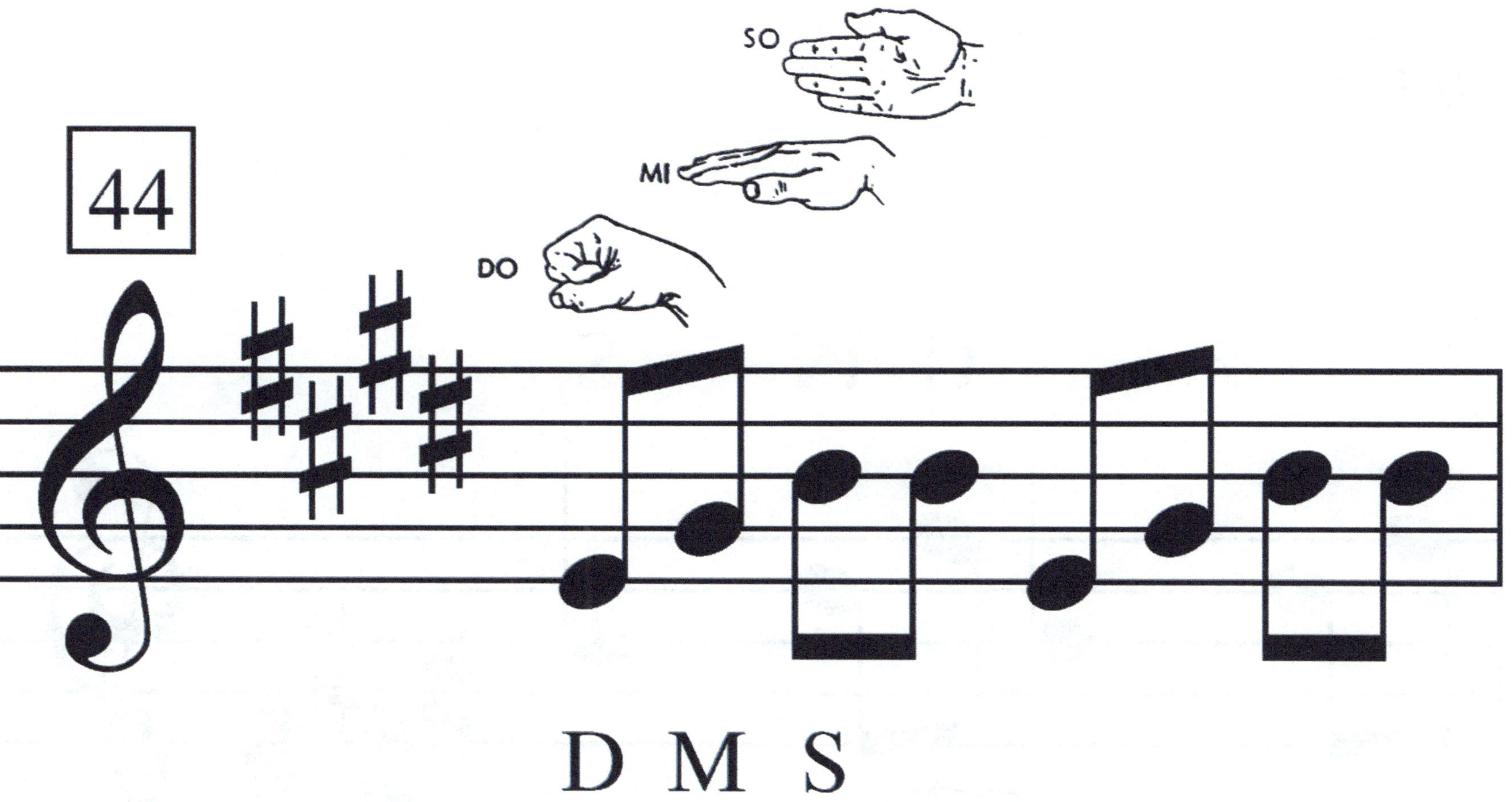

D M S

S-M-D

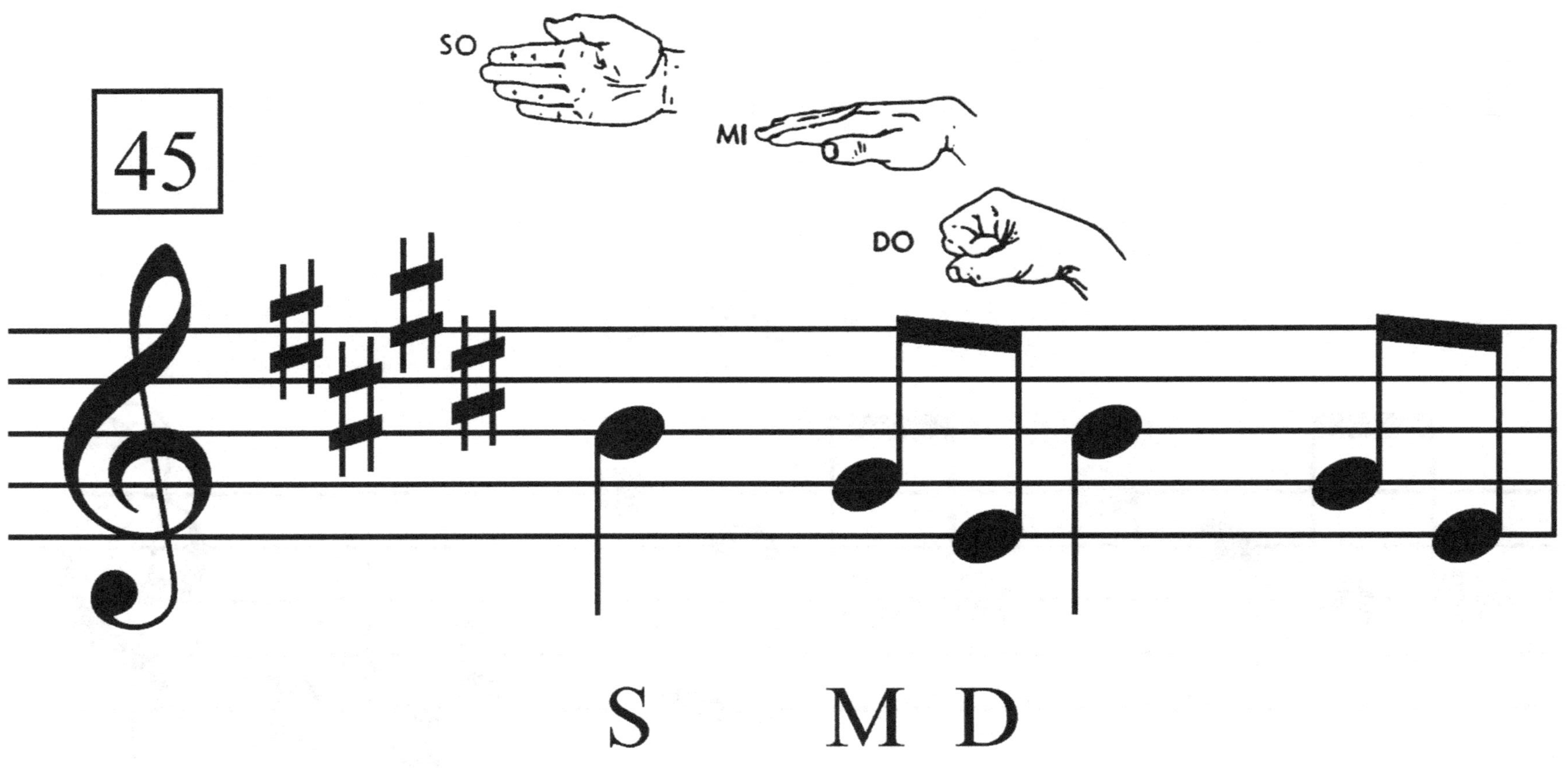

S-M-D

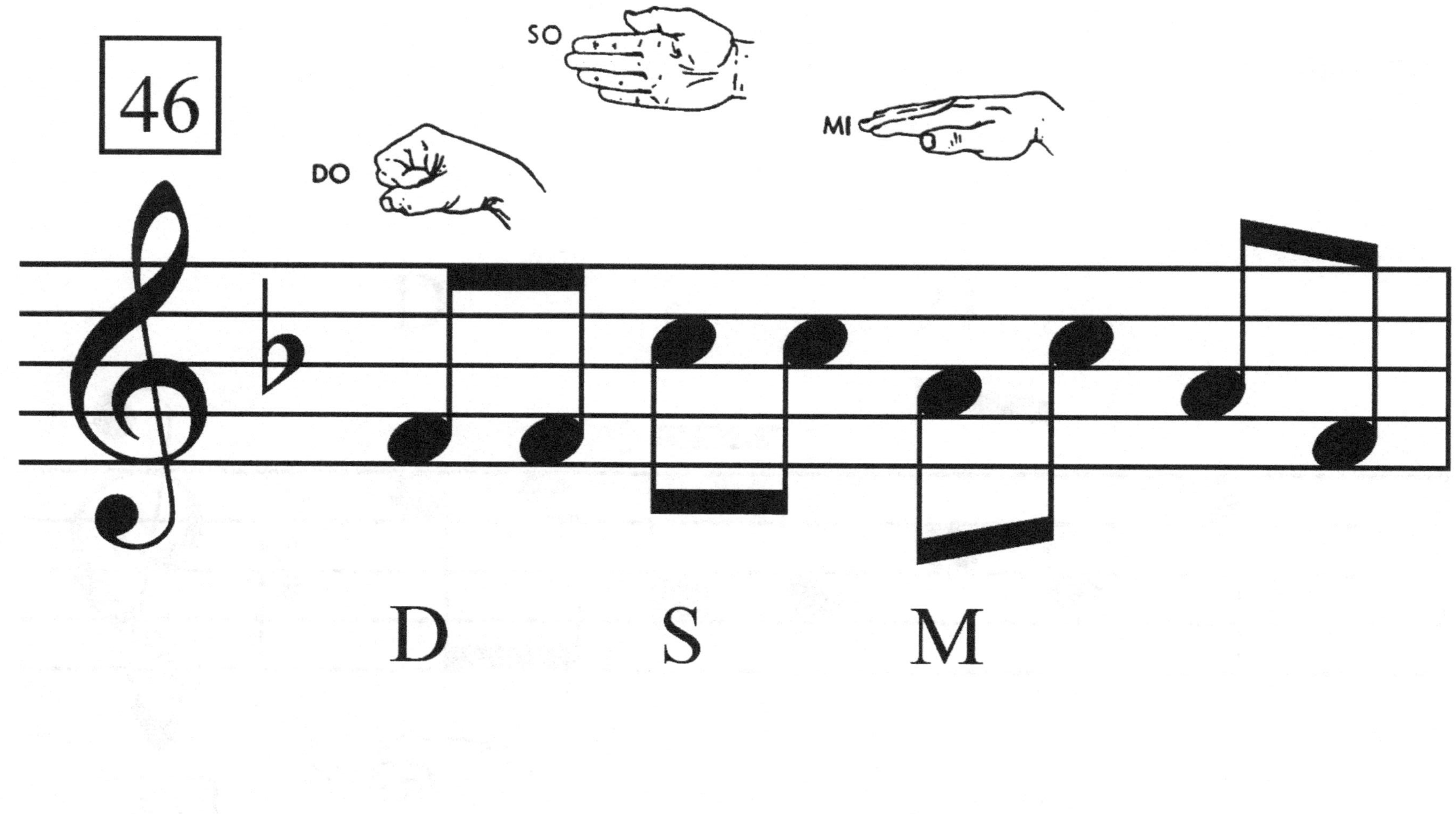
46
DO
SO
MI
D
S
M

S-M-D

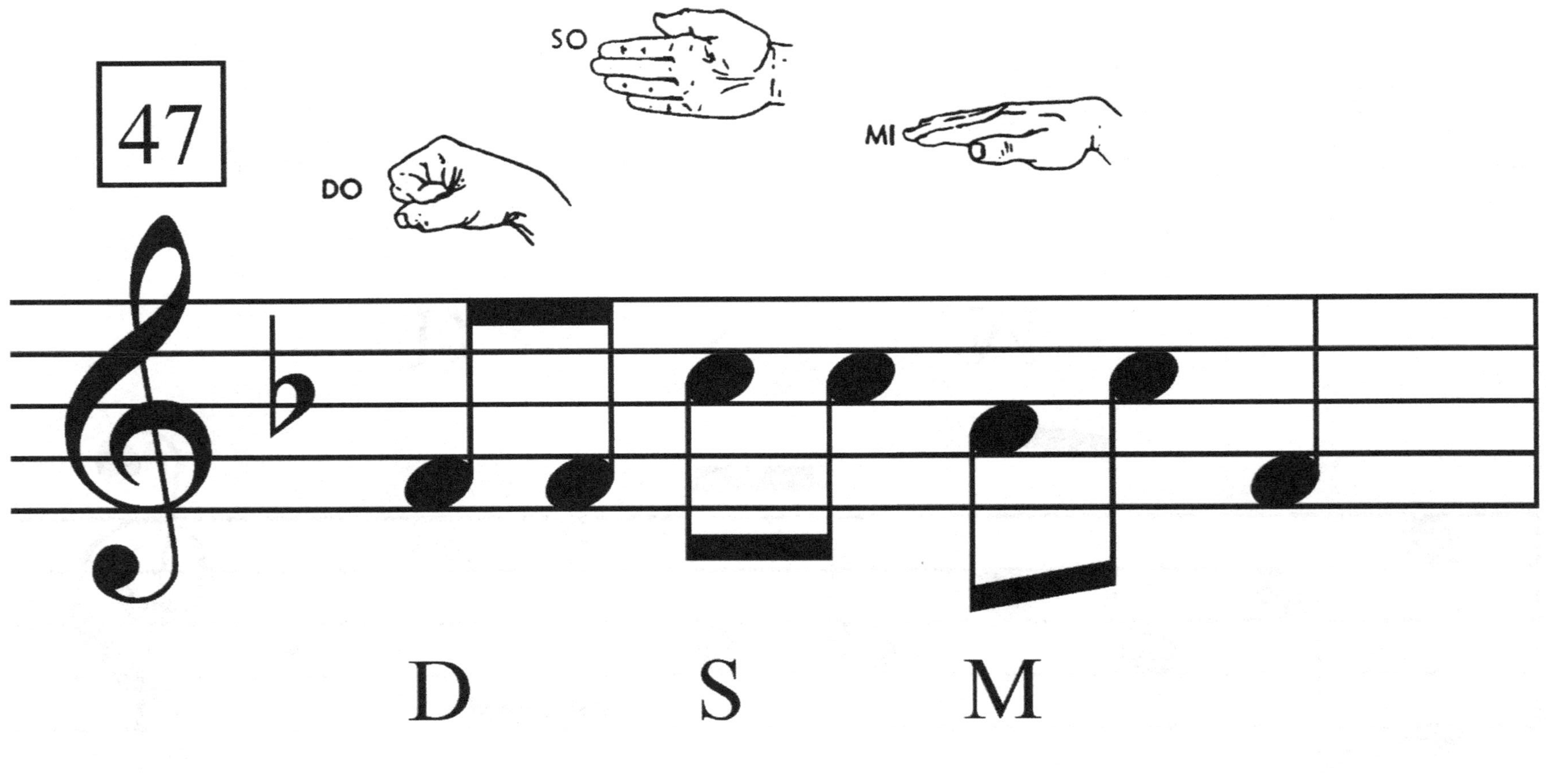

S-M-D

48

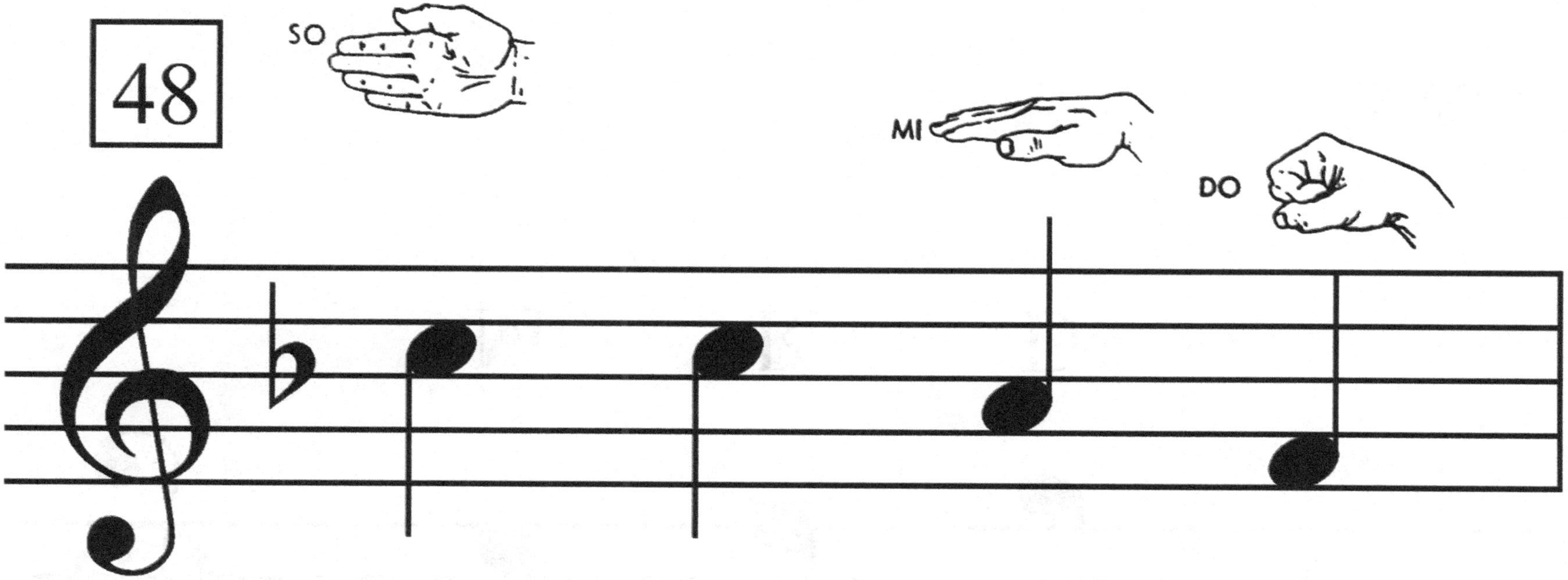

SO

MI

DO

S M D

S-M-D

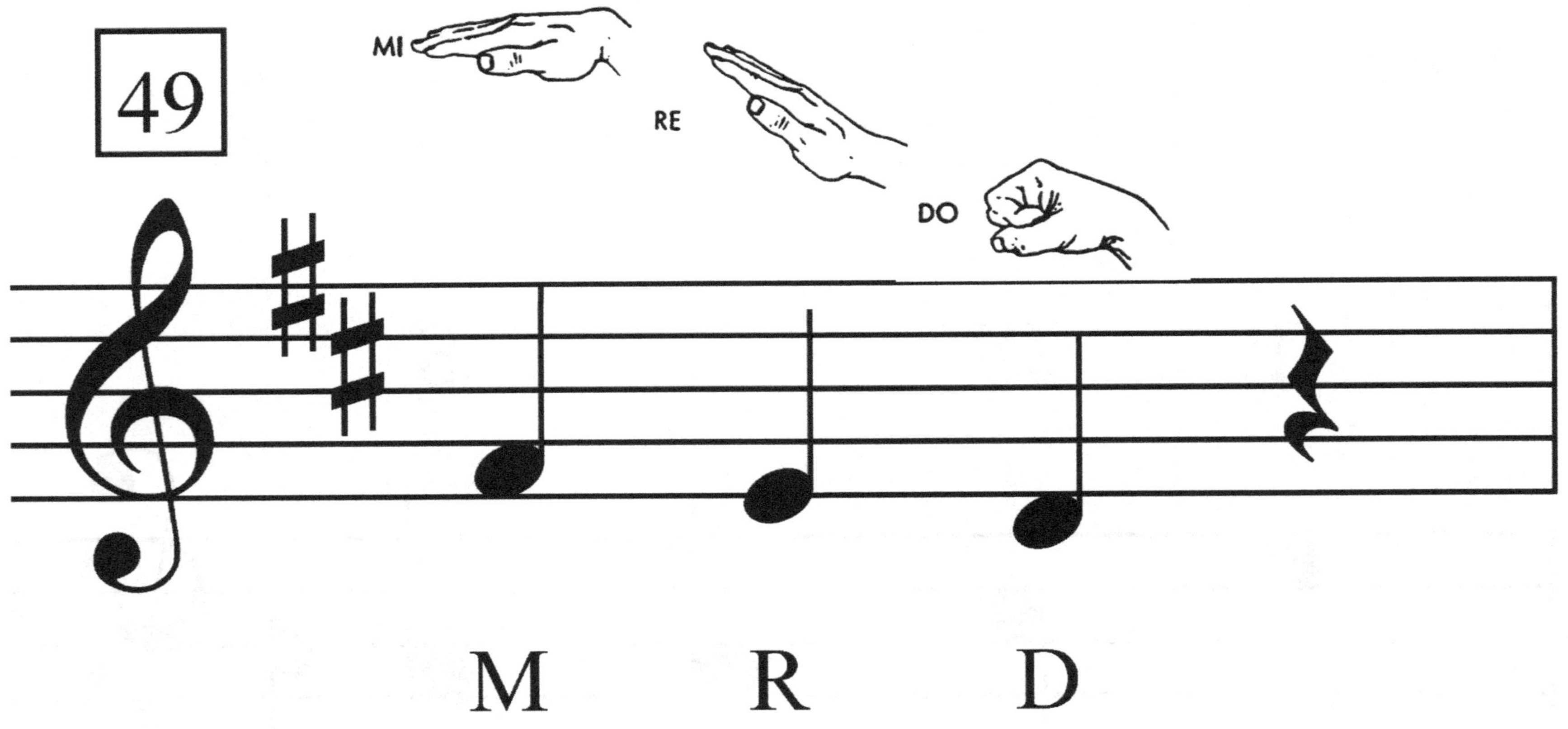

M-R-D

M-R-D

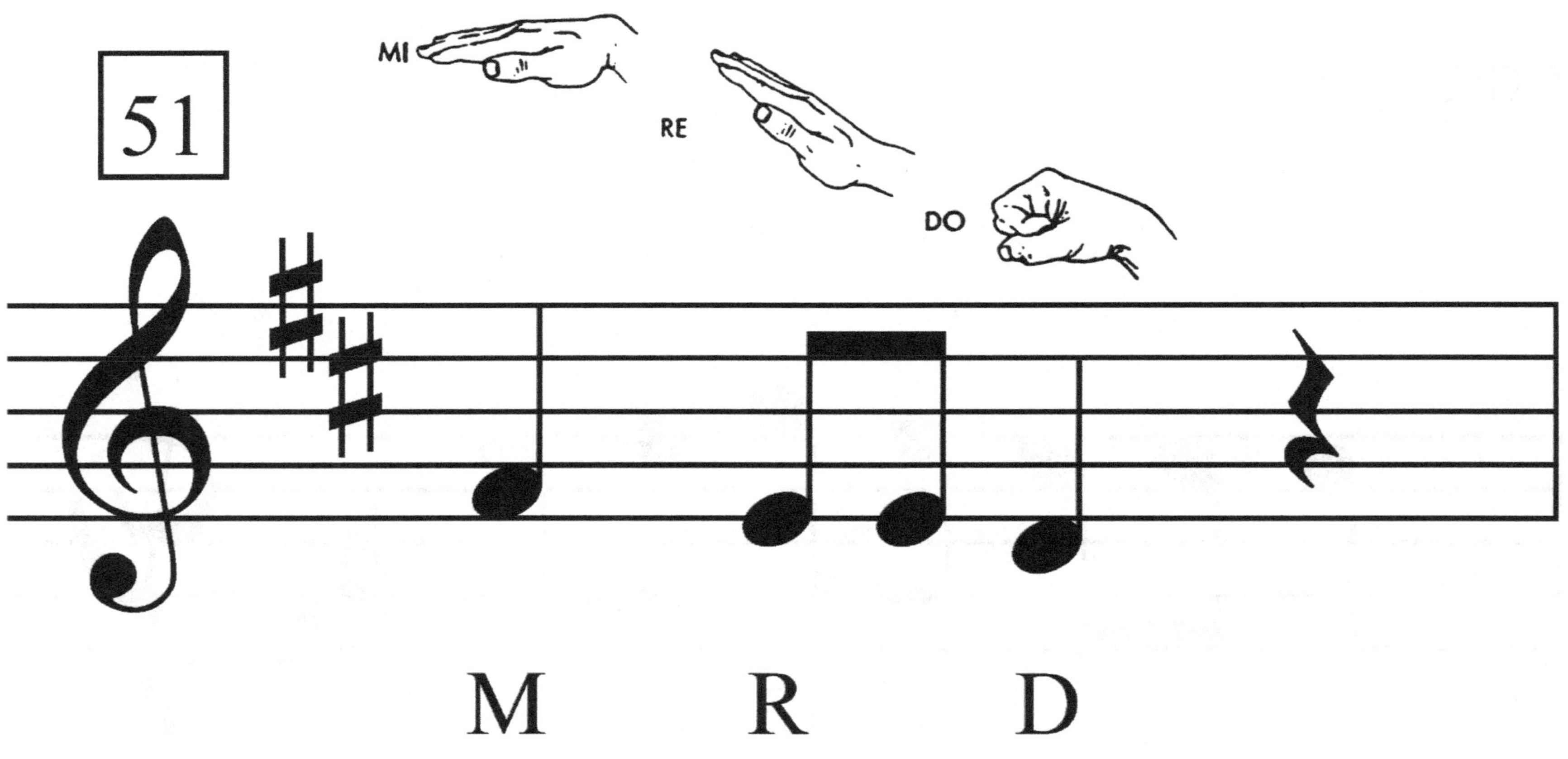

M-R-D

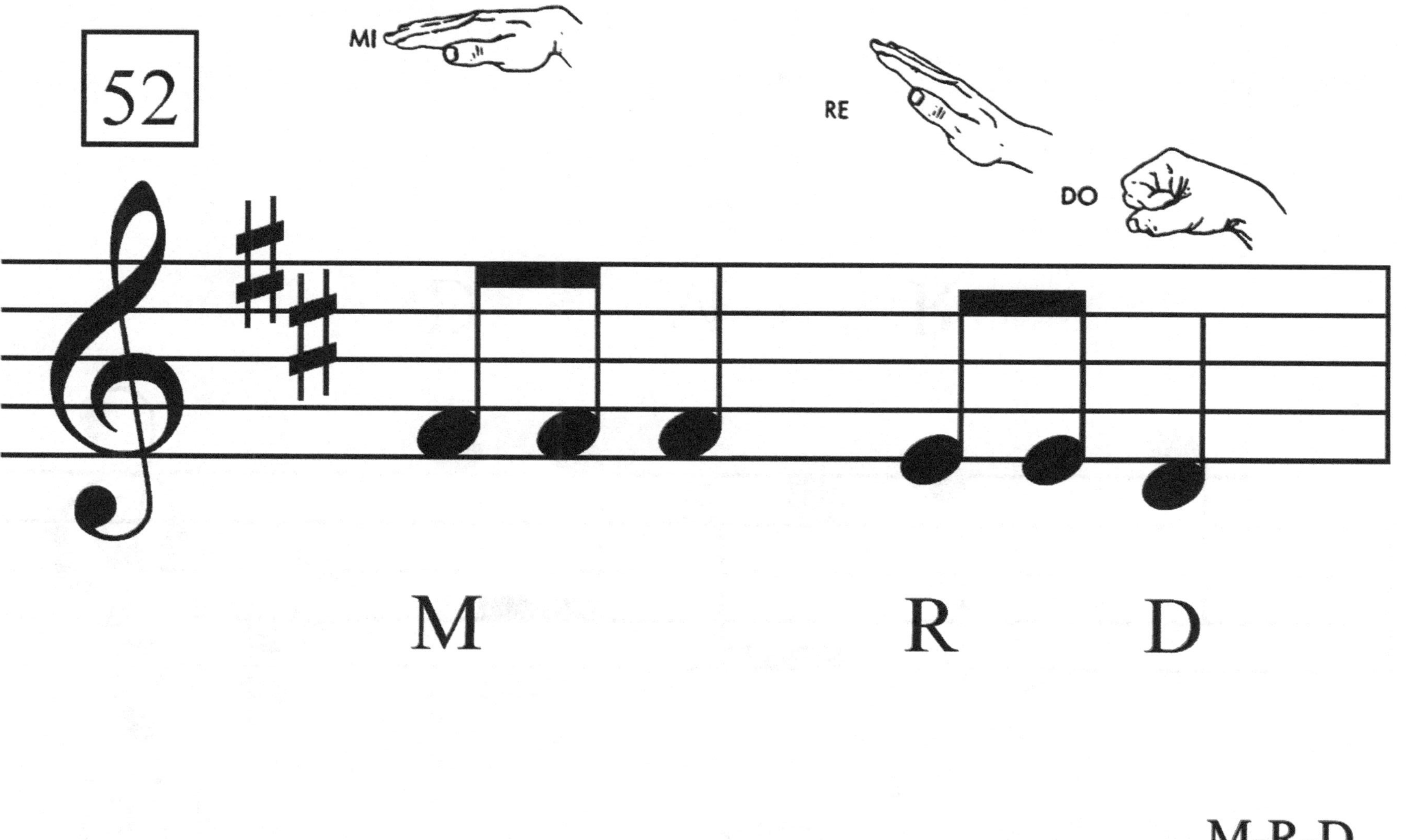

M-R-D

53

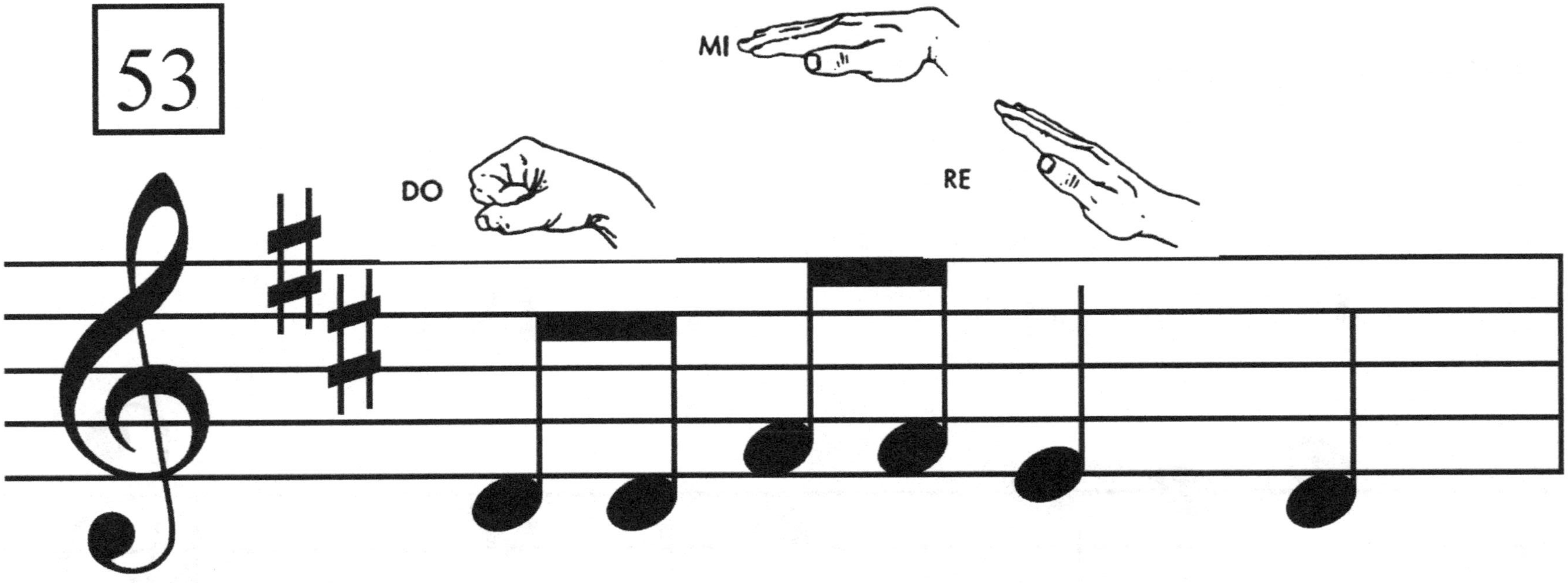

DO

MI

RE

D M R

M-R-D

54

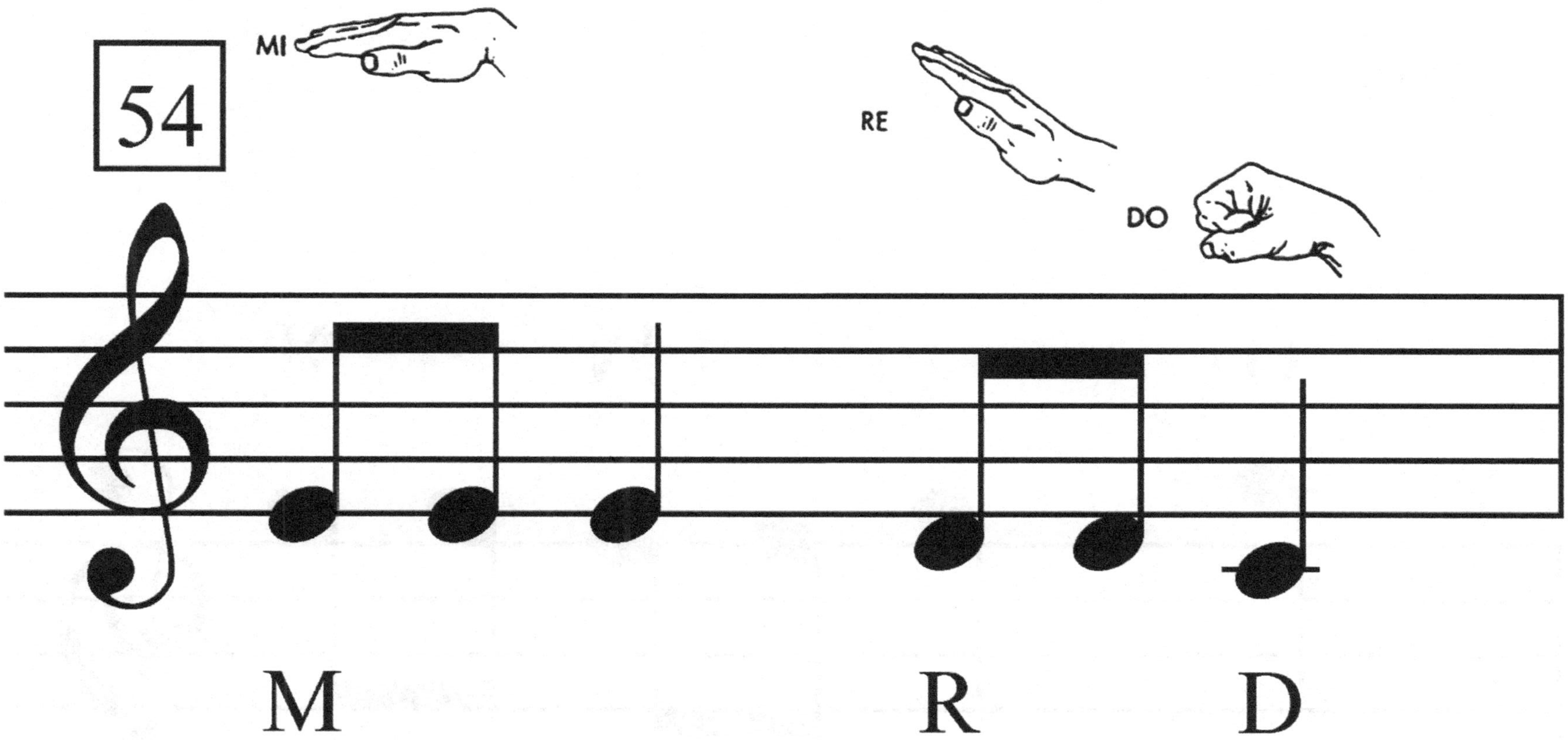

MI RE DO

M R D

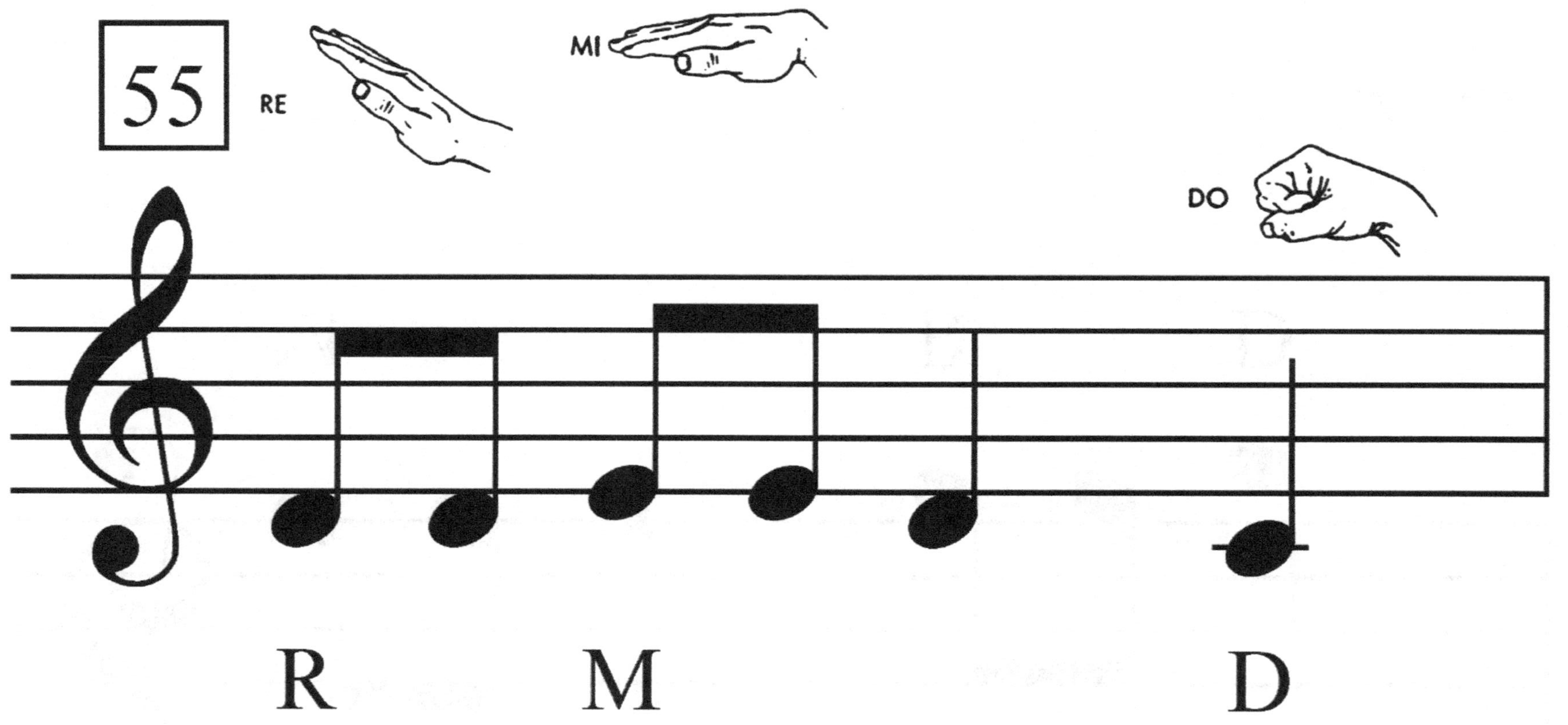

M-R-D

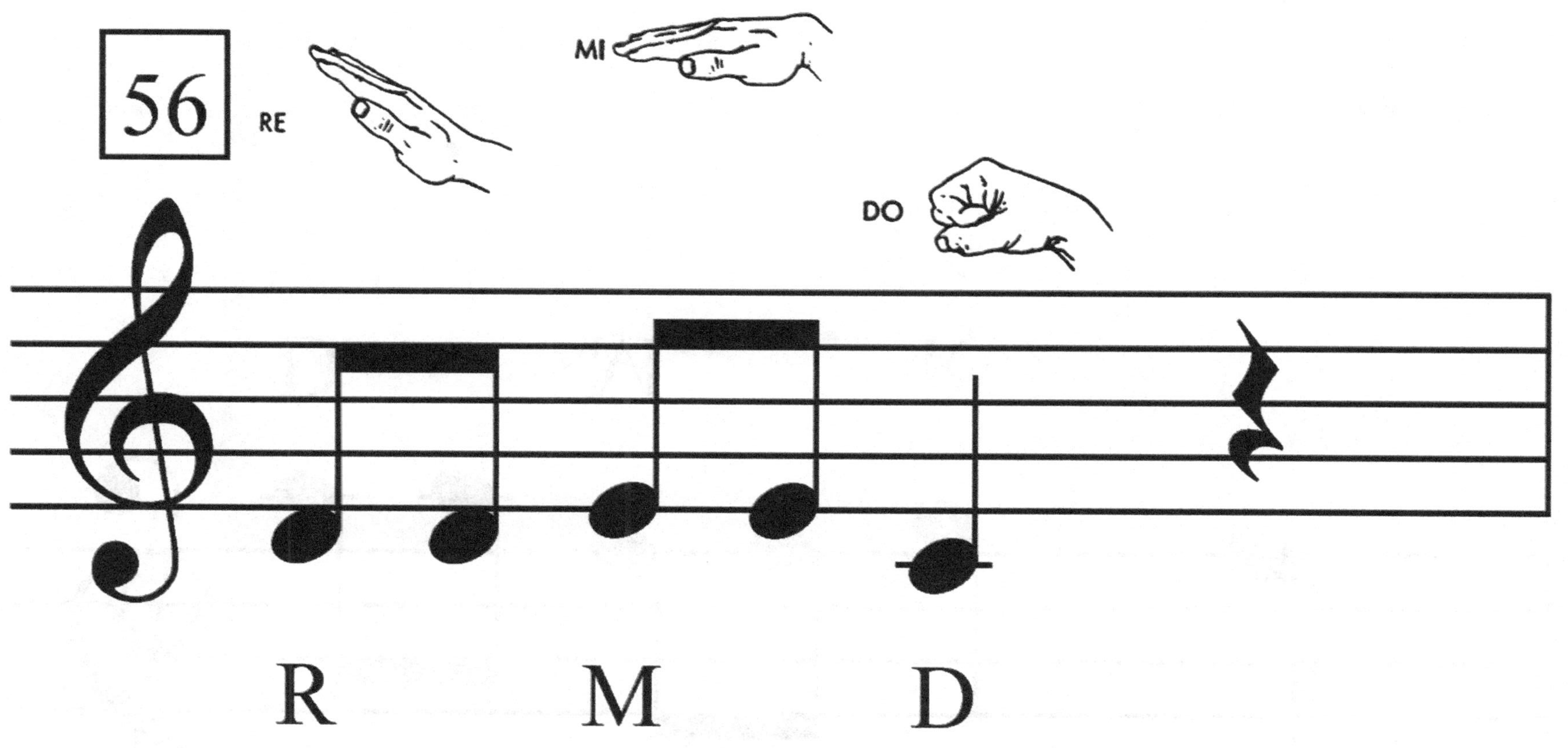

M-R-D

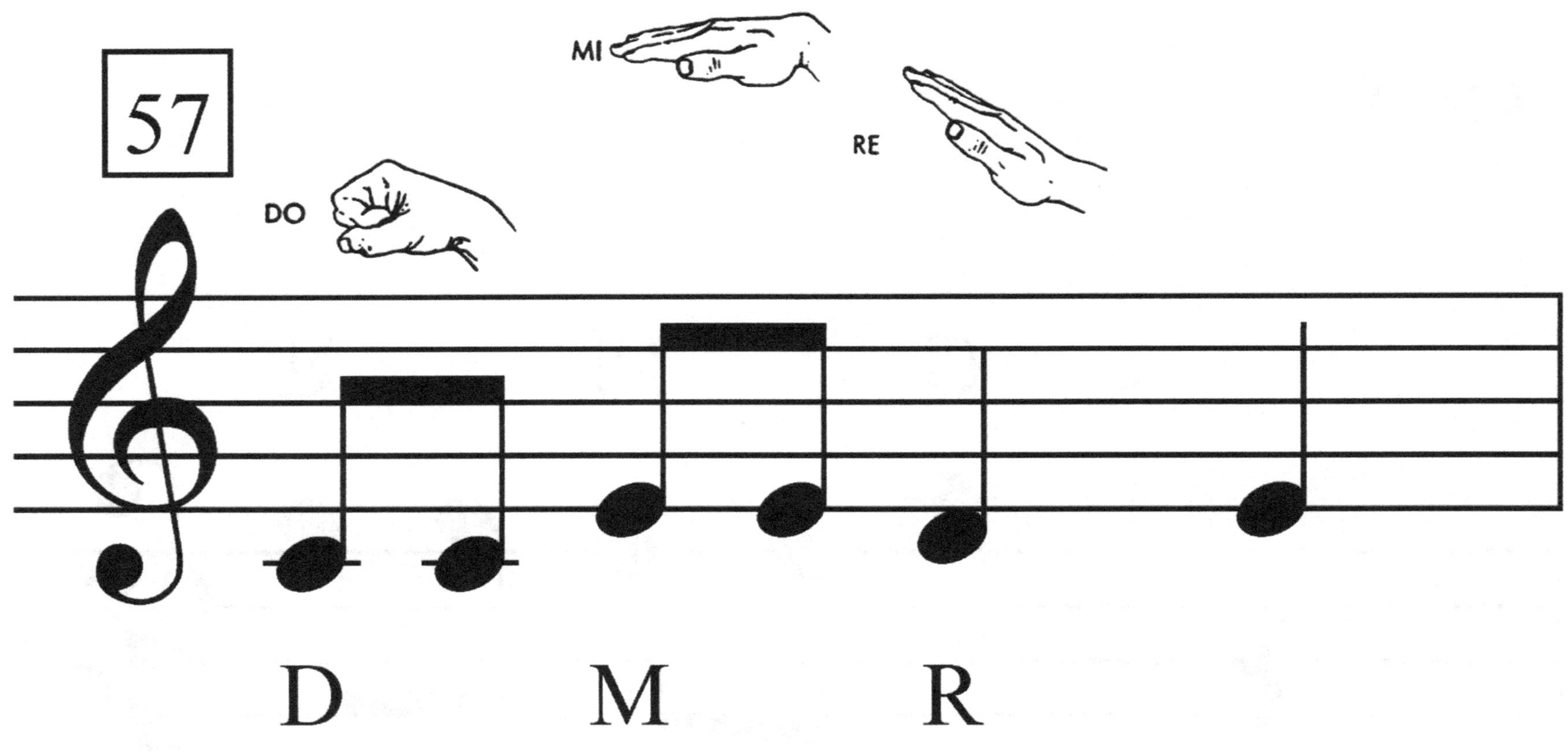

M-R-D

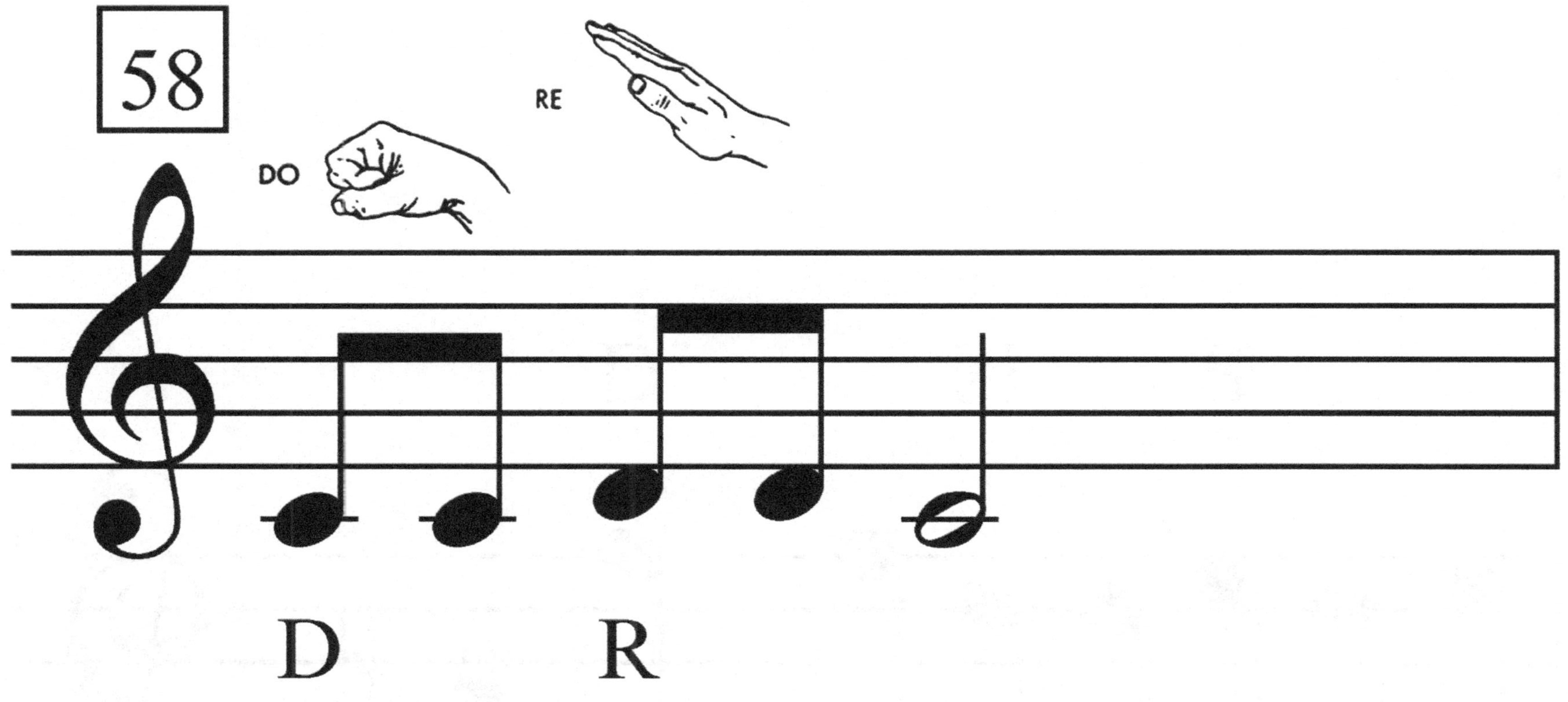

M-R-D

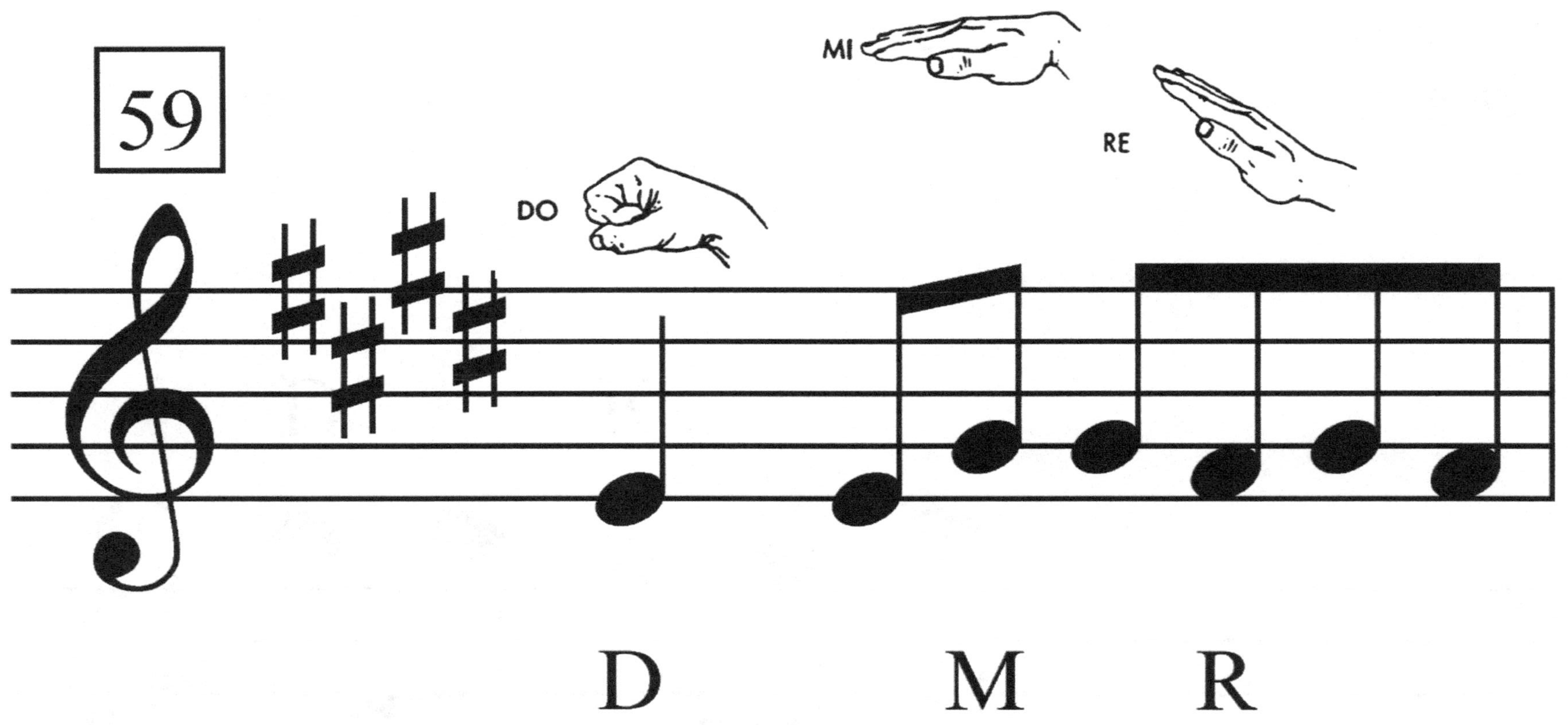

D M R

M-R-D

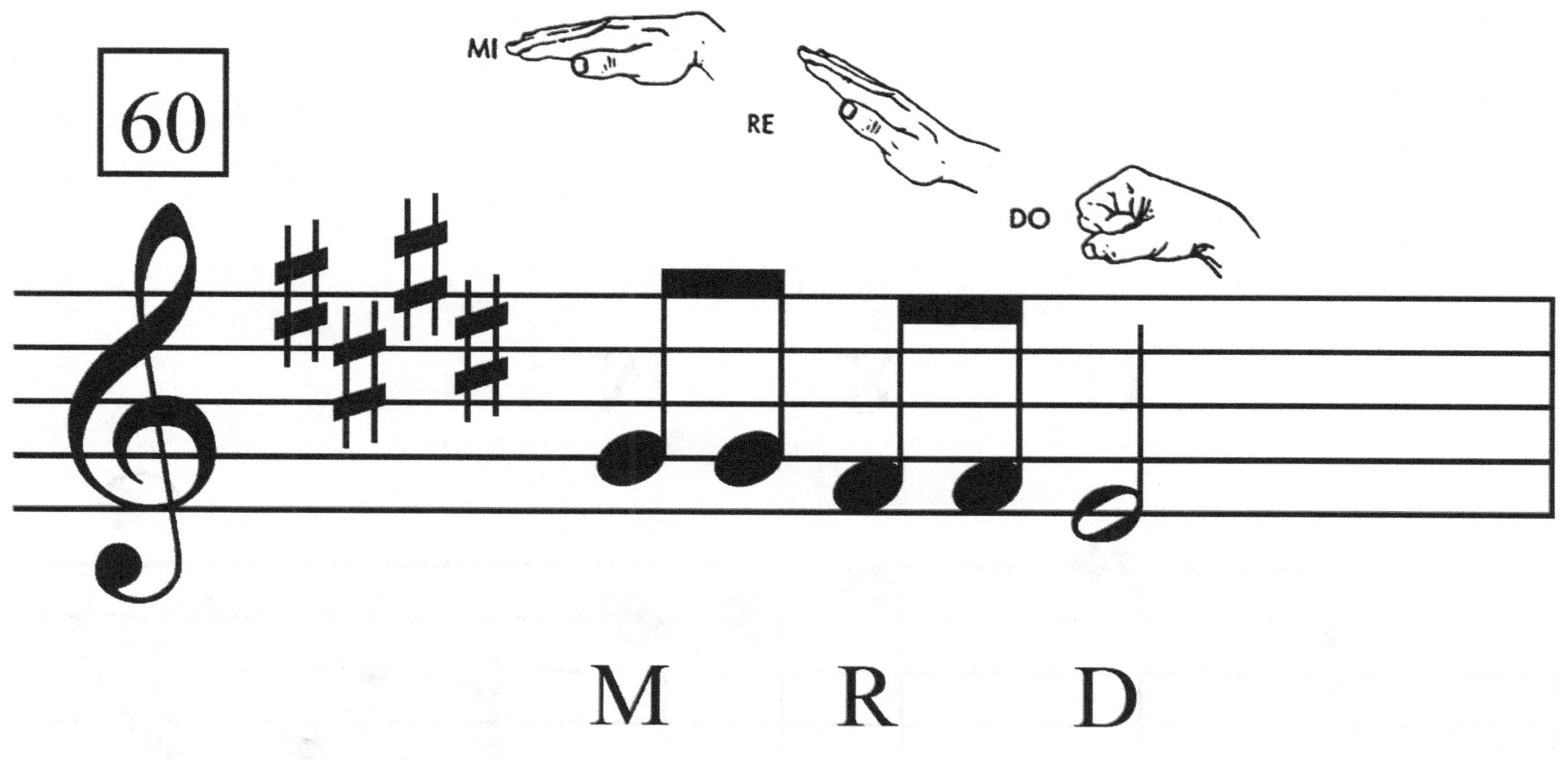

M-R-D

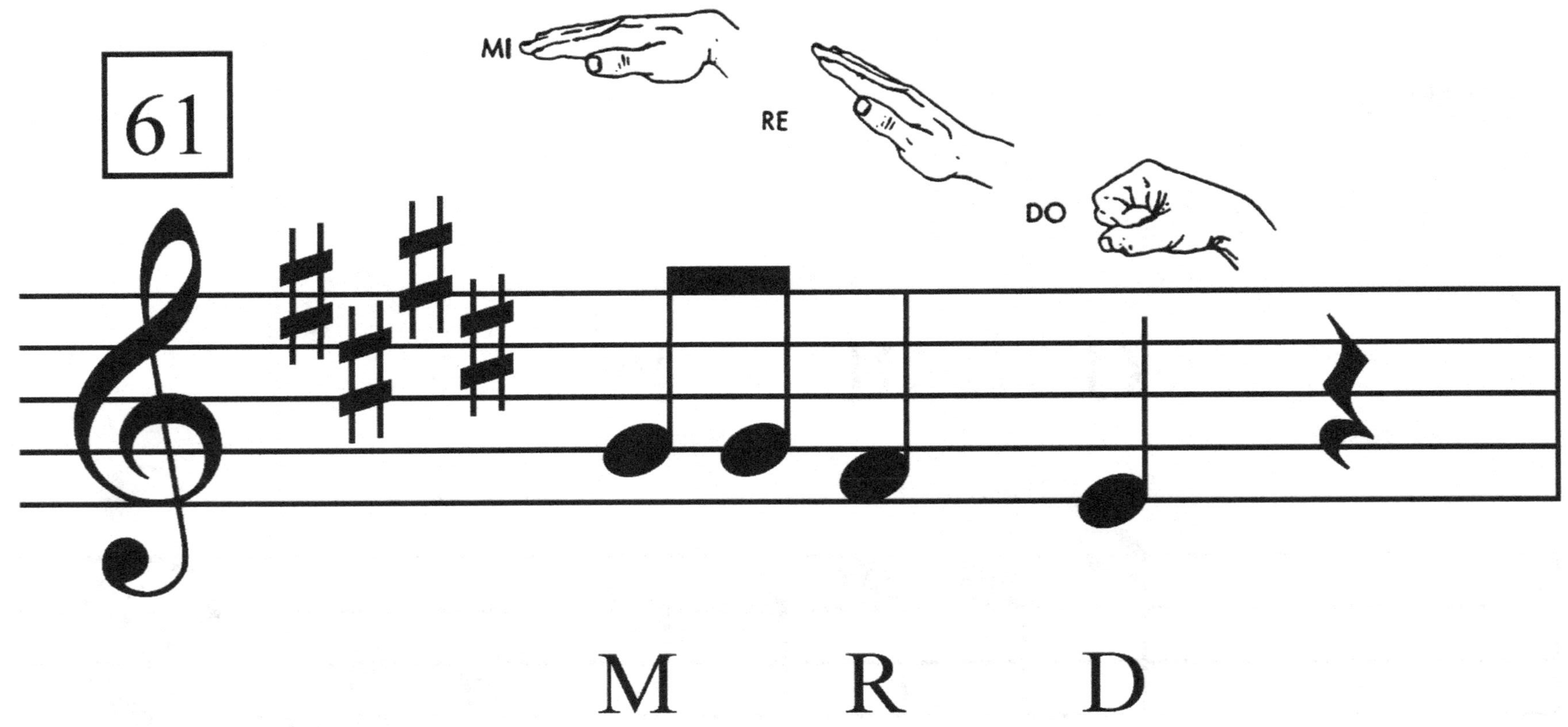

M-R-D

62

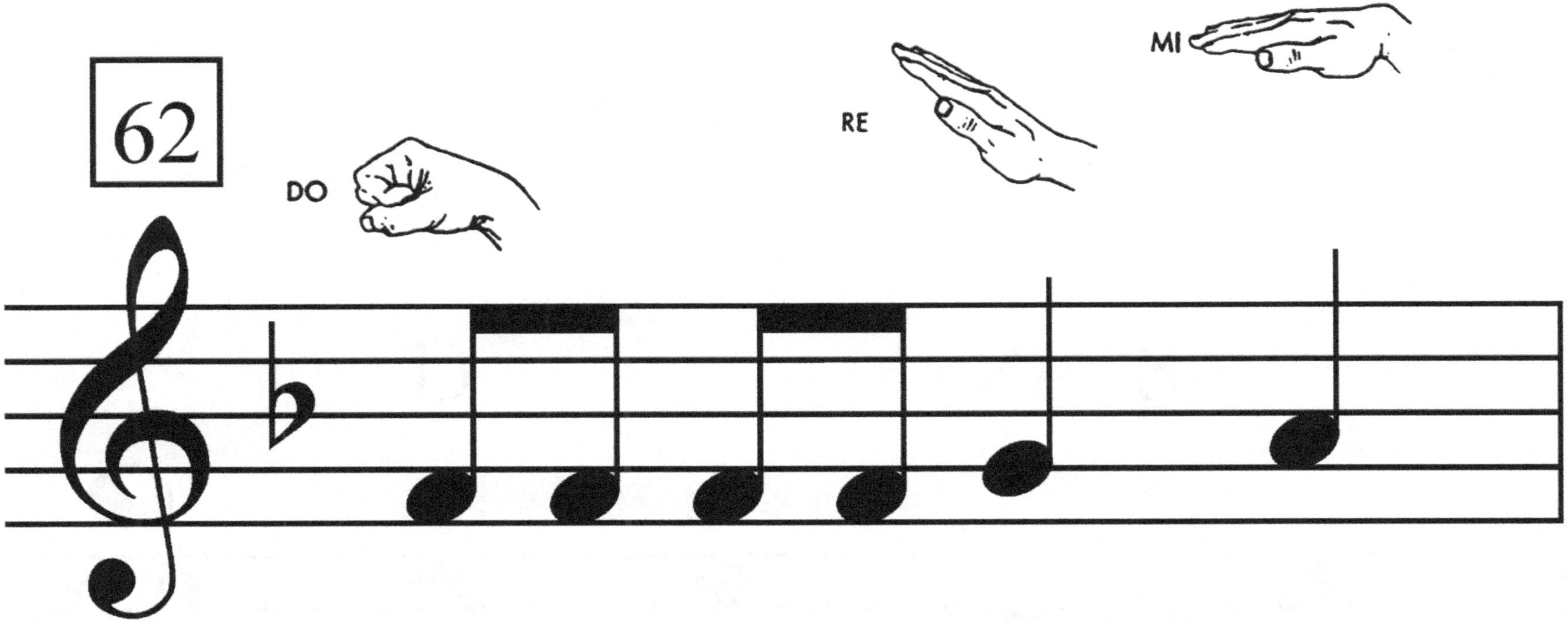

DO RE MI

D R M

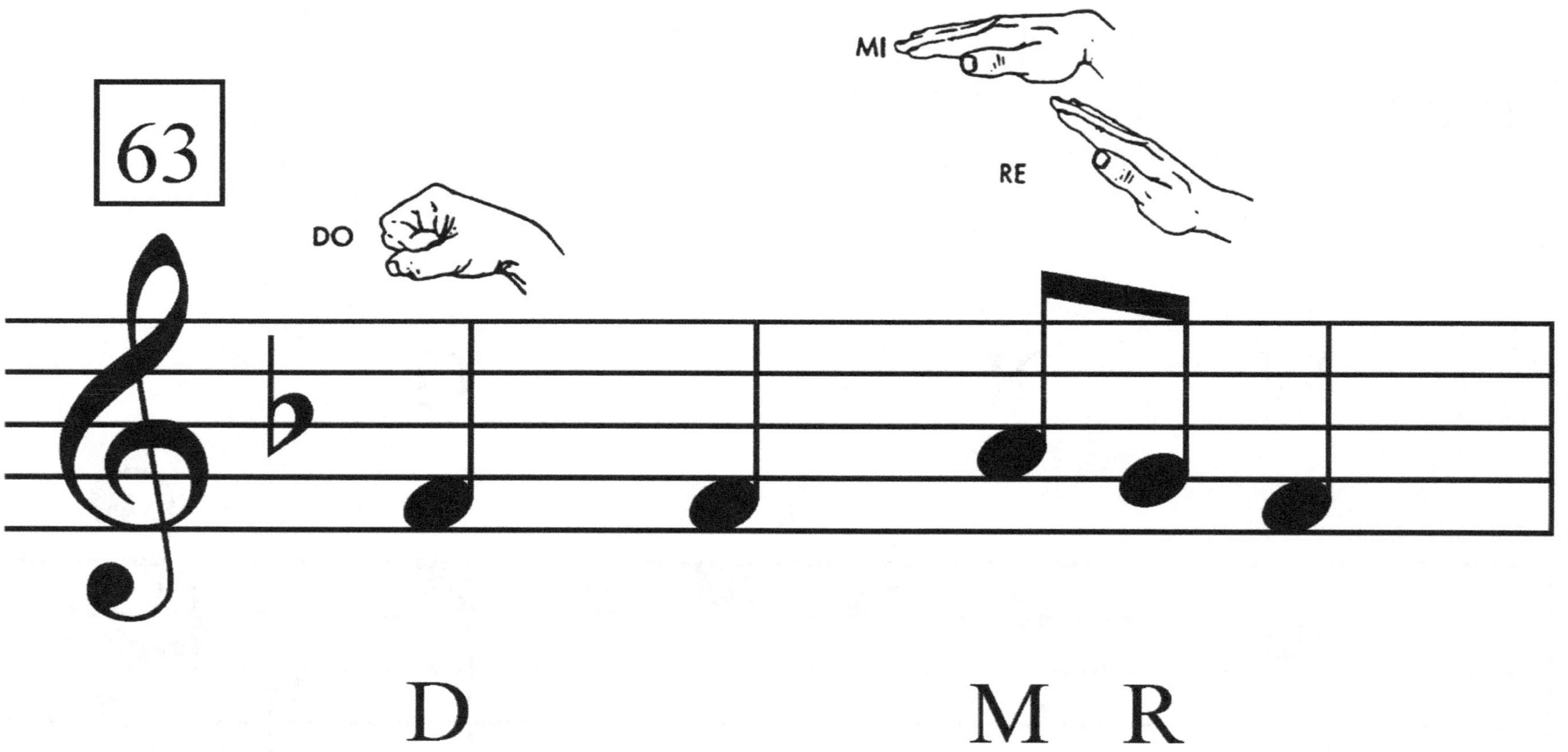

M-R-D

64

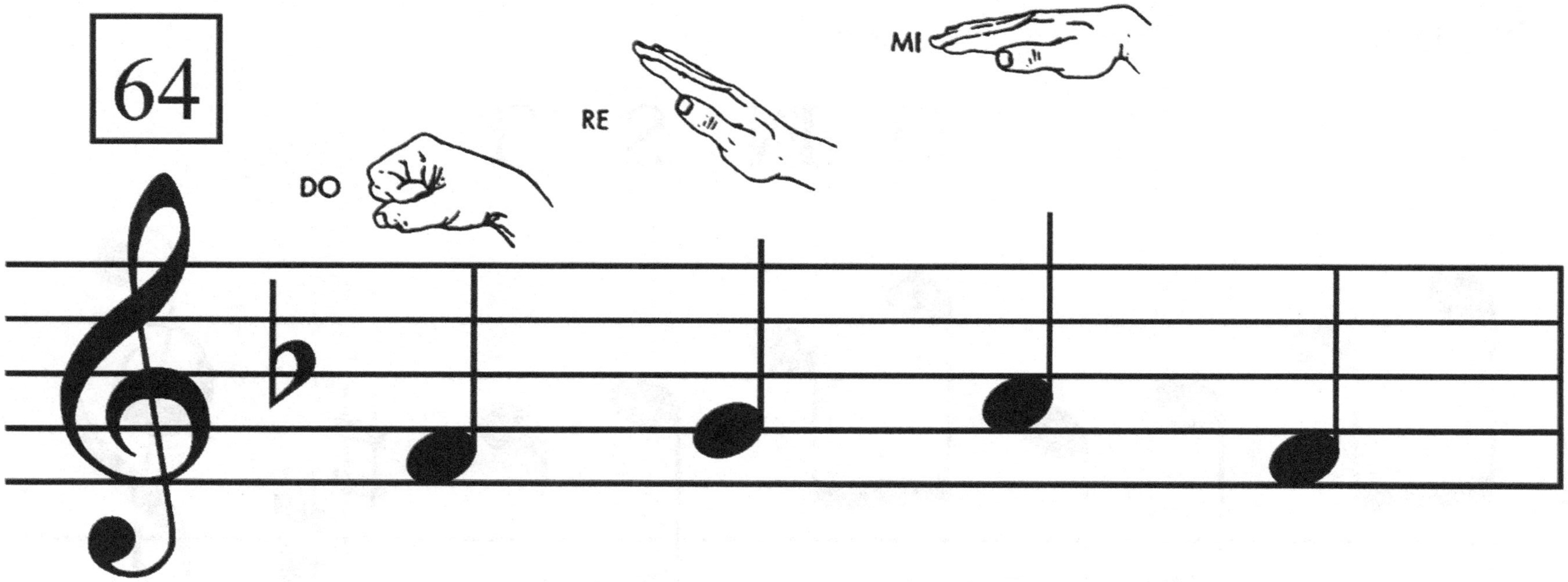

D R M

M-R-D

L-S-M-R-D

66

SO

LA

MI

DO

S L M D

67

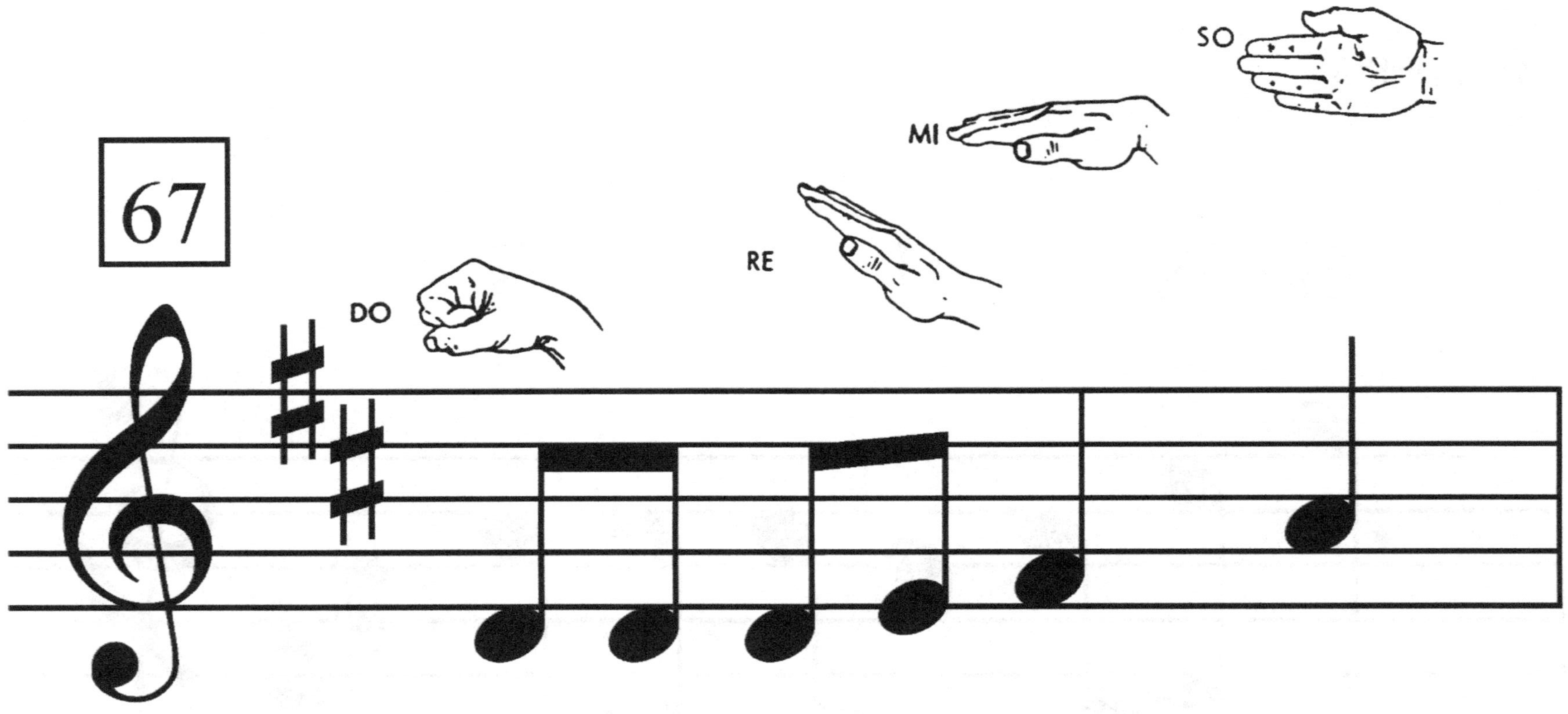

DO RE MI SO

D R M S

L-S-M-R-D

D L S

L-S-M-R-D

L-S-M-R-D

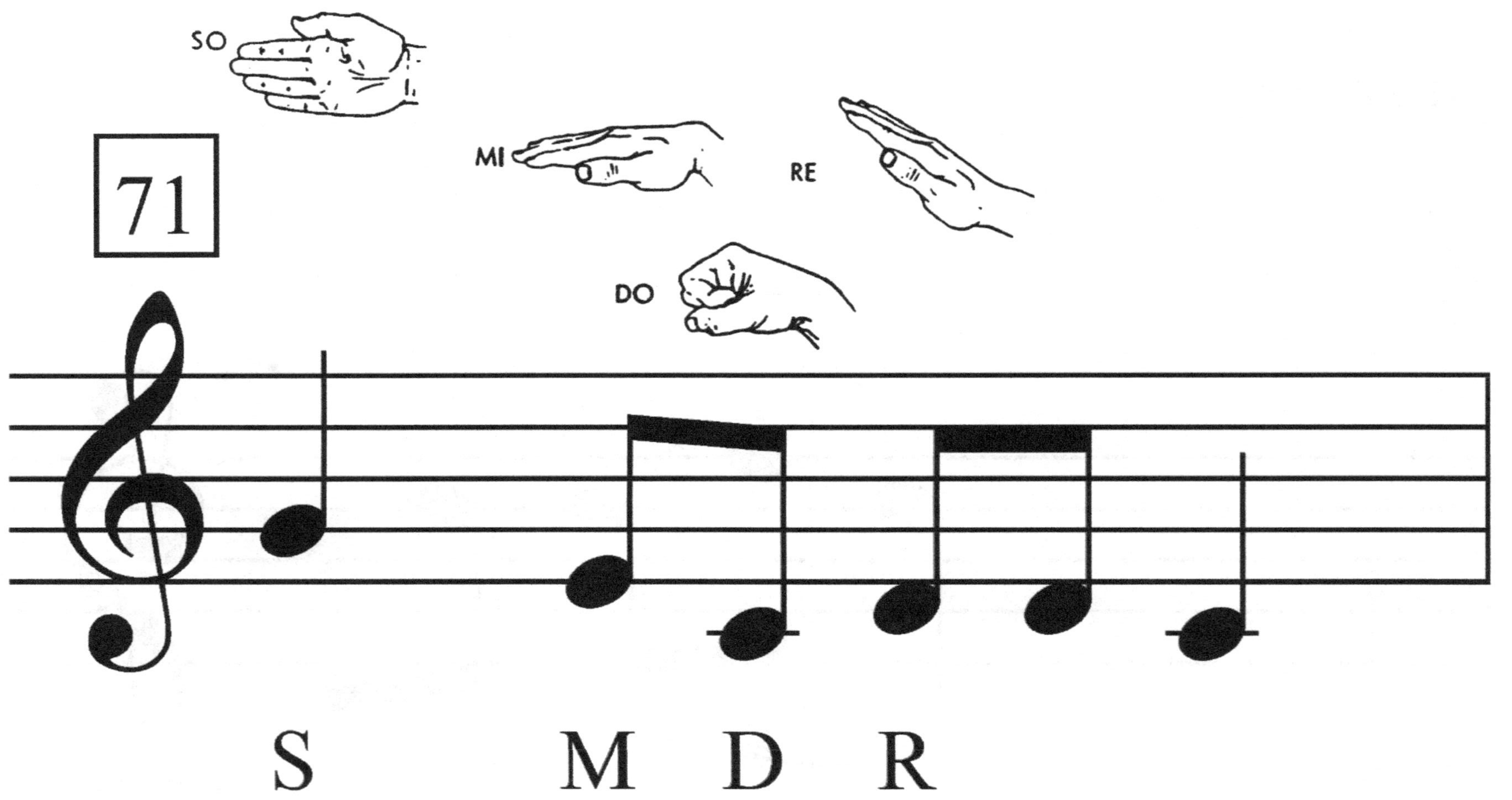
71
SO
MI
RE
DO
S M D R

L-S-M-R-D

L-S-M-R-D

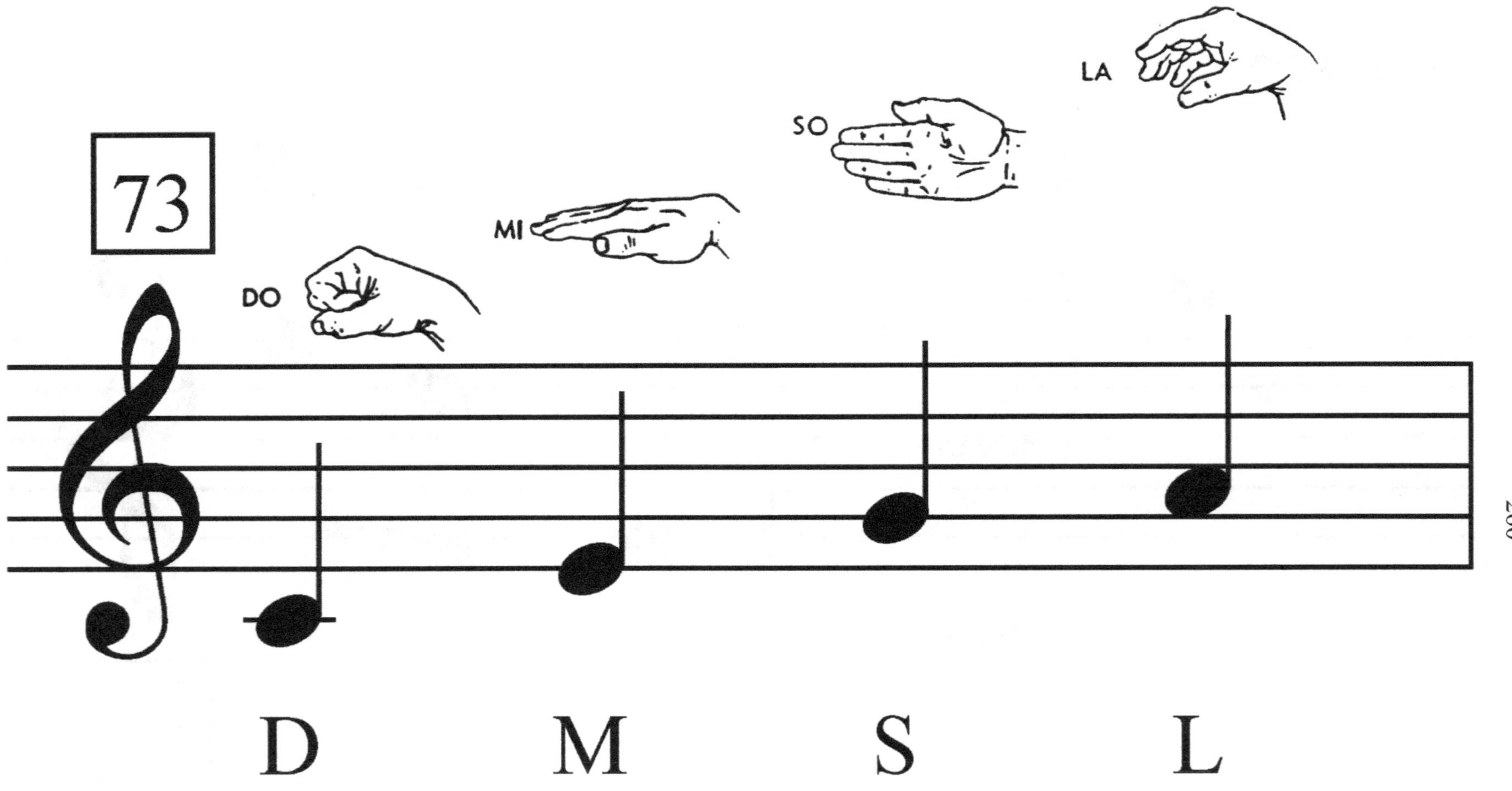

L-S-M-R-D

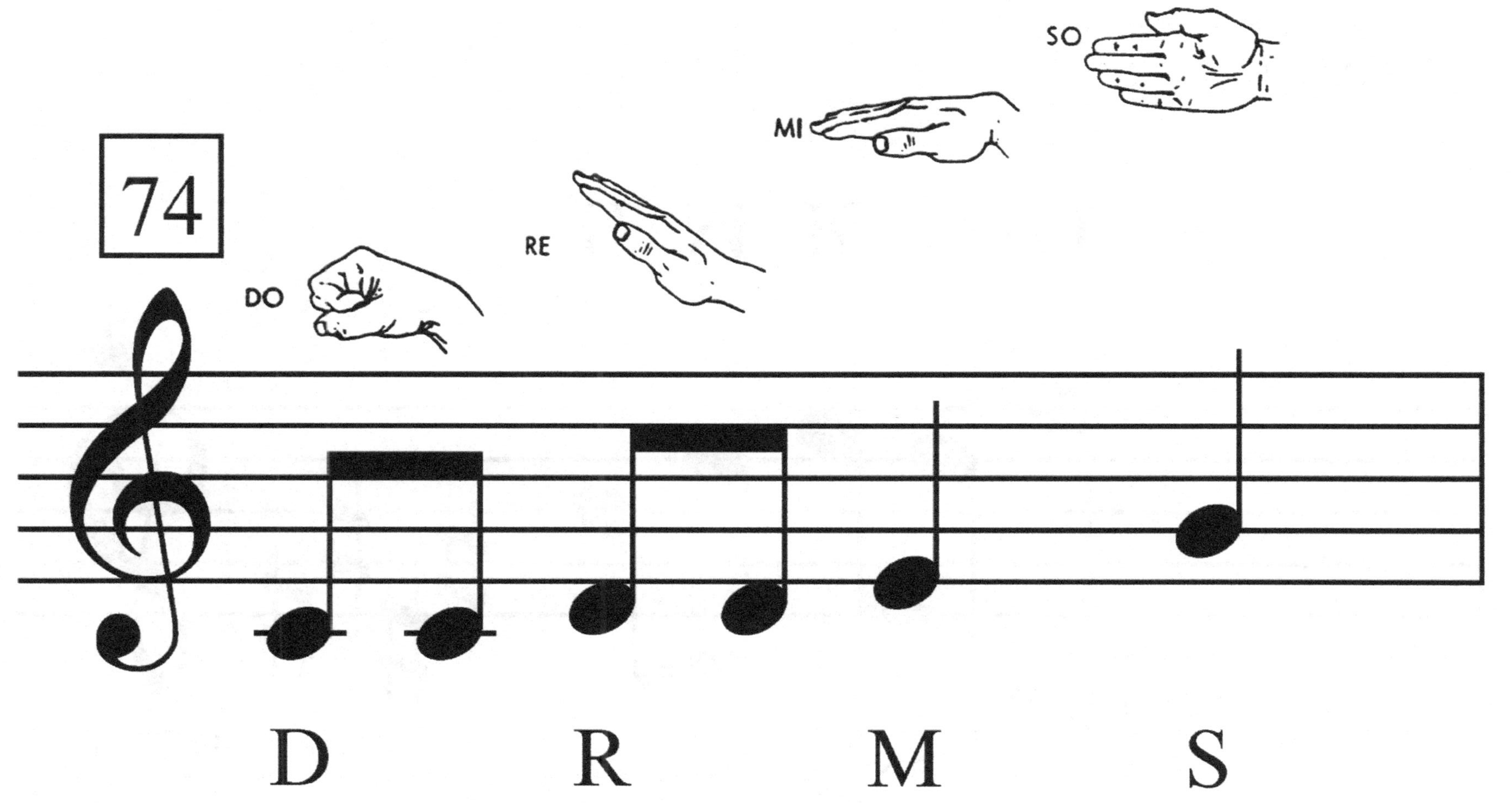

L-S-M-R-D

L-S-M-R-D

76

LA

SO

MI

DO

L S M D

L-S-M-R-D

77
LA
SO
MI
RE
DO
L S M R D
L-S-M-R-D

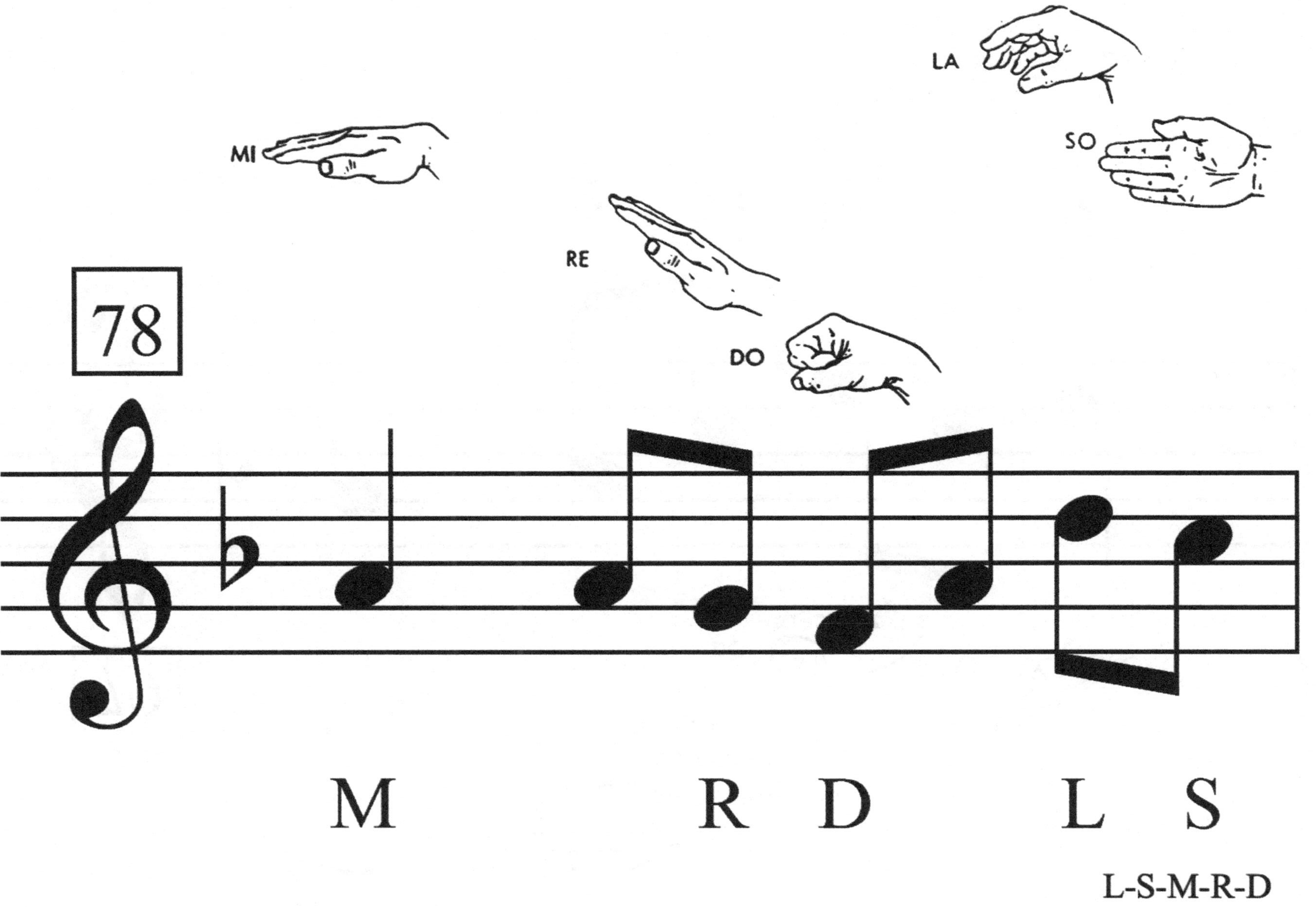
78
MI
RE
DO
LA
SO
M
R
D
L
S
L-S-M-R-D

L-S-M-R-D

80
LA
SO
MI
RE
DO
L S M R D
L-S-M-R-D

81
TI
LA
SO
FA
MI
RE
DO
T L S F M R D
T-L-S-F-M-R-D

82
SO
FA
MI
RE
DO
TI
LA
S F M R D T L L
T-L-S-F-M-R-D

83
TI
LA
SO
FA
MI
RE
DO
T L S F M R D
T-L-S-F-M-R-D

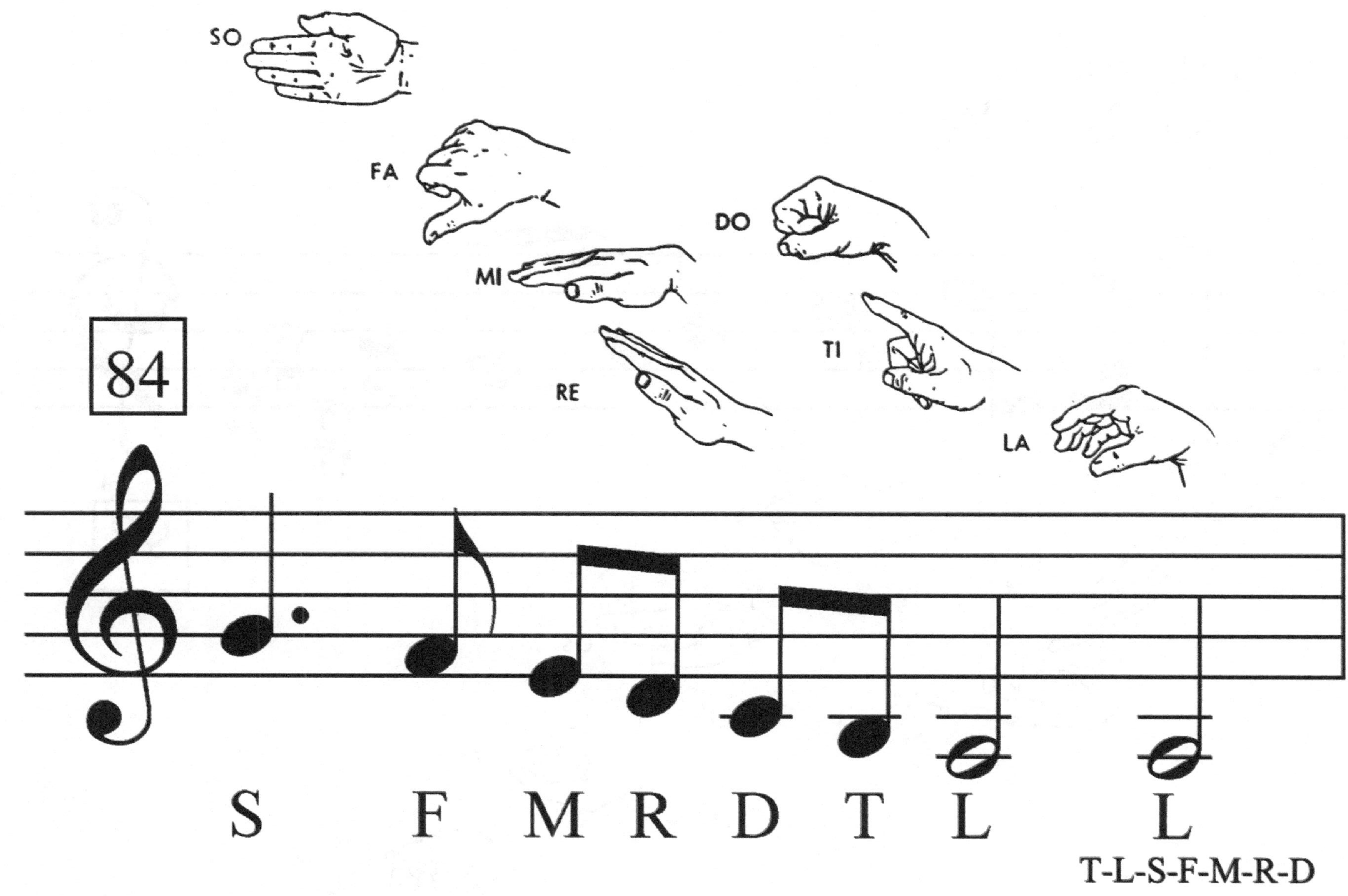
SO
FA
DO
MI
TI
RE
LA
84
S F M R D T L L
T-L-S-F-M-R-D

85
TI
LA
SO
FA
MI
RE
DO
T L S F M R D
T-L-S-F-M-R-D

86
SO
FA
DO
MI
TI
RE
LA
S F M R D T L L
T-L-S-F-M-R-D

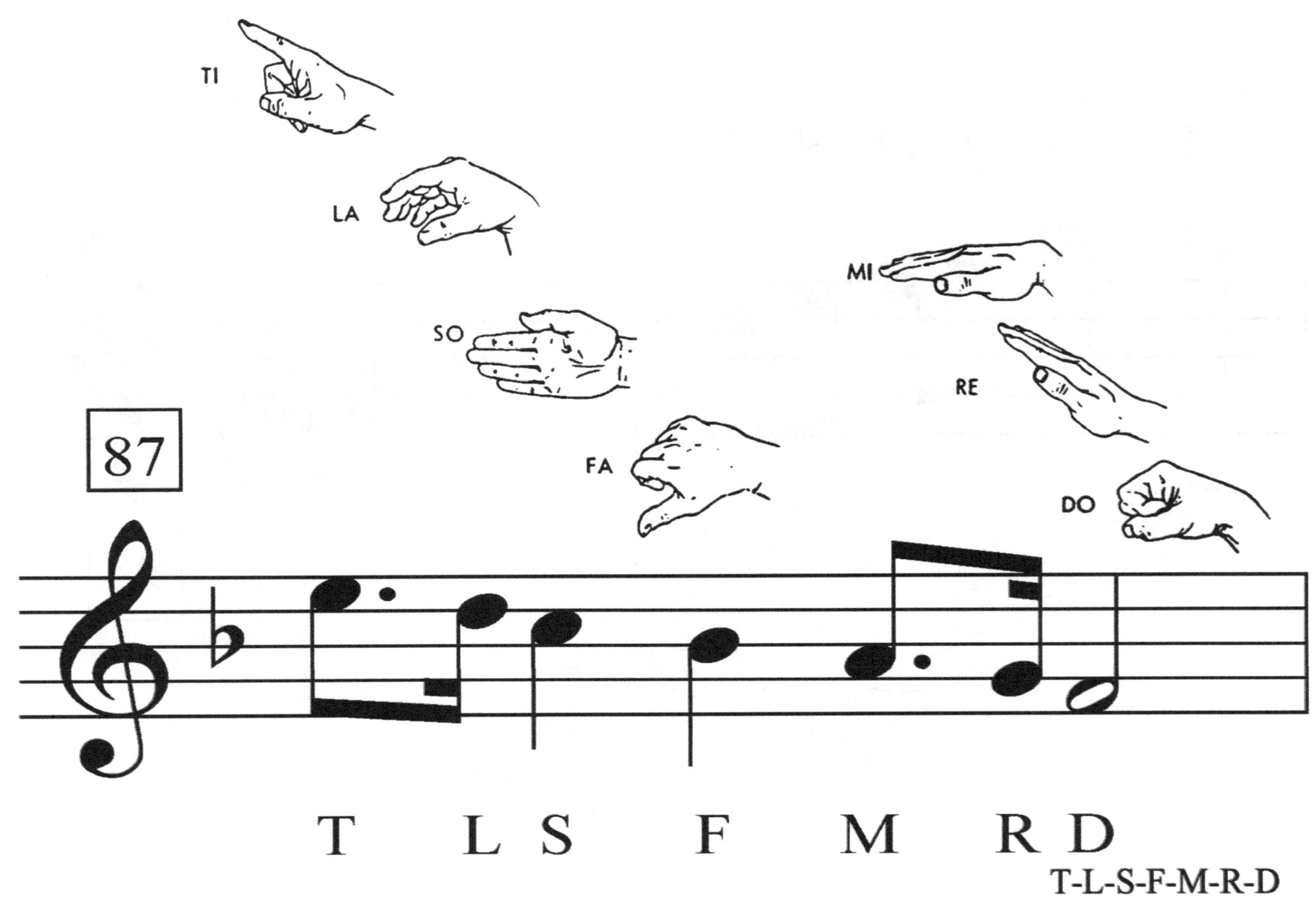
87
TI
LA
SO
FA
MI
RE
DO
T L S F M R D
T-L-S-F-M-R-D

88
SO
FA
MI
RE
DO
TI
LA
S F M R D T L L
T-L-S-F-M-R-D

89
DO
TI
LA
SO
FA
MI
RE
DO
D' T L S F M R D
D'-T-L-S-F-M-R-D

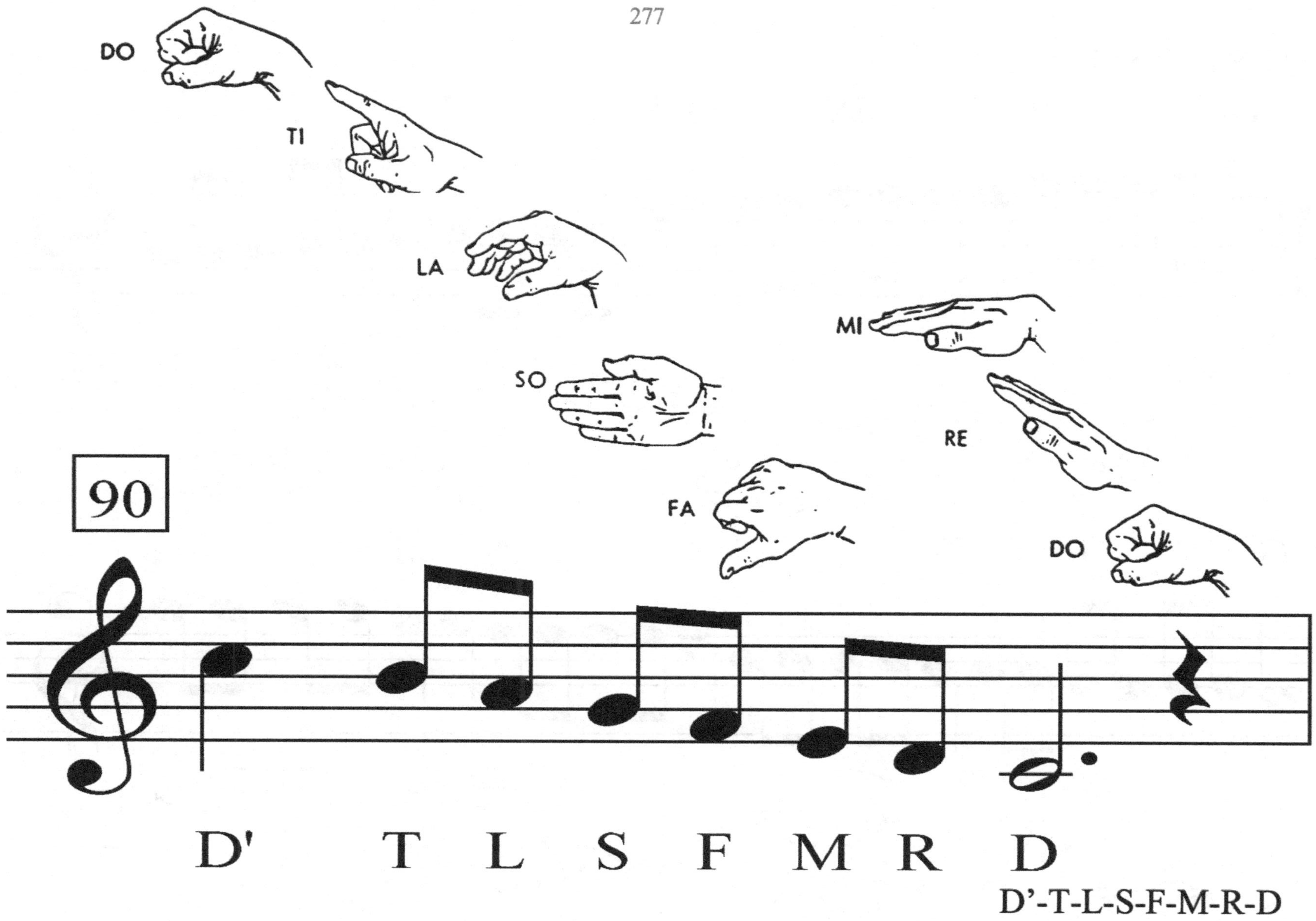

277

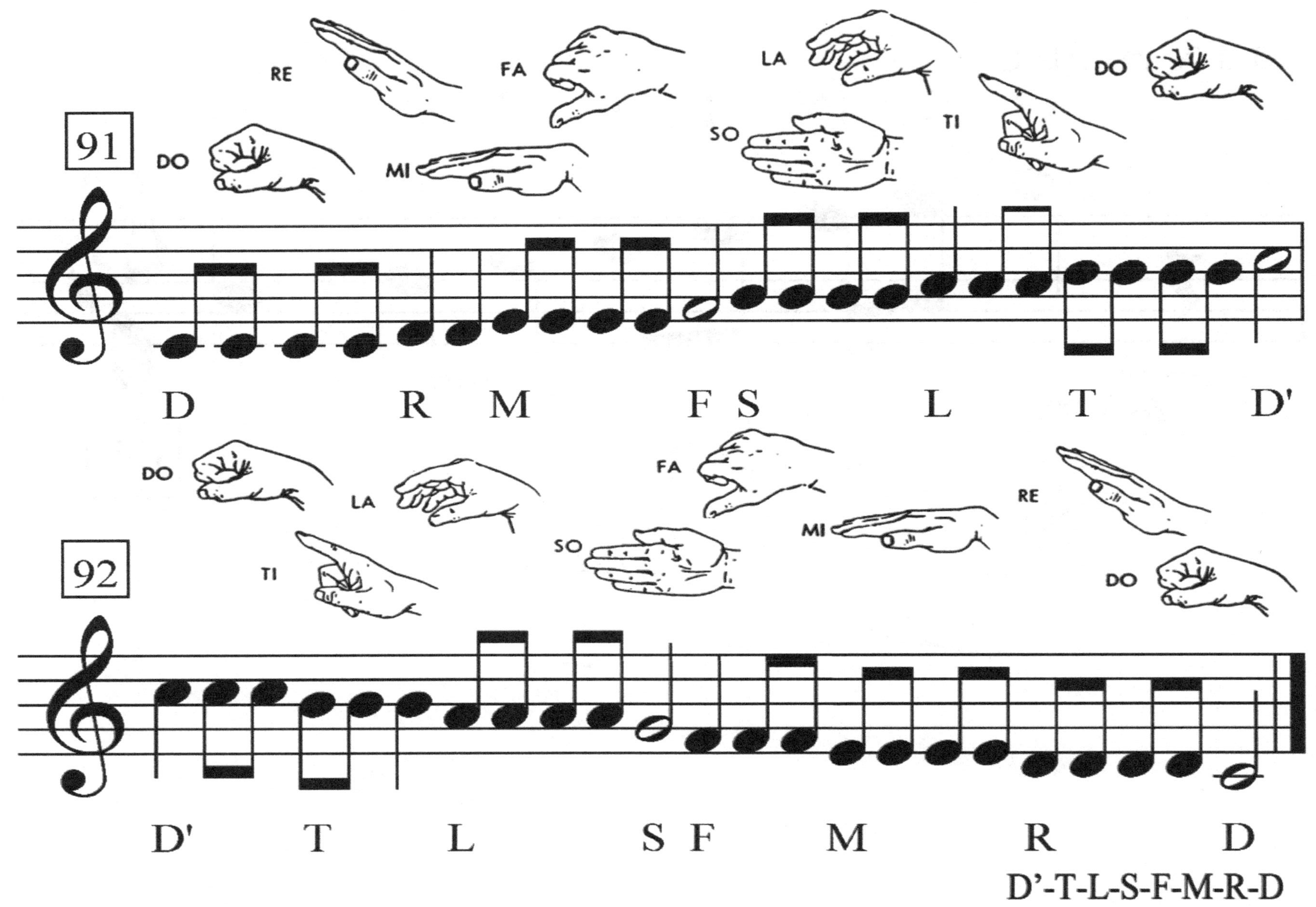
91
DO
RE
MI
FA
SO
LA
TI
DO
D R M F S L T D'
92
DO
TI
LA
SO
FA
MI
RE
DO
D' T L S F M R D
D'-T-L-S-F-M-R-D

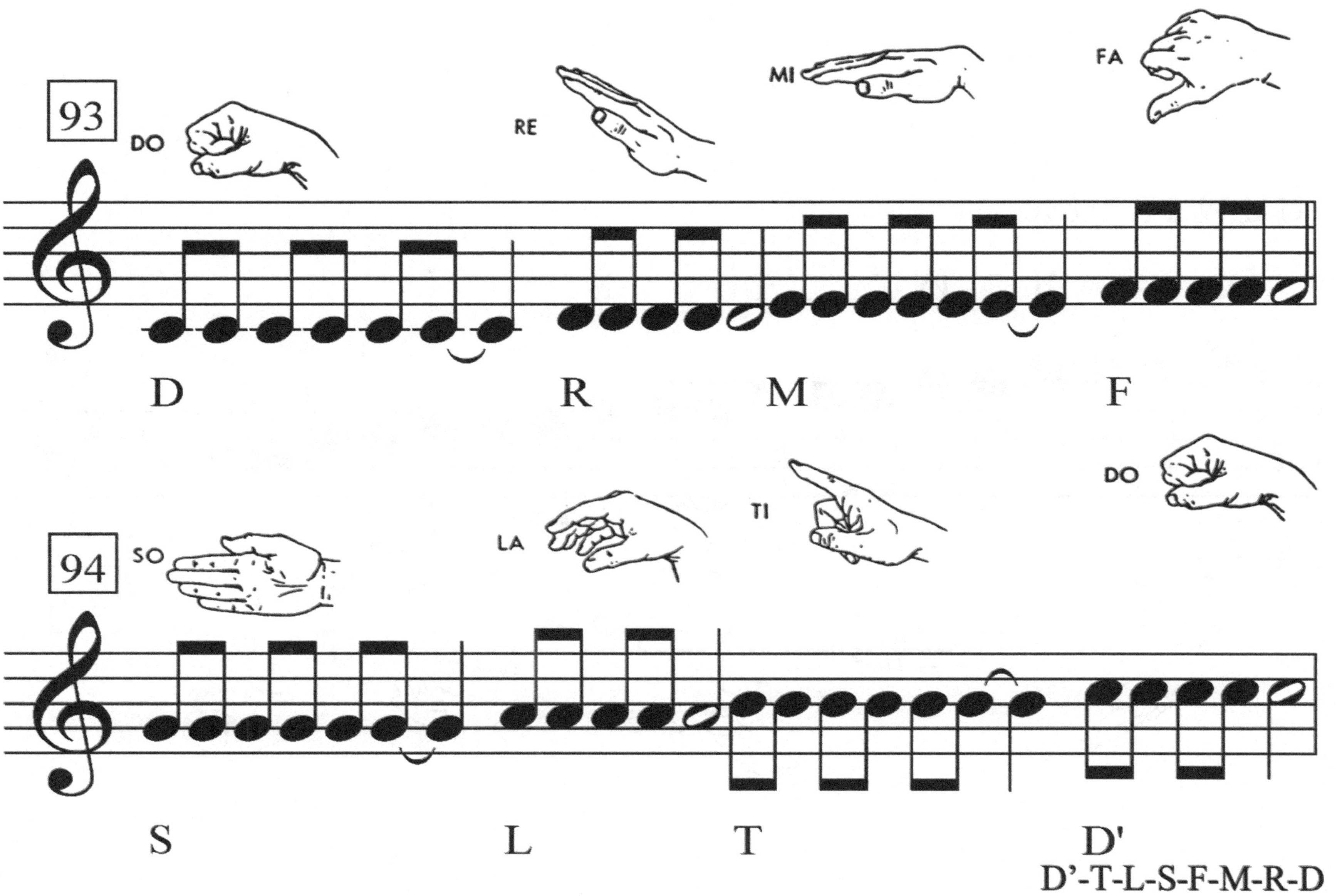
93
DO
RE
MI
FA
D
R
M
F
94
SO
LA
TI
DO
S
L
T
D'
D'-T-L-S-F-M-R-D

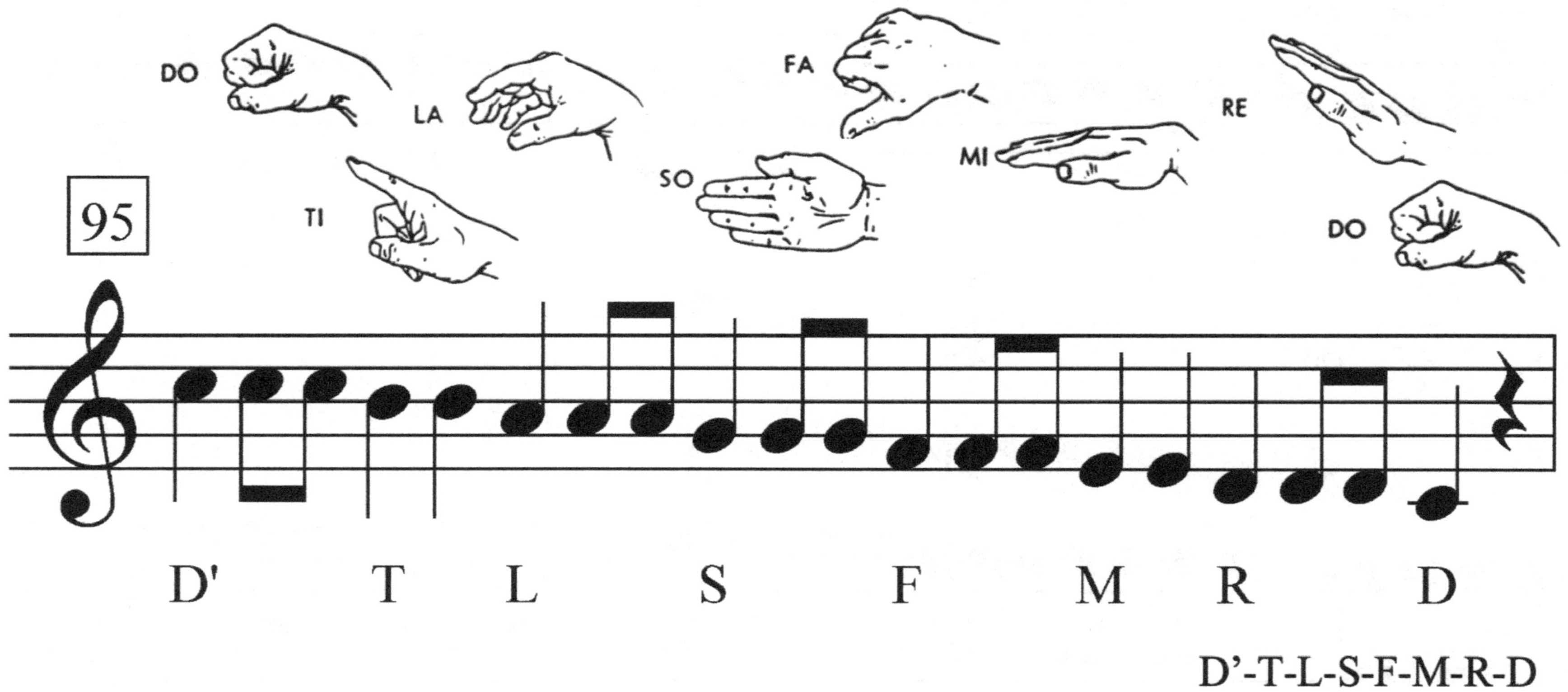
95
DO
TI
LA
SO
FA
MI
RE
DO
D' T L S F M R D
D'-T-L-S-F-M-R-D

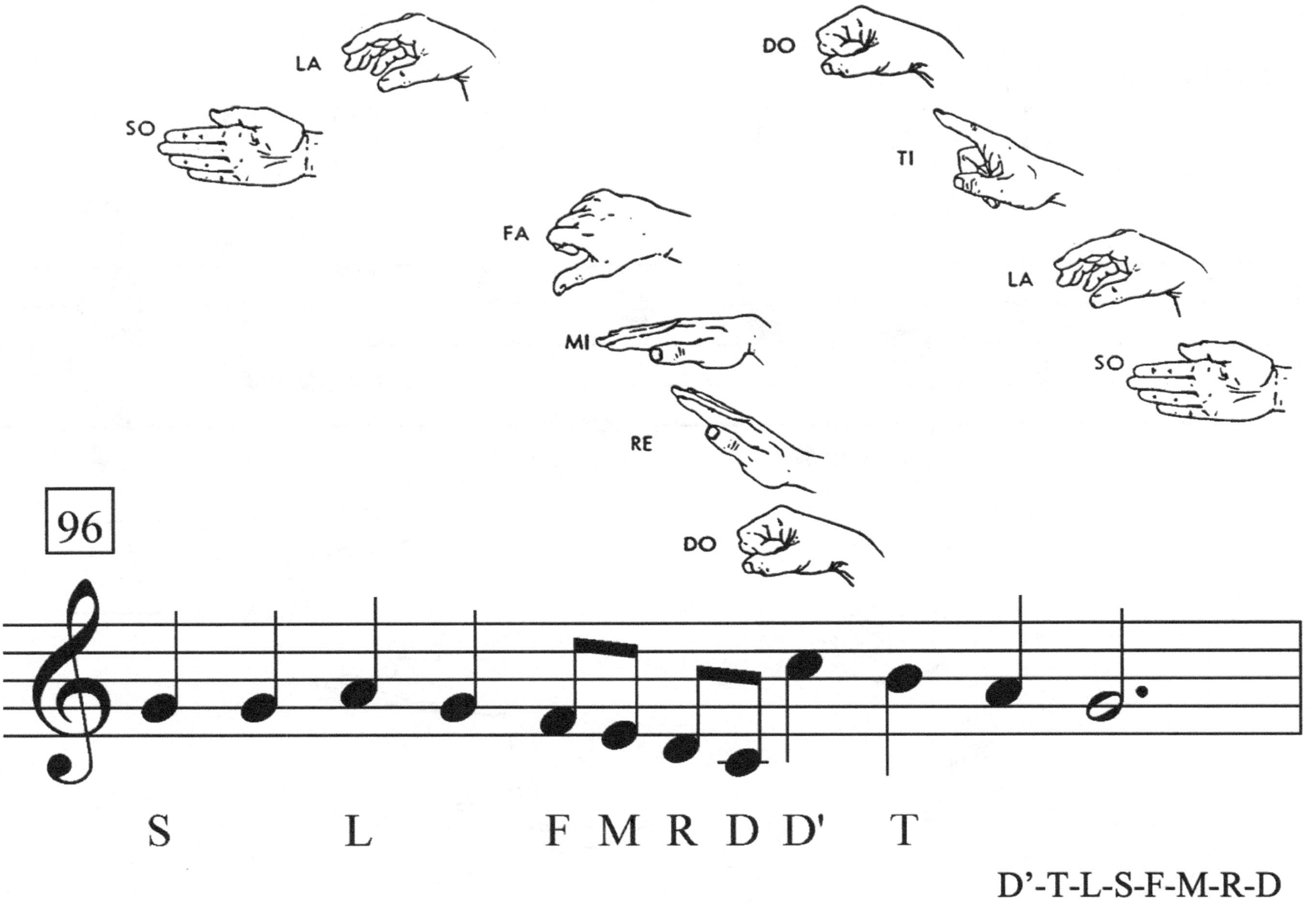

LA
SO
FA
MI
RE
DO
DO
TI
LA
SO
96
S L F M R D D' T
D'-T-L-S-F-M-R-D

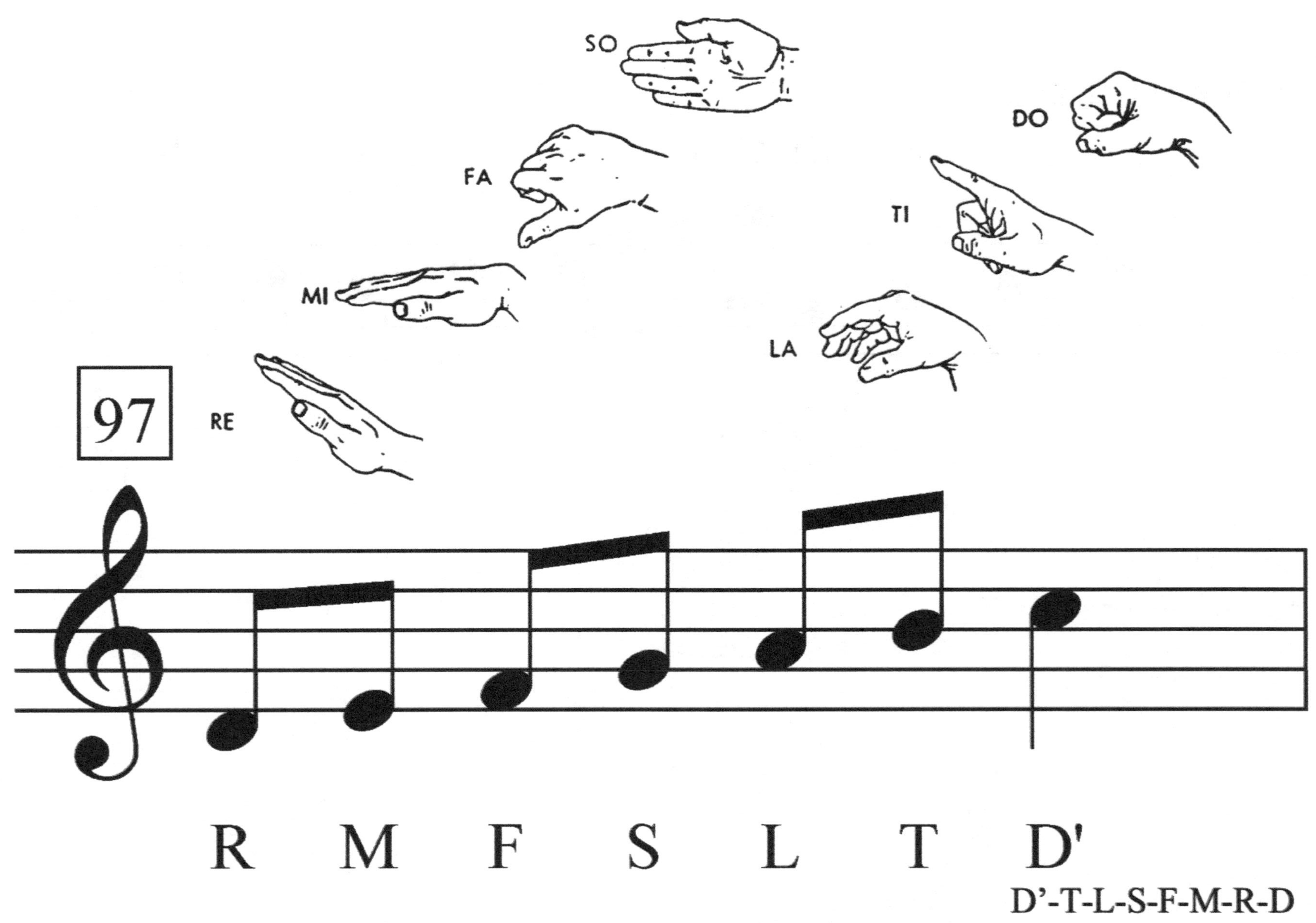
97
RE
MI
FA
SO
LA
TI
DO
R M F S L T D'
D'-T-L-S-F-M-R-D

Made in the USA
Las Vegas, NV
10 August 2023